# Accounts Current Book 4

Pittsylvania County
Virginia

1805-1812

*Gayle Austin*

HERITAGE BOOKS
2006

# HERITAGE BOOKS
*AN IMPRINT OF HERITAGE BOOKS, INC.*

### Books, CDs, and more—Worldwide

For our listing of thousands of titles see our website
at
www.HeritageBooks.com

Published 2006 by
HERITAGE BOOKS, INC.
Publishing Division
65 East Main Street
Westminster, Maryland 21157-5026

Copyright © 2006 Gayle Austin

Cover illustration by John Hill Carter Beverley

All rights reserved. No part of this book may be reproduced or transmitted in any form or by any means, electronic or mechanical, including photocopying, recording or by any information storage and retrieval system without written permission from the author, except for the inclusion of brief quotations in a review.

International Standard Book Number: 978-0-7884-4071-3

# INTRODUCTION

Accounts Current Book 4 covers the period between 1805 and 1812 in Pittsylvania County, Virginia. These are the closest documents to probate records in this county. The accounts current contain, among other things, records of the appraisement, inventory, accounts current and account sales of estates. They also contain the guardianship accounts and the division of estates. These records do not necessarily mean that the decedent left no will. They are merely a record of the above.

Three men, usually neighbors, were appointed by the county court to inventory the property as it was at the time of death and to appraise the personal property and return a written copy to court. If a sale was held of the personal property, the items were listed with the names of the buyers. Sometimes the values of the items from household goods to slaves were included. Often the buyers were family members; frequently even the widow participated in the sale. Three "subscribers" settled the accounts current of the estate with the executor. This was a means to check on the executor and has provided us with much valuable information.

The accounts current and guardianship accounts contain mountains of information that often cannot be found elsewhere. These accounts could remain open for a short time, but often were kept open for years with reports being made periodically to the court. Examples of the type of information they contain include lawsuits that were ongoing or settled, wives and children, the names of slaves, and the names of people owing notes to the estate. Land in another county or state owned by the deceased is often mentioned, revealing an entirely new area to be explored. In the account of Mathew Bates we learn that his "late wife" is now Mary B. Nowlin. The actual death date is given for David F. Patrick and in another account, we learn that "Abraham Shelton, son to John," is to be paid for planting 46 apple trees!

The occupations of many people in the county are also found in these records, as different people are listed for their services: the shoemaker, midwife, attorney, tailor, blacksmith, doctor, etc. The accounts current give a very good view of life in this era from the price of goods to what was of value to the people of that time.

The original records are held at the Courthouse in Pittsylvania County at Chatham. Microfilm is available at the Library of Virginia. In transcribing these records, I used the microfilm and then checked my work with the original book in Chatham. I have used the original spelling and have copied the book in its entirety.

The first three books containing the accounts current from 1770 have been published by Lucille Payne. With her permission, I include her glossary. Many thanks to Lucille for indexing this book and for her help and support in transcribing some of these strange words.

# ACCOUNTS CURRENT BOOK 4, 1805-1812

**AC 4, p. [none]**                                               **Inventory of Benjamin Harris**

In obedience to an order of court to us directed, we have proceeded to appraise the estate of Benjamin Harris, Decd, July 5, 1805.

Negroes: Solomon, Darker and her son, Peter, Anniea, 1 Bay Horse, 1 gray mare & two colts, 5 cow & two calves & bull, 4 yearlings & one bool, 4 sows 9 shoats 3 pigs, ox cart yoake & Lock chain, 1 Cutting box & blade, 1 Sword & Scabbord, 1 Shot Gun, 12 Cheers, 1 arm Do, 1 Follen Table, 2 small Chair, 1 Trunk & Red chest, 1 Case & seven bottles, 1 looking glass, 1 bed & bed sted Cord 1 sheet counterpin & bolster, 1 Do no bolster, 2 Do with bolsters under beds one sheet & counterpin each, 1 Round Table, 1 Lot of surveyers Instruments, 2 Trunks, Candle stand, small box & cradle, 1 cross cut saw & old spinning wheel, 2 old sythes & flax wheel, 2 axes, 1 pare of steelards, 3 wedges, 2 augers, 2 drawing knifes.

3 old bells & wheat sive, 1 small pine Table, 1 pine Cupboard, 1 grid Iron, 1 Tea Kettle, 6 Judgs, two butter potts, 1 large Iron pot, 2 pare and Irons, 1 Do, 1 pan handle & Tribot, 1 large bowl, & Candle mole.

6 plates, 2 Dishes, 4 Basons puter, 6 plates, 2 dishes, 1 small bole, E.ware, 1 Old sugar box, 4 barels, 1 with iron hoops, 1 pare of spoon moles, 3 Reap hooks, 1 hand saw, 1 broad ax, 2 Colters, 6 hilling hoes, 3 grubbing Do, 2 pair of Iron Traces, 2 swingle trees, 2 clevises, 2 pare of hames, 1 collar and pad, Do, 1 Churn, 1 tub, 1 ?pole, 1 grind stone, 2 w. cans, 2 wash bowls, 1 pare of and Irons, 2 plough hoes, 1 man saddle, 8 old books of different kinds, 1 woman sadle, 3 oven, 1 pot, 1 skillet, 4 volums of ?peregrame? pickles, 1 hone, 1 anville, 2 bellas, 1 chare, 1 Smith vise & 1 sledge hammer, 2 hand Do, 1 Shoeing Do, 3 pare Tongs, 3 cole chisssels 1 ?? widg & naile plate, 1 Book dramatic pieces, 1 bond on Charles Pistole, 1 Hhd of Tobacco 1253lb neet at 22/pk.

In obedience To an order to us directed bearing date June 1805 we have appraised the estate of Benj. Harris Deceast and find the amount as above stated given under our hands this 15th day of July 1805.
    W. Beavers, Christopher Robertson, Hezekiah Puryear         Total: δ455.13.0

Recorded: 15th of September 1806


**AC 4, p.1**                                                                 **Joseph Marks Inventory**

In Obedience to an Order of this Worshipfull Court of Pittsylvania County bearing date November Court 1804 we the undersigned have proceeded to appraise the Estate late the property of Joseph Mark Dec'd. in the following Manner viz:

1 Pied Cow, 1 Heifer, 1 Red Cow earling & Bull, 1 Small heifer, 16 Geese, 1 Cuting Box knife &c old, 1 Sorrell Mare, 1 Fodder stack & shucks 1 Parcel of Blades, 1 Parcel of unstript Tobo., 1 Parcel of unstript Tobo., 1 Stack of Oats, 1 Grine Stone, 1 Parcel of old Hoes & axes, 1 pare of Steelyards, 1 Frow & handsaw drawing knife and auger

1 Mans Saddle, 1 Womans Do, 1 Crose hackle, Bell Riddle and Dryer for fruit, 1 old flax wheel, 1 Ox yoak, 1 tray & old Sifter, 1 Parcel of shoemakers Tools &c, 1 set of Worping Spools, 1 old Barrel, 1 pare of rawhide traces Haimes, collar and, 2 Baskets & Double tree

1 Loom & Warping Bar, 1 Churn, 2 Tubs two Piggins, 1 Pail old, 1 Dish, two Small Basons, 2 Large Basons, 3 Spoons, a parcel of old knives and forks, a funnel, & ½ Dozen Pewter plates, 1 Large pot, 1 small Do, one dutch oven, 2 pr. Hooks, 1 pine chest, 1 Bed & Stead under Do, counterpaine & Sheet & Pillow, 1 Bead & Stead & Bolster Mat & Cord counterpaine & Sheet.

A parcel of Earthern ware, 1 large Juag, 6 chairs, 1 Slate, 2 pr. cards old, 1 pare of scales & weights, 1 old chest, 1 Spinning wheel, 1 pine table, 1 Bead & Stead Cord, sheet and quilt, Counterpaine and under bead, 1 Chest, 1 Pine table, 4 pales

1 hogshead, 2 ?Beguins? & Flax seed

Given under our hands this 8th December 1804
Joseph Rogers, Washington Thompson, Charles Shelton

After the above articles was appraised the follow articles was produced at an after day and appraised in the following manner

1 Bed and furniture & Stead, 1 Box of Earthern Ware, 1 Chest, 1 Cotten wheel, 2 chairs, 1 Dish, 1 plate, 2 Basons, 1 case of knives & folks [sic], ½ Doz Spoons, 1 Pistol, pr. Sad Irons, 1 Water stand & plate, Candle moles, 10 Lasts, 10 Small shoats, 1 Keeler, tops & shucks, 1 Hackle, 1 Bed quilt & 1 Blanket, 1 Basket

Given under our hands this 4th January 1805.              Total: δ15.15.6
Charles Shelton, Joseph Rogers

Recorded: 16th Day of December 1805

### AC Book 4, Page 3                                              Abr. Legrand's Account Current

1804 - Dr. The Estate of Abraham Legrand Dec'd in Acct. Currt. wt. Obadiah Owen & Jesse Wilson admrs. of Agness Legrand, Dec'd
To Colo. John Watson as per Acct. & receipt
To Cash paid Thomas Chaney? as per prov'd acct. & Inv'y.obtain'd.
Paid Ditto Cost of Warrant
1803 - Sundries as Per acct. Render'd
To Cash paid John Legrand as per debt & Cost Int. &c Obtained in Pittsylvania Court agst. the Estate of Abraham Legrand, Dec'd
To Sundries as per acco't. Vouchers &c render'd per Jesse Wilson.

Dec 30, 1803 By amount of Sales as pr. acc't. filed in the office
By parcel Tobo. priz'd & Inspected at Petersbg. & sold Colo. John Watson as per accot. & Receipt render'd after deducting 170 lbs Tobo put in said Hhd. Expenses &c.
By a Balla. due the admrs.

In pursuance of an Order of the Worshipful Court of Pittsylv'a. county to us Directed we have this day met & Settled the acct. Current of Obediah Owen & Jesse Wilson admrs. of Agness Legrand Decd who was administratrix of Abram Legrand decd. & find the above amt. by us Stated to be Correct agreeable to the Vouchers to us produced and that the balance of thirty pounds & four pence is due the administrators. Given under our Hands the 17th Jany 1806
Geo Adams, Ro. Harrison, Will. Ware - Commrs.              Total: δ154.17.02

Recorded: January 21st, 1806

### AC Book 4, Page 4                                                              Wm Mays' Inventory
Nov 13, 1805- The appraisement of the Estate of Wm. May, Dec'd
7 Shotes, 3 hogs, 1 ditto, 1 yoke of Steers, 2 Cows & Calves, 2 Heifers, 12 Geece, 1 Mare, 1 Colt, 1 Ditto, 2 Axes, 2 Hoes, 1 Coulter, 1 Swingletree Irons, 1 Spade, 1 Wedge & Mattock hoe, 1 pr.Traces & 2 chisels, 1 Loom, 3 casks, 1 Saddle & Bridle, 2 Hhds, 2 Skillets, 2 pots & 2 ?chits/chets?, 2 chairs & 6 plates, 11 Pewter plates & 2 Dishes, 2 Basons & 2 Slayes, 1 Bible & 2 Spelling Books, 1 Half Bushel, 2 feather Beds & furniture, 1 Ditto.

Agreeable to an Order of Court to us directed we have proceeded to appraise the Estate of Wm May, Dec'd. Given under our hands this 13th Nov 1805         Total: δ77.12.0

Sam'l Thompson, Geo. Robertson, Christopher Robertson Junr.

Recorded: December 16, 1805.

**AC Book 4, Page 5**                                              **George Sutherlin's Account Current**
John Sutherlin & George Sutherlin admrs. of George Sutherlin, Dec'd in acc't Current with the Estate of the said George Sutherlin Dec'd Dr: to amount of sales made on 10th Oct & to 6 December 1803

To Cash rec'd by George Sutherlin for Debts for the Estate
To 3 Hhds. Tobacco Weighing neat 4210 lbs formerly in the hands of Jno. Sutherlin
To 882 lbs Transfer Tobacco Do      Do
Cash rec'd by Jno Sutherlin
To this Sum due the Estate by the administrators
                                 Contra
By amt. of Bonds placed in the hands of Wm. Clarke
By the Commrs. appointed to Divide the Estate & by him Delivered to John Sutherlin
By amt. of Bonds assigned to Thomas Sutherlin by direction of the said commrs.
By amount of acc't rendered by Jno Sutherlin
By this Sum allowed John Sutherlin for his Services as an administrator
By amt. of acc't rendered by George Sutherlin
By this Sum allowed George Sutherlin for his Services as an administrator
By this Sum due the Estate by the administrators

In Pursuance to an Order of the Worshipful court of Pittsylvania county to us Directed, we have this day met & settled the account Current of John Sutherlin & George Sutherlin admrs. of George Sutherlin, Dec'd with the Estate of the sd. George Sutherlin Dec'd & find the above amount as Stated by us to be Correct agreeable to the Vouchers To us produced & that the Balance of Three hundred & Seventy Six pounds five Shillings & two pence is due the sd. Estate by the said adminrs. November 17th 1804
 Jno Wilson, Christopher Robertson, Geo. Adams          Total: $1707.14.0
Recorded: January 21, 1806.

**AC Book 4, Page 6**                                                        **Jno. Craddock's Inventory**
Inventory & Appraisement of the personal Estate of John Craddock Dec'd taken the 12th day of Nov. 1805
1 Bay Horse, 1 Sorrel Mare, 1 Brown Cow & yearlin, 1 Brown Cow & yearlin, 1 Brown Cow & yearlin, 6 Hogs, Howel & adds, 1 handsaw, 2 drawing knives, 1 Crows round shave Jinters [?jointer] & taper Bell, 1 pair of Cumpises Chizel & nippers, 1 pair of sheep shears & & 1 pair of Sturrup Irons, 1 Broad ax, 3 axes, 2 Mattocks, 1 Grubing hoe, 5 hoes, 1 Sithe & Cradle, 1 Colter & plow, 1 Curry Comb & Bridle, 2 Hides & a peace, 1 Loom, 3 Slays, 1 large pot, 1 Dutch oven, 1 Small pot, 1 Small oven, 1 tub Barrel & sheep skin, 10 plates, 3 Dishes, 3 Basons, 10 Spoons, 5 tin cups, Skillet, 2 Piggons. 1 Bed & bed stead, 1 flax wheel, 2 Jugs, 1 saddle, 10 chears, 3 old tubs, 1 Tool Box, 1 Bed & Bed sted, 1 Bed & Bed sted, 1 Cotton wheel, 1 meal Box, 3 flat Irons, 1 Case of knives & forks, 1 table, Crokery ware in cubport [sic], 1 Sugar Box & Coffey Mill, 3 Jugs & Butter pot, 1 grind Stone, 1 large Chest, 1 Looking glass, 1 Box Wafers, 12 Books, 1 Shaving Box & 2 Reasors, 1 Slate, 4 Voiles, 4 Bells, 1 Stack of Tops & Shocks, 1 Black Boar, 1 Sow & pigs, 3 Stacks of Blades,, 1 Stack of Oats, 5 sheep

Pittsylvania We George West, John Turner, Benjamin Ballinger & Owen West being first duly Sworn, have proceeded to appraise in Current money the personal Estate of John Craddock, Dec'd as above Certifyed under our hands the Date above Written.
Owen West, George West, John Turner

Recorded: February 17, 1806

**AC Book 4, Page 8**                                                            **Tho. Johnson's Acct. Current**

Charles Lewis & Gatrey Lewis, his wife administrators of Thos Johns Dec'd in acct. with the Legatees of said Johns Dec'd

To Amount of Sale £245.1.11
17 Negroes agreeable to appraisement £638.15.0
Increase & advance on above Negroes £190.5.0
Interest rec'd from Individuals £2.16.8
The hires of Negroes for 1800 £83.1.9
One track of Land sold Harmon Cook £60.0.0
The rent of land belonging to the legatees for years £43.17.6
    Total: £1263.17.10
  Part 1 Hhd. Tobo £7.2.3
  Cash furnished Edward Bannister £12.0.0
Balance as per Contra: £163.15.1
Memo Since the report we find the above acct. entitled to a Credit for £104.5.7
Amount Due: £57..7.4
Robt Devin, Nich's Parrish, Jno Parrish

### Contra

By Sundrie ticketts Rects prov'd accots &c
By Paying Abraham Johns his pt negroes being in number four & purchased at Sale
By Paying Elizabeth Johns her part negroes being three in number
By Paying Isaac Johns his part negroes being two in number & purchased at Sale
By Paying Jacob Johns his part negroes being two in number
By Paying Judith Johns her part negroes being in number three
By Paying Polley Johns her part negroes being three in number
By Paying Jos Johns his part negroes being 2 in number & purchased at Sale
By Paid Jeremiah Kessee for Sundries tickes
By Paid Sam'l Watkins as per Recit.
By 1000 lb pork Furnished by Jos Johns at the request of the administ.
By Cash furnished by  do  do
By  Pd Jos Johns for Services ren'd which is deducted from the charges made by the admin.
By admist. Services after charge of £15.1.7 for his services.
By Balance due the Legetees £163.15.1
Balance: £1283.0,1

In Obedience to an order of the worshipful Court of Pittsylvania we have Examined the papers & accots. of Thos Johns Dec'd so fare as lay before us and find the papers as appears to be legal to leave a Balance in favour of the Legatees to the amount of δ163.15.1 but further find a number of other papers which appears to us not to be properly established, we further Report that we did not examine any papers relative to the estate from the Twenty ninth day of December 1794 to the Sixth day of december 1799 there being no accurate accounts kept of the Same for these years. Given under our hands this fourteenth day of Feby one thousand eight hundred & Six.

                                              Robt Deavin
                                              Nich's Parrish
                                              Jno Parrish

Recorded: February 18, 1806

**AC Book 4, Page 10**                                              **A. Campbell's Inventory**

In Obedience to an order of the Woshipful Court of Pittsylvania county bearing date January Court 1806 to us directed, we being first Sworn, as the Subscribers have appraised in current money the personal Estate of Abraham Campbell, Dec'd and has reported thereof to Court as follows to Wit:

One Bay horse, Six Cows & yearling, One Brindle Hiffer and one Red yearling, Four head of Sheep, One Sow and four Piggs, One feather Bed and Bedsted and furniture, One Do Do Do Do, One Bedsted, Two Juggs and one Butter Pott, A parsell of old pewter, One funnel and pepper Box and 1 white Bole, Four knives and six Forks, One Coffee pot and parcel of Tallow, Four chairs, and one chest, Two potts and hooks and one Dutch oven, one frying pan, Eight casks, four old Tubs and one Gun, A parsil of Salt, Four old hogheads, Plantation utencils and Carpenters tools, One flesh fork, tools and flat Iron, Three Bells and one Bread Baker, one pan handle, Water Vesells, Table and chears, Shoe makers Tools, Two qurt Bolles, One old Saddle, Two Spinning wheels, Two pr cards and one flax Hackell

One pare hair Hames and currying Comb, One Bread tray, 2 Razors Horsflums, Brass lock and file Two Gimblets and one pr Sheep Shears

One Raw hide and Calf, One feather Bed, One Cow, One Candle Stick and pr Compases, Parcel of salt Pork

Given under our hands this 25$^{th}$ of January 1806
Thos Ragsdale, Jennings Thompson, John (X) Long          Total: $62.12.6

Recorded:   February 17, 1806

**AC Book 4, Page 11**                                              **Chas. L. Adams' Inventory**

In Obedience to the Worshipful Court of Pittsylvania, we the Subscribers, after being duly Sworn, have appraised the Estate of Charles L Adams as follows Viz:

1 young Bay Horse, 1 Bay Ditto, 1 Black Ditto, 1 Sorrel Colt, 35 head Hogs, 4 head Sheep, 5 Plows & 2 Coulters & 4 pair Geers, 10 old hoes, 4 axes, 1 pr Iron wedges & 7 Reap hooks, 4 Screw augers, 2 chezils, 1 frow, 20 head cattle Including 2 yok Steirs, 1 drawing knife, 2 Hand Saws, 1 Lock chain, 2 Cow Hides & 1 old Cart, 4 feather Beds & furniture, 8 old chairs, 2 cotton wheels & 1 flax wheel, 2 Tables, 1 Chest & 1 Corner Cubard, 2 Stone Jugs, 1 Tea kittle, 1 pr Stillards, 1 Shugar Box & Tea Canister, 1 Weirter, 1 Buter Pott, 1 Knife Box & knives, 1 looking Glass, a parcel of earthren ware, 1 Spade, 1 old chest, 4 Iron potts, 1 pot Rack, 2 Water pails, 1 half Bushel, 1 hackle, 1 powdering Tub, 1 Gum, 1 Loom

1 Negro man Primus, 1 Do Jack, 1 Do Woman Nan, 1 Do Do Aggey, 1 Do Do Turner & 2 children 1 Do Do Pattey, 1 Do Do Dicey

3 Slays & 1 Harness

Thos Farmer, John Eads, James Bruce           Total: $777.12.6

Recorded April 21, 1806


**AC Book 4, Page 12**                                              **P. Gilbert's Inventory**

By Virtue of an order of the Worshipful Court of Pittsylvania County, we appraised, being first Sworn before a Justice of the Peace for the said county, have Inventoried and appraised the Estate of Preston Gilbert Dec'd to us Shown as followers to wit:

2 yoke of Oxen, 7 Head of young Cattle, 19 head of other Cattle, 20 head of hogs, 4 Sows and 28 piggs 1 Sow, 10 head of Sheep, 1 Horse Prince, 1 Bay Mare Fance, 1 Ditto Do Poll, 2 Bay colts, 1 Bay mare Tiney, 1 Wheat Fan, 1 Cuting knife and Box, 60 Bushels Pie in the Straw, 2 Stacks oats, 1 Raw Hide

1 Ditto, 1 Waggon & 4 pair Geer, 1 lock chain, 1 Halter chair, 2 Bells & Collars, 1 Lot Blacksmith Tools
1 Parcel old Irons, 1 Still, 1 Ditto, 15 Beir? Stands, 1 crop Cut Saw, 4 Waggon Boxes, 5 pole axis, 1 Pair Iron Wedges, 1 old Spade & Shovel

1 Truckle Cart, 1 Grind Stone, 5 plow hoes, 4 weeding hoes, 5 Small ditto, 3 Coulters, 5 hilling hoes, 3 Grubing hoes, 1 Hand Saw, 1 old Ditto & 5 old Chisels, 1 Hhd jointers & 1 hand ditto, 1 Broad ax Foot Adz & Fro, 1 parcel old tools, 4 Mill Picks, 2 cotton wheels & 2 pair chards, 2 Potts, 2 Dutch ovens
1 Brass Tea Kettle, 1 Skillet, 1 Weaving loom, 1 Raw hide, 1 Dough Beatter, 1 Churn, 4 Water Pails
4 Pewter measures, 3 pewter Dishes, 4 Pewter Basons, 6 old pewter plates & 5 spoons, 1 Grist Iron & 1 old sword

Negroes: Lewis, Ben, Bob, Kajah, Tom, Caesar, Jack, Billey, Jesse, Grey
Charles, Dinah, Rachel, Easther, Fanny, Jenny, Alice, Pheby, Polley, Rachel Jun, 1 Ditto

1 Sash Door Walnut Cupboard, 1 Pannel Door ditto, 1 Crese & Bottles, 1 Large Trunk, 1 pair of stilyards
2 Jugs, 1 Clock Reel, 1 Chest, 2 Flax wheels, 1 Womans Saddle & Bridle, 1 Mans Ditto, 1 Womans Ditto
6 Feather Beds & furniture, 1 old Case, 1 Wire Sieve, 1 pair Saddle Bags, 1 Looking Glass, 1 Candle Stand
2 Brass Candlesticks, 2 Walnut Tables, 11 Chairs, 1 pair Compasses, 3 Buttor potts

5 Silver Table Spoons, 6 Ditto Tea Spoons, 5 Caskes, 1 parcel of Earthen & Glass ware, 2 cases of knives & forks, 1 Small Bor's gun, 1 Rifle gun, 90 Barrels Corn, 8 Pieces Walnut planks, 1 canoe, 6 Hogs

David F Patrick, David Hamick, Anderson Chick: apprs.     Total: £1922.7.6

The foregoing appraisement contains a true and perfect Inventory of the Estate of Preston Gilbert, dec'd, given under my hand This 19th Day of April 1806.
       John Gilbert, acting Exec.

Recorded: April 21, 1806

**AC Book 4, Page 16**             **M. Markham's Share of 906 Acres Land**

Pittsylvania Court, February 16th 1805
By the Directions of Isaac Coles, Thomas Anderson and Joseph E Haley, Gent, Commissioners appointed by order of court to allot To Mary Markham, Widow of John Markham Dec'd, her thirds of the lands of the said Decedent & we have surveys & lay'd off 302 acres, it being one third part of 906 acres lying on the north side of Bannister river & White horne Creek. Beginning at the mouth of Lick branch on the said river, thence up the said River as it meanders 120 poles to a mulberry tree, Thence New Line N 60° W 376 Poles to pointers in Coles line and thence along the same, N 52° E 82 poles to a white Corner N 4° E 66 poles to a pine, thence a new line S 60° E 53 poles to John Steels Corner dead pine with a small persimmon tree marked by it for a Corner, thence along Steels lines the same course continued 38 poles to a ____ on Lick branch aforesaid and down the same as it meanders to the Beginning.
       By Joshua Stone Surv.
We have this 16th Feby 1805 allotted the above 302 acres as the third of the sd Tract of 906 To Mary Markham, widow of John Markham, dec'd.
               Isaac Coles
               Thomas Anderson
               Joseph E Haley
Recorded: April 21, 1806

**AC Book 4, Page 17**                   **Sam'l Slates's Inventory**

In obedience to an order of the worshipful Court of Pittsylvania dated February Court 1806 we the under Written Subscribers after being first duly Sworn have proceeded to appraise the personal Estate of Samuel Slate Dec'd in current money viz:

To three pewter Measures & large funnel, To Lot of Pewter, To one other lot of Pewter, To Spoons & candle moles and parcel of knives & forks, To two Slates and five reap hooks and candle sticks, To Lot of Compass tools, To one Lot of Carpenters Tools, To wedges, stone hammer and ax, To Two Mataxes, To parcel of plows, To parcel of plow Geers, To one Grind Stone, To Two Bells & parcel of hoes, To three Cotton wheels, To one Small Shot Gun, To one large Shot Gun, To one Brass Skilet & one Iron Skilet To two Dutch ovens & one large pot, To parcel of old Irons & 2 Small pots & Hooks, To 1 loom & two flax wheels &c, To one Hackel & one Steell traps, To one lock chain, To one mans Saddle, To one feather bed and counterpain, To bed and bed sted cord & Some Cover, To three pare Cotton Cards and one large, To one Desk, To one bed and Sted and cover, To one other Bed and counterpin, To one Bed and Cover To three wire sives, to pare of flat Irons old, To eight chears and pare of Stilards, To one yoke of Stears To one red and white pide heifer & black & white heifer, To red heifer yearling and one white yerling To red Cow and Calf, To one Sorrel Horse, To one ox cart, To one Bay mare, To one Bay Colt, To 2 axes To Six Sheep and three __, To Sixteen geese, To one Still
Appraised the 8$^{th}$ Day of March 1806.     Total: £153.16.9
John Shelton, Heath Gardner, Abraham Chaney

Recorded: April 21, 1806

**AC Book 4, Page 19**                                                                                          **A. Campbell's Acct. Sales**

Amount Sales of the Estate of Abraham Campbell, Dec'd made the 25$^{th}$ of Jun 1806 by Nathan Adams & Francis Worsham, Exec.

| Item | | Buyer |
|---|---|---|
| 1 Cow & yearling | sold | George Shelton |
| 1 Hepher & 2 chairs | do | Tho Chambers |
| 1 yearling, 1 wheel " | do | E Campbell' |
| 4 head of Sheep | do | Jno Patterson |
| 5 Do of Hoggs | do | Tho Watson |
| 5 Hogheads | do | Stephen Hardy |
| 4 Barrels & 1 Gun | do | Tho Harness |
| 8 Casks | do | Wm Ricketts |
| 1 Pott & hooks | do | Jonas Waller |
| 1 Do Do | do | Francis Worsham |
| Box & Shoe Tools | do | Jno Elliott |
| 1 pr Iron Traces &c | do | N. Adams |
| 1 wheel | do | P. Worsham |
| 3 Water Vessils | do | P. Worsham |
| ½ Raw Hide | do | R. Campbell |
| 1 Do Do | do | A. Sutherland |
| 1 Coffee Pott | do | E. Campbell |
| 1 Bed Stead, 1 Chair | do | Levy Lewis? |
| 6 Pewter plates | do | N. Adams |
| 2 Do Basons | do | Tho Harness |
| parcel of Pewter | do | Jos Richaards |
| 1 Bowel & P Box | do | Jesse Richards |
| parcel of Tallow | do | Tho Harness |
| 1 qurt Bottle | do | N. Adams |
| 1 p W.Cards | do | J. Blakley |
| 1 p. Cards Sold N. Adams | | |
| 1 Hatchet | do | P. Worsham |
| Knives&c | do | N. Adams |

| | | |
|---|---|---|
| 1 Table | do | L. Hardy |
| 1 Jugg | do | Wm Thomas |
| 1 Do | do | J. Richards |
| 1 Butter pott | do | F. Worsham |
| 1 p Iron Wedges | do | James Blakley |
| 2 axes | do | Jesse Long |
| 2 Bells | do | R. Campbell |
| 1 Do | do | J. Richards |
| 1 Ladle & fork | do | P. Worsham |
| 1 Bread Ba Ker | do | J. Richards |
| parcel of Iron | do | Tho. Watson |
| parcel of Tools | do | Jno. Elliott |
| 2 Hoes | do | J. Waller |
| 1 smoothing Iron | do | Wm. Sawyers |
| 1 Grubing Hoe | do | L. Long |
| 1 Bottle | do | J. Richards |
| 1 Bed &c | do | Wm. Shelton |
| 1 Do &c | do | F. Worsham |
| 1 Bed Sted, Chears | do | E. Campbell |
| 2 Rasors &c | do | Tho. Harness |
| 1 funnel &c | do | A. Sutherlin |
| 1 Saddle | do | Jesse Richards |
| 1 Horse | do | R. Campbell |
| 1 Chest Sold J. Richards | | |
| 1 Bed &c | do | Jno. Maddin |
| 1 Cow | do | Thos. Harness |
| 246 lb. Pork | do | E. Campbell |
| 1 C Stick &c | do | N. Adams |
| 152 acres Land | do | E. Robertson |

Total: £268.16.4
Nathan Adams, Francis Worsham
Recorded: June 16, 1806

**AC Book 4, Page 21**         **Inventory & Sale of Estate of Richard Reynolds**

March 1st 1806 an Inventory of the Sail of Richard Runnels

Deceas'd
Nancy Reynolds
To 2 Pewter Dishes, 2 Basons 9 Plates, 5 Spoons, Salt Seller, To 4 Cut Knives & 8 fork, To 1 Looking Glass & 5 Phials, To Candle Stick and moles, To 1 Table, To 2 Jugs, 2 quart Bolles & tumbler, 1 Decanter, 3 earthern mugs, 2 Jacks, 2 earthen Bowls, tea pot, cruit & dram Glass, To 2 Bells & fire tongs, To 1 Cotton wheel and 1 one pair of Cotton chards
1 pr wool ditto, To 4 chairs, To 1 pail, piggin & Cairn?, To 1 chest, To 1 Pot, 1 oven, 1 Skillet & pot hooks To 1 Bed & Bed Stead & furniture, To 1 Ditto, To 1 axe & meal Sifter, To 1 Sorrel Colt

Dodson Burnett
To 1 Woman Saddle

John Winters junior
To 1 Bay mare
Total: £37.13.6

The above property Sold agreeable to Law by the Executors.

John Bennett

Recorded: July 21, 1806

**AC Book 4, Page 22**                                                **C. Keatts Acct Sales**

Memorandum of property Sold at Publick auction belonging to the Estate of Curtis Keatts, dec'd by William & Charles Keatts, Executors the 15th November 1804

Robert G Tucker          Dr.
To wheel & Cards with a Copper Kettle, 1 Shovl and tongs with Tub & piggins, 1 Skillet, Water pail and Table, 1 pair Stilyard & chains, 1 Feather Bed and furniture, 4 Barrels Corn, 4 Hogs, 4 head of cattle, 6 Stacks of Forrage, Shucks & Straw, 1 Barrel & mial, 1 Tub, chist lock & Bridle, 12 Fowls, Trunk & Blanket, 1 pair spectacles & Cash
Total: £31.13.0

William Tucker, Nelson Tucker, & James G. Keatts      Dr.
To 1 Lot of old Iron with wheel & Cards, To Pott hooks & Rack, To1 Stone pott & 2 wheat Seives, To 1 parcel of Earthern ware, To 24 Bason &c, 1 ol Cart, To Lot of Sundry articles
Total: £9.17.0

William Tucker & Peter Rieves      Dr.
To 1 hand Saw & pr of copper ??, To 5 Hogs, To Iron Steel Rat Trap & one heifer
Total: £7.8.2

Charles Keatts              Dr.
To 1 Flax wheel & pott, 1 spice mortar & Chisl, 1 yoke of Oxen &c
Total: £15.13.0

William Keatts             Dr.
To 1 Steir, one Lot of Sundry articles
Total: £8.9.0

Samuel Irby
To 1 Lot of old Iron, 5 Barrels Corn
Total: £7.15.8

Langhorn Scrugs            Dr.
To 2 Sows & Shoats with 5 Hogs
Total: £3.17.0

Drury Scrugs Sen          Dr.
To 1 Cross cut Saw
Total: £1.10.0

John & Henry Keatts          Dr.
To 1 Lot of Tools & Stone pott
Total: £1.1.6

Thomas Keatts           Dr.
To 1 Lot of Tools & earthen Ware
Total: £1.1.0

Nathaniel Farris            Dr.

To frying pan, fork and Saddle
Total: £0.7.6

Vincent Walker            Dr.
To 1 Grind Stone & Sundry other articles, 1 Grubing hoe
Total: £2.0.6

John Hunt                 Dr.
To 1 Stove Pott
Total: £0.4.6

Stephen Clement           Dr.
To 1 Jug
Total: £0.4.6

Benjamin Walten           Dr.
To Sundry articles, Cash, To Sundries
Total: £0.9.0

John Eads                 Dr.
To 1 Tub, candle mould, & Snuffers
Total: £0.6.0

John Turner               Dr.
To 1 Gun
Total: £2.3.0

Richard Keatts            Dr.
To 3 chairs, a Stack of Blades & Tub
Total: £1.11.8

George Davis              Dr.
To 2 Stears & Stack of oats, Cotton, 1 Bee hive
Total: £5.0.9

William P Davis           Dr.
To 1 Cow
Total: £3.12.0

William Darning           Dr.
To 1 Cow
Total: £4.0.6

Hugh Clement              Dr.
To 1 Cart
Total: £0.3.6

Caleb Farris              Dr.
To 2 Empty Hogshead
Total: £.0.7.4 ½

Benjamin Gossney          Dr.
To 5 Hogs
Total: £3.1.0

William Cox                     Dr.
To 1 Cow
Total: £3.19.6

Joseph Mays                     Dr.
To 1 Feather Bed & furniture
Total: £7.15.0

Jerimiah Mc Cullock             Dr.
To 2 Hogsheads, 1 Bag, Tub and Tobacco hoshead, 8 Fowls & Ramrod
Total: £1.8.11

Robert Tucker                   Dr.
To 4 Hogs
Total: £6.18.6

William Patterson               Dr.
To 1 Tub
Total: £0.4.1/2

James G Keatts        Dr.
To a parcel of Sundries & Hammer, 4 Tubs & Salt, 100 lb. Tobacco, 1 Ax and loose Corn
Total: £1.18.0

George Saunders                 Dr.
To Sundry articles
Total: £2.9.0

William White                   Dr.
To 5 Barrels Corn, 1 Hhd. Tobacco (Sold)
Total: £5.5.0

William Keatts, Charles Keatts: Executors
Recorded: July 21, 1806

## AC Book 4, Page 24            C. Keatts' Acct Current

William & Charles Keatts, Executors of Curtis Keatts, Dec'd against the Legatees.

| | |
|---|---:|
| To amount Wm Keatts acct | £3.11.6 |
| " Ditto George Davis's ditto | 1.11.0 |
| " Grasty? & Pannell ditto | 8.16.3 |
| " Richard Keatts do | 0.17.3 |
| " To So much Paid Wm Tucker p Rect. | 32.0.0 |
| " ditto pd Wm Tucker (Whisky) | 32.0.0 |
| " ditto paid Martha Tucker | 32.0.0 |
| " Cash paid Whitehead per accot. | 0.15.0 |
| " Funeral Expenses | 1.04.0 |
| " Cash paid appraisers | 0.09.0 |
| " Lawyers fee | 0.15.0 |
| " Cash paid Crier | 0.18.0 |
| " Wm Keatts for Negro Clothing &c | 3.14.0 |
| " Clerks Tickett | 1.14.7 |
| " Cash paid Shiff for Tax for 1804 | 1.07.2 |

| | |
|---|---|
| " Charles Keatts per accot. | 1.19.9 |
| " Cash paid for 1 quire paper | 0.02.6 |
| William & Charles Keatts, Executors for Services rendered | 26.00.0 |
| Total: | 149.15.9 ½ |
| By Amount of Sale | 161.0.0 |

Agreeable to an order of Court to us directed we have proceeded to state, Settle & adjust the accot. Current of Curtis Keatts, dec'd Rendered to us by the Executors of the dec'd which accot. We conceive To be Correct Given under our hands this 19th July 1806.
Armistead Shelton, Vincent Shelton, Sam'l Fuqua, John Stone jr
Recorded: July 21, 1806.

**AC Book 4, Page 25**          S. Pannill Gdn. Apt of D. Pannill's Orphans

The Heirs of David Pannill Dec'd
In acct. With Sam'l Pannill, Guardian.

1804
September 10th   Paid John White 2 Comms. Ticketts

1805
March 20        " Cash Paid Clk Pittsylva' P. Ticket
April 4   Robert Alexander Clk Campbell do
Aug 3   Cash Paid Clk Patrick        do
Sept. 12  Ditto paid Sheriff Campbell    do
          "  Paid John Brooks for land Warrant
          "  P. Rec't 21st August 1805
October 31 Cash paid Sto. Turner p. Tickett

1806
May 20   Cash paid Sheriff Campbell p. Tickett
         Cash paid Chas Lewis jun for 100 Fruit Trees to be planted on the
plantation in Patrick per Rect.& agreement
July 20 Cash Paid Clk Pittsylava per Ticket 24 cents
August 15 Commission of 5 per cent allowed in collecting £40
Balance due the heirs of D. Pannill dec'd this 15th day of August 1806      £21.1.8

Cr.     40.6.2

1804
Nov 28 By Charles Lewis for rent of Patrick Plantation this year

1805
Dec 28 Ditto    Ditto    Ditto for 1805

Interest on £5.12.11 3/4 from September 1805
By Balance due as above £21.1.8
In obedience to an order of the Worshipful Court of Pittsylvania County bearing Date June Court 1806 to us directed we David Hunt, Joshua Stone Sen, William Smith and Philip L Grasty having examined the account of Samuel Pannill Guardian with the heirs of David Pannill, dec'd and the Vouchers, find a balance due the heirs of David Pannill dec'd of Twenty one pounds 1/8. Given under our hands this 15th day of August 1806.
D. Hunt, Joshua Stone, Wm Smith, P L Grasty
Recorded: August 18, 1806.

**AC Book 4, Page 26**                      R. Thurman's Inventory

July 31, 1806-In obedience to an Order of the Court of Pittsylvania to us directed, we the Subscribers have this day, after being duly Sworn, appraised the Estate of Richard Thurman, Dec'd as followeth Viz:

To one Negro, To two Beds & furniture, To a parcel of old puter, To one flat iron, To nives and forks, To Sundry Lumber, To a parcle of Hogs, To eight head of Cattle, To Sundry lumber, To 3 head of Sheep, Ditto, To two horses

Thomas Farmer, John Edds. George Cox

Recorded: August 18, 1806

**AC Book 4, Page 27**                                                                                     **D. Pannill's Account Current**

Estate of David Pannill, dec'd  In account with Samuel Pannill Exor.

1805
July 4,1805-To Amount paid Wm Smith Pittsyl" for hauling Cotton from McDaniels to Chalk Level p. acct. ren'd me

July 22, "     -Cash paid Wm Mitchell per Rect.

Aug 3, "    - Cash pd Clk Henry for Ticket, Ditto pd Clk of Patrick ditto, Cash paid Wm Smith as a witness at Smith vs Perkins per Ticket, Cash paid Stew. Willis, Constable p. account & rect.

Aug 15, "    Cash paid Weavers In Lynchburg for Publishing Order vs Poor p. Rect., Cash paid Postage 1 Letter from J Roberson

Sept 13, " Cash paid Henry Banks attorney at law for fee at Suit vs Ball

Oct 15, "    Cash paid Thornbury & Miller their account per Rect., Hodgson & Thompson per note taken in & Rect., McCullock & Poore per note taken in & Rect., Israil & J P Pleasants per note taken in & Rect, Lyon & Webster per their account & Rect. 1020, M & J Conrad per their account & Rect., M. Kenn & McClelan for Interest on account per statement & Rect.

Oct 29, " Cash paid Clk Halifax per Ticket, Ditto   paid Ditto &c do, Ditto   paid    ditto      do, Cash paid Clk Halifax per Ticket

Oct. 31, "   Cash paid Sto Turner sheriff of Pittsylva' per account Ticketts & rect.

Nov 19, " amount paid George Herndon for David Pannill's 3 Bonds & Interest p. Statement & rect.

1805

July 4  By Balance due on Settlement per account returned To Court

July 8  Cash rec'd of Vincent Shelton in full, ditto rec'd of James Bruce, ditto rec'd of Ward Bruce, ditto rec'd of Henry Mitchell, ditto rec'd of Letty Mitchell Memo. acct., Geo Dejarnett in full his note, Reuben Dews? do, Cash rec'd of Jno Sally per Sam'l Marshall

July 16  Ditto rec'd of Samuel Fuqua, ditto rec'd of Joseph Robertson,  ditto rec'd of Thos. H Wooding

Aug 3 "ditto rec't of William Lewis, Ditto rec'd of John Swepstone, ditto rec'd of Thomas Dalton, ditto rec'd of John Smith Sandy river, ditto rec'd Martha Fountaine, ditto rec'd Ward Bruce, ditto rec'd West D Hurt, ditto rec'd Bev Shelton Bev, ditto rec'd Eliza' Boatman, ditto rec'd Joseph Yeatts, ditto rec'd Wm

Willis Memo. accot., ditto rec'd Wm Hoskins, ditto acct. John Sally, per S. Marshall, ditto Aug 21 Ditto rec'd of Henry Cross, Cash rec'd of Stephen Yeatts, Ditto rec'd of David Irby, Ditto rec'd of Jos Thacker

Sept 14 " ditto rec't. of Ben Lankford

Sept 18 " ditto rec'd of Leroy Shelton

Sept 19 " ditto rec'd Vinct Walker, do rec'd Spencer Medcalf, ditto rec'd Wm Williams, ditto rec'd Bev Shelton Gabl , ditto rec'd of Peter Perkins

October 15 "ditto rec'd of Joshua Lester

October 17 " Robert Mitchell for Balance due him by one

October 24, 1805- Cash rec'd of Bev Shelton Gabl., James Linn, N. Frizzle, Geo Lackey Sandy River, Armst'd Dudley, Wm Compton, Allen Thurmand

Nov 19 To Amt brought over £1513.18.8

1806

Jany 4- Cash paid James Logan for tax on Kentucky land per rect.,

Jany. 8 - Sto. Turner for cash in suit vs. Ro. Johns

Feby 19- Cash paid Sam'l Yeatts per rect., Joshua Stone Sen per do

Feby 27- **Cash paid Francis Chumbly per Rect.**

Mar 12- Cash paid William Smith attend' as Witness in case Irainer? per Ticketts & Recipt

Total: £1524.3.10 ¼

1806

Feby 1 – **By Amt' from Contra     £1311.2.3**

Feby 19 – By Cash rec'd William Beck, Sam'l Parsons, Wm McNeley, Wm Saunders, Oba' Taylor, Sam'l Yeatts, James Lewis, Hezk' Ripley, Adam Poore, Lemuel Colbert, Peter Perkins, James Barnes, John Harris, Leroy Shelton, Sam'l Fuqua, Peter Perkins, Thomas Willis, Ditto Ditto, Spencer Pace, James Moore

March 8 –Rec'd of Samuel Fuqua

March 12 -  Rec'd of John Hundley, Drury Owen

March 14 – Rec'd of Wm Williams Waggr'?

March 21 – Rec'd of Jorden George

March 27 – Rec'd of Jesse Rowland Sen

1805

Oct 24 – Amt brought over   £863.17.3 3/4

Oct 31 - Cash rec'd of Jno & Wm Williams, Ste Yeatts, Wm Shealds, Abra' Poor, Joel Neal for 2 Executions

Nov 2 - Wm Pannill, jr

Nov 8 - Wm B Banks

Nov 13 – Cash rec'd of Bartlet Smith

Nov 19 - Jos. Robertson, Ward Bruce, Abra' Shelton (John), Isaac Coles Junr, Bev Shelton Gabl.

Nov 25 – James Oliver

Nov 30 – Cash rec'd John Salley per S Marshall

Dec 7 – Cash rec'd Robert Bumpass

Dec 17 – Cash rec'd David Baggerley, Robert Love, John Simpson, Bev Shelton Gabl., Frs. McClanahan, James Moore, Rich'd Shelton, Sam'l Fuqua, John Rowland, Wm Saunders

Dec 26 – Thomas Collins

1806

Jany 4 – Chs Lewis for Jno Brisons Note, cash rec'd of Walter Hutcherson

Jany 6 – Cash rec'd of Peter Perkins

Jany 8 - Robert Johns

Jany 15 – Cash rec'd Caleb Tate

Jany 22 – Cash rec'd of Nevin Stewart, Joel Shelton, Wm Mc Neley, John Lovell, John McCritchard, Henson Spurling, James Moore, Robert Love, Jos Thacker, John Stone, jr.

Feby 1 – Cash rec'd Caleb Compton

March 12 – To account brought forward £1524.3.10 ¼

Apr 9 – Cash paid Clerks tickett in case vs Ball, Joshua Stone Sen for Cost, John Stone per the Clerks certificate, Clerk Henrico for copy of Record in case of Ryan &c intended as evidence in case vs Ball

May 20 – Cash paid William Tunstall, Clk Pittsylva' per Tickett

Jun 11 – ditto paid Ro & Walter Colquhoun per Rect.

July 7 – ditto paid  do  do         per Rect.

July 14 – ditto paid Sheriff of Campbell per Ticketts

1806

May 24 – By amt. from Contra £2333.0.10 ½

May 29 – Cash rec'd – Jas. Linn Per Wm Wimbish his admr.

May 31 – Cash rec'd of Saml. Irby

Jun 17 – Cash rec'd Lemuel Shelton, Jos Thacker, Jos Beavers, Bev Shelton Gabl., John Lewis, Walter Hutcherson, Jno Greggory Jr., Jno Greggory, Senr.  Do  Do,

July 22 – ditto rec'd Luke Matthews, Henson Spurling, Ro Love

Mar 27 – By amount brought forward  £1665.5.6

Mar 28 – Cash rec'd Francis P Coe, Ste. Shelton, George Cox, Sam'l Parsons, Robert Love, Jacob Barger Sen, Wm Beck, Zacha. Irby, Charles Bailey

Apr 9 – ditto Bry'. W Nowlin,  Geo McNeley

Apr 18 – ditto Leml' Shelton, Chas. Keatts, John Rowland, Bev Shelton Bev., Saml. Parsons Sen., Wm Shelton Capt., Cris. Bailey, James Love, Crispin Shelton

Apr 23 – ditto rec'd Crispin Shelton,  James Love, Wm Saunders, Joseph Robertson, Nathan Thurmond, James Moore, Jno & Wm Williams, Wm Watson jr

Apr 26 – ditto rec'd Peter Perkins, Do  Do

May 10 – ditto rec'd John Rowland, Wm Saunders, Bev Shelton Capt, Heza' Ripley

May 20 – ditto rec'd Robertson Shelton, Cris. Shelton rec'd 17$^{th}$ April last, ditto this day, John Steele

May 23 – ditto rec'd Coleman Shelton, James Moore, Geo Robertson

May 24 – ditto rec'd Peter Perkins

July 20 – Cash brought forward      £2917.8.8 1/2

1806

Aug 7 – Cash paid Wm Smith for his attenda. Suit vs.Ball in Richm'd D.Court per Recipt.  Cash pd Postage in summoning Colquhoun in suit vs. Ball

5 per Cent Commission allowing for collecting £2457.2.10 1/4
being the amount Collected since the last settlement.

To Balance due per Contra  £61.5.8

1806

July 22 – By amount bro forward   £2853.8.8
            By cash rec'd John Stone Jun, Ditto Ditto, West D Hurt, John Jenkins

Aug 7 -  ditto rec'd Wm P Davis, Jno McCritchard, Richard Shelton omitt'd for 4th January last, Jos. Leak 12$^{th}$ Feb 1805, Peter Perkins 7$^{th}$ Oct. last, Walter Hutcherson 8$^{th}$ Mar last, John Saunders 9$^{th}$ July 1805, ditto it being error in entering Cash to Thos Willis 17$^{th}$ Feby last, William Temple, Wm Adams, memo. Acct., John Hurt

Aug 15 – Balance due S Pannill Exec. £61.5.8

Balance: £3044.8.93 ¼

In Obedience to an order of the Worshipfull Court of Pittsylvania County to us written bearing Date June Court 1806 we David Hunt, Joshua Stone Senr, William Smith & Philip L Grasty have examined the account of Samuel Pannill Exor. of David Pannill, dec'd as above stated with the Vouchers and find a balance due the said Samuel Pannill Exor. of Sixty one pounds 5/8 as above stated. Given under our hands the 15th day of August 1806.
D. Hunt, Joshua Stone, Wm Smith, P L Grasty
Recorded: August 18, 1806

**AC Book 4, Page 36**                                    **Inventory of D. Slayden**

In Obedience to the Worshipfull Court of Pittsylvania by an Order from them To us Given, we have convend together at the late dwelling house of Daniel Slayden Dec'd and appraised the Estate of the said Deceast as followth:
1806 May 5

One Beadstead and furniture, One Do, One feather bead & bolster, One Cotton wheel, One do do, One old flax wheel, One chest, One Case of Rasors & hone, One large Bottle & quart do

One Cubbard, Five old chairs, Five Bowls at g'd?, Some earthern ware, Some potters ware, One copper coffe pot, One spice Morter, 1 snuf bottle, One jug & one butter Pott, Three Basons, three dishes, eight plates & 7 spoons, One puter Tankard, Six knives & 12 forks, Fore pare shares, One sarch?, Two Small looking glasses, One pare sad irons, Parcel of lather, Two skillets, One dutch oven

Three pots, 2 pare of hooks, One frying pan, One hand Saw, One plow & colter One pare hames & traces One dutch plough and 2 hoes, One plough hoe, Two augurs & 2 Drawing knives, One chop ax, one Fro, Some old iron, Three Bells & 2 Collars, One claw Hammer & wedge, Two Mattocks, one grubbing hoe, two Broad hoes, Two hilling hoes & two old hoes, One pole ax, One water pail & piggin, One Fat Tub & cirn, One whip Saw, One pan handle

One jointer crow. & Foot Adds, 1 table & cloth, One pair of Stillards, Three raw hides, One cythe & cradle, One pare cards & one candle stick, Two be hives, One Saddle & two Bridles, One Horse, 1 Small Trunk

One old Hhd & some Casks, One mare, One cow & calf, One heffer, One pole ax, One pare horse Phlems

Armica a Woman Slave, Sillar a Girl Do, Polley a Do Do, Phillis a Woman Slave, Billey a Boy        Do

The half of a Cart & Steers. May the 6th 1806, Five barrows, One Sow and Pigs, Six Gees, One Small Barrell
As Witness our hands:
Creed Tanner, Martin Daniel, Samuel Walker
Recorded: September 15, 1806

**AC Book 4, Page 38**                                    **Jno. Dupuy's Account Current**

DR  The Estate of John Dupuy Dec'd  In account with Silvanus Stokes Admr.

1800

Feby 6th – To Stamp paper, cash paid James Meador, Edmund Tunstall, to the auxtioner For crying property, Spirits for the Sale of the hogs, Clerk of Pittsylvania Court, David Pannill

1801

Feby 16 – To Stockley Turner for R. H. & Co., to Clerk of Pittsylvania Court

Oct 19 – To William Irby for the Direct Tax, To Doctor James Linn, To the Sheriff of Pittsylvania

1802

Jany 1st – To Champness & J Terry for goods for the use of the Children, To John Motley for the board of Susanna Dupuy 12 months

Feby 17 – To Paid William Hall for Schooling Do, To Sally W Dupuy for Goods purchased for Susannah Dupuy

1801 (omitted) To ditto for bordering Polly Dupuy 12 months

1803

March – To goods purchased for Susanna Dupuy

May 16 - To Champ & J Terry for Do

Dec 29 – To Edmond Fitzgerald for board of Susannah and Polly Dupuy, To Abe Echols for Schooling both

1804

Feby 20 – To 1 Blanket, pr shoes for Children, Goods for Susanna Dupuy

March – To Do for Do

June 15 – To Do for Polly Dupuy

June 28 - To Do for Susanna Dupuy

Sept 17 –one Saddle and Bridle for Do

Oct 14 – To 1 pr Silk Gloves for Do, To Boarding Do 9 months, To Do of Polley Dupuy 8 ½ months, To Paid Smith Lawson for Schooling Polly, To 1 Spelling Book for Susanna Dupuy

1805

Jun 22 – To Goods purchased for Susanna Dupuy, to Sally Dupuy for goods for do

July 22 – To Goods purchased for Do

Oct 15 - To 1 pr Shoes, 1 Silver Thimble, To bord of Susanna Dupuy to this Day, to 1 pr Shoes for Polly Dupuy, 1 Quire paper for Do, James M. Williams for Surveying & dividing the Land &c, to this Sum pd to Sundries by Mrs. Dupuy agreeable to Voucher filed.

1800

Feby 5 - By the amount of sale due 5 Aug 1801, By James Farmer for Rent, By James Sawyers for hire of a Negro

1801 – By James Farmer for Rent, By James Sawyers for hire of a Negro

1802 – By Hubbard Farmer for Rent, Joseph Mart for hire of a Negro

1803 – By Hubbard Farmer for Rent, By Stewart & Sheets for hire of a agro (sic) (Negro)

1804 – By Hubbard Farmer for Rent, By hire of a Negro

1805 – By Hubbard Farmer for Rent, By Grigory Durrarn for hire of a Negro

In obedience to an order of the Worshipful Court of Pittsylvania County Bearing date December Court 1802 we have Stated and Settled the account Current of the estate of John Dupuy Dec'd with Silvanus Stokes the administrator agreeable to the within Statement Given under my hand this 15 day of Sept. 1806.
D Coleman, Clem't McDaniel, J M Williams
Recorded: September 13, 1806

**AC Book 4, Page 40**                                                   **Nathan Tate's Inventory**

Agreeable to the within order we have convened together at the house of Nathan Tate Dec'd and appraised the said Estate as follows to wit:

2 hammers, 1 Case Knives &c, Shoe Tax & alls, 1 Doz Flints, 1 Iron Skillet, 2 Vials
Appraised by us this 13 October 1806
Robt Walters, Geo Dodson, Jno Clopton

Sworn to before me
Benj Watkins
Recorded: October 20,. 1806

**AC Book 4, Page 41**                                                   **Nat. Thacker's Inventory**

The Inventory of Nathaniel Thackers Estate Dec'd praised by James Hart, Elisha Burton & Alexander Mahan

One White cow & Calf, One Red Cow & Calf, One pided Cow & Calf, One pided Do & Do, One Pided Heifer, One Pided Stear, One Brindle, One Pide Heifer, 6 Head of Sheep, One Grind stone and Iron axel, One Whipsaw, saw, One Box Iron and heaters, One Cross Saw, One Sorrel mare & cold (sic), One Sorrel mare, One pair of Stillards
Two Saws, 4 Drawer knives, 4 Augurs, a parcel of Cooper Tools, Four Reap Hooks, A parcel of Shoe makers Tools, Two Boxes Lumber, One Foot Adz, One Rifle, gun, shot, pouch, horn, ¼ powder & a small piece led, 2 pair of Sheep Shares, 4 Dishes & 8 plates, 7 Spoons, Candle Stick and Snuffers, One Hackle, One Tin Funnel, One pepper Box, 6 knives and seven forks, 2 pair Cloth shears, 3 Basons, 2 lb Steal & 15 lbs iron, Three Stone Jugs and one Butter pot, 3 Mugs, 2 Qurt Bottles, 1 snuff Do, 8 phials & Ticklers 1 Jug, old Brass, pr Saddle Bags, 1 Dutch Oven, 1 Skillet, 1 hone, 1 pot and hooks, curry comp (sic), 1 pot, 2 pair hooks, 1 lock chain, Baking Iron & poker, One still, One Case and 8 bottles, 7 Bee Stands, A Parcel of Casks & Tubs & hand bucket, One Brass Cock, 5 Casks, 1 Cask, 1 Barrel, 1 flesh fork, & Ladle, a parcel of water vessels, Bedstad and Cord, One Chest, 6 Chairs, One Double plated padlock & file, One Table, one feather Bed under Straw do & sted, 2 Sheats, 2 Blankets, Bed quilt Bolslter, 2 Pillows, One Spinning wheele, One Negro Boy Samuel, One Negro Boy Moses, One Negro Wench Juda,, Frank a Negro woman 12 Shoats, 2 sows & 4 pigs, one cutting knife & Box
Recorded October 20, 1806

**AC Book 4, Page 43**                                **Wm Williams' Account of Sales**
To the Worshipful Court of Pittsylvania This is to Certify the sum arising from the sale of the personal property of William Williams, Dec'd

Amount Sale: £7.3.2

Cash on Hand £14.12.0
Total: £21.15.2
Anthony Holloway admin.
Recorded: October 20, 1806

**AC Book 4, Page 44**                                          **William Williams' Inventory**

Where as the worshipfull Court of Pittsylvania did at February Court last Grant an order and appoint Francis Cornwell, Joseph Flippin & George Cook to appraise the personal property of William Williams Dec'd in compliance with the same after being Sworn we met at the House of John Yeaman the ninth of October 1806 and made the following appraisement to wit:

One feather Bed and Stead, 1 chest, 1 pole ax & hilling hoe, 1 pair of money Scales, 1 Bible and Hymn Book, 2 History Books, 1 Slate, 1 Tin pot & Spoon, 1 Spanish Saddle, 3 Bottles, 1 Bottle & 3 Vials 1 Ink stand, Raisor Lancet & Sugar box, 1 Jug, 1 Sword & knife, 1 Rundlet & Canters, 3 gimblets, Hammer nippers & shoe buckles, 1 Tin Cup, 1 Ciphering & Singling Book
Given under our hand this day and Date above Written
Francis Cornwell, George Cook, Joseph Flippen
Recorded: October 20, 1806

**AC Book 4, Page 44**                                  **Appraisement of W. Garners Land**

Agreeabe to an Order of the Worshipful Court of Pittsylvania, we have this day been Viewing the 2 tracts of land of William Gardner, Dec'd and have apaised the same to Three hundred and Sixty pounds Current money. Witness our hands this 23 day of September 1806.
Henry Burwell, Shadrack Boaz, James Fulton
Recorded: October 20, 1806

**AC Book 4, Page 44**                                   **William Mitchell's Inventory**

Pursuant to an order of the Worshipful Court of Pittsylvania we the Subscribers being first duly Sworn have appraised the personal Estate of William Mitchel, Deceased as follows Viz:

1 Bay Mare, 1 Roan Horse, 1 Filley, 13 Head of Hogs, 2 Sows & 7 Shoats, 3 Large Hogs, 11 Small Do, 2 pr.Spancels, 1 Pied Cow & Bell, 1 Steer, 2 Small work Steers, 1 Red Heifer, 1 red Brindle yearling, 2 Cows & 1 yearling, 3 calves & 2 cows, 2 yearling, 3 Sheep

36 Ducks, 1 Grind Stone, 1 Riddle?, 1 pr Smith Tools, 1 plow share, 1 Mattock, 3 axes, 3 hoes, 3 old sythe Blades, 1 Dung fork, 1 pitch Do, 1 coal Rake & Shovel, 1 hoe, 3 Augers, 1 hand Saw, 1 pr Crows & 1 Jointer, 2 Drawing knives & 1 Gouge, 1 plow hoe, 1 Chisel & 1 grubing hoe, 1 pr Stillard & 1 Gun, 1 Table & Bag feathers, 1 Bed sted Bed & furniture, 1 Bed sted Bed & furniture, 1 Bed sted Bed & do, 2 Casks & 1 powdering Tub, 1 old Side Saddle, 2 Juggs

1 Flax Hackle, 1 Lanthron(sic), 1 Tea Canister, 3 pr Cards, 1 Side Leather, 1 Flax wheel, 1Slay, 1 Counter Pane, 1 Chest, 2 Meal Bags, 2 Tea Canisters, 1 Set Tea Cups, Saucers & Spoons, 2 Earthen Bowls &1plate10 pewter plates , 3 Ditto Dishes, 5 Knives & 6 forks, 1 Slate & 1 Gimblet, 1 pr Scissors & 1 earthen plate, 2 Rasors, 2 candle sticks & 1 pr Snuffers

1 Hoan & 1 Bottle, 5 chairs, 1 cupboard, 9 Books, 1 Shoe Brush, 1 Tea Chest, 1 Wool hat, 5 hogshead & 1 meal Tub, 3 potts, 1 Dutch oven, 1 pot Rack, 1 pr Tongs & old pot, 1 Ladle & 1 flesh fork, 1 Candle moal & 1 Ladle, 1 Spinning wheel, 1 Washing Tub, 1 Half Bushel & 1 Fat Tub, 2 Water Pails, 1 Loom, 1 Fat Tub & 1 pail

1 powdering Tub, 8 Bee Gums, 4 Reap Hooks, 1 pr flat Irons, 2 pocket Books, 2 Bells, 5 Fray Irons & 1 open ring, 2 negro Women (nothing), 1 pr money scales, 1 pr Iron Wedges, 1 pr compasses, 1 hand Vice & 1 chisil, 1 old pewter Bason & 3 Tin cups, 2 Bridle Bells, 1 clevice & 1 Twisted Ring, 1 Hawmany? Pistle 2 Bridles, 1 Clevice Rod & screw, 1 Trunk, 1 pewter Bason, 1 Churn, 1 Firken Butter, 1 Butter pott

5 pr Breaches, 1 cap, 2 coats, 1 great coat, 3 pr overalls, 5 Jackets, 1 Black Silk Hankerchief, 2 pr Gloves, 1 Linen shirt, 3 cotton Ditto, 2 pr Yurn Stockings, 1 pr thread Ditto, 1 pr Silver Sleeve Buttons, 1 Silver breast Buckle, 1 Frow, 1 Habit & apron, 1 Ditto & Ditto, 1 Hat, 1 handkerchief, 1 apron, 8 caps, 1 Bonnet & 1 cloak, 1 Gown, 1 pr yurn Stockings, 2 pr cotton do, 1 pr Pockets, 1 pr Silver Shoe Buckles, 1 Bunch of Fillets
Total: £166.14.5    November 15$^{th}$, 1806
John Witcher, Pleasant Fears, George Benaugh
Recorded:  November 17, 1806

**AC Book 4, Page 49**                                    **Edward Robertson's Inventory**

Agreeable to an order of the Worshipfull Court of Pittsylvania directed us, we the Commissioners have proceeded to appraise the property of Edward Robertson Dec'd as Was in the hands of Mary Amy, his widow. To Will one Negro man Slave Cotter and known by the name of Joshua and we consider him to be worth four Hundred Dollars current money 12$^{th}$ Dec 1806.
Jennings Thompson, James Soyars, Joseph Richards
Recorded:  December 15, 1806

**AC Book 4, Page 49**                                    **John Craddock's Account Sales**

The following is an account of Sales the Estate of John Craddocks Estate 28 November 1805

Samuel Pannill 1 Horse
Capt John Ward 1 mare
Ruben Hubbard  1 Dish And Cradle
George Dejarnate  foot ads, 1 Taper Bit, Shock
Langhorn Scruggs  1 Howel
Grose Scruggs 1 crose
Thomas Collins 1 howel
Capt John Ward 1 Chisal
Greose Scruggs 1 drawing nife
Samuel Pannill 1 pr Coopers compasses
Capt John Ward 1 Drawing nife
William Clark 1 Hand Saw
Thomas Collins 2 round Shaves
Drury Scruggs 1 Curry Comb
John Douglas 1 pr Sheap Shers
Thomas Collins 2 Stirrip(sic) Irons
Grose Scruggs 1 Hogshead Jointers
Edward Douglas 1 Broad Ax
Robert Bumpass  1 Pole ax
Drury Scruggs Sen 1 mattock
To  1 Do
Capt John Ward 1 Grubing Hoe
Andrew McHaney 1 Hoe
Drury Scruggs 1 Bell
John Douglas  2 Bells
Andrew McHaney Sen 3 hilling Hoes
Thomas Collins 1 Soop Spoon
Cap John Ward 1 Weeding hoe

Langhorn Scruggs 1 pole ax
Nathan Batterton 1 do do
Stephen Dove 1 Froe

Samuel Pannill 5 Sheep and Bell
William Worsham 1 Boar
Langhorn Scruggs 1 Sow And pigs
Ann Craddock 5 Barrows
Samuel Pannill 1 Black Cow
To 1 Brown Do and Calf
Ann Craddock 1 cow and calf
Samuel Pannill 1 yearling
Enock Organ 1 Shock oats
Ann Craddock 1 cock Blades
Drury Scruggs 1 Blade Stack
Capt John Ward 1 Do Do
Thomas Collins 1 Stack tops and Shucks
Ann Craddock 30 Barrels Corn
To 5 Do Do
Thomas Collins 3 ½ Barrels corn
John Douglas 4 Gees
Drury Scruggs 1 table
Andrew McHaney 1 flax Wheel
Thomas Scruggs 6 chairs
Ann Craddock 1 larg pot
Do Do 1 Piggin
Robert Bumpass parcel puter
Ann Craddock Do Do
To 1 Loom
To 1 Dutch oven
To 1 Pot and 1 hoocks (sic)
Thomas Collins parcel raw hides
Ann Craddock 1 Washing Tub
To 1 chist

Ann Craddock 1 feather bed and furniture
Andrew McHaney 1 Jug
Benjamin Waller 1 Do
Joshua Baber 2 chiers
Ann Craddock 2 do do
George Dejarnate 1 Slay
Andrew McHaney 1 Do
Ann Craddock 1 Slay
To 1 meal Chist
To 1 skillet
George Dejarnate 1 pr flat Irons
Daniel Glass 1 holter chair
Andrew McHaney 2 Decanters
Drury Scruggs 1 Dish, 1 Bole
William Craddock 1 Butter pott
To 1 coffee mill
Andrew McHaney 1 Jug
John Turner 1 Slate, Lead pencil
Ann Craddock 1 looking Glass
Benjamin Waller 2 pr cards

Thomas Collins 1 Book
John Lester 1 bible
Andrew McHaney Sen 1 Book
John Turner 1 Book
Elebeth Craddock 1 coffee Pot

Abraham Black 1 mans Saddle
George Dejarnate 1 Brok Bottle
To 1 pare Horse fleams
Wm Craddock 3 Sasers, 2 cups, 3 Spoons
William Worsham 1 tin sugar Box
To 1 Dish
William Craddock 1 Tin Cannister
To 1 Grind Stone
Thomas Collins 1 Set Knives and forks
Langhorn Scruggs 4 tin cups
Thomas Collins 1 Bason
To 3 Vials
To 1 Bed & furniture
To  Do  do
Langhorn Scruggs 1 Pewter Dish
Total: £134.5.2
Thomas Collins Admr.
Recorded: December 15, 1806

**AC Book 4, Page 52**                                                                 **M. Bates' Account Current**

The property of Mathew Bates Dec'd Sold by the administrator. The first Day of October 1805 & October 1806 each sale a 15 months credit

1. Charles Irby
2. Delaney Holden
3. Joseph Franklin
4. Thomas Parsons
5. Tho B Jones
6. James Bates
7. John Deurman
8. Robert Posey
9. James Moore
10. John Irby Jun
11. Robert Hubbard
12. Edmund Bingham
13. Dudley Farthing
14. Allen Woodson
15. Henry Glass
16. Josiah Rice
17. Thompson Robertson
18. Daniel Camron
19. George Robertson
20. Joseph Mays
21. Lucy H Bates
22. Jo B Dawson
23. Emanuel Jones
24. Robert Oaks
25. Stephen Coleman
26. John Lewis

27. Allen Womack
28. Nancy D Bates
29. John Mihellos
30. Martin Farmer
31. Beverly G Shelton
32. David Nowlin

Thomas Jones 1 Silver watch
William Irby 1 Horse

1801
To Cash paid Jacob Sanders, Higginbotham & Company, David Panill, Sam. Irvin, John Wimbush, William Linzy, John Stamps Dos?, William Wimbush, Thos. & E Jones, Armstad Shelton
Total: £45.13.6

To cash paid for Clerks Ticket at Sundries, Thos B Jones on accompt of British Debt, Thos B Jones, to ditto pd John Adams for crying the Sales, for Spirits at Defferent Sales
Total: £63.16.52

Contra

1801
By cash Received of Sam. Irvin Lynchburg, Wm Woodson, Crop of Tobacco 1800, Thos. Lintecomb
Total: £117.1.9

The Estate of Matthew Bates Decd Dr in acct. with David Nowlin administrator
To amount of money paid away as pr page 3  £63.16.5 ½
To boarding, Clothing, Schooling 5 Children from Xmas 1800 to Xmas 1806. The raising. Feeding & Cloathing 2 Little Negro Children included.  £240.0.0
To an allowance for raising Horses  £53.6.1
Balance: £726.19.1
Money & Bonds in the hands of the Executor £369.7.6 ½
Mrs.Nowlin, late Widow of Mr Bates 1/3 part  £123.2.6
The childrens Part       £246.5.0 ½

Cr

By cash received as pr Page 4  £117.1.9
By amt of Sales as pr Pages 1 & 2  £208.8.4
By amt of Corn, Cotton , Flax, Brandy, Rye, Hogs amounted to £61.0.0
Which Were appraised but made use of before the Sales
By the Hire of the Children's part of the Negroes & the Interest of their money from Xmas 1800 to Xmas 1806 £240.0.0
Balance: £726.10.1

In obedience of the Annexed Order of Court we have Settled & adjusted the acct. Current of the Estate of Matthew Bates Decd with David Nowlin adminstrator and find a Balance of £246.5.0 ½ due The Children of the said Matthew by the Administrator after deducting the Sum of £123.2.6 for the Widow's Part. We have also allotted to Mary B Nowlin late Widow Susie? D Dicey as her Dower of the Slaves . We have allotted the administrator the above Sum of £53.6.1 because of the Horses then a Colt was appraised to 7.10 & sold for £30.0.6. 3 pounds more that were sold  were foal'd after the appraisements and that it is right not to Charge the articles made use of out of the Crop made 1800 as we considered his charge for raising the Children to have been very moderate.
Isaac Coles, Allen Womack, John Adams
Recorded: January 19, 1807

**AC Book 4, Page 56**                                             **Chs. Williams Inv'y**

Agreeabe to an Order of the Court of Pittsylvania to us Directed, we the Subscribers being first Sworn have appraised the Estate of Capt Charles Williams Decd This 20$^{th}$ Day of Decem 1805 to Wit:

Jacob a Negro man, Samuel Do Do, Dick Do Do, Gabriel Do Do, George Boy, Peter, Do, Sary wench, Phibby Do, Milley Do, Little Sary girl, Judy Do, Pigg Do, Henry Do

1 Bay Horse, 1 Mare & colt, 1 Horse, 1 Do, 2 Steirs, 1 Heifer, 3 Cows, 2 Do, 1 Bull & Heifer, 2 yearlings, 1 Bull Cow & Calf, 1 Steir & Heifer, 3 cows, 1 yearling & cow

2 yearlings, 1 cow & 2 Heifers, 1 Do, 1 Steir, 1 Cow & Calf, 8 head Sheeps, 8 fatning Hoggs, 15 sml Hogs, 1 sow, 1 Waggon & 4 pr Gair, 4 old Hogsds, 1 Grind Stone, 25 Geese, Pewter Queens ware Copper Skillet, Bottles qt jarrs, Qurt Jugg & Sad Irons, 1 Case with 10 Bottles, 1 Pine Table, 1 old Desk,
1 Black Walnut Table, 1 old Chest
1 large B. W. Chist, 2 Shot Guns, 1 Bedstead & furniture, 2 Do Do complete, 1 Do Do, 1 Do Do, 1 old flax wheel, 3 Sythes & 2 cradles, 3 plows & Stocks, 1 pr Sheep Shears & nippers, 5 axes & Hammer, 11 Hoes, 2 Grubing hoes, froe & 3 wedges

1 foot adz, 1 pr Steelyards & 3 R Hooks, 1 Drawing Knife, hand saw, 2 Gimblets, 1 Chizel, Coopers adge & auger, 1 X cut saw, 1 old pit saw Do, 3 Rat traps & 1 Hog crose, 12 tight casks & 1 Hogs head,
2 Runlets, 2 Churns, 2 large wheels, 1 Cutting Box & Knife, 4 Potts, 1 Dutch oven & Skillet, 1 wash Tub, 3 Piggins & 1 Churn, 1 weaving Loom, 2 pr Harnesses & 3 Slays, 3 Bee Stands, 9 Cheirs, 2 Powdering tubs & 1 Hogs'd, 2 wheet sheaves, 140 Barrels Corn, parcel Taned Leather, Decanter pitcher, looking glass & tumbler, Water Pail & Stand, 1 Side Saddle, 1 mans Do, 250 lbs Seed Cotton, 7 lbs Picked Do, 1 Chamber Pot, Hackled flax, 20 Bushels wheat Tops, Blades & husks, 1 sml Stack of oats, 5858 lbs Tobacco prised & parsell'd
Total: £1313.7.8
P. Wilson, William Astin, Geo Adams, Jno Wilson, Appraisers
Recorded: January 19, 1807

**AC Book 4, Page 59**                                             **Ro. Bruce's Inventory**

December 31, 1803 agreeable to an order of the worshipful Court of Pittsylvania to us Directed we Wm Smith, Wm Dove & Wm Lewis Jr being first Sworn have proceeded to appraise the Estate of Robert Bruce Decd as follows:

1 Pided Heepher, 1 black cow & yearling & Bull, 1 Bed Bedstead Cord & Mat, 1 Bed, Bed Stead Cord & Mat, 1 pair Bed Blankets, 1 Iron Kettle Damaged & Hooks, 1 Cotton wheel, 1 Hand Saw,
1 Plow Hoe, 1 Grubing Hoe, 1 Bell, 1 Straw Knife & Box, 1 pr Haymes & traces, 1 pine table,
1 pr Sad Irons, 1 Raw Hide
Total: £16.15.6
William Smith, William Dove, William Lewis Jr
Sam'l Pannill administrator

A List of Debts due the Estate of Robt Bruce Decd
Wm Smith & Thomas Gransty £20.5.5 ¾
Money lying in the hands of David Pannill & not appropriated by him £8.4.8 ¼
Sam'l Pannill admr.. £28.10.2

The Following is a List of the Sale of Robert Bruce Dec'd December 31, 1803 accounting the Sum of Thirteen Pounds 18/8 as Below Ward Bruce gave his bond for 1 Horse which he traded away Supposed to belong to the Estate

Sam'l Yeatts

To 1 Pided Heepher, 1 cow yearling & 1 bull

Lucy Bruce
To 1 Bed, Bed Stead Cord & mat

Betsy Bruce
To 1 Bed, Bed Stead Cord & mat

Polly Mustaine
To 1 pr Bed Blankets, 1 pr Sad Irons, 1 pine table

Jos Mays jr.
To 1 Iron Skillet & Hooks Damaged
1 Bell

Champion Mays
To 1 pr Haymes & traces

Thomas Bruce
To 1 Straw Knife & Box

Henry Gosney
To 1 grub'g hoe, & plow hoe

Eliza. Mays
To 1 cotton wheel

1 cow hide Executed by Sheriff for taxes
1 Hand Saw Executed by Sheriff for note
Sold by me   Sam'l Pannill Admr.
Recorded: February 16. 1807

**AC Book 4, Page 61**                                      **Ro. Bruce Account Current**

1804  Dr Estate of Robert Bruce in account with Samuel Pannill, Admr.

May 22 – To cash $1.40.2 Clerks ticket £0.8.4 1/2

July 17 – amount of Debt to Estate of David Pannill per rect.  £10.11.10
July 26 - Cash paid William Dove per his account & Rect. £1.10.0

Novem 22 – Cash paid Polley Mustain in part her Claim entered on back a Bond in her possession 19$^{th}$ June £1.2.0

Decem 4 – Cash paid Polley Mustain pr Rect. £20.1.0

1805
Deduct for our Charge £1.20.0

January 2 – Cash Paid Wm Dove 1 Days Service appraising Estate per Receipt £0.3.0

1807
Jan 7 - To 5 pr cent commistion on receiving £43.8.2 ½
Add Ward Bruce's Bond ren'd him as per Contra £10.10.0, 5 pr cent on this amt. Rec'd & negotiated £2.13.9

Bal due the Estate of R Bruce £6.18.4

1804
January 17 - By cash Received of Wm Smith & Thos Grasty per Wm Ssmith £10.2.5,

Apr 28 – Cash pr Do Do  £10.2.11 ¼

May 22 – Cash pd David Pannill in his life time from Thos Grasty & W. Smith £8.4.8 ¼

Novem 22 – Cash Received of Polley Mustain per Wm Dove in full loan Due in full of her note Rendered Wm Dove who was Secy.

1805
August 21 – Cash £0.13.6

1806
Febarury 19 – Cash Received of Samuel Yates in full his note & Int. £8.13.0

July 22 – Cash Received of Thos Bruce in full his note per Francis Chumney, Constable, Do of Do for Int on Do, Do of Elizabeth Mayes pr Do for Note, Do of Do for Int on Do, Do of Champness Mayes per Do for note, Do for Do for Int on Do, Do of Joseph Mayes jr per Do for note, Do of do for Int on Do, Ward Bruce Note for £10.10.0 Rendered him by order of legatees

November - Cash Received of Lucy Bruce for her note rend', Do of do for Int on Do, Do Receiv'd of Elizabeth Bruce for her note Rend'. Do of Do for Int. on Do, Receiv'd per Francis Chumney, Constable
Total: £43.8.3 ½
By Balan due per Debit £6.18.4

In Obedience of an Order of the Worshipful Court of Pittsylvania County to us directed bearing date April Court 1806  to us directed we Samuel Stone, William Lewis Son of Charles and Zachs. Lewis have examined the account Current of Samuel Pannill Admr. of Robert Bruce Dec'd and the Vouchers produced before us agreeable to the Charges on the within account and find a balance due the said Robert Bruce Dec'd of Six pounds, Eighteen Shillings & 4p. Given under our hands this 2nd Day of January 1807.
Samuel Stone, William Lewis, Zas. Lewis
Recorded: February 16, 1807

**AC Book 4, Page 63**                                                                                   **Cottereel's Account Current**
Andrew Cottrill In Account for William Beavers

1803
January 1 - To Expences at Sundry times at my house, to amount your Bond to Claiborn Settled for, To amount of Ann Cottrills acct vs you as proved before Wm Wilkinson, To account James Colquhoun's account  vs you, To amount James Givins account vs you Proved before Wm Beaveers, To cash paid Sheriff for you by me per Receipt, To amount your account with Wm Wright proved before Capt. Beavers, To George Shelton for Sundries per accot. # 2. To Sundry Smiths work done at Thos Wilkinson's proved before Wm Wilkinson, to cash paid George Shelton officer for fees where was Cash in Warranting, To Eppy Boothe paid for you To Claerks Ticketts
Total: £44.14.8

To Expenses in Keeping the Stud horse before he was Sold 99 Days
To Commissioner on Property Sold 5 P. Cent.

Total: £53.7.11

Cr

By amount Sale your property to wit:
1 Grey Stud Horse, 1 cow
10 Blls. corn
money collected from Prewet
By this Sum Charged George Shelton
Due Capt Beavers
Deduct 3p Per Day for Keeping the Horse
Due Capt Beavers

In Obedience to an Order to us directed by Pittsylvania December Court we have exmined the accounts current between Andrew Cottrill & William Beavers & find the balance above Stated to be Just in favour of William Beavers. Given under our hands this 2$^{nd}$ Day of February 1807.
Alex Brown, James Soyars, George Robertson
Recorded: February 16, 1807

**AC Book 4, Page 64**                                                      Sutherlin's Account Current

Dr. The Estate of George Sutherlin Dec'd In account Current with Thomas & Adams Sutherlin.

1804
Janay - To Cash pd Shff for Clerks Tickets
Oct – Ditto pd Do
Feby – Ditto Surveyor of Pittsylvania
June - Ditto Shff of Ditto

1805
Feby – Ditto Ditto for Clerks Ditto
March – Ditto Ditto for Clerk District Court
Jany - Ditto pd Carter Mickleberry per note proven

1804 Ditto pd Shff for Clerk Pittsylvania
Nov – Ditto pd Ditto Tickets

1805
Aug – Ditto pd Ditto Ditto
Feby – Ditto pd Ditto
March – Ditto pd Ditto
Aug – Cash pd Shff for Clerks tickets

1807 – Do pd Ditto for Do Smiths Cost
Januy 7 – Ditto pd John Wilson per rect.
Januy 10 – Ditto Wm Beavers per acct.

1806 Cash lent George Sutherlin by Thos Sutherlin June 13$^{th}$ 98, Copy of the Will, Ditto of Settlement

Feby 2 – Cash pd Robt Wynne Dr per his rept., Ditto pd James Sutherlin as per his acct., Ditto Do Do Do, Ditto pd Robt Mickleburrough his account, Ditto Adams Sutherlin his acct. proved

Current acct. rendings by John Sutherlin
This sum allowed John Sutherlin for his Services administrator

Amount acct. Rend'd by George Sutherlin
This Sum allowed George Sutherlin his Services as adm.
Cash pd Absalam McDaniel for the Sum alow'd him by the Will
Ditto pd George Sutherlin for bed left him in will

To this Sum for Negroes that was will to the Legatees of George Sutherlin, Dec'd
agreeable to his will & which was Sold by the administrators.

1 Bond put in the hands of W Clark attorney at law & made use of by the sd Clark
To Thomas Sutherlin for his Serv' for acting as Executor
To Adams Sutherlin for his Services as Executor
Cash paid John Sutherlin his part in full per his recipt
Do pd George Sutherlin per his recipt
Ditto pd William Sutherlin per rect.
Ditto pd James Sutherlin per rect.
Ditto pd John Givin Per ricpt
Ditto pd Rob Mickleburrough per reipt
Ditto pd Absalum McDaniel per recpt
Ditto pd William Smith per rept
Ditto pd Thomas Sutherlin
Ditto pd Adam Sutherlin

1805
May 18 – By account Sales made by the administrators on October 10 & December 6th 1803
By cash Rec'd pf Geo Sutherlin for Debt On the Estate
By amount of Sales made by the Executors

In Pursuance of an Order of the Worshipful Court of Pittsylvania county to us directed we have this day met and Settled the account Current of Thomas Sutherlin and Adams Sutherlin Exec. of George Sutherlin Dec'd with the estate of sd George Sutherlin Dec'd and find the above account, as stated by us to be correct agreeable to the Vouchers to us produced and that the balance of one hundred and Sixty eight pounds, Seventeen Shillings and Six Pence, one farthing is due the sd Excts. from the sd Estate. February the 16, 1807
Rich' Jones, James D Patton, Nath'l Wilson
Recorded: February 16, 1807

**AC Book 4, Page 67**                                                                                       **Wilson's Acct. Sales**

Account of Sale of the Estate of John Wilson, Dec'd
One Shot Gun, one mans Saddle, One Sett of Waggon huhs with Irons, One Sett of Do with Ditto, Three Horse Bells, chains, Sundries old Irons, Iron, One Cutting knife & Steel, 2 collers, One old Cutting Knife, One Negro Woman, One Negro woman, Five Books, One Pair Saddle bags, one bed & furniture, One walnut Table, one cupboard & ware, 9 chairs, pine table, three raw hides, Shovel & Tongus, 2 old guns
James Wilson, John Wilson, Henry Wilson: Exors
Recorded: April 20, 1807

**AC Book 4, Page 68**                                                                                              **Wilson's Inventory**

In obedience to an Order of the Worshipfull Court of Pittsylvania we the appraisers being first Sworn do appraise the Estate of John Wilson, Dec'd and return an Inventory thereof to the Court as follows:

One Negro man, One Negro man, One negro Woman, one Negro girl, One Negro Woman, One feather Bed & furneture, 2 old Chests, Shovell & tongs, one Shott gun, 1 walnut Table, 1 pine Ditto, 2 old Guns, 9 Chairs, one cupboard & the Contents, 6 Books, augers, Chisells & drawing knives, 1 Saddle, 3 Dutch plows, 4 colters, old Waggon Irons, 1 lock chain, Barr Iron 4 Iron Wedges, 2 Barr Shear plows, 2 cutting knives, 6 Horse Bells, 5 pole axes, 4 hilling hoes, , 3 Seyths, Cradle, 1 Grind Stone, Horse Geers, Iron Kettle, 2 Polls & one Scillett, pewter & knives & forks, 1 Pair Saddle bags, Stilyards & Hammer, One pitt saw, 1 grid Iron, 4 flesh forks & Ladle, 3 Grubing hoes, one bay mare, 18 head of hogs, 10 head Cattle, 30 head of Gees, one yoke Steirs, one Cart, 4 reap hooks, 1 pr Stilyards, 10 head sheep, 1 set of Razers & strap, one flax Hackle, Three Raw cow hides

Total: £604.1.0
Samuel Walker, Royal King, Peyton King
Recorded: April 20, 1807

**AC Book 4, Page 69**                                                                                    **Mrs. Pannill's Dower**

Mrs Pannill's Dower Negroes were Valued by us to viz: £415
Dean £120, David £45, Prew £60, Milly £90, Sally £75, Kiah £10, Frederick £15 Griffith Dickinson, Vincent Shelton, Isaac Coles

Pittsylvania Janury 1 1807
We have in Obedience to the above Order lay'd off & allotted to Bethenia Pannill widow of David Pannill Dec'd her dower of the Slaves of said Decedant to wit Dean, David, Prew, Milly, Sally, Kiah & Frederick
Griffith Dickenson, Vincent Shelton, Isaac Coles
Recorded: April 20, 1807

**AC Book 4, Page 70**                                                                                    **H. Ford's Inventory**

In obedience to an Order of Pittsyva' Court February 1807 we the appraisers to wit: Creed Tanner, Jackson Walters and William Ragland have conven'd to the appointed house of Henry Ford Deceas'd on the 19$^{th}$ Day of February 1807 and after being qualified do report as follows, viz:

1 Bed bedsted & furniture, 1 Do Ditto & Ditto, 1 Bed stead & parcel feathers, 2 barrells Seed Cotton
1 Hamper & pick Cotton, pees & veseles, 1 bag of Cotton, 1 Side Saddle, 2 old Barrells & Salt, 1 weir Sive,
1 bag flax old & plunder, 1 Shott Gun, 1 Crib Bridle, 3 books, 1 Walnut Table, 1 pale, 1 Chest, 1 looking Glass, 6 chirs, 1 Sad Iron, 1 Candle Stick, 1 pr Shiers & Tribet, 1 sml blue baskit & its Contents, 1 cruit, 1 Lott knives & forks, 1 sml Bell, 1 Steel trap, 1 Decanter, crewit, Tumble, dram glass, & salt seller, 2 Gimblets & file, 1 pitcher, 1 qt bottle, 5 Earthern plates, Coffee Ware, 1 Tin Pepper box & file, 1 Tin Tumbler, 1 old Table, 1 flax wheel, 1 Tub & piggon, 1 large Iron pott, 1 Hackle, 1oven, 1 pott & skillet, 2 pott Racks, 1 pott & 2 pott Hooks, 2 Spinning wheels, 3 pr Cot. Cards, 1 Tub, 1 Piggen, 1 Case & 2 Razors, parcel pewter, 1 Tin coffee, 1 copper Teas Kittle, 1 Shovell, 4 plow hoes, 5 hilling Hoes, 3 Weeding Ditto, 3 Grubbing Ditto, 4 pole & 1 bro'd ax,
1 X Cut Saw, 1 coller, 1 lock Chain, 3 pr. Chain traces, 1 pr. Stilyards, 3 pr. Swingle trees

4 pr. Hames, 1 cutting Knife, 10 Wedges, 2 Drawing Knives, 1 Hand Saw, 6 Chesells, 1 Clivis & 2 Iron Pins, 4 augers, 2 Gouges, 2 Hammers & 1 Taper bell, 5 Horse Sheers, 3 Bridle bells, 2 plains & Stock, 1 hdg'd croze, 3 Sythes & Cradle, 2 britch bands & 3 Collars, 2 mans Saddles, 1 bridle, 5 Sheep Skins & pr. Ps.Lethers, 1 Half Bushell, 2 reap Hooks, 1 Trumpitt & part of reap Hook, 3 raw hides,
40 Barrels Corn, 24 ½ Bus wheat, 1 Grind Stone, 1 ox cart, 1 Cutting Box, 2000 lb oats, 450 lbs fodder in the Granery, Parcel Straw, 1 Grey Colt, 1 Sorrell Colt, 1 bay mare, 1 Grey Ditto, 1 Bay Horse, 410 lbs Bacon, 26 lbs Fatt, 3 butter potts, 2 Jugs, 2 Bags, 4 Tubbs, 2 Sifters & bred tray, 1 Chirn, 3 Casks,
1 Emp HH'd, 1 Hdd., 2 Ditto, 4 Ditto, 1 Tub, 1 Cow & yearling, 1 Do, 1 Do & Calf & Bell, 1 Do,
1 Bull, 1 Cow & Calf, 1 Hefier, 1 Ditto, 1 Cow, 1 Do, 1 Heffer, 1 Cow & Calf, 1 Steer, 24 Gees,
15 Sheep & 9 lambes, 21 Hogs, 1 Top Stack, 1 Heffer yearling

Negro Will, Ditto Betty, Ditto Lucy, Ditto boy Charles

Feby the 27 1807
Negro Edy, Ditto Allen, 1500 lbs of Fodder, 1200 lbs Tobo, One ox ring & Staple, Stack of Shucks,
Foot adds & 1 Clevis, 1 Fro & 1 howel, one Hone, 4 Slays, One old muskit
Total: £711.6.0
Creed Tanner, William Ragland, Jackson Walters
Recorded: April 20, 1807

**AC Book 4, Page 74**                                                   **Wm. Mitchell's Inv'y**

We the apprasers of the Estate of William Mitchell Dec'd do apprase the Balance of the Estate as follows:

Three Sides of Lether, One Sow & five Shots, 25 Chickings & Six pence, 1 small hammer, One pair of Specticles, One Cuting Box & Knife, One Hogg
Peter H Clark, Executor, Pleasant Phares, John Witcher
Recorded: May 18, 1807

**AC Book 4, Page 74**                                             **Tho. Martin's Account Current**

The Estate of Thomas Martin Dec'd In Acct. Current with Leonard Dove, Exor.

1800 – To cash Flk Pitt per Ticket

1801 – Ditto     Ditto
Ditto Elisha Williamson Constable per acct. recpt., John Thrusher's Witness to prove Thos Martins Will per order & rect., Ditto for Stamp Paper to appraise the Estate of Thomas Martin Dec'd

1802 - Ditto paid Net Amount Constable pr Rect., amount of your Execution account against your Testator

1807 – Cash paid William Tunstall Clk pr Ticket

June 13 – Services of attending the Sale and collecting as below.
Bala' due the Estate of T Martin, Dec'd £49.6.6

1800
Oct - By amount your Execors. Purchase at Sale
Edm'd Bingham   Do
Thomas Simpson Sen Ditto
James Famborugh  Ditto
Milley Martin      Ditto
Thomas Simpson jr   Ditto
James Love       Ditto
Burdet Roach  Ditto
William Simpson  Ditto
Samuel Yeatts  Ditto,
Jesse Kesee Ditto
John Simpson  Do
Cash rec'd for 2 Cream Potes, 1 bottle & Basket
Cash rec'd of Elijah Cundiff For 9 Barrels Corn which he owed
Ditto rec'd of Elisha Cundiff for his note
Memo' Livicey Martin's bond of £4.17 for her purchasen at sale is not yet collected

In obedience to an Order of the Worshipfull Court of Pittsylvania County to us directed we have Examined the account Current of the Estate of Thomas Martin Dec'd and Leonard Dove, Exor. And the Vouchers produced before us, we find the balance due the said Estate of Eighteen pounds, thirteen Shillings and Eight pence. Given under our hands this 13$^{th}$ Day of June 18 Hundred and Seven.
Nathan Glenn, Wm Smith, William H Stone
Recorded: June 15, 1807

**AC Book 4, Page 76**                                                   **Geo. Herndon's Inv'y**

Pittsylvania County, we the apprasurs met agreeable to us Order of Court was maid for the apprasement of George Herndon Dec'd Estate and after being first Sworn we Proceeded as followeth

To One Horse, To One Cherry Chest, To one Cherry Do Do, To one Bed & Bedstead & furniture, To one Bed Do Do, To one Bed Do Do, To two bed & bed Sted Do, To two colter wheels, To four pare of Cards, To two flax wheels, To three Irons & one Spice Morter, To Elevin Chiars, To three Tables, To one Cash & bottle, To Puter of Sundarys Sorts, To five tin Cups, To Six Knives & nine folks, To four Water Vessels & two trays, To one coffee mill, To Pots & two Dutch ovens & two Skillets
To Earthen Ware of Sundry Sorts, To three Glasses & one Jack & one funnel, To one Gun & one pare Sillard, To one Lanton & four Boks & one Trumpet, To one woman Saddle & one Grid Iron, To Earthen pots & two Slays, To one Negro Woman & Child
The hole amount: £208.13.8
Peyton Graves, David Vance, Wm Witcher Executor, Richard Burnett
George Herndon Decd
Joseph Tolar
Recorded: June 15, 1807

**AC Current Book 4, Page 77**                                                                                   G. Shelton's Inv'y

1803
Octob 20 – An Inventory of a balance of property of the Estate of Gabr'l Shelton Dec'd which was not appraised the first Day to Wit:

Parcel of Flax, Do Blades, Corn Suppos'd to be 34 barrels, Parcel leather, 1 CowHide raw, Parcel fodder, Do Rye Supplos'd to be 10 Bushels, Do Rye in Stacks, 1 oat Stack, 1 Stack Tops and Sucks (sic) within same, 1 old Sythe & Cradle, Parcel Seed Cotton out for B. Shel. G., Beverley Shelton's part of Cotton
Henry Kay, Thos Payne, Beverley Shelton
Recorded: June 16, 1807


**AC Book 4, Page 78**                                                                                   Stockton's Inventory

Inventory & appraisement of the Estate of John Stockton, Dec'd

1 Bureau & Candle Stand, 1 Folding table, 1 Square Do, 8 Split bottom Chairs, 2 large Trunks, 2 Small Do, 1 Desk, book case & Books, 1 large Folding C. Table & 1 Square Do, 1 Cupboard & its Contents
1 Square Walnut table, 6 Windsor Chairs, 6 Split Bottom Do, 2 Fire Skreens, 2 looking Glasses, 1 Shott Gun (Bursted), 1 tea Tin (large), 12 Cloke Pins, 4 Silk Embroidered Pictures, 6 Prints in frames,
2 Crpetts, 1 Bed & furniture, 1 Do & Do & Stead, ! Womans Saddle, 2 Split bottom chairs, 1 Tin Trumpet & 1 Reel, 1 Square Pine table, 1 Bed & furniture &c, 1 Do & Do &c, 1 Do & Do, 1 Do Do, 1 Do Do, 2 Beds

6 Setts Window Curtains & 1 mantle Cloth, 1 Band Box, 8 Sheets & 4 new Counter Pens, 2 Worked Counterpanes fring'd, 1 bed quilt & 1 Counter pain, 1Bed quilt not finished hexegon Work,
Part suit Bed curtains, 3 table Covers, 6 furniture Do, 3 Pair bed blankets, Kitchen furniture,
2 Cotton wheels, 2 flax Do, 1 Sorrel mare Colt, 1 Bay mare Do, 1 Bay Horse Do, 1 Bald Eagle Horse,
1 large bay mare, 1 Dark Horse, 1 Do do, 1 Brown mareColt, 1 Bay Colt, 1 X cut Saw & 1 Pit Do,
1 X cut Saw & 2 Hand Do, 1 large Still, 1 Small Do, 11 head Sheep, 1 Grind Stone, 1 Riding Chair Harness

1 cuting box & knife, 1 Waggon & Gears, 1 old Do & 2 pair Breeches, 1 pair cart wheels
3 ploughs &c, 3 Cotton Do &c, 1 Sett Black Smith's tools, 50 lbs Iron In Parcels, 1 bar Share Plough &c, 1 Small Do Do, 1 Pair Stylards, 40 lbs old Iron, 19 Hhds. & Casks, 1 Small Steal Trap, 1 Crow Bare, 1 large Bell, 1 large Bell, 31 head hogs, 1 Hackle, 3 Tin Funnels & 3 brass cocks, 3 Waggon Boxes, 3 Broad axes & one froe, 1 Sett Irons for Cutting mill Stones, 6 Hilling hoes & 6 Grubing Do,
6 axes, 1 pair Iron Wedges, Carpenters tools, 5 old Shovels & 11 Reap hooks, 1 Parcel Tobo., 1 Ditto Bill for 1649 lbs Iron, 3 Cows & yearlings, 1 Stear & 2 work Bulls, 1 Heifer, 1 Cow & 2 yearlings,

1 Pair Saddle bags, 1 Negro Woman Milley, 1 " Man Harry, 1 " Charles, 1 " Jack, 1 " Harry,
1 Boy Nero, 1 Woman Tiller & Child Amanda, 1 " Cabel, 1 " Dorcas, 1 Girl Chaney, 1 " Mary,
1 " Lucey, 2 Boys Hallaway & Ned, 1 pewter, 2 Potts, omitted, 1 Cow & Calf, 1 Sow, five Shoats,
5 Small pigs, 1 large Pott & Skillet, An account against Edward Popejay for rent, 1 Trunk, 1 Bed &
furniture, 1 Bed Do Do, 1 Bed Quilt & 1 Counter Pane, 1 Pair Sheets, 1 Worked Counter Paine,
1 Negro Girl Phillis
Total: £1830.15.10

We the undersigned being first duly Sworn agreable to an Order of the Worshipful Court of Pittsylvania County have appraised all the Personal Estate of John Stockton Dec'd Shown to us by the admrs. Of the said John Stockton, Dec'd as Stated above. Given under Our hands & Seals this 18$^{th}$ Day of July 1807.
Jas. Hopkins,. Caleb Hundley, Nich' Parrish
Recorded: July 20, 1807

**AC Book 4, Page 82**                                               Gilbert's Account Current

The Estate of Preston Gilbert Dec'd In account current with John Gilbert, Exor.

1806

Jany 1 – Paid the Estate of Patrick Henry For rent of long Island
Paid the Sheriff Tax &c per Rect. Granted Rich'd H Luck per. Rect, Joseph East per. Ditto, Rich'd H Luck per Ditto, Oliver White per Ditto, Wm Brown & Co. Do, H. Davis &Co. per. Do, H. Davis &Co per. Do, Allen Thurman, Mitchell M. Gallion. Clerks Ticket, Do Do, I A Wayne J M Gordon, Chas. Hodges, for 2 tobo notes, Philip Payne for 4 Barrels Flour which paper in Superfine, for Services rendered.
Total: £83.8.0
Balance Due the Estate: £34.18.10
Total: £118.6.10
By amt. Of Sales & the Tobacco & wheat sold: £118.6.10
Balance due per Debit: £34.18.10

Agreeable to an Order from the Worshipful Court of Pittsylvania County to us directed, we have proceeded and settled the acct. Currant of Preston Gilbert, dec'd with John Gilbert Exor. And find a balance due the Estate of £34.18.10. Given under our hands this 13$^{th}$ Day June 1807.
Rich'd H Luck, Harden Chick, John Luck
Recorded: July 21, 1807

**AC Book 4, Page 83**                                               Chrisp. Shelton's Invent'y

In obedience to an Order made by the Worshipful Court of Pittsylvania to us Directed for the appraisement of the Estate of Crispin Shelton, Dec'd we appraised as followth to Witt: May 12$^{th}$ 1807

1 Negro Man Gruff, 1 Do Do Castelleo, 1 Do Do Major, 1 Do Boy Patrick, 1Do Do Stuart, 1 Do do Billy,
1 Do Do West, 1 Do Woman Luce, 1 Do Do Phillis, 1 Do Do Lydia, 1 Do Do Aggy, 1 Do Girl Sally, 1 do
Do Stella, 1 Do Do Jenney

1Bay Horse, 1 sorrel Ditto, 2 Roan colts, 5 head Sheep, 13 head Cattle, 17 Ditto Hogs, 1 Ox Cart,
1 Grind Stone, 1 wheel bearing, 1 Harrow Iron Tooth, 3 Plow hoes, 8 Hilling Hoes, 4 Colters,
4 axes, 1 Broad ax, , 1 Hand Saw, 4 Screw Augers, 3 chizzels, 1 Jointer, Bill and Stock, 5 plain Do Do, 1
Smoothing plain, 2 Drawing Knives, 1 Cutting Box and Knife, 2 Cradles and 3 Sythe Blades

3 reap hooks, 2 Setts plow Geers, 3 Bells, 2 Iron Wedges, Box with Sundrie tools, 1 wire Seive,
2 mens Saddle, 1 Side Ditto, 3 Bridles, 1 log chain, 1 X cut Saw, 3 mataxes, 1 Grubbing Hoe,
1 Foot adds, 1 pr Compasses and rule, 1 Round Shave, 1 Hatchett, 1 Tommy Hawk, 1 Barrel auger,

2 Taper Bitts and one Stock, 1 pr Sheep Shears, 6 feather beds and furniture, 4 beds Steeds, Cords and Mats, 1 Walnut table, 1 pine do, 1 Pine Cupboard, 2 large Hair Trunks, 1 Small Do Do, 1 Pine Chest, 1 Case of Bottels, 1 Shott Gun, 5 Slays, 1 Tin watering Pott, 1 Revised Code, 1 Hennings Virginia Justice, 1 Laws United States, 2 Latin Dictionaries, 2 Ditto Grammers, 2 Ditto Corderie?, 2 Ditto Erasmus, 1 Columbian Orator, 1 American Preceptor

1 American Selections, 1 art of Speaking, 1 Gutheries Geography, 1 Enticks Dictionary, 1 young mans Companion, 3 English Grammers, 3 Testamemts, 1 bible, 1 prayer Book, 1 Scotts Lessons, Books of Difference, , 1 bell metal Skillet, 1 Brass candlestand, 2 Iron Ditto, 1 Copper Coffee Pott, 1 Do Tea Kettle, 7 Butter Potts, 3 Stone Jugs, 1 Tin Gallon Pott, 1 Pewter Pint Do, 8 Pewter Basons, 3 Do Dishes, 8 Do Plates, 9 Do Spoons, a Parcel knives and forks, 2 Decanters, 3 Cotton wheels, 1 small Ditto, 2 Dutch ovens, 1 large Pott, 1 Small Do, 1 Ditto, 1 Do Pott Rack, 1 Do Grid Iron, 1 pr Do pot Hooks, 1 Iron Ladle & Skimmer &c, 1 pr Do, Shovel, tongs & poker, 2 Ditto Fire Dogs, 1 pr. Flat Irons, 1 loom, 1 Chafin Dish, 1 Trevitt, 1 Tin funnel, 1 moweing Sythe, 1 Brier Syth, 1 Coopers adds,
1 Frow, 1 pr. Stamp Irons, 1 Sythe, anvil, Hammer, 1 Sett Center Bitts, 1 Gun Lock, 1 pr. Marking Irons, 1 Brass Cock, 1 Spaid, 2 Bridle Bitts, 2 Damaged Slates, 2 Hogshead , Croses & Gouge

1 Saw Rest, 1 pr large Nippers, 1 Sett Shoe makers tools, 1 Trough Digger, 2 Squares, Sundrie Kegs with Paint, 2 pr Saddle Bags, 2 Pains Glass, 2 Tubs and 3 Pails, 1 Sifter, 3 Trays, 2 Bee Stands, 2 Blowing Horns, 1 pr Shell Brass, 1 Iron Spice mortar, 3 Clivises and two Swingle trees, 1 ox yoke,
1 Ditto, 1 Small Skillet, a parcel of tins, 3 Wine Glasses and 2 Tumblers, 2 pepper Boxes and 2 Salt Stands, 1 Tumbler and Vials, Sundrie Vials containing Some medicine

1 Bottle with camphire, 2 Tea Potts, 2 Sugar Dishes, 1 Cream and mustard Pott, 2 Waiters and a parsel of tin ware, 2 Bowles, 15 Earthern plates, 4 Earthen Dishes, 1 Bottle spet's Turpentine, 3 Black Bottles
2 Cupboard locks, 1 Pitcher, 1 Snuff Bottle, 1 looking Glass, 16 Barrels, 3 Boxes
9 Casks, 1 Rundlett and 1 wood funnel, 1 Still and pewter worm, 1 Pr. Stilyards, 6 Hogsheads and 2 small Do, 1 parcel Irons, 1 piece German steel, 9 Geese, 9 Chairs, 1 Yoke Oxen, parcel peucian blue,
2 Casks & 2 Hds., 1 Sett Razors, Strap & Box, 1 Hone, candle molds, Snffers,
Total    £3628.95.0
Zach's. Lewis, Nathan Glenn, Avery Mustain, Appraisers

The foregoing is a Perfect Inventory of Cris. Shelton Dec'd Estate as far as have Came
Into Our hands.
Susanna Shelton, Chs. I Shelton, Abra. C Shelton, Execs.
Recorded: July 20, 1807

### AC Book 4, Page 89                                                                                          Burnett's Inv'y

In obedience to an Order made by the Worshipful Court of Pittsylvania and to us Directed, we being first Sworn do now proceed as follows to appraise the Estate of Thomas J Burnett, Dec'd July 17th 1807

Parcel of Pewter, Parcel of tin ware, 1 Pitcher, parcel Castings, 19 Head Cattle & 2 Bells,
1 Grey Horse, 1 Bay mare & colt, 1 Ditto   Ditto, 7 Stone Jugs, 4 quart Bottels, Glass ware, Earthern Ware, 1 Shott Gun, 1 Table, 2 Chests, 9 Chairs, 2 flatt Irons, 2 Cotton wheels, 1 flax wheel, 1 Sml. Table, 1 Feather Bed & furniture, 1 Ditto   Ditto   Ditto, 1 Ditto   Ditto   Ditto, 2 Ditto   Ditto   Ditto
Knives & forks, 20 lbs Feathers, Pr Sml. Steelyards, Casks, 1 Black Horse, 1 Sythe Blade & Cradle, Sundry Tools, Water Vessels, 1 Looking Glass, Pr money Scales, Pr Wool Cards, 8 head Sheep, Stock of Hogs, 2 Pr Cotton Cards, 1 pr. Wool Ditto, 8 head Gees, 6 Bee hives, 3 Slays, Sml. Hackle,
1 Negro man Harry, 1 Ditto woman Cloe, 1 Ditto   Ditto Vilett
Total: £1424.89.0
John Ward Min., James Arthur, Wm Burnett, John F Dalton
Recorded: July 20, 1807

### AC Book 4, Page 91                                                                                          Wm. Waller's Inventory

William Wallers, Dec'd Estate appraised

1 Steir, 1 yoke of Bulls, 1 Heffer, 1 cow and yearlin, 1 cow and yearlin, parcel of Hogs, old Iron, Flat Irons and Hammers, Plantations Tools, Crosscut Saw, Plows and Gears, Cutting box and Knife, Pots and ovens,, Water Vesels, Some Sithes and Cradles, old Saddle, 2 Beds and furniture, 2 Beds and furniture, 2 old Guns and 3 wheels, tubs and Jointer, books and Safe, Pewter Knives and forks, Cubard and old Saddle bags, Iron Wede(sic) And old Tools, 1 mare and Colt, pare of Steelyards, old Negro Peter, old wench Mary, Fellow Little Peter, Boy Tom,  Wench Lucy,  Girl Rachel,  Girl Nance, boy Manuel,  Girl Doll,  Girl Miriah,  Boy Carter,  Boy York, Gray mare and Colt, Mare Colt
Thomas Moore, Stephen Yates, William Haymes
Recorded: August 17, 1807

**AC Book 4, Page 92**                                                                                          **Ford's Account Current**

The Estate of Henry Ford to William Thompson the Exeor.

1807

March – Paid Ambross Haley jr by E Ford
1 muskett, 3 bushels wheat paid Ambross Haley
Cash paid Elijah Creel 2 vouchers
March 7 – Cash paid Francis Daley for making coffin for the Dec'd
Cash paid Sil Vaden for Crying Property at the Dec'd Sale

April 10- Cash paid Jarrald Ford for 5 bushels of Corn

April 25 -  paid Elisha Ford in Bonds & accts.
Paid Thomas Shelton & James Murphy
This sum paid Jarrald Ford per Voucher

April 29 This sum paid Johnson Lansdiwn Do

May 4 -  paid Benjamin Terry Senor
To five Bushels of Corn for Carriage of Tobacco

May 25 – The sum paid John H Hendrick per Tho. Shelton
Paid Thomas Shelton for 1 weather proved by T. Chaney
Paid Jarral Ford 9 months Interest and his pro acct.

Jun 11 – paid John Fords pro. Acct.
Paid Daniel Slayden Do
Paid Josiah Shelton Do

Jun 13 -  paid Benjamin Watkins part of Bond
Paid James Walker

July 10 – Paid Thomas Chaney pro. Acct.
Do paid the same for whiskey
Paid Francis Duly per Acct.

July 13 -  paid Sam'l Carter for the Season on One mare
Paid Wm Ragland for his Services account apps.

Aug -  paid Sheriff Pitts' Tax & leavies for 1806

Paid Achiles Whitlock per Voucher
Paid Beverly Barksdale bonds and prov'd accts.
Paid Same Int. on the above Bonds
To this sum allowed William Thompson for his Services as Exec. Of the Estate
Total: £208.7.6

Cr

1807

Feby By Sale of Sundry Property
Feby 27 – Elisha Ford
**Bond on Johnson Wall**
Part of Hhd. Tobacco
John Ford
Beverly Barksdale for 896 lbs. Seed Cotton
**Cash rec'd of Beverly Barksdale**

Aug  Cash rec'd f Harris Brown
Balance In favour of the Estate:  £8.15.2

In obedience to an Order of the Worshipful Court of Pittsylvania to us Directed we the under written Subscribers have this day proceeded to Settle the account Current of the Estate of Henry Ford, Dec'd with William Thompson the Exor. And find that there is a ------- in the hands of the Exor. At this time to the amount of Eight pounds fifteen Shillings and two pence as will appear from the Debits & Credits in the foregoing Page . Given under our hands this 11$^{th}$ Day of September 1807.
Sto. Turner, Wm Shelton, William Ragland
Recorded:  September 21, 1807

**AC Book 4, Page 94**                                                                                             **Thomas's Account Current**

The Estate of John Thomas, Dec'd
To Durrett Richards Dr.
1806
To Bal. Due on account Currant Settled 19$^{th}$ Oct 1805: £22.2.10 ½

May 9 – To Paid Asa Thomas bal. Of two notes  Joice Thomas vs you

July 15 –To Paid an Execution Jean Read Guardian of  Thos. Read & John & Chas. Thomas
To pd an Execution Thomas Fisher vs you

Prov. Eq. To
Interest on Do from 13$^{th}$ Feby 1801 to 25 Dec 1806
To pd an Execution vs you William K Harrison a pincelsic of Jean Read
Interest on Do from the 30$^{th}$ Dec 1800 to 25 Dec 1806
To bal. Of yr note To Dav'd Smith
To Interest on Do from 5 Dec 1799to 25 Dec 1806
To yo'r note to Durrett Richards in fav. Of Nath'l Thomas Dec'd due 26 June 1800
To Interest on Do to 25 Dec 1806
To pd John Freemon & Rob. Wilkins for building a Tobo. House on the land of Jno Thomas.
To pd Richard Johnston for notifying  the commissioners to Settle acct. current Octo. 19 1805 & paying Asa Thomas his Ferriage

To pd John Rogers for going to Pittsylvania County Court to proves yo'r Will
To Cash expended going to Danville to Settle acct. Current 1806

To Paid Jno Walters agent for the orphans of Nath'l Thomas vs Jno Thomas  See it.

To Pd my ferriage going & coming to Settle acct. Current 19th Oct. 1805

1800
April 14 -  To Paid Matt Terry balance of a bond given by Jacob & Jno Thomas & assigned by said Terry to Jeffrys and Richards

per. Contra            Cr

By one tract of land whereon John Thomas, Dec'd Sold to John Lewis for $671
By errer in addition & Calculations of Interest
By Balance due D Richards.
Total: £212.9.3

Pursuant to an Order to us directed from the Court of Pittsylvania County we have Proceeded to examine & Settle & adjust the acct. Current of Durrett Richards with the Estate of John Thomas, Dec'd and we find the Vouchers To us Produced a Bal. Due said Richards of Ten Pounds, Seventeen Shillings and Six pence. Given under Our hands this 1st Day of August 1807.
Ro. Payne, James Hillyer, James D Patton
Recorded: September 21, 1807

**AC Book 4, Page 97**                              **Thomas's Account Current**

The Estate of John Thomas
To Asa Thomas Excr            DR.

1806
June 26 – To Paid the Shff of Pitts' for Clks Ticketts

1807
May 27 -  Pd Rich'd N Venable a fee for Pleading in Defence of a Suite brought by Wm Thomas and Halifax Court.

June 18  - pd the Clk Pittsy'.

July 21 – Do Orlando Smith part of a prov'd Acct.
Do Paid Sundry Sheriffs Tickets

Cr

1806
June 26 -  By Cash Rec'd of James Dix for two lots in Milton No 10  11

1807
July 21 -  Do Francis Epperson in part of the rent of land

Pursuant to an Order to us directed from the Court of Pittsyl' County we have proceeded to Examine, Settle & adjust the acct. Current of Asa Thomas with the Estate of John Thomas, Dec'd and we find from Vouches to us produced a balance due said Asa Thomas of  Five Shillings & eleven Pence, half Penny. Given under our hands this 1st Day of August 1807.
Ro. Payne, James Hillyer, James D Patton
Recorded:  September 21, 1807

**AC Book 4, Page 98**                      **Pannill's Account Current**

The Estate of David Pannill Dec'd In account with Samuel C Pannill, Exor.

Cr

1806
Aug 15 - To Balance due on Settlement p. acct. return to Court p. the Commisioners.

Oct 11 - Cash paid Wm B Banks for fee in Case against Irvin

Oct 22 - Cash paid Clk Franklin p. Tickett

Oct. 28 – Cash paid William Smith Cost of Suite Mead against him

Nov 18 - Cash paid Stokley Turner former Sheriff Pittsyl' for Ticketts

Dec 8 - Cash paid John Wickham fee in new case against Ball P/ Rect.
Cash paid Clerk D Court in Richmond for tax on writ against Ball
Cash paid Balls Execution for Cost per George Hays Rect.

1806
Aug 16 - By Wm G Parham for Cash

Aug 20 – James Linn Per John Lewis
Ditto Ditto Per Thos. Payne
Ditto Ditto Per Wm Wimbish
Isaac Coles Colo. For Cash
James Lewis Do
Ben Oliver Do
James Hunt
Amos Farris
Ditto Ditto

Aug 28 - Abra. Shelton Chloe

Sept 26 Chloe Shelton
Spencer Medcalf
Robert Love

Oct 22 - John Gregory
William McNeley
Philip Johnson

Oct. 28 Michael Mitchell
William G Parham
John Lester
Henry Worsham do
Henry Arnold Do
Daniel McGregger Do

Nov 18 - Peter Perkins 2nd May Last
Edmund Tunstall
John Bruce overseer

Dec 8 – Thomas Self
James Linn
Samuel Parsons, Senr.

Dec 16 – George McNeley
Nathan Thurmond Senr.

1806 To amount brought over

Dec 7 - John Dabney Paid him for fees Per account & Rect.

Dec 25 - Nathan Glenn Per notes taken in & rect.

1807
Jany 3 – William Smith P. note & Rect.

Jany 26 - Cash paid Sheriff Tickett in Case of Ryburn P Ticket

Feb 18 - Cash paid Samuel Calland cost of suite for land in Pittsyl' Court
Cash paid William Yancy Sheriff pittsylv' for Ticketts
Cash paid Clerk Pittsylv' for Do
Ditto paid John Dabney For his fee Per. Rect.

March 13 - Cash paid Clerk of Campbell per 2 Ticketts

March 17 - Cash paid Sheriff of Pittsylvania for Ticketts
James Linn for error in receiving money Per John Lewis

1806
Dec 16 - Amount brought over
By Robert Love for 20 Barrels Corn Received on account land

1807 Jany 3 - Charles Lewis jun. received
Chloe Shelton Do
Edmund Tunstall Do
Thomas Wells Do
William Parker Do

Jany 5 - William Pringle Do

Jany 21 – John Harris Do
John Lewis Do
Nathan Thurmond Sen Do

Feby 18 - William Bolling do
Sandy river Stone Do
Leroy Shelton Do
James Linn Do
Thomas Self Do
Crispin Shelton Do
Michail Mitchell Do
Joseph Robertson Do
Joseph Polley Do
Nathaniel Jones Do

Feby 20 – William Pannill Do

March 17 - Thomas Richardson Do
Rubin Mitchell Do
Abraham Shelton Bev Do
Crispin Shelton
James Linn Do
John Saunders Do
Thomas Self Do
Nathan Thurmond Sen Do
Drury Owen
To Amount Brought over

April 22 – Cash paid Briant W Nowlin Per Rect.
Cash paid Sheriff Pittsylva'
Ditto Clerk Halifax P. Tickets omitted 20th Aug 1806

May 7 - Cash paid Hartwell Allen cost in suit of Oliver Per Statem't & Rect.
Sam'l Parsons Sen Per Rect.

Jun 3 – Ro. & Waller Colquhouin Per Rect. Your Bond taken in
Cash Paid Isaac Tynes Constable for Cost of Settling Joseph West account Per Rect.

1807
Mar 17 - By amount brought forward
Beverly Shelton (Bev, rec'd
Henry Croff Do
Joseph Thacker Do

April 14 - Gabriel Shelton jun Do
James Linn Do

April 15 - Grasty & Pannills Do
Ditto Ditto
John McCritchard Do
Jsoeph Smith Do

April 22 – Nathaniel Faris Do
John Watson Do
John Patterson Do
John Harris Do
Leonard Dove Do
Gabriel Shelton Do
Briant W Nowlin Do
James Craine Do
William Williams Waggo. Do
Joshua Hardy Do
Charles Keatts rec'd

May 2 – Grasty & Pannills Do
473 ½ lbs Bacon rec'd Ro. Love on 9th

May 20 - John Jenkins
Edward Nunnelee
Grasty & Pannil's

June 3 - Rubin Mitchell
Grasty & Parnills
Ditto Ditto

June 17 - William Burns
George McNeley
John Rowland Sen.
Chloe Shelton
William Williams Waggo.

1807
Jun 17 - To amount brought over

July 24 - Commision of 5 P Cent allow'd on Collecting £2253.1.9 since the last Settlement.
Bethenia Pannill paid her 1/3 part of the money now due the Estate as P. acct. above Stated & her Rect. Heirs of David Pannill Dec'd for the bala. Of the money now on hand as stated in this acct. it being two thirds now in the hands of their guardian as will appear from the account of the guardian this Day Settled

1807
June 17 – By amount brought over

June 24 - Jesse Rowland Sen. Rec'd

July 9 – Richard Wal

July 21 - Grasty & Panills
John Hoskins
Negro Pannills Drewry

In obedience to an Order of the County Court of Pittsylvania bearing Date June Court 1807 to us directed we have examined the account of Samuel Pannill, Exor. Of David Pannill, Dec'd and the Vouchers attending the Same agreeable to the account was above Stated, and find at this day all the moneys which has come into his hands as Exor. Since the Settlement in 1806 is fully appropriated. Given under our hands this 24th Day of July 1807.
Wm. Smith, Wm Wimbish, Philip L Grasty
Recorded: September 21, 1807

**AC Book 4, Page 103**                                                           **Pannill's Gdrs. Account Current**

Dr. The Heirs of David Pannill Dec'd  In acct. with Samuel Pannill, Guardian    CR

1806
Aug 20 – To cash paid Sheriff Pittsylv' Per Tickets

1807
Feby 9 – Ditto paid Register of land office Per Rect

Feby 18 – Ditto paid Clerk Pittsylva" Per Ticket
Ditto Paid Sheriff Pittsylva' Do

Mar 13 – Ditto Paid Clerk of Campbell Do
Ditto Paid land Tax in Patrick P. Rect.

July 24 - 5 Per Cent Comms. Allowed on Collecting £42.12.8

Bala. Due the heirs this Day

Cr
1806
Aug 15 – By Bal.due Per account Return to Court

1807
Jany 3 – Cash rec'd of Charles Lewis jun for rent of land in Patrick for 1806

Feby 18 – Ditto rec'd of Frederick Shelton for rent of White Thorn land for 1805 Per Jno Lewis
Ditto rec'd of Fred Shelton for rent of white thorn land for 1806

April 30 – Cash rec'd of Wilmouth Crowder for rent of land for 1805 & 1806 in Halifax

July 24 - Interest on £21.1.8 from 15$^{th}$ August 1806 to 24 July 1807

By bal. Due as above
Samuel Pannill Exor. Rec'd for Bala. Due the Estate of D Pannill Dec'd Per his account this Day Settled By the Comisioners.

In Obedience to an Order of the Worshipful Court of Pittsylvania County to us directed bearing date June Court 1807 we have examined the account of Samuel Pannill Guardian with the heirs of David Pannill, Dec'd agreeable to the within Statement with the Vouchers attending the Same and find the balance due the heirs this Day to be one thousand and thirty seven pounds, Shillings & eight Pence /4. Given under our hands this 24$^{th}$ Day of July 1807.
Wm. Smith, Wm Wimbish, Philip L Grasty
Recorded: September 21, 1807

**AC Book 4, Page 105**                                          **Thomas's Gdn. Account Current**

Nathanael P Thomas To Asa Thomas Guardian            Dr

1805
Nov 4 – To pd John Epperson one half of his attendance a Witnes vs John Walters

Dec 14 - 1 Pr. Shoes

1806
Apl 10 - 1 pr. Do

Aug 2 - Half of 2 qts whiskey for Amey & Children

Nov 29 – Pd Ditto D. McDaniel for 7 ½ months schooling at $5 pr. Year

Dec 25 – Pd Thomas Bouldin part your acct.
1 pr Double Soled Shoes

1807
Jany 31 - Pd John Epperson as pr. Rect.
Pd William Eddings for making a Suit of Clothes & omit'd 24$^{th}$ Dec 1805 as pr. Rect.

March 28 – 1 pr Shoes, mending 1 pr. Do

Apl 25 - Pd for your board with John Epperson last year & Interest

June 27 - Pd John Eppersons order for making 2 pr overalls.

Cr
1806
By pd D. McDaniel on Thos. Bouldin's Store

Dec 25 - By one half of the hire of Patience's Children to John Epperson for this year

1807
Apl 25 - Cash Rec'd for Part of Abrams hire for 1806 Including Int 14/4 ½
One half of the Rent of land to John Freeman & Jonas Fishnick for last year

Balance due Asa Thomas
Pd the Clk of Pittsa' half of 52 Cents
Do Shff Do half of 84

Oct 1st - 9 months board at £11 per year
Services Rendered as Guardian

At the Request of Asa Thomas we have examined the above acct. and find the Necessary Vouchers Produced 19th Oct 1807
Lawson H Carter, Jere Terry
Recorded: October 20, 1807

**AC Book 4, Page 106**                              **Thomas's Gdn. Account Current**

William Thomas To Asa Thomas Guardian              DR

1805
Nov 4 – To pd John Epperson one half his attendance as Witness vs. John Walters

Dec 14 - 1 pr. Shoes

1806
Apl 10 - 1 pr Do

Aug 2 - half of 2 qts. Whiskey for Aamey & Children

Nov 29 – Pd Drury McDaniel for 7 ½ months Schooling at $5 per year

Dec 25 – Pd Thomas Bouldin as Pr. Rect.
1 Pr Double Soled Shoes

1807
Jany 31 - Pd John Epperson as Pr Rect. 2 of 3
Pd Wm Eddings for making a Suit of Clothes omit'd 24th Dec 1805 Rect.

Apl 4 - 1 Pr Shoes

Apl 25 - Pd for your Board with John Epperson last Year &10.00 Interest2/

June 27 – Pd John Epperson for making 2 Pr overalls 2/

Cr

1806
Nov 22 – By pd D McDaniel in Thos. Bouldins Store

Dec 25 – One half of the hire of Patience and Children to John Epperson last year

1807

Apl 25  Cash rec'd for part of the hire of Abraham for 1806 including Interest at 14/4 ½

One half of the rent of land to John Freeman & James Fishnick last year.
Total: £15.13.7 ½
Balance due Asa Thomas: £1.0.7 ½
To pd the Clk. Of Pitts. Half of a Tickett
Do Shff Do half of 84 Cents

Oct 1 – 9 months Board at £11 pr. Year
As services your Guardian

At the request of Asa Thomas we have examined the Within acct. and find the necessary Vouchers produced 19th Oct 1807
Jerry Terry, Lawson L/H Carter
Recorded:  October 20, 1807

**AC Book 4, Page 108**                                                                                                          East's Inv'y

Agreeable to an Order of Pittsylvania Court to us directed we have proceeded to appraise the Estate of Obedience East, Dec'd as follows viz:

One Cow & Calf (brindle)
One Red Heifer & Calf
One black Heifer
Total: £131.18.0
Drury Scruggs, George West, John Ward jun.
Recorded:  October 19, 1807

**AC Book 4, Page 108**                                                                                                    Twedwell's Inventory

In obedience to an Order of the Worshipful Court of Pittsylvania County bearing date the 16th of June 1794 we the Subscribers have appraised the Personal Estate of William Twedwell Dec'd in Current money as follows viz:

7 head of Cattle, young and old, 1 old Sorrel mare and Colt, 3 feather beds and furniture, 4 Chests, 2 Tables and a Bottle Case, 3 pots and one Dutch oven, 1 frying pan, Grid Iron, box Iron, 1 heater & Ladle, 2 Stone Jugs, one earthen pan and buter pot, 3 earthen plates and 3 pewter Basons, 2 Do Dishes and five plates, 3 basons & Salt Cellar, 6 Do Spoons, Tin ware, Iron candle Stick, a parcel of Books,
a parcel of Wooden vessals &1 churn, 1 flax wheel and 1 cotton wheel Do, 2 meal Sifters and one wheat Riddle, 2 Sythes and a Parsel of old Iron Tools, 1 meal Tub, one Womans Saddle, 1 mans Saddle and a pare of Sadle bags, 2 Glass Tumblers, looking Glass, 1 pint pot, 1 Set of Knives & forks, Iron Pot Racks and one pare of Fire Tongs, 2 Pare of Cotton Cards, 1 Sow and four Shoats
Total: £54.16.0
     his
James (X) Nelson, W Wilkerson, Esors
    mark
Tho. Wilkinson, John Wier, Abia. Cheathan
Recorded: October 19, 1807

**AC Book 4, Page 109**                               Wilson's Account Current Sales

Account Sale of Tobacco belonging to the Estate of John Wilson, Dec'd/

4169 lbs Manchester Inspected Tobacco at 39/    £81.5.10
24th Apl 1807
James Wilson, John Wilson, Henry Wilson Exors.
Recorded:  November 16, 1807

**AC Book 4, Page 110**                               Tucker's  Gdn. Account of Keatts

Nov 5, 1807 Parkskell Keatts Dr to N. Tucker
Contra           CR

1807
March 27 – To cash paid
To cash pd the Clerk of Pitts.
To land tax for 1804
To Do for 1805

April 25 – To cash paid
To a Balance due on a Bond on Wm White
To Bond on Wm White
To Do on Wm White
To Do on Vincent Walker
To 10 gls. Brandy at 5/
To 1 pr Boots

Commision for my Trouble

By cash Rec'd of Z Lewis
By Do of Jeremiah McCullock
By bond on Wm White
By Do  on Do
By Do on Do
By Do on Vincent Walker
7th Nov 1807

In Pursuance of an Order of the Worshipfull Court of Pittsylvania to us Directed,  we have proceeded to adjust the account Current of Nelson Tucker as Guardian of Pascal Keatts and find that they are pricepely balanced after allowing sd Tucker £3.11.2 ½
As commission for his trouble.
Philip L Grasty, John Hunt, Stephen Clement
Recorded:  November 16, 1807

**AC Book 4, Page 111**                                             B. Smith's Inventory

An Inventory of the estate of Booker Smith, dec'd by William Witcher, jun., Henry Atkinson, & Moses Kerby

Negro Jack appraised to £75, Sylva a woman Do £70, Lucy a Woman Do £90, Hanar a Woman Do £90, Tom a Boy Do £75, Emanuel a Boy Do £60, Cealy a Girl Do £60, Mary a Girl Do £50, Easter & her Child Sophia Do £105, Squire a boy Do £90, Agy a Small Girl Do £45, Amy a Girl Do £30

A Black mare & colt, A Bay mare, A Bay Horse, A Black Horse, A Small bay Horse, A year old black colt, 1 gray Do Colt, a Cutting box & knife, 5 Pr. Chains including a lock Chain, a pr. Haims, 7 hilling & Weading hoes, 2 Grubbing hoes & a mattock, 4 Plow hoes, a Parcel of Clevises, Swingle tree & Coulter, 4 axes & a froe, 2 Sythes & Cradles, 5 Reap hooks, a Saw, 2 augers & a Chizzle, 16 head of Sheep, a yoke of Steers & cart, cupboard, X cut Saw, 1 Shot Gun, 1 Shot Gun draw Luped,
1 bedstey bed & furniture, 1 bedsted bed & furniture, 1 Loom, 1 Cotton wheel, 1 check Rule, 1 flax wheel, 1 Chest, 1 old Trunk, 1/2 Doz. House Chears, 1 Grind Stone, 4 Cows & 4 yearlings, 8 Cow hides, 1 Sow & 2 Shoats, 7 hogs in Pen fattening, 2 larger in Pen Ditto, 7 Volumns of Hums History England, 7 volumns of nature Displayed, 3 Volumns of the Cookenors, 1 Violin
Jno Smith, Saml' Smith, Admints.
William Witcher, jun, Henry Atkinson, Moses Kerby, appraisers
Recorded: January 18, 1808

**AC Book 4, Page 113**                                                                                    **Twedwell's Account Current**

Dr. The Estate of William Twedel Dec'd to Wm Wilkinson the Surviving Extor.          CR

To 7 Barrels Corn for the Widow, To 3 Do Rye, 5 do wheat, To work at Sundry times for Do, To 2 Bush'ls Salt for Do, To 199 lbs Pork, To finding leather & making 3 pr. Shoes, To Tanning 2 Hides,
To pork delivered Thos. Wilkinson, To Cash pd Do for the Estate, To Do pd Rob. Payne as Per Voucher, To Do pd Wilkinson, To Do pd John Wilson by Ste. Barker, To Do pd Barksdale B.,
To Do pd Mrs Twedell at 12/6, To 33 lbs Beef Cash, 1 ½ galls. Brandy, To cash paid Tho. Wilkinson, To Wintering Cattle Sundry times, To Services rendered the Estate by Jas Nelson as Exor.
Total: £42.11.0

To Ball. As Per Contra

By 1 Mare & Colt James Nelson took to himself, By Sundry articles of the Estate to wit: 1 Bed Cord, 1 Tub, 40 Gall. Cask, taken by Do, A 60 Gall. Do, a Screw auger, By Rich'd Hintons bond, Sam Constables Do, By Juddgt.. W Wright as Per Rect., By consideration for Conveying the Widows life Estate in a tract of land to Benj Twedell
Ball. Due the Estate: £17.16.3
Pittsylva. County to wit:

In obedience to an Order of the Worshipful Court of the County aforsd bearing Date the 16th Day of Nov. 1807, we the Subscribers have Convened & proceeded to State, Settle & adjust the account Current of the Estate of Wm Twedel deceas'd with Wm Wilkinson the Surviving exor. & it appearing to us by the Will of the Testator that he bequeathed all his personal Estate of what nature kind or quality Forever to his wife Abigail during life & after her death to his Son in law James Nelson the other Extor. , his heirs & assigns. Forever that the said James Nelson took the duty of an Executor wholly upon himself, that he made no sales of the personal Estate agreeable to law & Custom but departed this life not having kept any regular account of his transactions, that such his neglect & misconduct render'd it altogether unpracticable for us to make any other adjustments of his transactions, than as above Stated. Given under our hands this 1st Day of December1807.
William Payne, Isaac Hill, Samuel Walker, Thomas Brown
Recorded January 18, 1808

**AC Book 4, Page 114**                                   **Division of Mays Estate**

In pursuant of an Order from the County Court of Pittsy. To us directed bearing Date Pittsylvania Dist. Court 1807 we have allotted & divided the real & Personal Estate of David Mays, Dec'd among the Several Distributees of Said Dec'd as directed in Said order herewith returned as follows to Witt: we have allotted that Mrs. Fanny Mays widow & Relict of said Dec'd Shall have the following Slaves as her dower Slaves as one 3$^{rd}$ part as sum as can be done to with: Negro man Moses £120, Woman Siller £90. Child Winny £20, Woman Nelley £75, girl Lucy £55, child Letty £20. Total amt. £380.00, we have also allotted Smith Mays Rachel, the younger £60 & Child Bird £20. Total £80 also allotted Smith Mays boy Jere £33.00, boy Robert £40. total £73.00. Drury Mays Girl Aggy Value £75 as his lott also allotted to Rhubin Mays boy Allen £33.00 & boy Jesse to Total £73.00. also allotted David Mays boy James £40.00 & girl Charity £45.00, Total £85.00. Also allotted to Gardner Mays a Negro man CesorValued to £120.00, also allotted to Sally Mays Lad John Value to £120.00, also allotted to Patsey Mays Woman Rachel 9oldest) Valued to £90.00, also allotted to Polley Mays Woman Aggy (oldest, Valued to £90.00, all of which is done as near as the Caluation of that family of Negroes would admit of,

we then proceeded to lay of & alott the said Dec'd lands as Ordered among the above Distributees, which by the assistance of Mr.James M Williams as Surveyor, we have done as follows. We have allotted to said Fanny Mays Widow & relict of said Dec'd the Martion house with 180 acres of land adjacent lying on the east side of Lick branch Valued to £300.00 as her dower of land, we have also allotted to Smith Mays 85 acres of land on the same Side of Lick branch adjoining said Dower lott near Garder Mays mill Valued to £70.16.8, we have also allotted to Armist'd Mays 93 ½ acres lyin on the West Side of Said Lick Branch, being the lower lott & adjoining Jno Fitzgeralds lands Valued to £99.3.0. We have also allotted to Rubin Mays 93 ½ acres on Same Side of Lick Creek being the upper lott with the tavern house valued to £99.3.0, we have also allotted to Sally Mays 118 acres of land on the Waters little Sandy Creek being the lott lying & may be more fully known by the South east lott Valued to £35.9, also we have allotted to Patsey Mays 86 acres known by the North east lott bordering on Wallers lands valued to £72.00. WE have also allotted to Polley Mays100 acres known by the north West lot adjoining Flippins lands Value'd to £72.14. We have also allotted to Gardner Mays 100 acres known by the South West lott adjoining Stamps land value'd to £65.00. We have also allotted to Drury Mays 83 acres lying in the County of Halifax on Pole Cat known by the lower lott & adjoining the lands of Meads Anderson Value'd to £85.10.0, We have also allotted to David Mays 107 acres lying in said County of Halifax & on Pole Cat being the upper lott with the in mantion House & adjoining the lands of Gardner Mays Sen& valued to £85.10 .

   The widows Dower of land is not Intirely her thirds but from situation & quantity of acres of the Differrant tracts it appears difficult to fix it otherwise. The widow appear'd satisfy'd & Contented it should be as allotted. The remainder was as equally Divided as the Several Situations & forms of the Different tracts would admit of & we further took in consideration after each Child had drawn his proportionable part & lots of Slaves. We then allotted each Such lots of lands as would leave them as little in Debt to each other as possible, all of which was done the most advantageous way to the best of our Judgments we also find each legetees proportionable part of land & Negroes to be £165.13.10 & that Armsted Mays from the Division is Indebted & rec'd over his proportions £6.9.2 & Rubin Mays on the same Score the sum of £6.9.2 & David Mays on the same Score the sum of £4.16.2 & Gardner Mays on the same score the sum of £19.16.2 & that the following legatees has not Rec'd there porportionable part & is to receive from the four above allotted to legetees found Indebted to each the Sums as follows. Smith Mays to receive £14.17.2, Drury Mays the Sum of £ 5.3.10, Salley Mays the Sum of £10.5.10, Patsey Mays the Sum of £3.13.10 & Polley Mays the Sum of £2.19.10. Given under each of our hands this 12$^{th}$ day of February 1808.
Benj. Watkins, Rob. Walters, Thomas Shelton, John Shelton
Recorded: February 15, 1808

**AC Book 4, Page 117**                                  **Division of Jno Dupuys Estate**

In obedience to an Order of the Worshipful Court of Pittsylvania County bearing date January Court 1808 to us directed we have proceeded to lay off and Divide the lands of John Dupuy Dec'd between the

Distritutees of the said Dec'd leaving to the Widow of the said Deceased her Dower already assigned her to Wit:

To Caleb Anglin in right of his wife Susannah, one of the Distributees of the said Dec'd one Hundred and Six acres be the same more or less and bounded as follows to wit: Beginning at a white oak upon the Clift of the River Hill in the dower line thence the same South 84 degrees east 74 poles to a Dead pine by a Spring South 30 Degrees east 120 poles to pointers in the back line upon the mountain, North 21 degrees east 170 poles to a pine Stump north 63 degrees west 114 poles to a post oak in Stokley Turners line, thence his line South 38 degrees west 108 poles to a post oak corner, thence a new line South 57 degrees West 30 poles to the Beginning at the value of one Hundred and Seventy Dollars, also to Polley Dupuy the other Distributee of the said Dec'd fifty five acres be the same more or less and bounded as follows to Wit: Beginning at the said white oak upon the said Clift, thence along the Dower line to Meekes line, thence his line to the River Banister, thence down the said river as it meanders to the said Turners line, thence his line to the said post oak corner, thence the aforesaid new line South 57 degrees west 30 poles to the Beginning including the low grounds of the said Dec'd at the Vallue of Three Hundred and thirty Dollars making a Difference of One Hundred and Sixty Dollars half of which the said Polley Dupuy is to pay to the said Caleb Anglin in right of his wife Susannah with interest from the Date hereof until paid. Given under our hand this 1st Day of Feby 1808.
Champness Terry, Step. Coleman, David Neal
Recorded: February 15, 1808

## AC Book 4, Page 118                                                                                                       Mayes' Inventory

In obedience & agreeable to Order of the Worshipful Court of Pittsylvania we the Subscribers being first Sworn as the law Directs have Convened together on 31st day of July 1807 at the late dwelling house of David Mayes Deceas'd & have appraise'd the Estate of Said Deceased in Current money as follows, to Wit:

1 negro Man Moses, 1 negro Woman Cyller, 1 negro boy Jesse, 1 negro girl Winney, 1 negro Woman Nell, 1 negro Girl Aggy, 1 negro Girl Lucy, 1 Girl Letty, 1 Boy Robert, 1 man Cesar, 1 Girl Rachel,
1 Woman Aggy & Child Byrd, 1 Boy James, 1Boy Allen, 1 Woman Ann & Child Edmond, 1 Girl Rachel, 1 Girl Charity, 1 Boy Jessy, 1 lad John

2 young bulls, 2 " Heffers, 1 Ditto, 1 Cow & yearling & bell, 4 Cows & 3 Colors, 1 Bull yearling, 1 blind mare, 1 Grey mare & colt, 1 Bay Horse, 1 Sorrel Horse, 1 black mare colt. 1 sorral Horse,
1 Shott Gun, 1 Ditto, 1 feather bed & furniture & Sted, 1 Ditto Ditto & Diito & Ditto, 1 Ditto Ditto Ditto & Ditto, 1 Ditto Ditto Ditto & Ditto, 1 old Chest, 1 old reel, 1 cupboard, 1parcel pewter,
1 parcell of queens & Tin ware, 1 looking glass, 7 old Chiers, 2 Winsor Chears, 1 Ladies Saddle,
1 Table, 1 Chest, 2 sml. Trunks, 1 pr. Sad Irons, Knives & forks, parcel old Pewter, 1 Book case, Razors box & Horse phleams, 3 Slaytes, 1 water can & Tumbler, 1 Table, 3 cotton wheals, 2 flax wheals, 1 Loom & Gears, 1 pr. Cotton Cards, 1 Parcell water vesells, fire Dogs, 1 Dutch oven,
1 Iron Skillett & lid, 1 pott & Hooks, 1 large Pott, 1 Kettle, 1 frying Pann, Parcell Hoes, 7 Pole axes, 2 Grubing hoes, 7 Plows & Coalter, Plow Gear, 1 Hackle, 1 Cutting Knife, Parcell old Irons, 1 Parcell coopers Tools, parcel old augers & Chisells, parcel old Irons, 1 Pr. Steeyards, coffee mill & Bell
parcel old tools, parcel barrels, parcel Wagon tire bands & boxes, 1 Grind Stone, Iron Wedge, fire Dogs, 1 sml. Barrell, 1 hammer, old wire sieve, 2 sythes & cradles, sawmill irons, wagon irons, one wagon & hind geer, old Irons

1 yearling, 1 Heefer, 1 Hiffer, 2 Cows Halves, 7 head hogs, 1 bay Horse, parcel Tobacco, 3 hoes,
2 Grubing hoes, plow gear, 2 Iron wedges, 2 reap hooks, 1 Plow & Coulter, 1 Hand Saw, 1 Cottonr wheel, 1 Iron pott, 11 Hogs, 18 Sheep, 24 Geese, Parcell Corn Suppos'd 45 barrels, Parcell Tobacco Suppos'd 900 lbs, 2 Hhds. Ditto suppos'd 2600lbs, parcel Fodder (blades), 1 top Stack & Shucks,
1 Black Horse, 3 Raw hides, 2 stacks oats, 2 sml. Stacks fodder (Tops), 11 bushells wheat, 1 paracel old Irons, 1 Desk & book case, 1 Walnut Chest, 7 Winsar Chiars, 1 Tea table, 1 Tea chest, 1 folding table, 1 feather bed & furniture & sted, 1 Heffer, 1 Sml. Bull
Total £1569.8.6

Signed: Thomas Shelton, jr, John Shelton Senr., John Fitzgerald
Recorded: February 15, 1808

### AC Book 4, Page 122 — Ro. Farguson's Inventory

In obedience to an Order of the County Court of Pittsylvania, we the undersigned have apprais'd the Personal Estate of Robert Ferguson Dec'd which was in possesion of Millicent Ferguson til her Dec'd. And make the report of the same to the sd court 13th Feby. 1808.

One feather bed & furniture, One chest and Small truck, One pr. Fire Dogs, one Hackll, One Warming Pan
Total: £10.2.0
Jas Hart, Hanson Dyer, Wm Dyer, Walter Lamb (SEAL)
Recorded: February 15, 1808

### AC Book, Page 122 — James Nelson's Inventory

Agreeable to an order of the Worshipful Court of Pittsylvania County, we have this 30th Day of December 1807 convened at the late dwelling house of James Neson
Dec'd & after being first Sworn do appraise the Estate of Said Dec'd as follows Viz:

1 waggon & hind Swingle tree, 3 Grubbing hoes, 2 Bro'd. Axes, 2 pole axes, 1 lock chain, 1 pr Gear Hames, 3 pr. Hames, 2 pr. Traces & parcel old gears &c, 2 Colters, one leather ditto, 1 Doble Swingle tree & Clives, 5 old hoes & Shovle, 2 augors, 1 Sml. Swingle tree & Curry Comb, 1 bay mair, 1 Sorrel mair, 1 young bay mair, 1 Gray mair, 1 Sorrel mair, 1 Sorrel mair, 1 Sorrel Horse, 2 Sides & peace of Leather, 1 Sithe & Cradle, 1 old Bed Sted, Parcell unbroken flax, 4 Juggs, 2 bottles, 1 Bed Cord, 1 box & parcel of old Irons, 2 Hammers &c, 1 Sad Iron, 1 old Saddle, 1 Spinning wheel & 2 Spindles, 2 large pewter Basons, 1 Dish, 6 plates, 1 Sml. Bason, 4 spoons, 1 Tin bason, 1 Tin Tea pott & Knives & forks, 4 Vials, 1 Slate, 2 pencils & looking Glass, pr. Saddle bags, 1 old Gun, 2 pare of cards, 2 Small Books, 1 cup & two Saucers, 7 Books, 3 Slays, 1 pr. And. & Irons, 1 Trunk, 1 pine Chest, 1 Bed Stead Cords and hide, Bed and underbed, 3 Blanketts, 2 Beds and Bed Steads, 3 Blankets, 1 Cupboard, 1 Table, 2 chairs, 6 lbs of moshean Cotton, 70 lbs of sead cotton with blue included, 1 Emty Tub & Round Shave, 1 meal Sifter, 1 foot ads, 1 hand saw, 1 fro, 1 Sithe blade, 1 bell, 1 Drawing Knife, 1 Wedge, 1 spinning wheel, 1 loom, 1 slay, 1 pair of harness, 1 dutch oven, 1 pair of hooks, 1 pott hooks, 1 Washing Tub, 1 large pot, 1 pail, 1 piggin, To parsel of Bacon, To parsel of Corn, 1 Tob. Top Stack & Shucks, 1 Stack & parcel of Blades, 3 Bridles, 1 Collar, 1 Cow and Calf, 1 Top Stack & 2 sml.Blades Stack
Samuel Walker, Creed Tanner, Francis Cornwell
Recorded: February 15, 1808

### AC Book 4, Page 124 — Peter Wilson Guardian Account

An Inventory of the Estate of William Wilson orphan of Peter Wilson, dec'd
Taken by Peter Wilson his Guardian

Oct-Nov 1806
1 Negro Man Harry, 1 " Boy Osborne, " Girl Eda, a Bond on William Linn and James D Patton due 1st Jany 1807

1807
Augt. 27 - a Bond on Ro. Norman & Wm Cobler due 1st Jany 1807, Cash, A bed and furnature
P. Wilson
Recorded: February 15, 1808

### AC Book 4, Page 124 — Peter Wilson Guardian Account

An Inventory of the Estate of Peter Wilson orphans of Peter Wilson dec'd taken by John Wilson, his Guardian

1 Negro Man Dick, 1 " Boy Rob, 1 " Girl Lucy , Cash received of George Adams, Exor.
Churchill Beirns & William Wares note Given 14$^{th}$ December 1805 paid in twelve months from date
John Wilsons Bond for hireof Dick till the first day of Jany 1807
Anderson Tucker & William Coblers Bond for hire of Boy Bob till 1 Jany 1807
Henry Perkins & William Wares Bond for hire of Girl Lucy till June 1807

Jany 1807   Jno Wilson
Recorded : Februray 15, 1808

**AC Book 4, Page 125**                                                  **Peter Wilson's Guardian Acct**

The Inventory of the Estate of Mead Wlison Orphan of Peter Wilson dec'd taken by Peter Wilson, his Guardian

Oct 1806 – 1 Negro Man Isaac,  1 " Woman & Child,

Nov 1, 1807 – Chrstiana, I Bed and furniture

Aug 27 – Cash, a Bond on Geo. Adams due 5$^{th}$ Feby 1808.
Recorded:  Feby 15, 1808

**AC Book 4, Page 125**                                                  **Abraham Martin's Inventory**

In the obedience to an order of the Worshipful Court of Pittsylvania to us directed we have proceeded to appraise the personal Estate to us Shown of Abraham Martin, Deceased as followeth to Wit:

One Negro Jude, One Girl Esther, One Girl Ede, One mare and Coalt, One pided Cow and yearling, One Cow and yearling, Two Sheep, One four plane drawing knife and fro, One jug, One pigen, pole and Realer?, One dish plate, spoon and fork, Four chairs, One Colter, one pair traces, one plow, one Swingletree and plow, Axe hoe, Three narrow axes, one Iron wedge, One Coopers adze, one round shave and one Croze, One hackel, one hand saw, one Curry Comb, one old hoe, One mattock, One cask, two old Tubs, one Can, One pair Tonggs, one chain, one dutch ov'n, One old kettle, two pots, two pair of hooks, One old wheel and Churn and Scales, One Dish, two basons, four plates, three spoons, One Sett of knives & forks, one pair of wool Cards, One raw hide, one Table, one bench,  an old hogshead, One hogshead, one Whipsaw, One pale, one Gum, Two baskets, one half bushel and box, One jug. One gun, one tray, One Chest, 2 baskets, one testament, One barrel, 1 bedstead and Cord, One meal Tub and bee gum, One meal bag, one pair of sheep Shares & bell, One old Saddle, One bridle, one grind stone, One bulk of tobacco, One stack of blades, One parcel of Cotton, One pair of Cotten Cards, One bed and Counterpin & Quilt, 1 bed & Counterpin, One bed and Sted and Cord, One Parcel of old feathers, One bed, One churn
Robert Finley, Wm Becke, Isaac Stone
Recorded:  April 18, 1808

**Book 4, Page 127**                                                  **Able's Chelton's Inventory**

A list of the property of Abel Cheltons dec'd  The 12$^{th}$ Day of February 1807 Viz:

1 Iron Potts, Pewter, 1 Beds, Bedsteads & furnature, 1 loom and Harness, 1 Spinning Wheel, 1 pine chest, 1 Grubbing Hoe, 1 Bell,, Barrel Corn, Bushel wheat, Ditto Rye, 1 large Stone jugg, 1 par Sad Irons, 1 Flax wheel, 1 Razer Case with 3 Razors, 1 Small pine Chest, 1 Looking Glass, 1 small Butter pott, 1 pr. Cotton Cards, a parcel of old iron, Knives and forks Box, 1 Bag dry'd Apples, Water Vessels, 4 chairs, 90 lbs Seed Cotton, Sml Barrels & 2 Basketts, Tubs and 2 Gums bees & Salt, Smal

Trays and 1 Sifter, 1 Side Soal Leather, 1 Case Bottles and one wine glass, 1 sack bag, 1 pine table, 1 Shott Gun, 1 Side Leather

We the appraisers having being first Sworn have Examined the above and find it to be correct. Given under our hands this Feby 1807.
Dan'l Price, Chas. Payne, Stith Wynne
Recorded: April 15, 1808

**AC Book 4, Page 128**                                                                 **Christopher Hutchings' Inventory**

In obedience to an Order of the worshipful Court of Pittsylvania County bearing date July 1807 to us directed we being first Sworn as the law directs, have appraised in Current money the personal estate of Christopher Hutchings deceased and report thereof to the Court as follows:

Lewis Negro man, Jack a Negro man, Bett a Negro Woman, Aabraham a Negro boy, Harry a Negro boy, Ben a Negro boy, Cato a Negro boy, Juno a Negro Girl

One sorrel horse, One Sorrel mare and Colt, Stock of Cattle, Stock of Sheep, Stock of Hoggs, Plantation utensils, One Feather bed and furniture, One ditto Do Do, One ditto Do Do, Shoe makers tools, One grind stone, Four bells, Kitchen furniture, One large spinning wheal and two Small Do, Parcel old pewter, One Syder Cask, One old Cart, Parcel old Books, Parcel Earthernware, One Glass tumbler and Cruett, Parcel Tinn Ware, One chest, One looking glass, One Stand of Bees, One Pr. Old Steelyards, One Table, One pr. Tongs, Five old Chairs, Three old Bedsteads, Two Gimblets, Two Sythes and Cradles, One loom, Two Jugs, Two butter potts, One flax Hackel, One old Skillet and spice morter, One frying pan, One pr. Wedges, One Pr. Money scales, One Whip saw, One Drawing knife, One old Case and Bottles
Amt of Cash on hand
Whole amount £3944.21.0
Given under our hands this day of July one thousand eight hundred and Seven.
Joseph Richards, Rich'd Proctor, Wm Walton

The within is a true Inventory of the Estate of Christopher Hutchings Dec'd. Given under my hand as Executor.
Moses Hutchings
Recorded: May 16, 1808

**AC Book 4, Page 130**                                                                 **Thos. Elliott Act. With Admrs.**

The Estate of Thomas Elliott deceased in acct. Current with M. Hutchings and James Soyars, Admrs. With the will, Anex'd.

1800
Feby 1 7 – To cash paid Sam'l Elliott, To So much paid the Clerk of Pittsy. County, To So much Paid the Sheriff Pittsylvania, To So much Pd Collector of the Direct Tax, To So much paid the Commissioners, To Paid Nathan Adams as Cryer, To So much Paid for Stampt Papers

June 5 - To Paid the widow her Part of the Deceased personal Estate

1804
Dec 3 – To So much paid William Elliott on acct. of Jas. Elliott, To So much Paid Simon Elliott in full per. Rect., To Paid the Clk. Of Pittsylvania and Coroner for Recording Inventory & acct of Sales & Coroner's fees, To So much allowed the Admr. For Services, To So much Deposited in the hands of James Soyars for the Benefit of Peter Elliott.

Cr

By Amount of Sales
By Cash Recv'd for 2 slaves Executed
Rent of 2 Plantations
Recorded: March 27, 1808

**AC Book 4, Page 131**            **The Estate of Abraham Campbell**

1806-The Estate of Abraham Campbell Deceased To Nathan Adams and F. Worsham Executors of &c.  DR

To Amt. Paid as Per. Rect & tickes
To Amt. Given to E Campbell by Cont of Legatees
To Amt. Do Rich'd Campbell Ditto

1807
Feby 23 To Do pd Thos. Watson his part of Estate

Mar 14  To Do pd E. Robertson by Jesse Richards
Mar 16 – To Do paid Wm Thomas on part of Legacy
Mar 17 To Do pd T Harrison in Ditto
Mar 23 To Do paid E Campbell in Ditto
To do paid P Worsham in Ditto

Apr 3 – To Do pd B Kirby in Ditto
To Do Due Nathan Adams in Ditto

June 19 – To Do paid Jesse Richards per Rect.

July 13 – To do paid Lucy Worsham for P. Worsham
July 20 – To Do paid Jesse Richards Attorney for B Kirby

Aug 10 – To Do Pd F Worsham per Rect.
Aug 15 - To Do pd E Campbell per Rect

Spt 21 - To Do Pd William Thomas per Rect.
To Clerks Ticket for Order of Settlem't acct.
To Do for Rec'g Acct. Current
To Compensation for the Executors

June 2 – To Amt. Pd. Thomas Watson p. receipt
To do Do Jesse Richards per Do
To Do Wm Thomas per Do p. Do
To Do F. Worsham Per Do
To Do E Campbell Do
To Do P. Worsham Per Do
To B. Kirby P. Do
To N. Adams Legacy

1806 The Estate of Abraham Campbell    CR
By Amt. Of Sales as P. Acct.
By Cash Rec'd of John Hall
By Do Rec'd of J Richards
By Cash left by the Testator
By Interest on E Robertsons Bond for £83.7.6 from 25 Jany 1808 to 2 June 1808

Agreeable to an order of the Worshipful Court of Pittsylvania we the Subscribers have Stated, Settled and adjusted the account Current of the Estate of Abraham Campbell Dec'd With Nathan Adams and Francis Worsham the Executors of sd Campbell's Will and find the account with corresponding Vouchers as above Stated. Given under our Hands this 2th Day of June 1808
Tho. H. Wooding, M. Hutchings, Allen Stoekas
Recorded: June 20, 1808

**AC Book 4, Page 132**                                                                                              **Wm Witcher's Inventory**

Agreeable to an order of the Worshipful Court of Pittislvania We Joseph Hatchett, Daniel C Edwards, Joseph Hames and Moses Kirby being first Sworn as the law directs has appraised the Estate of Wm Witcher, dec'd as follows, Viz:

53 Head of Hogs, 14 Piggs, 1 Negro Woman Sarah, 1 Negro Child Patsey, 1 Do Do Cindy, 1 Do Girl Cely, 1 Do Child Anna, 1 Do Woman Tamer, 1 Do Do Betty, 1 Do Boy Peyton, 1 Do Do Child George, 1 Do Do Phebe, 1 Do do Stephen, 1 Do Child Anderson, 1 Do Man Bob, 1 Do Do Abram, 1 Do Do Jacob, 1 Do Boy Will, 1 Do Girl Phillis, 1 Do Man Sam, 1 Do Woman Hannah, 1 Do Child Syller, 1 Do Do Mary, 1 Do Woman Bathsheba, 1 Do Child Sophia, 1 Do Girl Rose, 1 Do Boy Edmund, 1 Small bay horse, 1 Large Do Do, 1 Roan Horse, 1 yoke Steers, 1 Do Do, 1 Brindle Steer, 1 Red ditto, 4 Cows & their Calves, 1 Red Cow,, 5 Head Cattle, 6 Head ditto, 5 Head do, 8 Head Sheep, 12 Bee Stands, 12 Hilling Hoes, 1 Shovell, Parcel old Leather, 1 Bed stead and furniture, 1 Bed Do & do

134 yards Cotton Cloth, ¾ Do Do Do, 12 lbs spun cotton, 1 pine Chest, 1 old Trunk, 1 pine chest, 9 large Juggs, 1 large Butter pott, 1 Do Do Do, 1 Small Jugg and Butter pott, 1 Dozen earthen plates, 1 Dozen pewter ditto, 2 pewter dishes, 3 Basons and ½ Dozen spoons, 7 Knives and 6 forks, 2 pepper Boxes, 5 Cups and Saucers & ½ Doz. Tea spoons, 2 Broken Mugs, 2 Tea potts, 1 salt stand , Butter Boat & Bowl, 1 Coffee pott & 1 spice Mortar, 7 pr. Old Cards, 1 Pewter quart Polt, 2 pr. Shears and 2 old knives, 1 candle stick and Snuffers, 1 Flat Iron, 1 Box do & Iron bowl

1 Tea Canister and old Ladle, 1 old Candle Mould & pewter and funnel, 1 Wirel Sifter and Seive, 1 Barrel seed Cotton, 30 lbs pick'd Cotton, 15 lbs. pick Cotton, 29 lbs Wool, 5 Bags, 4 old Barrels, 3 Runlets, 3 Barrels, 1 Grind Stone, 9 old Meal Bags, 2 Cotton Wheels, 1 Flax wheel, 3 old Sithes and cradles, 9 Reap Hooks , 4 Casks, 1 Jointer, 2 Cider Casks, 1 old Hogshead, 1 pr. Saddle Bags, 2 Tumbles and Water pitcher, 1 Case, 6 Case Bottles, 1 Ticklet & 4 phials

6 potts, 2 ovens, pr.pot hooks and Frying Pan, 4 p. Greers with Haymes, 3 Collar & 3 Bridles, 1 pr. Beech bands, 1 Saddle and Bridle, 1 Gun powder horn and shott bags, 1 Jack Screw and Cross Cutt Saw, 10 Axes, 5 Grubing Hoes and 1 Mattock, 2 Bare shares, 6 old plow Hoes, 3 old Coulters, Bed pinn and Iron, 3 old 2 Breast Chains, 2 slays, 2 Lock Chains, 2 pieces Steel, 508 6p. Nails, 1 p. old Saddle bags, 500 6 X 8d Nails, Old plantation tools Consisting of Augers, Hand Saw, Drawing knife, Foot adds, 1 Cutting Knife, Rake and Steel, ? Rollers, Chain and lap ring, 1 Flax Hackle, and pr. Old Hames, 7 Padlocks and 5 Keys, 1 Piggan and Cann, 1 Bible, 1 Webs Justice, 1 pr. Stillards, 1 Cherry Table, 7 Chairs, 6 Bells and Collars, 1 old Wagon, 10 Hides and 2 Skins leather, Cutting Box Irons, 1 Sett black Smith's Tools, 1 pr. Money Scales 3 phials physic.
August 4, 1808
Total: £1896.2.3
Joseph Hatchett, Daniel Edwards, Joseph Hames, Moses Kirby

The foregoing appraisement Contains a true and perfect Inventory of the Estate of William Witcher, Deceased except the Crop now growing. Some grain on Hand and four hundred and forty Seven pounds in money left in Hand by the Testator and ten pounds, fourteen Shillings and one penny Cash remaining in the Hands of William Witcher, one of the Subscribers from the Sale of Tobacco for the Testator.
John Witcher, Wm Witcher, Executors of Wm Witcher, Dec'd
Recorded: August 16, 1808.

**AC Book 4, Page 137**                          **Patrick's Acct. Current**

The Estate of David F Patrick in account with Sa'l Pannill, Exor.

1807
June 26 – By Cash on hand at the death of Dav'd F Patrick

July 23 – Cash rec'd of Robert Aalexander

August 21 – Robert Alexander

August 29 – By 1 Bay Steed Horse due 19$^{th}$ August 1809

October 14 - Cash Rec'd of Robert Alexander
Jermiah Pannill for Balance due at Division of Negroes Fall 1806
Interest on Ditto

November 10 – Cash Rec'd of Robert Alexander

November 14 – 50 Gallons Brandy

December 15 - Cash rec'd of Robert Alexander

December 22 - Cash Rec'd of Jeremiah Pannill for his bond

1808
January 13 – 5 1/2 Bushels Wheat at Lynch's Mill

January 22 – Amount Rec'd of Robert Alexander

February 6 -  3 Hhds. Lynchburg tobo.    4272 lbs
Deduct for turning up do
John Lynch for 7960 Bushels wheat that was stor'd in his mill

February 9 – Henry Wade Sen. For 24 feet Top fodder

February 23 – 550 lbs. Blade fodder, 600 lbs Sheaf Oates

March 12 – 27 feet Top fodder, 350 lbs. Blades do
Robert Cobbs for shuck

April 27- 2 Hhds. Lynchburg Tobo.    2708 lbs.
Deduct Turning up.

May 2 – 2 Hhds. Lynchburg tobo.        2849 lbs
Deduct turning up

May 18 – Jas. Arnold Sen for amt. rec'd in Tobo. Enter'd on bond to D.F.P.

June 6 -  Ann Craddock for Rent of land for the year 1807, & 60 lbs. Lynchburg Tobo.

June 21 -  Jonadab George for Season of mare

July 6 -  David  F Patrick for balance due him by me at his death the 20 June 1807

So much then due
So much due 17th April 1808
Interest on £190.1.4 the amt. Due at the death of David F Patrick til 1st of May 1808 at Which time his Bond to Thomas Collins was due.

Pursuant to an order of the Worshipful Court of Pittsylvania to us directed we Wm Smith, Saml. Stone, & P L Grasty have Examined the account of Saml. Pannill Exor.of David F Patrick, Deceased, With the Estate of the said decedent with the Receipts and other exhibits and do report a Balance in favour of the Estate of David F Patrick of Forty five pounds, 16/1 1/4 which Balance will be due 29th August 1809 as will appear from the Credits on the Within account. Given under our hands this 25th day of August 1808
Wm Smith, Saml. Stone, Philip L Grasty

1807
July 4 – To Postage Letter to Lady
July 8 – To James Pernberton for Tax Per Rect.
Ditto  ditto for Serving Cap' s vs Alex'd & Security
July 10 – 72 Gallon Whisky
July 18 – 72 Gallon Rum Per Order
July 29 - David Spencer Per Rect.

August 1 – Postage 1 Letter to Lady
August 7 - William Collins for 1 Coffin Per Rect.
August 14 - 11/4 Yards Black custring?, 7 1/8 yds Black cambrick, 2 yds Ribbon, 1 3/4 yds. Chambry, 2 yds Ribbon, 3 Hanks silk, 3 Binch wire, 2 paste boards, 1 pair selk Gloves
August 20 - 74 Yards Cat Gutt, 1 1/4 Yards Ribbon
August 22 - Jacob Jones Per Rect., 40 Grams Rhubarb
August 31 - Cash paid John Jenkins

September 10 - Cash paid Clark Hubbard Per Rect.
September 19 - 1 lb Sugar P. Lady, 1 lb. Coffee, 5 Yards N. Cotton, 14 lbs Ginger

October 2 - Cash paid Cornelious McHaney Per Rect.
October 8 - David Spencer P. Rect.
October 10 - 16 lbs. Iron
October 13 - 1 Yard Ribbon, 1 Yard ditto
October 20 - 50 " 10 d. nails
October 21 - Cash paid Wm Yancy Sheriff Pittsy. per Rect., Cash paid Commitioner Per Rect..

November 2 - 1000.8dy nails, 1 P. N. Cottons, 1 ps. ditto
November 7 - 1 days Work of Waggon & Team and finding Halling Shingles from Tho. Baileys to Pittsylvania Quarter.
November 14 - 1 Doz Nedles, 1 E. Dish, 1 ditto, 2 E. dishes, 2 Spelling Books

November 28 - 1 Tumbler, 1 mug, ¼ lb. Pins, 1 1/2 Doz E plates, 1 china Bowl, 6 lbs Sugar, 1 Candlestick 6 lbs. loaf Sugar, 1 Coffee pott, 1 Coffee mill
November 30 - 16 1/4 Sole Leather, 1 Syde upper leather

December 1 - 1 Sett knives and forks, 5 1/2 lb. Sole leather
December 5 - 1 Tea Kettle, 4 lb. Coffee, 1/4 lb.Tea, 1 Tea pott, 2 Bowls, 1 pott, 1 frying pain
December 9 - 1 Sack Salt, 100 20 d. nails, 1 Iron pott Rack, 100 12 d. nails, 2 Days work of Ox Cart and 2 Yoke oxen, Halling Corn at Campbell quarter 26th last month
December 15 - John Black P. Rect.
December 16 - 2 Tobo. Hhds. Complete, 100 6 d. nails
December 19 – 2 1/4 lbs. Blesterd Steel
December 25 - 1 Tobacco Hhds. Complete

December 26 – ¼ lb. Peper?, 100 d. nails

1808

January 2 -  John Black for halling 1 load Corn P. Rect.
January 9 -  Halling 9 loads Wheat to Lynch' and finding
January 21 -  David G. Talbot for his proven acct & Rect.
January 25 -  10 lbs. Suar, 16 lbs Cotton, 100 8 d. nails

Feby. 17 -  Cash left with Mrs. Patrick to pay Mr. Vaughan
Feby. 20 - 28 lbs. Iron, 1 lb. Coperas
Feby. 27 -  Thomas Bailey per Bill & Receipt, 1 Bushell Salt, 2 pair Lines

March 5 -  1 lb. Coperas, Cash paid Robert John Per Rect.
March 17 - Cash paid Sarrah Leveston Per Rect., Cash paid Doctor George Cabbell per Rect.

April 2 -  1 pair Cards, 1 oz. thread, ½ gal. molases
April 5 - 2 lbs. & 10 oz. Blistead Steel
April 7 - 20 lbs. picked Cotton at West's Machine
April 15 -  John Turner Per Rect.
April 19 -  William Worsham for 48 Bushels oats P. Rect.
April 25 - 1 pair lines
April 27 - 1 butter pott, 9 ½ lbs. Sugar
April 29 - Cash paid John Dabney his acct. for Fees P. Rect.
April 30 - 15 lbs. Iron

May 2 – Ferryage of 4 Hhdgs. Tobacco Waggoned
May 14 - 1 Bushel Salt, 1 Jug, 1 Gall. Molases, 500 20 d.. nails, 500 12 d. ditto
May 17 - Cash paid Clerk Pittsylvania P. Tickets
May 19 - Cash paid William Cobbs Per Rect.

June 1 - 500 90 d.. nails, 2 Stocks Locks, Jas. Pemberton Shff Campbell for Tax and new Rect.
June 6 - Anne Craddock in full for mauling Rails per Rect.
June 10 - amt. paid William Collins Per Rect.
June 11 -  James Pemberton Shiff Campbell per 2 Rects.
June 25 -  10 1/2 lbs Cotton, 2 Scythe Blades

July 9 - 2 Pewter dishes, Hank Silk

July 14 -  Thomas Collins for amt. of Bond due 1st May last Taken in ditto ditto due 1st May 1810 taken in 220.10.0, deduct the interest for promp paymt.
July 20 - Philip L Grasty per Rect.
July 23 - 1 Bed Cord, ½ lb.alspice

August 9 - William Worsham Per Receipt, Owen West per Bill & Rect.
August 22 -  Benjamin Waller p. Rect.
August 23 - Thomas Baily per Rect.
August 24 - paid William Yancy Sheff Pitts.
August 25 - Samuel Pannill & Co per Recipt, 10 lbs. Sugar, 4 lbs. Coffe, 1 lb Shott, 1/4 lb powder @ 6/ the 24th Interest

5 Per cent comms. allow'd on Collecting £367.3.6 at being the Bal. after deducting the Money in hand at the death of D. F. Patrick.
Balance in favour of the Estate which will be due 29th August 1809 as Will appear per contrac under date of the 29th August 1807.

1807 Mr. David F Patrick in account with Samuel Pannill

January 6 - By Balance due Per Bond
January 8 - add Errors, Behathaland F. Patrick for 1 Gallon Rum 10th May last, ditto for 1 Sack Salt 14th October last, ditto for 1 doz. neadles 15th November, 1 oz. Camphor 3 October last you think Boung?-

February 9 - Cash received of William Moerman

March 13 - ditto received of Robert Alexander

April 15 - ditto received of Wm & Sam'l Harrison Per Rect.
April 17 - 5 Hhds. Lynchbyrg Tobo. 7113 lbs, deduct for Turning up for Hhg., due in Twelve months per note.

May 2 - Thos. Wiatt for Bal. due on S F/T Harrison & Co note, Do Do for Int., Int on do till 14th Instant
May 27 - Cash rec'd of Lewis Duvall
May 28 – Tobacco 200 lbs, William W Cobbs for Striping, prising & carrying his part Tobo. to market 545 lbs., Wm McCatlester for carrying 412 lbs Tobacco

1807 To amount Brought over

January 24 - To cash paid Benjamin Waller P. note
Benjamin Waller for assennt on acct corn
January 30 - 2 Barrel Corn left with you by Wm W. Cobs

Feby. 3 - 4 knitting pinns, 1 nutmeg
Feby. 6 - Value paid William Reine Per Note
Feby. 16 - 1 lb. Sugar, ½ quire, 1/2 Gal rum
Feby 20 - Cost of Recording power of Atto. in Campbell, Cash paid John Dabny fee &c vs Ro. Alexander
Feby. 25 - 35 lb. Iron

March 5 - Cash paid for 1 Vial Laudeinum
March 6 - 1 Gallon Molases, 1/2 Bushels Oysters, 1/2 Bushel ditto about 1st December last
March 9 - 1/2 Bushel ditto Per Boy Simon
March 13 - Thos. Collins for your Bond due 1st Octr. Next, Deduct allowance he makes you
March 14 - 1 Syde upper Leather
March 18 – 2 ¼ quarts port wine
March 23 - 4 Knitting pins, 1 almanack, 1 Vial Emelec Tartar, 1 Yard Velveat Ribbon, 1 Yard ditto
March 24 - Cash paid W Edenfield for medicine

April 7 - 35 lbs Iron per Boy Adam
April 15 - Cash
April 18 - 1 Bushel Salt Per Adam
April 21 - Cash paid for 2 Vials Laudnurn
April 22 - paid Postage Letter to Lady

May 12 - Cash paid for 9 Oranges
May 16 - 1 quart Rum, 1 paper Pins, 1 Stran necklace
May 20 - 1 Vial Elexir Vitrial
May 23 - Cash paid for 2 Vials Laudinum
May 28 - 1 Bed Cord & per Stephen

June 6 - 4 3/4 pints rum, 1 Vial Elex Vetrial, William Black in part yr note to Wm Eads, Thomas Cooke for bal. of do, 1/2 Gallon Rum

1808

Janury 1 - amount your Smith's account for 1807

July 6 - Estate of David F Patrick for balance due you by me at your death 20th June 1807
So much then due
do due 7th April 1808

1808 July 6

It will be recollected that I have this day balanced this account as if it had been done on the day of the death of David F.Patraick and have entered the interest on the amounts due that day 190.1.4 to the Credits of his Estate which will appear by a Reference to that account and the interest is entered up in that account to the 1st May 1808.
Saml. Pannnill

Mr. David F. Patraick To Saml.Pannill for Smith's work

1807

Febry 12 - To upsating 1 pair Wedges & nailing on old Shoe

May 23 - Shoeing 1 horse per Boy George, finding & Nailing an old pair behind
May 28 – Laying one plow hoe, 2 ½ lbs. Iron per Boy Will

June 11 - Pinting 1 Phoe, Strapin 1 do, 4 lbs Iron

July 4 - penting 2 plow hoes with forket points, Making one frisen'd, 3 lbs Iron
July 28 - Shoeing 1 Horse before per Boy Simon

August 28 - finding & nailing on pr shoes

October 17 - Shoeing 1 Horse before pr Benjamin Waller

Dec 21 - Shoeing 1 Horse before per Boy George

Making 1 Staple for Waggon

This account was commenced in the name of David F. Patrick in his lifetime and Continued in his name to the end of the year.
Recorded: September 19, 1808

**AC Book 4, Page 145**                                                            **John Hodnett's Inventory**

In obedience to an order of the County Court of Pittsylvania bearing date July Court 1807 we the Subscribers being first Sworn before James Johnson, Gent. have appraised So much of the personal Estate of John Hodnett Deceased as was produced by Lucy his Widow, Administritex

1 Bed furniture, bed stead &c, 1 Walnut Desk & Toylett, 1 Looking Glass, parcell old Books, 6 coverleats belonging to beds, 1 Walnut Table & Toylett, 6 Winsor Chairs, 1 waterstand, 1 Walnut cupboard, Earthen & Glass Ware, 1 pewter Bason, Broken fire Dogs, 1 Sand Seave, Flax Seed, 12 Bushells Wheat, 3 Tubs, 1 pine Chest, 1 Side Saddle, 1 Bed furnature & Stead &c, 1 Check real, 1 Small Walnut Chest , 1 Cotton wheel, 1 Loom, 1 450 Slay, Square Walnut Table, 8 Rush Chares, 1 Shott Gun, 1 Bed furniture & Stead, 1 Ditto Ditto Ditto, 1 Spice morter, 2 old Candle sticks and Coffee pot

parcel old pewter, knives and forks, 1 Hyme Book, 1 p. fire Dogs and Tongs, parcel pickled pork, & tub, Ditto Leather, parcel seed cotton, 1 parcel pickled pork & Tub, Ditto wool, 3 Stove pots with Butter & fat, 2 Small Tubs and Churn, 1 Tray and parcel of Flax, 1 pewter Candle mould and Sad Iron, 1 meal Tub, 1 Cotton wheel, Wood Ware, Skillet and Small pot,, ¼ grind stone &c, 1 large Iron pot and Hooks, 1 Dutch Oven and top, 1 Meal Sifter and Tray, To 6 1/2 pr. Cast Wheels, 1 p. Haymes Traces &c, 1 Hammer auger &c, drawing knife, 2 Axes and Mattox, 1 p. wedges, 2 plow hoes and Swingletrees, 8 old hoes, Old Saddle, 1 Saddle, 1 Sythe and Cradle, parcel Flax, 35 Barrels Corn, Bottle Spirits Turpintine & 2 phials, 197 lbs. Pork, 1 Roan Mare, 1 Sorrel Colt

1 Bay mare, 1 Bay Colt, 1 Bay Colt, 1 oat stack, 1 White Heiffer & 2 Red ditto, 1 Spotted Steer yearling, 1 Cow and yearling, 2 ditto Ditto, 2 Yearlings, York young Steers, 12 Sheep, 3 Blades Stacks , 1 Stack and shuks, 1 Ditto Ditto, 2 Cows, 7 Shotes, 13 Geece, 1 Fro, an old ax, 3 hogs, 1 Negro boy Jere, 1 Ditto Moses, 1 Ditto , Woman Phillis, 1 Ditto Boy Daniel, 1 Ditto Woman Dafney & 2 Children Phillis and Barnett, 1 Negro Man Sam, 1 Ditto Girl Jincey, parcel Tobacco
Total: £657.3.1 1/2
Benj. Terry, Benj. Terry jr., Daniel Motlley, Saml. Motley
Recorded: September 19, 1808

**AC Book 4, Page 148** **Wimbish of Neal Account Current**

Mr. David Neal orphan of Ste. Neal dec'd Acct. Current with William Wimbush, Adrm. of Jas. Linn dec'd former Guardian

1803
MR. 15 To Cash Paid Mrs Neal for board

June 11 Cash

July 23 ditto

Sept. 24 ditto

Dec 22 ditto

Dec 30 Paid John Wimbush per account 1802
Paid Champness Terry ditto

1804
Jany. 3 Cash paid Edm'd Fitzgerald p. acct.
ditto paid W A Allen 24th Dec last for Tuition per acct. & rect.

April 7 Cash

July 14 ditto

Jany 1 ditto it being 1/2 of the Amt. Paid Jon. Stone for Land &c Per your request
Amt. paid for Negroes Expsek per account.
Commis. of 5 p. cent on 497.8.11
Sto. Turner & Co. for Mans Saddle
Interest
Balance due on Stone acct. This is not settled

Octo. 18 Balance due

1803 CR

Feby 19 By your proportion of the Estate of Stephen Neal dec'd as appears to us from a Statement by Comms. formerly appointed to allot to the widow her part
1/2 of Hire of Negroes due 1st Jany 1803
½    "           "    1804
½    "           "    1805
½    "           "    1806
½    "           "    1807
½ Rent of Plantation due 1st Jany 1807
Thomas Neal for the Hire of Negro Woman Dice for 1803 & 1804
She being a slave which the Said Thomas has no part nor Interest in the half of which we entered to his Credit
1 Negro Woman Dice & child which you sold Vachel Clement and Jas Linn dec'd his Bond, The half of which was payable 1st May 1805 and the Balance 25th Dec 1805.

1806 Oct 8 -Int. is calculated up til 18th Oct 1806 except on £65 due 25th Dec. last
By Bal. of Interest


1808 Oct 18 - By Bal. due P. Contra £491.2.1

In obedience to an order of the County Court of Pittsylvania bearing date May Court 1806 we have examined the Account of William Wimbush, admr. of James Linn, dec'd who was Gardian of David Neal orphan of Ste. Neal, dec'd and find a Balance due D. Neal of Four Hundred and ninety one pounds 2/1. Given under our hands this 18th day of October 1806.
Wm. Smith, J. Williams, Champness Terry
Recorded: September 19, 1808

**AC Book 4, Page 150**                                              **S. Neal's Account Current**

DR the Estate of Stephen Neal, dec'd in acct. current with William Wmbish, admr. Of James Linn, dec'd who was admr. Of Stephen Neal, dec'd.

1808
Augt. 15 To Cash paid Taxes as per 1800 p. Rect.
ditto p. Clk hs. Per 2Tickets
1808 Bal due

Augt. 15 By 1 Hhdg. Tobacco which appears to us was received by J. Linn and not accounted for on a former Settlement.
Bal. P. Contra
With interest from 6th Nov 1801
Total: £16.16.5

In obedience to an Order of the County Court of Pittsylvania and bearing date August Court 1808 we have Examined the account of William Wimbush admr. of James Linn dec'd, who was admr. of Stephen Neal dec'd With the Estate of Stephen Neal dec'd and find a Bal. due the Said Estate of Eleven pounds 15/2 aagreeable to the above acct. Given under our hands this 15th day of August 1808.
Wm Smith, J M Williams, Champness Terry
Recorded: September 19, 1808

**AC Book 4, Page 151**                                              **Wimbish Gdn. Of Neal Acct. Current**

Dr. Mr. Thomas Neal orphan of Stephen Neal dec'd In acct. Current with William Wimbush, Admsr. of James Linn dec'd former Guardian

1801 To Cash paid Chas. Irby for Tuition

1803 Paid Mrs. Neal for yr Board

Dec.   Paid W A Allen for Tuition  p. Account & Rect.

1804  Pd. John Wimbush per acct. for 1802

Jany 3 Paid Edm'd Fitzgerald for Board
Cash 23 July 1803
ditto 18th Dec

Jany 8 Cash
Services of Exps. of Servant & horse
a Trip to Guilford

1805 Paid Champness Terry per acct.

Jany 8 Cash

1806
Feby. 5 Paid Abra. Neal for 1 Horse
Cash Omitted July 1803
Cash paid Jno. Stone 1 Jany last on acct purchase of land
Paid for Expences of Negroes &c Per account
amt. yr account at Stinkin River Store
David Neal for the hire of Negroe Woman Dice for 1803 £12.7 & 1804 £5.0.0.  She being a Slave which you have no Interest in the half of which hire is entered to your Credit.
Sto. Turner & Co.per account 23rd Dec 1802
ditto ditto for Cash 7$^{th}$ Nove 1803
Commis. on 423.12.13
Bal. Interest
To Medicine  account
1806 Oct 18 Bala. £474.18.9

CR

1803
Feby 19 By your Porportion of the Estate of Stephen Neal dec'd as appears to us from a Statement by Comms. formerly appointed to allot to the Widow her part.  £310.15.4
½  of the Hire of Negroes due 1st Jan 1803
"                                                     1804
"                                                     1805
"                                                     1806
"                                                     1807
1/2 Rent on Plantation
Bal. of Interest Acct.

1806
Oct 18 By Bal Pr. Contra £212.2.4

In obedience to an order of the County Court of Pittsylvania bearing date May Court 1806 we have examined the acct. of William Wimbush admr. of James Linn dec'd who was former Guardian of Thomas Neal and find a Balance due Thomas Neal orphan of Stephen Nead, dec'd of Two hundred and Twelve pounds Two Shillings & 4p agreeable to the above account. Given under our hands this 18th day Oct. 1806.
Wm. Smith, J M Williams, Champness Terry
Recorded: September 19, 1808

**AC Book 4, Page 153**                                                                                                   **David F. Patraick's Inventory**

Agreeable to an order from Pittsylvania Court to us directed We William Mc Allester, George Gilbert and John Luck and John Gilbert being first Sworn have proceeded to appraise the Estate of David F Patrick as follows Viz:

1 Bay Steed Horse Said to be got by Boxer 4 yrs old last Spring, 1 Sorrel ditto Got by Quick Silver 3 years old, 1 Dark bay steed colt got by Whip 1 Year old, 1 Sorrel mare about 12 years old
This much
Appraised August 26 1807 & one silver watch
William McAllister, John Gilbert, John Luck, George Gilbert

1808 Sam. Pannill Exor.

April 19 We George Gilbert, John Gilbert and John Luck have this day proceeded to appraise the balance of the Estate of David F Patrick as follows Viz:

1 walnut Cubbord, 1 Do Chest, 1 Do Table, 1 Do Desk and Book Case, 6 Chires, 2 Small Do, 1 Domestick Medicine, 1 Bible, 1 Jeffersons Notes, 1 Gutherys Grammers, 1 Testament, 1 Hymn Book, 1 Costicks Domocrasey Unvailed, 1 Miscellanies, 1 Collumbian Orator, 1 Scotts Lessons, 1 account Pelew Islands, 1 American Preceptor, 1 Costicks Ferrable Tractoratins, 1 Acts of Congress, 2 Spelling Books, 4 Fathers Legacy to his daughter, 1 Jays Diseaptery Malgta, 1 China Bowl, 1/2 Doz do Cups and Saucers, 1 Tea pott, 2 Razors, Cases Shaving Box & hone, 1 Looking Glass, 1 Do, 7 Hogs, 6 Shotes, 17 Pigs

1 wriding Chain & Harness, 1 Bay Horse, 1 Gray Do, 3 Plows and Gare, 1 Pr. Traces & Haymes, 1 Bull, 1 Do, 1 Cow and Calf & Bull, 1 Do & yearlings, 1 Do & Do, 1 Do & Do, 1 Mare, 1 Do, 2 Small Do, 1 Cow, 1 Heffer, 1 Do, 3 Do, 1 Gun, 1 Sword, 1 Case and Bottels, 2 Jugs and Butter Pott, 1 ox Cart, 1 Grind Stone, 1 Spade, 1 Cutting Box and Knife, 4 Wedges and Reap hook, 1 Iron Tooth Harrow, 4 axes, 14 Hoes, Hilling and Grubing, 1 auger & old Saw, 2 Caulters, 1 Froe, 1 plow hoe, Old Iron, 1 whip saw, 2 Bells, 1 Pott, 1 Do & hooks, 1 Iron Kittle, 1 Frying Pan, 1 Saddle, 1 Sifter, 1 Cotton Wheel, 2 Tubs, 3 Pails Water,, 1 Chock Reel, 1 Trunk, 1 Do, 1 Do, 1 old Walnut Table, 1 mans Saddle, 1 Do, 1 Womans Do, 1 Halter chains, 1 pr. Saddle bags, 4 Feather Beds and furnature, 1 Churn, 1 Tea Kettle, 1 Tribbet bed

1 Negro man Jim, 1 Do George, 1 Do Simon, 1 Boy Baccus, 1 Do Reubin, 1 Woman Jenn, 1 Child Isbel, Girl, 1 Girl Lette, 1 Boy Jonathan, 1 Do Darby, 1 Woman Lucy, 1 Girl Child Hannah, 1 Girl Sarah, 1 Woman Nan, 1 Boy child Jere George, 1 Girl Bette, 1 Do Dafney Rucker, 1 Do Dilee Rucker

1 Coffee mill, 1 Coffee pot, 2 Supe Spoons, 8 Table Do, 6 Silver Tea Do, 2 Bowls, 2 Do, 1 Bason, 1 ½ Doz. Earthern Plates, 4 Earthan Dishes, 1 mug, 1 Tumbler, 2 Earthan Salts, ½ Doz. Knives and forks, 2 Peppers, 2 pr. Cotton Cards, 4 Table Cloths, 4 Towels
Aprl 19 1808
Cash on hand at Death
George Gilbert, John Gilbert, John Luck, Saml. Pannill Exor.

**AC Book 4, Page 157**                                                                      **D.F Patrick's Inv'y Account of Sale & List of Balances**

The following is a list of Debts due David F Patrick at his Death as near as can well be ascertained by the Said Patrick not having kept any regular accounts of what was due him and also owed to a Considerable amount of which he also left no account the most of Which however was due on Bonds.

Saml. Pannill in his private Capassity owed
Robert Alexander Do
James Arnold Do
Benj. Waller
David Hambrick
John and Sarah Luck

1808
April 20 Saml. Pannill, Executor
Amount of appraisment & cash on hand at Death of D F Patrick as on the other Side

Total amount of Personal Estate £2199.14.1/4
Saml. Pannill Esor.
The following is a list of Sales of part of the Estate of David F. Patrick mostt Subject to waste which Sale took place 29$^{th}$ Augus. 1807. Viz:

Mitchel M. Gallion 1 Silver watch
Littleberry Epperson 1 old Sorrel Mare
Saml. Stone 1 Bay Mare steed Got by Boxes
Clack Stone 1 Sorrel Steed Got by Quicksilver
John Kent 1 Brown Steed Colt Got by Whip
Total: £125.3.0
Saml. Pannill Exor.
Recorded: September 19, 1808

**AC Book 4, Page 158**                                              *Linn's Gdn. Account Current*

DR The orphans of John Pannill Dec'd in Account with William Wimbush, Admr. Of James Linn dec'd who was Guardian in right of his wife, Nancy, former Guardian.

1799
Sept. To paid William Wimbush & Co P. Acct.

1800- John Wimbush & Son P. ditto. Ditto ditto,

Jany. Paid Crier at hiering
15 yards Linnen
Colquhoun & Gatewood p. acct.
Obadiah Johnson for Shoes

1801 Board 3 orphans 3 ½ months, Paid Crier at hireing

Jany. Paid for Spirits at hireing, Cash furnish'd the Orphans, Cash pd. Exp. To School & returring, Ditto pd. Jos. Woodson for Schooling, Ditto ditto, Ditto paid W. Smith for Sundreries, Ditto paid E Dismukes for Schooling, Ditto pd. Ross & Douglas for Books, Ditto pd. Jno. Wimbush & Sons, Ditto pd. John Motley, jr., Ditto pd. Fed. Tax p. Rect., Ditto pd. 5 Tickets 18 cents, Ditto pd. Nancy Adams for Services, Ditto pd. P. Butler do, Ditto pd. Mrs. Ashlock, Ditto pd Mr. Scurlock

1802
Jany. 9 month Board in A J Pannill, Cash paid Jos. Woodson for Schooling, Ditto paid Crier at hireing,

Ditto furnished the orphans, Dotto pd Exps. Goings and Returning to & from School, Cash paid D. Pannill p. acct., Ditto pd John Wimbish & Son
Total: £257.14.3

Credits

1799
Sept. 12 By Balance as Stated by Commissioniers Viz. for
David Pannill Bond on Which Interest is to be paid annually @ 5 p. cent £1724.9.9
On demand this day £714.15.4 1/4
Due 1st Jany. 1800 £178.17.10 1/8

1800
Oct. 25 Rent of Store House Lott & &c
Jany. 1  hire of Long Jim, Jim Thornton, Jacob, Euclid, Easter and Children, Lett and Children, George, Jack and John, A parcel of Bricks sold G Deckenson, Rent of Field above the Wash, Tunstall's, Interest on D. Pannills Bond at 5 per Cent

Oct 25 Rent of Store House Lott &c

1801
Jany. Hire of Euclid, Jacob, Easter and Children, Jim Thornton, Long Jim, Jack, John, Lett and family, George, To rent field above slash, "     Rolands, To Interest on David Pannills bond @ 5 per cent

Oct 25 Rent Store House Lott &c

1802
Jany.  Cash paid Ross and Douglas for 1 Book, Do Oba. Johnson for Shoes, Do pd. Mr. Tuck for Weaving, Do pd. Nancy Adams for Services, To 9 Month Board of 2 Orphans

1803
January To 12 Months Board for 1 Orphan, Cash paid Cryer at hireing, Ditto Sheriff Pittsylvania for Land, Tax for 1802 per Recipt, Ditto Ditto 1801, Cash Paid Jesse Woodson for Schooling, Board of Ditto 1 Year, Cash Paid Abra. Neal for 3 pr. Shoes, Ditto Paid a Pedler for 1 pr. Ear Drops, Ditto paid R. Ashlock for making 3 pr. Shoes, Leather found for ditto, Cash Paid Rawlins for 3 pare Shoes, Ditto Paid Nancy Adams for her Services, Ditto ditto ditto, Dotto Paid John Wimbish & Son, Ditto Paid John Wimbish jun., Ditto Paid Pannill & Smith

1804
January
Boarding 3 Orphans 1 Year , Cash Paid Cryer at Hireing, Ditto Paid E Thomas Jeweller, Ditto paid Thomas Colquhaun & Co., Ditto paid 6 pr.Slippers, Ditto paid 4   ", Ditto paid 1 Fan, Ditto Paid Small Trunks, Ditto paid 3 Smelling Bottles

1802
Jan.
By Hire Negro John, Jacobl, Euclid, Jack, long Jim, Jim Thornton , George, Easter & Children, Lett & Children, Rent of Field Above the Slash, Interest on D. Pannills Bond @ 5 per Cent

Oct. 25  Rent of Store House Lott. &c

1803
Jany 1 By hire of Negro long Jim, Jim Thornton, Euclid, Jacob, George, John, Jack, Betty, Lett & Children, Easter & Children, Rent Field Above the Stash,    "     Tunstalls,   " Tavern House, Interest on D Pannills Bond at 5 Per Cent

Oct. 25 Rent Store house Lott &c

1804

Jany hire of long Jim, Jim Thornton, John, Euclid, Jacob, George, Jack £23.12.0 ( he died received in prop. for the time he lived), Betty, Lett & family, Easter & family., Rent Tunstall field, "      Slash field, "     Tavern House, "     Store House &c, Interest On D Pannills Bond @ 5 per Cent

1806
Jany Cash paid for 3 pr. Silk Gloves, Ditto pd. 6 pockett Handkfs., Ditto pd. 2 pr. Ear Rings, Ditto pd 1 Stran Necklace, Ditto pd. Mrs. Glenn for weaving, Ditto pd Mrs. Saunders, Ditto pd. Nancy Adams, To Cash paid Jno Wimbush & Son, Ditto pd Jno. Wimbush jr., Amount yr. Store acct.

1805
Jany, Board 3 Orphans 1 Year @ $50 ea., Cash paid Crier at Hireing, Do pd Nancy Adams for her Services,, ¾ yard Lac'd Cambrick, John Wimbush jr. per Acct., Thomas Davenport & Co., Amount of Store Acct., Board 3 orphans 1 Year @ $50, 2 Gallons Brandy for hireing in Jany last, Sundries furnish'd V. Walker for Negro Jack when Sick, Paid V Walker for his Service as Doctr. to Jack, Paid Mrs Rowland as Mid wife, Paid Crider at hireing, Jas. McCain Singing Master, 2 Dressing Boxes, 1 Stran Necklice, 3 pr. Blk.Silk Goves, Amt of Store acct., Board 2 Orphans 6 Months ea., Ditto 1 Do 1 Year, Paid Jno. Wimbush & Son for 1 Hat 28th Apr, 1801, Ditto ditto 1 Hat 23th Augt., Ditto ditto 1 Slate & 3 penciles 29th Oct. 1803


1805 Jany
Amount Brought over, By hire of long Jim, Jim Thornton, George, Jacob, Euclid, John, Betty, Lett and family, Easter & family, Rent of Tunstalls field, "     Slash field, "     Tavern House, "     Store House, Interest on D. Pannills Bond at 5 per Cent

1806
Jany hire of long Jim, Jim Thornton, George, John, Euclid, Jacob, Nat, Betty, Chaney, Winney, Easter & family, Rent of Slack field, "      Tunstalls, "     Tavern House, "     Store House &c,
Rent of Rowlands place to Henry Rowland for 6 years past @ $5, Over charge in paid John Wimbush & Son 1802. it should be 57.16.2 1/4 instead of 69.17.11/4 makes a difference of £12.0.11, Interest on 1724.9.9 it being for D, Pannills Bond renidered from 1st Jany 1805 till 15th March 1806.

March 15 1806 To Paid John Wimbush for 1 Trunk 2nd March 1804, 5 1/8 yds dk Callico, 8 2/3 " blk. Cambrick, 5 "     ", Balance of Interest £532.6.6, Allowance for tranacting the Estate of the orphans £129.1.0, Balance due the Orphans £4027.17.7 ½, To 1 Woman Saddle the price of which cannot be assertained at this time, By Amount Brought Over
Mar. 15 Balance of Interest Acct. £537.6.6
By Balance due per Contra £4024.17.79

Pursuant to an Order of the Worshipful Court of Pittsylvania County bearing date December Court 1807 directing us to State, Settle, and adjust the Accounts of the Guardianship of James Linn dec'd who was Guardian in right of his wife Nancy former Guardian of the orphans of John Pannill dec'd with William Wimbush admr. And after examining the account as Stated above and Such exhibits as produced before us find a Balance due the Orphans of John Pannill dec'd of Four Thousand and Twenty Seven pounds 7 3/4 of which Three Thousand Eight Hundred & Twenty Seven pounds 7 3/4 was due 17th March 1806 and Two Hundred pounds & 2/ due 1st Jany 1807. Given under our hands this 16th day of April 1808.
Joshua Stone, Sen, William Smith, Philip L Grasty
Recorded: June 20, 1808

**AC Book 4, Page 166**                                                                                                               **N. Pannil Gdn.**

Dr. The orphans of John Pannill dec'd in Account with Nancy Pannill Guardian

1795
Jany To Paid William Todd for his Services as Crier at hiering p. T & D Pannills Accot., 5 yds Cotton for 1 of the Negroes Per Acct., Paid John Wimbush & Son for Sundirias for the orphans Per account, Wimbush & Pannill ditto, Paid Clerk Pittsylv' P. Tickett

1796
Jany 1 Paid Crier at hireing, Wimbush & Pannill for Primmer, Paid Thos. B McRoberts atto. fee for Conveying Tittle of land Sold G Dickinson P. Rect., John Wimbush & Son for Sundries furnished the orphans P. Account.

1797
 Paid Crier at hireing, Paid D Pannill for Brandy at hireing, " John Wimbush & Son for Sundries for the Orphans P. acct., ditto ditto, Wimbush & Pannill for 9 yds Green Wild Cose?, Paid Sharp Lumpkin P. acct & Rect.

Credits

1795
Jany 1 By hire of Negro George, Easter, Toby, Jacob, John, Jim, Jack, Euclid & Jim, Letty Rent of Tunstalls field, "      dry fork, "      Tavern House

1796
Jany 1 hire of Negro Toby, Easter & Children, Long Jim & Jim Thornton, Jacob, Jack, Euclid & Letty, George, John & Rent of Tavern house, Rent of Tunstalls field, "      field above Slash, "           "

1797
Jany 1 Hire of Negro Toby, Easter & Children, John, George, Jacob, Jack & Euclid, long Jim, Jim Thornton, Letty, To Rent of Field above Slash, "      Tavern & field between, "      Road & Stinken River, "      of dry fork, "      Tunstalls

1797
 Amount Broughjt forward, To Paid Crier at hireing

1798
 Jan 1 Amount Paid David Pannill for building Store Room, moving Counting Room & Lumber Room and finding Materials and Provisions for Carpenters & Masons, Paid Samuel Pannill for articles for the orphans per his account, John Wimbush & Son for Sundries for the orphans, 2 pr. Shoes from W Wimbush & Co., Paid James Linn for Shoes for do

Cr

1797
Jany 1 By Balance due per Account Stated by the Commissioners 15$^{th}$ Dec 1795  £795.0.11 ½, Ditto ditto , Ditto ditto 3$^{rd}$ Feby 1797 £346.0.3, Memo the above £1724.9.9 is due deposited in the hands of David Pannill Payable 1$^{st}$ January 1805 with Interest at 6 pr. Cent from 1$^{st}$ January 1797 in which Interest is to be paid annually

1798
Jany 1 Cash rec'd for interest till this time, Hire of Negro Jacob £15.2.6, Easter & children £1.17.6, Toby £12.10.0, Jack, Euclid, George & John £69.18.0, Letty £8.4.0, Long Jim and Jim Thornton £35.10.0 Rent of Tavern House & field between the Road & Stinkin River £1.10.0, Rent of dry fork £0,5.0,

Rent of field above the slash £6.0.0, Rent of Store house Lot &c from 25th October 1793 till 25th Oct. 1797 £80.0.0, Interest on David Pannills Bond @ 5 per Cent

1799
Jany 1 1 Years Rent of Store House Lot &c, Hire of Negro George £13.13.6, Euclid £27.6.6, Jim Thornton, Jacob £17.12.6, Easter & Children £1.13.6, Toby £12.10. but died 1st July following £6.5.0

1799
Jany 1 To paid Crier at hireing, Paid Jas. Linn for 4 pr. Shoes, Paid William Wimbush & Co for Sunderies furnished orphans, John Wimbish & Son for ditto, Balance of Interest Account Carred to Contra £67.5.1

Sep. 12 Allowed for transacting the business of the orphans Estate
Balance due the Orphans £2618.2.11 ¾

1799 Amount Brought Over
Jany 1 By Rent of Field above Slash, " dry fork, " on the Road, " Tavern House, Interest on David Pannills Bond at 5 Per Cent., Balance of Interest Account brought from Contra

Sept. 12 By Balance & Contra

Persuant to an Order of the Worshipful Court of Pittsylvania County to us directed bearing date September Court 1807 directing us to Settle and adjust the account of Nancy Pannills Guaradianship with John Pannill's Orphans and after examining the Said Account and exhibits before us find a balance due the orphans of John dec'd of Two Thousand Six Hundred and Eighteen Pounds two Shillings and 11 ¾ as Stated above one thousand Seven Hundred and Twenty four pounds 9/9 of which is stated to be in the hands of David Pannill on Interest at five per Cent as this account will shew under Dale of 1797 Seven Hundred and fourteen pounds 154 1/4 due the 12 September 1799 and one Hundred and Seventy Eight pounds 17/10 1/2 due 1st day of January 1800. Given under our hands this 3 day of December 1807
Joshua Stone Sen., William Smith, Thomas Anderson, Philip L. Grasty
Recorded: June 20, 1808

**AC Book 4, Page 171                             Pannill Gdn. A.C.**

The Heirs of David Pannill in Account Current with Saml. Pannill

1807
July 24 By Balance due per acct Settled & Returned by Commisr. £ 1037.7.8 1/4
Hire of Negro Jack for 1807 due 1st January next £12.0.0

1808
Jany 6
Cash rec'd of Bailey Street in part his note £4.10.0
Saml. Pannill & Co for George Davise note & Int. £8.3.2

March 19 Bailey Street in part his note £7.15.0
Cash rec'd of Bailey Street in full his note & Int. £9.18.0

April 4 James Overby for his half of Rent for 1805 and 1806 £3.0.0
Ditto ditto for Rent for 1807 £3.0.0

Aug 25 Estate of David Pannill for two thirds of £477.5.2 ½ the neet amount Collected Since 21st July 1807 per account Settled with the Commissioners to be return'd by them to Pittsylvania Court £318.3.5
Interest on £103 ½.7.81/4 from 24th July 1807 £67.9.6 ½

1807

October 21 To Cash paid Sheriff Pittsylvania Tax P. Rect 55 cents

1808
Jany 1 Bethenia Pannill for 1 year Expence P. Rect. £26.10.1 ½

April 9 Cash paid Sheriff Pittsylvania Per Ticket 90 cents

May 17 Cash paid Clerk Pittsylvania per Ticket

July 16 Cash paid Sheriff Halifax per Ticket

August 25 Samuel Pannill & Co for amt. Paid Abraham Shelton, son to John for 46 apples trees to be planted on the land purchas'd of Gabriel Shelton Son to Gabriel
To cash paid Sheriff Pittsylvania per. Ticket
5 p. Cent Commis. allow'd for transacting the Estate of the Heirs of D. Pannill dec'd of £58.6.0 the amt. rec'd.
Bal. Due the heirs this day  £1448.11.2 ½

Pursuant to an order of the Worshipful Court of Pittsylvania County Court bearing date June Court 1808 directing us to State, Settle & adjust the account of Samuel Pannill's Guardianship of the orphans of David Pannill dec'd, we have, in obedience to the Said order, examined the Account as Within Stated with the exhibits and find the Balance due the Heirs of David Pannill dec'd of Fourteen Hundred & forty Eight pounds 11/23. Given under our hands this 25th day of August 1808.
Wm Smith, Saml. Stone, Philip L Grasty
Recorded: September 19, 1808

**AC Book 4, Page 172                                      J.Morton gdn. Account Current**

Jasiah Morton To Joseph Morton his Guardian            Dr.

1803
To Boarding you from Jany 1803 to Jany 1804 one year £9.0.0

1805
Jany To Boarding you from date to March following £12.0.0

April
Cash paid Tuition £4.16.0, To Boarding you at Dr. David Rices one Session £6.0.0, Tuition for the Same time while at Dr. Rices £2.8.0, To 5 yards home spun linen £0.12.6, To 4 yards Ditto £0.8.0, To 5 yards mixt Cloth for a Coat and pantaloons £0.15.0

1806
Dec  To Boarding you with Wm L Turner at Banister Academ one Session £5.0.0,  To Tuition @ Ditto £3.0.0, To one Selector Teteree, £0.4.6, To one Dictionary £1.7.0

March 29
To March bought of Nathaniel Harris , To 1 ¾ yards fine blue Cloth £3.3.0, To 3 yards black fancy Cord £1.6.3, To ½ yard Buff Cassemore £0.10.0, To 2 yards brown Holland £0.8.0, To 1 Do linnen, 4 hanks of silk £0.6.9, To 3 Sticks twist, two Doz.large buttons £0.9.8, 1/6 Doz. Small gilt buttons £0.1.9, To 3 yards Superfine linnen £1.0.3, To 1 quire Writing paper £0.1.6, To 2 yards blue Coating £1.4.0, Cash paid James Borden for making a Satule £0.12.0, To cash paid John Figg for making a Suit of Clothes £1.4.0
To 5 yards home spun Gean? Cloth £0.15.0, To 2 yards mixt Cloth £0.4.0

1807
To Boarding you £9.0.0, To Tuition the same year £2.0.0, To 6 yards home spun Linnen £0.18.0

To 12 Ditto Ditto Cloth £1.10.0

1808
To Boarding you £9.0.0, To 9 yards home Spun linen £1.7.0, To 4 ½ Yards home spun linen £0.9.0
To Cash paid Midwife fees £1.16.0, Note this charge was Omited in the above.

Josiah Morton            Cr

1803 by the Hire of your Negro Girl one year £10.0.0

1804 by Ditto Ditto £10.0.0

1805 Ditto Ditto Ditto £8.0.0, By the hire of your Negro Boy Phill one year £6.0.0

1806 By the Hire of your Negro Woman Judy £7.0.0, By the Hire of your Negro Boy Phill £8.0.0

1807 By the hire of your Negro Woman Judy £6.0.0, By the Hire of your Negro Boy Phill £9.0.0
1808 By the Hire of your Negro Woman Judy £6.0.0
By the Hire of your Negro Boy Phill £ 12.0.0
Recorded: September 19, 1808

**AC Book 4, Pge 174**                                              **S. Pannill's acmpt Currt.**

Dr. the Estate of David Panill dec'd In account with Samuel Pannill Exor.

1807

Aprl 1 To Cash Pd Wm Smith as a witness at Suit vs. Irvine per Rect. £1.1.1, William Adams Halifax for his account disputed £0.3.4, Cash paid Chas. Johnson pr. Execution P. Sheriff Statement and Rect. £4.2.6

April 29 Cash paid Ticketts on Suit vs. Ball £1.5.0

Oct 17 ditto paid Nathaniel Craddock as a Witness in Suit vs Stogdon per Rect. £0.12.9

Oct 21 Cash paid Clk of Henry Per Ticketts , Ditto paid Sheriff of Pittsylv' do, Ditto paid Saml. Lovell P. Rect. £0.1.9, Ditto paid Sterling Willis do £0.10.6

Oct 26 ditto paid Clerk & Sheriff of Hallifax Per Ticket £1.7.11

Nov. 17 To Cash paid Sheriff Pittsylv' Per Ticketts £3.10.9

1808
Feby 17 Thomas Mustaine paid him P. Bond & Rect.£0.2.7 ½, Cash paid John Lewis for part 1 Tickett £0.3.10

Mar. 30 ditto paid Isaac Tines Constable Per Rect.£0.6.3 1/2

Apl. 19 ditto paid Sheriff Pittsylv' P. Tickett £
Ditto paid ditto    ditto £0.6.3 1/4

Apl. 29 ditto paid John Dabney attorney P. Rect. £8.11.0

May 17 ditto paid Sheriff Pittsylv' Ticketts £8.14.0

June 11 ditto paid Sheriff of Campbell £0.6.3 1/2

July 16 ditto paid Clk. Halifax £0.4.9 1/2

CR

1807
Aug. 18 By Daniel Shelton Sen. Rec'd £6.8.3 3/4

Aug. 30 John Jenkins rec'd £3.0.0, William Parsons rec'd of Ster. Willis Constatt. £0.10.6

Sept. 2 Cash rec'd of Patsey Doss Memo acct £0.2.3 1/2

Oct. 21 James Stewart rec'd £3.19.0 1/4, Robert Orkes rec'd in full £0.4.4, John Lovett £0.8.2
Cash rec'd of George Hairston for Morton on Laniers Delivery Bond quashed in Pittsyl' Court £0.19.6

Nov 17 Peter Perkins rec'd £36.3.1, John Bruce Overseer £11.16.1, Cash rec'd of Luke Matthews Memo Acct. £ 0.0.9, John Hogdon rec'd Per James Stewarts order on the Sheriff of Campbell £5.7.0

Dec. 23 Jacob Barger Sen. P. Saml. Lovell Constable £1.6.2, David Hunt rec'd £0.13.0

1808
Jany 26 Cash rec'd of Nat Terry Memo Acct. & Interest £0.15.6

Feby. 17 Thomas C Stone in full £3.0.0.3/4, George Cox £1.17.3, William Robertson Hatter £0.2.9
Reubin Mitchell rec'd of M. Mitchell £3.18.0, Grasty and Pannill £60.6.8, Samuel Woosley rec'd 21$^{st}$ Oct. last £0.6.0

Mar. 17 Wiatt Ellis and No £0.3.8, Cash rec'd of Rowland Jones on acct. Ticketts £4.4.9, Ditto ditto ditto on acct. Land Warrant £2.8.3

Mar 23 William Williams Wagg'o Per S Pannill & Co £0.13.0, Robert Love for 20 Barrels Corn , Deduct for hauling ditto Per his rect. £8.0.0, Joshua Hardy rec'd in full £2.7.1.1/2, Sandy River Store rec'd of W Beck £12.11.1 1/2, Ditto ditto rec'd for Geo. Lackeys note & Int. in acct to Frizzle Per P. R. Gillmore Deduct Commis' retain'd by Gilmore £4.2.4, William Waller rec'd £23.9.5 1/2, William Tucker rec'd £9.19.0

1808

July 16 Cash

Augst. 25 ditto Clk Campbell, Ditto Sheriff Pittsylv', Ditto do do, To 5 Per Cent Comms. Allow'd on collecting £548.5.6 1/2 as P. Contra £27.8.3
Bal. Due the Estate £477.5.2 1/2

1808 August 25 To the Heirs of David Pannill for 2/3 of the above Balance enter'd to their Credits with Saml. Pannill, Guardian £318.3.5 3/4
Paid Bethenia Pannill Widow of D. Pannill, dec'd her 1/3 part of the above Balance per her Rect. £159.1.8 3/4

1808 Mar 23 By Amount Brought Over £209.3.1 3/4
John Jinkins for Cash in full £1.11.0 1/2

April 5 Robert Love for 306 3/4 lbs. Bacon £10.4.6
Apr 19 Samuel Linn acct. p. H. Wimbish £92.15.6 1/2

July 21 John Harris rec'd In full £2.5.5, James Linn 17 May £33.0.0, Ditto ditto , Deduct for enter'd 17th May £50.6.8, George McNeley £11.16.1

Augt. 25 Grasty & Pannills Omitt'd 21st Oct. last £9.0.5 ¼, Ditto ditto rec'd from 17th Feby. Last till this day £108.17.0 ½, Saml. Woosley? rec'd in full £0.5.8
Total £548.5.6 1/2

By Bal. P. Contra £477.5.2 1/2

Pursuant to an order of the County Court of Pittsylvania bearing date June Court 1808 to us directed, we have examined the account of Saml. Pannill Exor. of David Pannill dec'd with the decedent's Estate as Stated above with the Exhibits and find the account to be balanc'd up till this day. Given under our hands this 25th day of August 1808.
Wm Smith, Saml. Stone, Philip L Grasty
Recorded: September 19, 1808

**AC Book 4, Page 177**      **Lucy Hodnett's Dower**

Persuant to an order of Feby Pittsylvania Court 1808 appointing Commissioners to allot to Lucy Hodnett widow of John Hodnett, deceas'd her Dower in the land of her Deceas'd Husband &c., I have surveyed and lay'd off 40 acres of land being one third part of 120 acres which the Said John Hodnett dec'd Siezed including the Mansion House. Beginning at 2 Gums at the head of a branch, thence a new line N. 53° E 130 poles through the plantation to a Red Oak in the out side line, thence N 78 W 130 poles to 2 Maples on the Spring branch, thence up the said branch as it Meanders 70 poles to a white oak near the Spring, thence S 10 ° E 14 poles to a white oak on the old Road and S 61 E 24 poles to the Beginning. Which said 40 acres is allotted by the Said Commissioners to the Said Widow for Dower &c. Done the 27 day of February 1808. By Joshua Stone S.P.C.

Agreeable to an order of the County Court of Pittsylvania Made at last February Court, we Champness Terry, Jeremiah Terry and Robert Clopton have allotted to Lucy Hodnett, Widow of John Hodnett deceas'd forty acres of land as directed in the plat and certificate hereunto annexed, also the following Slaves To Wit: Moses, Daniel and Jinney, also one pound thirteen Shillings and four pence which makes one equal third in the Value of the slanes, also that she retain one third of the personal part of the Estate already sold agreeable to the Sale. Given under our hands this 27th day of February 1808.
Chanpness Terry, Jeremiah Terry, Robert Clopten
Recorded: October 17, 1808

**AC Book 4, Page 178**      **H. Micklerough's Inventory**

In obedience to the Worshipful Court of Pittsylvania Co. we have appraised the Estate of Henry Michelborough, Dec'd viz:

1 negro man, Joseph £135.0.0, 1 Negro man Lewis £120.0.0, 2 Negroes, Clary and her Child Hannah £120.0.0, 2 Negroes Easter & her Child Nancy £120.0.0, 1 Negro boy Wiley £60.0.0, 1 Do Do Ratley £50.0.0, 1 Do Do James £40.0.0, 1 negro Girl Isbell £40.0.0, 1 negro boy Stephen £30.0.0

14 head of Cattle £24.0.0, 30 head of Hoggs £9.0.0, 1 horse & 3 raw Hides £19.16.0, 1 mare & yearling Colt £25.10.0, 10 head of Sheep £6.0.0, 2 pare of plow Gare £1.4.0, 2 plow hoes and clevises £1.2.0 1 pare of Cast Coxes £0.3.0, 2 Colters and one plow hoe £0.9.0, 5 Hilling hoes and 3 weeding hoes £1.6.0 2 Grubing hoes & 5 Axes £1.14.0, 2 Wedges and a box of old Iron £0.9.0, 2 Cotton Wheels and 50 lbs. Bare Iron £1.13.0, a parcel of Corn and oats £10.15.0, 1 flax wheel £0.15.0, 2 Sithes and Cradles & 2 Juggs £0.16.0, a parcel of Cotton & 3 bee hives £3.3.0, 1 Curecomb & a parcel of bacon £18.1.6, 3 butter potts and 1 Spice morter £0.13.0, 2 Tin Candle molds £0.1.6

1 Tee Kettle and a parcel of Lumber £1.4.0, a pare of worpen bears & boxes £0.6.0, a parcel of Cleane oats and one Wheat Sive £0.13.6, 1 pare of old Irons £0.6.0, 1 Shovel and 1 flat Iron £0.4.6, 4 beddes and furnature £40.0.0, 8 Setting Chires £1.0.0, 1 Desk and walnut Chest £1.6.0, 3 pare Cotton Cards £0.12.0 1 Looking Glass £0.7.6, a Cubboard and furnature £3.0.0, 1 Wire Wheat Sive £0.7.6, a parcel of old books £1.10.0, a parcel of old Puter £2.8.0, 1 Set of Knives and forks £0.7.6, 3 dutch ovens £0.18.0 3 potts and hooks £2.5.0, 2 pott racks and one Skilet £0.12.0, 1 Gridiron, Shovel &c £0.10.0, 2 bolls & 1 brass cock £0.6.0

1 Negro Girl Ailey £75.0.0, 1050 pounds of inspected Tobacco £9.9.0, a parcel of Tobacco £7.16.0 1 pine table and 1 folding Table £2.0.0

Total: £993.19.6
May 12, 1809
Daniel Sullivan, Hezk. Puryear, Thomas Worsham
Recorded: June 19, 1809

**AC Book 4, Page 180**                                                   **Inventory of Chas Payne Inventory**

Inventory of the property of Charles Payne Dec'd March 22, 1808

Negroes Cretia and three children, Abram, Hurt & John $600, 1 Sorrel Horse 75, 1 Bay mare 70 1 Bed and furnature, bed Stead and Cord 30, 1 Do do do do 35, 1 do do do 6, 9 Winsor Chairs 2.25 1 Black Walnut Desk 10, 1 Black Walnut folding Table & Toilett 6, 1 Black Walnut Cubboard and Earthen Ware 15, 1 parcel of Books 5, 2 Brass Candle Sticks 1.25, 2 Decanters 1.50, 1 pair of hand Irons .50, 1 Trunk 2, 1 Waiter .50, 1 Blue pine Chist 1, 1 Jug .50, 1 Trunk 1, 1 Bridle & Saddle 5 1 Fiddle .50, 4 Butter potts, 1 Jug, 2 Ticklers & 2 Bottles 2.50, 1 Churn and Firken .75, 1 Small Trunk 1 2 pair of Iron Wedges 3, 3 plow hoes and 1 Coalter 3, 3 Weeding and 2 Hilling hoes 2.50, 2 Grubing hoes 2.25, 2 Axes 1.50, 2 pair of plow Geers 4, 1 Bee Stead 1.50, 1 Tobacco Hhds .75, 1 parcel of old Iron .25, 1 Cutting Box .50, 1 Red Cow and Calf, 1 White Cow, 1 Red Cow & Red Bull 30, 1 Dutch oven 2, 3 potts and 1 skilet 4, 1 pair of flat Irons 1.50, Tub and two pales .50

Agreeable tp the above order to us directed we met and apprais'd the above articles as pr. Statement. Given under our hands this 20th day of March 1809.
Jas. D Patton, Silas Heston, Thomas Stewart
Recorded: March 22, 1809

**AC Book 4, Page 182**                                                         **John Waller's Inventory**

Pursuant to an order of the Worshipful Court of Pittsylvania County to us directed We Creed Tanner, Joseph Flippin, Robert Walters and Noel Waddill hath Conven'd together the late dwelling house of John Waller, Deceas'd on the 24th February 1809 and after Being first Sworn do proceed to appraise the Said Estate brought before us as followeth:

February 22, 1809
Five Sows and 15 pigs, Three Sows and 10 pigs, One Sow and 10 Shoats, Five Hoggs, Eleven Sheep, one yoak of oxen, One ditto, One ditto, One Cart, Three Cows and Calves, Three Cows, two Heefiers, Three Heifers, four Cows, One Bull, one Sorrel Horse, One Black mare, one Sorrel Ditto, One Bay Horse, one filley, One wagon hind gear, Swingletree & lock chain, One Still & Eleven yearlings, Five mattocks and one Grubing hoe, Five Weeding hoes, one pole ax, Five hilling hoes, three Colters, 5 Stocks and two Swingle trees and Clives

One Set of harrow hoes, three Iron Wedges, One X Cut Saw, two pair Iron traces, Three back bands and belly bands, Three pair of Haymes, one Whip Saw, Four bells & Three Collars, One Drawing Knife, Screw auger, 5 Hand Saw, One adze Frow and hammer, ibe broad ax and auger, One jointer, one pair of Stillards

Parcel of old Iron, two horse collars, One bridle and Saddle, One Grubing hoe, three plow hoes & one old hoe, Two old Sithes, two Sows & five pigs, Three Sithes, three bee hives, Two thousand weight of loose Tobacco, One hogshead of old Tobacco, Four hogshead of tobacco, Five hogshead & one barrel, one Cutting knife, Three hogshead, four Cow hides, Blade fother, one Calf Skin, One cask, two hogshead One cash, four casks, One rum hogshead full of cotton, One bag of collard and cake, One tub of fat One Jug and Honey, dry'd fruit, Parcel of Soap, Six oats Stacks, One walnut leaf Table, One desk, one Walnut Chest with drawers

One small Trunk, One Walnut Chest, One pine Table, one case & Bottles, 3 plow hoes and 1 ax, 1 Case of Iron Blacksmiths Tools, Wheat in the Straw, ditto' one cupboard, Eight deer skins Case of Razors and horse phlegums, Eleven Chairs, One Turean, half Doz. Green Edg'd plates, 3 Dishes 1 Bowl, 1 Teapot, 1 Castor, pair salt seltars, 2 wine glasses and Decanter and Mustard pot, 6 Tea spoons, nine Table spoons, 1 Bread pan and Milkpot, 1 Soup Spoon, 8 Knives and 12 forks, 2 Brass candle Sticks 1 Tea Cannister, old Waiters, 13 Vials, 2 Books, 1 looking Glass, 3 Wheat Sives, Small piece of blistea'd Steel, 1 pr. Of Sad Irons, one slate, 4 pewter Basons, 9 pewter plates, 2 pewter dishes, 2 pr. Sheers, Shovel and Tongs, Brass Skillet, 1 Bason and Butter & some old pewter, 1 Pitcher and Sugar, Some Butter, 1 Chest, 2 flax wheels, 1 Bed and Blanket sheet, Bolster and stead, 1 Bed and Sheet and Quilt and Bolster 1 Bed and Sheet and Two Quilts and Bolster, 1 Bed and Sheet, 3 Quilts, Bolster and pillow and Stead, one Bag of feathers, one Bead and Sheets & Counterpine and blanket and Quilt and bolster, two pillows, bead stead and Cord, One Bed, two Counterpins, one blanket, one Sheet and bolster and bead Stead and Cord, One Bead, one Sheet, two Counterpins, one blanket, Quilt, bolster under Bead and Cord

One pair of Cards, Six white plain Counterpins, Six checked Counterpins, Three notted Counterpins, One Lock chain, One oven and lead, one do, one pot tribet & hooks, Two pots and hooks, one spice mortar, Two Iron pot racks, one flax Hackle, One Lamb, one slay & old Harnesses, Two pair chards, one pair Wool Chards, Three Cotton Wheels, one flax, One table, four tubs, three pails & two piggions, One pistole and 1 pot and Hooks, One Beadstead & Card, two old Wheels, One Rum hogshead with Pork, Parcel of Bacon and Some beef, Three barrels & Churn, a parcel of Soap tallow, One Steel trap, one copper tea Kettle, Two Barrels, one Chirm, old pot of Butter, One hundred Barrels of Corn

One negroe Man Known by the name of Cupid, One Negro man the name of Adam, One negroe woman by the name of Silva, One Negro Boy by the name of Ben, One Negro Girl by the name of Patty, One Negro Boy by the name of Alfred, One Negro man by the name of Harry, One Negro man by the name of Sy, One Negro woman by the name of Philis, One Negro Girl by the name of Isbel, One Negro Boy by the name of Peter, One Negro man by the name of Abram, One Negro man by the name of Daniel, One Negro woman by the name of Reah, One ngero Girl by the name of Mary, One Negro Boy by the name of Jerry, One Negro Woman by the name of Hannah

March 18
One Shot Gun, one old Musket, One bay Horse, One bay Horse Colt with stair & snip, One bay do do, Some unbroken flax, Two boxes, Sixteen Gees, One 3 hoe Harrow, 2 pare fire dogs, Some Potatos Plantings, One Seale Skin trunk, One mans Saddle, One do do

Total: £1827.18.9
Creed Tanner, Joseph Flippin, Robert Walters, Noel Waddill

We also find in the possession of the Estate of Mr. John Waller Dec'd the following bonds and accounpts as follows:
Wm Wilkerson bond £4.4.0, Do Do £16.5.0, Joseph Slayden bond £31.11.8, Christon Huser Do £60.0.0, Do £30.0.0, Presley Dodson Do £24.14.6, Asa Thomas Do £7.11.10, James Colquohoun Do £300.0.0, Do Do £300, Do Do Rect for 2 hhgs. Tobacco, Elisha Dodson Bond £6.0.0, Cash in hand £0.3.9, Samuel Walkers acct. £31.4.6, One Loan office certificate for Seventy one Dollars and 79 Cents.
Total: £543.18.6 ¾
Creed Tanner, Joseph Flippen, Robert Walters, Noel Wadill
Recorded: March 21, 1809

**AC Book 4, Page 188**                                             **Calland's Inventory**

An Inventory and appraisement of the Personal Estate of Mr. Samuel Calland Dec'd Viz:

36 Large Hogs @ $4each, 36 pigs @ $3/ each, 35 Grown Sheep @10/, 11 young Lambs @4/6, 1 Grey Horse @$70, 1 Dark Bay Do $40, 1 Bay mare , 1 Black Horse, 1 Bay mare, 1 Bay mare, 11 Milk Cows @ $10 each, 2 Large Steers $12 each, 1 yorke of Work Steers $25, 1 yoke young Steers $12, 8 yearlings $17, two year old Cattle @$6 each, 1 ox Cart, 2 yokes and a Lock Chain, 4 young Calves, 6 Dutch ovens and Lids, 2 spare Dutch ovens Lids, 6 Frying Pans, 1 old Frying pan and 1 Ladle, 3 Small Iron Potts, 1 Iron Tea Kettle, 2 Copper Kittles, 1 spice Mortar and Peste, 2 pair Sad Irons, 2 Large Iron Potts, 4 pair Pott hooks, 1 Grid Iron and Bread Toaster, 7 Pewter Basons, Jack Screws, 1 pair Stillyards, A parcel of old Iron, 4 old Sythe Blades, 2 Large Barrel augers, 2 Screw Do, 1 Tool Adze., 1 Cross Cut Saw, 9 Bar Share Ploughs, 4 Coulters & Stocks, 1 Lock Chain, 1 X cut Saw, 1 Pole ax, 1 Mattock, 3 Grubing Hoes, 6 Hilling Hoes, 3 Hilling Hoes and 2 weeding Do, 1 Cutting Box & Knife, 2 Double Trees & Irons, 1 Iron Toothed Harrow, 3 Iron wedges, 1 chisel & Clivis, 7 Bells, 1 pair wagon Boxes Bands &c,, 1 Froe, 1 old Plow Hoe, 2 Shovel Plows Stocks &c, 3 pair Plow Geer, 1 Small Kegg containing Ssundry pieces of old Iron, 1 Shovel Plows Stocks &c, 1 Straw knife, 1 small keg containing Sundry pieces of old Iron 1 Copper Coffee Pott, 2 Large Juggs, 2 Small quart Jugs, 1 spice mortar, 1 Demi John, 1 large Jugg

1 Well fixed Rifle gun, 3 Shott Guns, 2 Mens Saddles, 1 old womans do, 1 new womans Saddle, 1 pr. Saddle bags, 1 Pair Pistoles & Portmanteau Holsters, 2 ½ Sides Sole Leather, 1 Large Rippskin, 2 sodes upper Do, 2 pr. Old saddle bags, 1 pr. Scales & weight, 1 Candle Box, 1 1 Bed and furnature, 1 Bed &c do, 6 Fine Cotton Counter panes $6 each, 1 Course Cotton Do, 2 Checked Counter panes 2 hall worn Cotton do, 1 pair old Linnen Sheets, 14 1/2 Pair new Cotton Sheets , 1 Suit new Cotton Curtains, 1 Suit Calico Do, 1 Suit new Callies Do , 1 Larage Trunk, 1 Bed Furnature &c, 1 Bed do, 1 new Desk, 1 new Ledger & Journal, 1 Walnut Table, 1 Back Gammon Table, 1 Tea Table, 1 Shaving Glass, 1 New flax wheel, 1 Sett Surveyors Instruments, 1 China Press & its Contents, 1 Clock, 1 Side Board, 1 Desk and Book Case, 1 Tea Chest, 2 Looking Glasses, Dozen Prints in frames, 4 Bird Picures in frames, 3 Prints in frames, 1 knife and spoon Case, 8 Trunks Large and Samll, 1 Desk, 1 Large Chest, 1 Check Reel,, 1 Walnut Foldling Table, 1 Bed and furnature, 1 Bed Furniture &c, 1 Bureau and Table, 1 Walnut Cubbard & its Contents, 1 Painted Do & its Contents, 1 Dressing Glass

1 Silver Watch, 1 square Walnut Table, 1 Case and Bottles Compleate, 5 Flower Potts, 1 Terrestrial Globe, 1 Silver Coffee Pott and Caster, 1 Silver Tea Pott, 1 sugar Dish & 1 Cream Pott, 6 Salt Stands @ $6 each, 1 Sett of Mahoganny Tables, 1 Side Bord, 1 pair Mahoganey Tea Tables, 1 Desk and Book Case, 1 Dozen Large Prints in frames, 2 Large Looking Glasses, 4 Silver Candlesticks, 1 Violin, 1 pair Fire Dogs, 1 pair Tongs & Poker, 1 Tea Tray, 2 pr. Money Scales & Weights, 1 doz Silver Table spoons & 1 Divider, 1 Razor Case Strap &c

10 Vol Smalletts History of England, 12 European Magazines in Boards, 12 Monthly Reviews, 4 Scotts Magazines, 1 European Do, 4 Naval Chronicles, 1 Spy Glass, Guthries Grammer, 1 Vol. Mc Kinzie on Health, 36 Vol on Various Subjects, 5 Vol Buchans Physician Elegant Extracts &c, 18 Vol on different Subjects, 2 Vol Ramsey Poems, 3 Vol Adams defence, 4 Vol Prideux Connection, 10 Vol Enciclopedia, 5 Vol Domestick Encycloped a, 8 Vol Humes History , 5 Vol Russels Modeern Europe, 6 Vol Gibbons Empire, 4 Vol Robertson Charates, 2 Vol Johnsons Dictionary, 3 Vol Elements of Erudation, 6 Vol Chesterfields  letter, 2 Vol. Select Plays, 1 Vol Cardiphonia

3 Vol Miscellanicious Vol, 6 Vol Popes Works, 4 Vol. Rottins Belle Letters, 4 Vol Don Quiotte, 2 Vol Modern Travel,  4 Vol Posseshomes, 9 Vol Shakespeare Plays, 1 Vol Junuis Letters, 1 Vol Dodridge Vise & progress of Religion, 2 Vol Bowens Geography, 1 Farmers dictionary, 2 Vol Sheredans Dict., 1 Vol Paleys Pholophsy, 1 Vol Baileys Do, 5 old Books

3 Beds Furnature, 1 Small Dressing Table, 1 Hand Bellows, ½ Doz Leather Bottomed Chairs, 10 Winsdor Chairs, 2 arm chairs, 1 pair old Fire Dogs & 1 pair Tongs, 1 Bed Furniture, 1 Large Still Cap & worm,

1 Loom, 1 pair of Swifts, 1 Cotton wheel, 1 Grind Stone, 1 pair Cart wheels

1 Negro man Abram, 1 negro Lad James, 1 negro man David, 1 negro man Leonard, 1 young Negro woman Aba, 1 negro woman Agness, 1 negro woman Hannah, 1 yellow Lad Bob, 1 young Negro man,
1 negro woman Juda, 1 young girl Sally, 1 young woman Chloe, 1 young girl Ame, 1 woman & her child Dinah, 1 young Negro Lad Jack, 1 young Girl Delsey, 1 Little yellow Girl Dolly, 1 Little Boy Lorenzo,
1 Little girl Prirrter, 1 negro girl Susan, 1 negro woman Polley & her child Lewis, 1 little Negro girl Edy,
1 Small Negro girl Sally, 1 Do   Do Milley, 1 Little Boy Stephen, 1 Little Girl Mary

1 old Riding Chair & Harness, 4 Candlesticks & 2 pair Snuffers, 1 spice Morter, 3 Chafing Dishes, 2 Large Butter Potts, 2 Large Juggs, 1 Butter Pott & 4 Cocks, 507 Bar Iron, 3 Butter Potts, a parcel of leather,
7 Large Tight Cask, 11 Small Do, Waggon Tire supposed to weigh 60£, 2 Large Butter Potts, 3 Tubbs,
1 Large Sugar Box, 1 Large Walnut Chest, 1 old Pine Do, 3 Vol Latin Books, 5 Vol Small Do, 3 Small Gilt Trunks, 1 pair Stilyards, 3 new Pole Axes, a parcel of Cuttery the remains of the Store, 3 Tin Tobacco Boxes, 6 Stock Buckles, 17 pair Knee Buckles, 1 pr. Waffle Irons, 3 Large Tin Canisters, 1 Still Cap and worm, 1 Small old Still &c

Property in the Possession of Doct. Callaway
1 negro Boy Daniel, 1 yellow Girl Lucy, 1 young woman Darkie & her child Randolp
Total amot. of the manor Plantation including Doc Callaways £3152.16.1

The property on the Glebe Plantation viz:

1 Dark bay mare & colt, 1 Roan mare, 1 Black mare, 1 Blind Sorrel Horse, 1 young Roan Horse, 1 Dark bay young mare, 1 dark bay colt, 1 dark bay do, 36 Grown Hogs, 35 Shoats and Piggs, 2 Large Sows,
25 head of Cattle, 1 yoke work Steers, 1 do young do, 1 ox cart & Lock Chain, 4 Coulters fixed compleate,
3 Iron Wedges,  1 froe & 1 Claw hammer, 4 Mattocks, 8 Hilling hoes, 1 Spade, 1 shovel, 1 cutting Box & knife, 3 pair Plow geer, 3 Shovel Plows, 1 Sett Breast Chains, 6 poll axes, 1 hand do, 2 old Grind Stones, 2 Sythes & Cradles, 1 Hand Saw, 1 Chissel, 1 Gouge, 1 auger & 1 drawing knife, 1 pair Steelyards, 1 yellow girl Lucy, 1 Do " male Frank, 1 negro man Dick, 1 negro woman Lindey & her child Nat, 1 yellow woman Aggey, 1 negro Lad Benjamin, 1 yellow woman Betty, 1 negro Boy Peter, 1 Do   " William, 1 Do Girl Rilah, 1 Little yellow Boy Belly, 1 "      Gabriel, 1     " girl Sukey, 1 negro man Daniel
Total Amt. Property on the Glebe Plantation £1298.16.6

Property on the Sandy river Plantation viz:

1 mill Cap Worm &c, 1 ox Cart, 21 head of Cattle @ $7each, Waggon Tire Bands Supposed to Weigh 61lbs, 1 pair Stillyards, 3 Augers & 1 chisel, 1 pair Iron wedges and 1 froe, 2 Waggon Bands, 5 Reap Hooks, 2 Coulters and Stocks, 1 Scythe and Cradle, 1 old Muskett, 1 grind Stone, 1 Cutting Box and Knife,
4 Shovel Plows , 2 Clives, 3 Sett Plow Gears Compleat, 15 old Iron, 1 Lock Chain, 1 Bay horse blind,
1 Dark Bay Horse, 1 young Sorrel Horse, 1 Bay Mare, 1 Small Sorrel Colt, 1 Dark bay Do, 7 Hilling Hoes,
2 Mattocks, 2 Grubbing Hoes, 4 Potts Axes, 1 Drawing Knife, 1 yoke oxen, 3 young Calves, 28 Grown Hogs @ $3 each, 30 Shoats

1 Negro man Squire, 1 Do  Do Mike, 1 Do Woman Betty & her child Chloe, 1 do Boy Lewis, 1 Do  "  Leas
1  " James, 1  "  woman Rachel, 1  " child Jinsey, 1 " Girl Clary, 1 old Woman Libby, 1  " Boy Harry,
1 " Girl Cindy, 1  "  " Sarah, 1 man Philip
Total Amt of Property  on Sandy River plantation £1118.8.9

Property on Dan River Plantation Viz:

1 Yoke work Steirs, 1 young Do Do, 1 ox cart and lock chain, 1 Road Waggon, 13 yearlings, 1 Grind Stone, 15 Head grown Cattle $10 each, 3 Head grown Do $4 each, 7 Head young Do $4 each, 1 old Bay Horse , 1 Chickasaw Horse, 1 Sorrel Mare, 1 Roan Mare, 1 Sorrel Colt, 13 Grown Hogs 21/ each, 18 Large

Shoats 7/6 each, 20 Piggs 2/ each, 6 Shovel Plows & 4 Stocks, 4 Poll axes, 1 Lott of Plow Geers , 6 Hilling Hoes, 1 Hand Saw, 1 pair Small Stillyards

1 negro Man George, 1 " " Jack, 1 " Woman Lydia, 1 "    " Molley and her Child Ned, 1 " Creasey & her child Christian, 1 "  Lad Jeremiah, 1 " Girl Fanny, 1 " Lucy, 1 " Isbell, 1 " Boy Randolph, 1 " Girl Rose, 1 " Boy Moses, 1 " Man Patrick
Total Amt. Of Property on Dan River Plantation £1200.8.0

Amo't of Property on the Manor Planation £3152.16.1
Amt. Of Property on the Glebe Plantation £1296.16.6
Amt. Of Do on the Sandy river Plantation £1118.8.9
Amt. Of Do on the Dan River Plantation £1200.8.0
Total Amt. Of the Whole Persoanl Estate £ 6768.9.4

Agrreeable to an order of the Worshipful Court of Pittsylvania to us directed we whose names are hereunto Subscribed have proceeded to apprase all the Personal Estate of Samuel Calland Dec'd as Shown as agreeable to the foregoing Statement. April 19, 1809
Jas. Hopkins, William Walker, Moses Kerby

1809 April 19th the above named James Hopkins, William Wallker and Moses Kerby made oath in Court that the foregoing appraisment was made by them according to the best of their Skill and Judgment.
Will Tunstall C.P.C.
Recorded: April 17, 1809

**AC Book 4, Page 198**                                                            **Shackleford's Inventory**

Am Ivventory and appraisement of the Estate of Thos. Shackleford Dec'd taken this Day above written.
May 12th 1809

One Feather bead and furnature &c, One Mare and Coult (sic) Saddle & Bridle, Two Chest , 1 Cupboaard 1 Cow and Heifer, 6 Jugs and two Butter pot, 4 Bottles, 1 Coffee pot, 1 Decanter, 1 loking Glass, 1 Candle Mole, 1 Slate, 6 phials, a parcel of pewter, a parcel of Earthan ware and Knives and forks, 3 ps. Shares, 1 pr. Scissors, 2 potts, 2 Skillets, 1 pr. Pot hooks, Flesh fork, Skimmer and spoon, Candle Stick and Snuffers, 1 Meal Sifter & 2 Mugs, 1 Cotton wheel & 8 Chairs, 1 Gun & a parcel of Books, 1 sesero? auger, 2 water pails, 1 Raw hide, 4 Basketts, 1 Hogshead, 2 Barrels & 2 Washing tubs, 2 plows & Set of Geer, 2 Hilling Hoes & 1 Coulter, 2  Axes, 1 Mattock and 1 grubing hoe, 1 Snuff Bottle and 1 Claw Hammer, 1 Taylors goos & 1 pr. Flat Irons, 1 pr. Cotton Cards
Total: £50.1.3

In obedfience to an order of the Worshipful Court to us directed we have proceeded to appraise the Within property to the best of Our Skill and Judgment.
William Betterton, Jon. B Dawson, Jesse Buckley
Recorded:  May 15, 1809

**AC Book 4, Page 199**                                                      **Division of Saml. Callands Estate**

In Conformity to a decretal order of the Worshipful the Court of Pittsylvania County pronounced on the 15th of May 1809 in the Suit in Chancery in Sd Court depending in which Samuel Calland in plfts. and Elizabeth Calland Administratrix of Samuel Calland dec'd, Henry G Callaway and Anna his wife , William Callaway and Elizabeth his wife , Ralph Calland , Booker Calland and James Calland defendt's . We the undersigned three of the Commisioners in Sd. Decretal order for that purpose named and appointed have proceeded to divide the personal and real estate of Samuel Calland dec'd as far as was practicable and the parties Concerned, Wishes being unacted upon a large landed estate in the state of Kentuckey and number of little Tracts of land in Pittsylvania of little Value. The Division of Which at this time might have operated prejudically to the parties adopting the Valuation of the Sworn appraisers of the Negroes belonging to the estate made but a month or two back as their Valuation at this time, We have allotted to Elizabeth Calland the widow as Dower one thirds the following Slaves to Wit: one Negro Boy Bob Valued at £115, one woman Judy £85, one man Leonard £115, one Negro man David £90, one woman Fanny & her child Dinah £100, one girl Dilsy £60, one Lad James £110, one Girl Susan £65, one woman Agness £50, one Girl Anny 60, one boy Lorenzo £35, one Girl Edy £60, one young man Nimrod £120, one girl Dolly £45, one Ditto Printer £25, one man Aabraham £120, one young woman Abbey £90, one woman Polly and her Child Lewis £110, one boy Obediah £65, one boy Stephen £30 and one girl Sally £100. The Total Value of which Said Negroes to assigned to Mrs. Calland we find to be 1640£ and according to the Standard which we have adopted leaves a balance due her by the other parties in the Score of the Negroes of five pounds ¾ as the third of the whole Stock of Negroes would be. £1645.3.4

The remaining two thirds of the Negroes we hane Divided by Lott as follows. To James Calland Lott No 1, one man named Dick £110, one woman Chloe £100, one girl Sally £45, one boy Peter £70, one Girl Lindey £37.10, one girl Fanny £80, one Lad Benjamin £100, the total Value of which Said Seven Negroes so allotted to James Calland by ballot, we find to be £552.10, leaving a balance due him of £6.15 as his proportion of the Negroes should have a mounted in Value to th Sum of £549.5.0

According to the Standard accepted Lott No 2 has in Like manner been assigned to Samuel Calland the Plltf. and consists of the Slaves following to Wit: one man Daniel£115, Lindy and her child Nat £100, one Milly £35, one Boy William £60, one boy Moses £35, one man Jack £100, one yellow girl Lucy £75, one Girl Jinney £30, the total of which sd. Nine Negroes in Value we find to be £530 leaving a balance due from him Sd. Samuel Calland of fifteen Shillings.

Lott No 3 has in like manner been assigned to Booker Calland and Consists of the following Negroes to Wit: one man Mike £110, one Woman Aggy £100, one girl Ritah £45, one Boy Lewis £60, one woman Lydia £50, one Girl Lucy £70, one boy Sias £75, one boy Gabriel £30, the total Value of which Sd. Eight Negroes we find to be £540 leaving a balance due to sd. Booker Calland of nine pounds 5/.

Lott no 4 has by us been assigned in like manner to William Callaway in right of his wife Elizabeth formerly Elizabeth Calland, one man Phillip £110, one woman Betty and her Child Chloe £110, one Girl Isbel £45, one boy James £68, one woman Liby £25, one Lad Jeremiah £100, one yellow Boy Billy £40, one girl Clary £60. The total Value of which Sd. Nine Negroes we find to be £558.leaving a balance due from sd. William Callaway of Eight pounds 15/.

Lot No 5 has been assigned by us in like manner to Henry G Callaway in right of his wife Anna, formerly Anna Calland, and contains the following Slaves to Wit. One man Patrick£115, Creasy and her Child Christian £115, one girl Sarah £30 and boy Harry £45, one woman Hannah £30, one man George £100, one woman Rachel £95, one girl Sukey £25. The total Value of which Sd. Nine slaves so assigned sd.Henry G. Callaway we find to be £555 leaving a balance due from him of five pounds 15/.

Lot no 6 has by us in like manner been assigned to Ralph Calland and consists of the following Slaves to wit : Frank a man of the value of £115, yellow woman Betty£100, Girl Rose £50, boy Randolph £35, Girl Mary £30, one man Squire £100, one woman Molly and her child Ned £120, The total Value of Which sd. Eight Slaves we find to be £550 leaving a balance due from sd. Ralph Calland of fifteen shillings. We then proceeded to the division of a Quanity of Inspected Tobacco being the crop of 1807, 1808, and 1809 between the Said and the other Defendants and Samuel Calland the Pltts. according to the respective intents of each as Will more fully appear by the two papers, one marked A and the other B which is here with Submited as forming a part of this report. We then proceeded to ascertain the advancements made by the deceadant in his Life time to the Defendants Henry G Callaway and Wm Callaway and found that Henry G Calloway has received in cash and property to the amount of £1257 amd William Callaway the sum of £1190 in Cash and property and the parties, all Wishing it, the four Tracts of Land that we then proceeded to divide were allotted.

To Samuel Calland, Ralph Calland, James Calland, and Booker Calland the Two Callaways agreeing to let the land go agst. their advancements as far as they Would go and were valued at cash price to putt them on an equal footing with the Said Henry G Callaway and William Callaway Whose advancements as above. we found to be prancipally in Cash to Ralph Calland was allotted by Ballot the home plantation Subject to the Dower as herein after more particularly by expressed and after an allowance for the dower as Life estate of Mrs. Calland Valued at £921.12 the sd. Land so assigned to Ralph Calland including the following tracts to Wit: a tract bought of Jefferson of 785 acres, one bought of 400 acres of Walker 75 acres and two of Gordon Containing 354 acres Some of 300 patented to Samuel Calland and other adjoining of two hundred in all making 2124 acres to Samuel Calland was allotted in like manner the Glebe plantation which after making an allowance for the dower which was laid off to the widow as is here in after described was Valued in like manner to the Sum of Eight hundred and forty one pounds 12/ the sd. Land so assigned to Said Samuel Calland as aforesaid including the following tracts to Wit: One tract of 593 acres bought of Spraggins and one other of Williams of 100 acres making in all 693 Subject to the dower of Mrs. Calland herein after more particularly described to James Calland was in like manner allotted Sandy River estate which after allowing for the dower was Valued at £900 the said estate so assigned to James Calland Containing the following tracts of land to Wit;

One tract of land bought of Morton 1053, several small tracts of McGruder containing together 108 acres, patented to Samuel Calland fifty acres and one tract bought of Allsup, 180 acres; in all 1391 acres Subject to the Dower as life Estate of Mrs. Calland herein after more partically described.

To Booker Calland in like manner was allotted the Dan River estate which after deducting for the Dower estate carved out of the Same was Valued to £860 and which sd. estate so assigned to sd Booker Calland Contains the following tracts of land to Wit: one tract bought of Yeamans of 300 acres, one Ditto of Peay of 150 making in all 450 acres Subject to the dower estate of Mrs. Calland as in here after more particularly described.

We assigns to Mrs. Calland as her Dower in the home tract of land 509 Acres including the mansion house and all other houses erected on the plantation. The boundaries of which are as follows to Wit: Beginning at a white oak in Reids order line thence new lines N 17 E 60 poles to a walnut in the field 165 E 440 poles to pointers in the old line thence With sd. old lines including a tract bought of Walker to the Beginning.

We also assigns to Mrs. Calland as dower in the Glebe plantation 176 acres the Boundaries of which are as follows to wit: Beginning at Blakeleys Corner Post oak thence a new dividing line N 3 West 310 poles to pointers in the old line, thence taking the back lines and round to the Beginning excluding all the buildings.

We also assigns to Mrs. Calland as Dower in the Sandy River estate Containing 300 acres the boundaries of which are as follows to wit: Beginning at a white oak Corner in the old patent tract thence a new dividing line N 89 E 165 poles to the back line, thence following the back lines including a tract of 901 acres bought of Magruder to the Beginning excluding all the buildings and we also assigns to Mrs. Calland as Dower in the Dan River estate 96 acres the boundaries of which are as follows to wit: Beginning at the mouth of a Ditch on the river bank, thence new lines south 32 poles to a Stump N 84°West 36 poles to a Poplar West 64 poles to a white oak S 85 ° W 105 poles to the Back Line, thence along the back line and with the meanders of the river to the Beginning excluding all buildings in laying of the Dower. We beg leave to report that we had a due regard to quality of Soil quantity of acres and State of improvements all which is respectfully submit'd to the Court. In Witness of all which we the undersigned Three of the Commissioners named in sd. Directal order have the 3rd day of June 1809 hereunto subscribed our hands.
D. Coleman, W. Beavers, Jas Hopkins

Proportion of Tobo. On hand at the Death of Saml. Calland allotted Mrs. Calland as her third inspected in 1807 Total: 15992 pounds

Of the foregoing crop 15992 Weight as above is assigned to the Widow as her third bearing a balance due by her to the Legatees of 380 lbs. of Tobacco.

Proportion of Tobo. on hand at the death of Samuel Calland allotted to Mrs. Calland as her thirds inspected in 1808. Total: 8049 lbs

The other assigned as third of the Crop to Mrs. Calland being her part of the crop of 1808 leaving a balance of 797 lbs due the Legatees.

Proportion of Tobo. on hand at the death of Saml. Calland allotted Mrs. Calland as her thirds inspected at Lynchburg 1809 viz: Total: 7094 lbs

The above assigned Mrs. Calland for her thirds of the Crop 1809 Leaving a balance due the Legatees of two hundred & ninety four pounds Tobo.

Will. Callaway 9888lbs (1807-1808)
H G Callaway 9888lbs "
R. L/S Callahan 9888lbs "
Sam'l Calland 9888lbs "
Bowker Callahan 9888lbs "
Jas Callahan 9888lbs "

Recorded: June 20, 1809
**AC Book 4, Page 206**                                                       **Abel Chilton Acct. Current**

Dr. the Estate of Abel Chilton dec'd In account with John Worsham

1807
Feby 10 To 1 pint Brandy

Feby 14 Gallon Brandy furnished at Sale
Cash paid the Cryer
Hire of Berry Worsham from the 20 Aug 1806 till Xmas

June 13 paid James Colquhoun per acct., Paid James Colquhoun & Co ditto, Paid Thomas Worsham, Paid Rebeckah Chapman, Paid Gidion Mitchell, Paid a Clerk's Tickett, My commission for Transacting the Business, Balance Due John Worsham £39.0.3

Cr

1807
Feby 13 By amt of Sales, By his 11th part of 2 Hhds. Tobo. After deducting all expense, By ditto 2 ditto By ditto 1 ditto refused, By balance due in old acct., By 11 Chickins, By his 11th part of 1 Hhdg., Tobo. deducting expense, By balance due Jno Worsham , Total: £39.0.3

We the subscribers do Certify that we have in Conformity with an order of Court Stated and Settled the acct. Current of Abel Chelton dec'd with Jno. Worsham, the administrator and that we have found the Vouchers Sufficient agreeable to the Charges and a Balance due Said Worsham of Thirteen pounds three Shillings and 10p as will appear Within. Given under our hands the 17th day of Jan.1809
Ro. Payne, James Gatewood, Daniel Price
Recorded: June 19, 1809

**AC Book 4, Page 207**                                                       **C Shelton's Acct. Current**

Dr. The Estate of Crispin Shelton dec'd In Account Current with Beverley Shelton and Vincent Shelton Exors.

1794 Feby To Cash paid Funeral Expenses £1.16.0
March 5 Ditto paid P. Henry for advise Per Rect. £1.4.0

March 21 ditto paid Chrispin Shelton as auctioneer for his Services 3 days £3..0.0
2 Quires Paper £0.4.0

1796 4 gallons spirits for the Sale £1.4.0

Feby 25 Cash paid Wm Tunstall Clk. Per Ticket £0.7.4
Ditto paid Andrew Ronald atto. Per Rect. £1.4.0
Ditto paid Sto Turner D Shff Per Rect. £0.5.0

1801
Feby ditto paid W Tunstall Clk Per Ticket £2.12.6

1803
Dec 2 ditto paid D Call atto. at Suit of Spears & Co P. Recit. £6.7.6

1804 Mar To cash paid W Tunstall Clk. P. Ticket £0.8.5

April 8 ditto paid J Ellis D Marshall for amot. of Execution J Hopkins Surviving partner of Spears & Co Per Statement & Rect. £204.4.0

May 23 Cash paid John Dabney atto. P. Rect.£1.4.0
Expense going 3 times to Richmond £9.0.0
Paid E Sydnor Agent for James Murdock Surviving partner of James Murdock & Co Per Statement and Rect. £110.2.2
Paid Wm Tunstall Clk Per Ticket £0.19.2
Paid W. Yancy D. Sheriff Per Ditto £0.7.6
Paid Sto Turner for 17 Tythes for Crispin Sheltons Estate Per Rect. £0.5.0
Balance of Interest acct. Carr'd to Contra £146.1.7
Total: £199.0.1

1808
Jany 4 This Sum allowed the Executors for trouble of transacting the business of the Estate £30.0.0

Balance due the Estate £115.1.8

1795 Mar 21 By amount of Sales this Day due £301.4.5
Deduct for 1 Certificate sold Arm. Shelton it being assets in the hands of yr Executor £1..2.0
Interest at 5 per Cent till 14 Jan 1808

1807 Aprl Amount rec'd of William Payne for old account £3.7.9.1.6

1808 Jany 14 Amount rec'd for 1 Certificate Sold 10st Nov. 1802 £28.0.3
Amt. Rec'd for 1 Certificate sold 14th Jany 1808 £13.10.0
Bala. Of Interest acct £146.3.7

1808 Jany 14 By Balance due Per Contra £490.4.0

Total: £115.1.8

In obedience to an order of the Worshipful Court of Pittsylvania County to us directed, we have examined the account of Beverley Shelton and Vincent Shelton, Exors. of Crispin Shelton, dec'd With the Estate of the said decedant With the Vouchers agreeable to the Within Stated Account and find a balance due the Said Estate of one hundred and fifteen pounds, Eleven Shillings and 8p. the 14th Day of January last .
Given under our hands this 1st Day of September 1808
Joshua Stone, Isaac Coles, Wm Smith

Recorded: July 17, 1809

**AC Book 4, Page 209**               **F. Irby's Acct. Current**

The Estate of Francis Irby Dec'd in acct Current with Nathan Glenn, admr.

1795 May 18 To Cash paid William Smith £8.8.10
May 9 Cash for the Clerk of Pittsylvania £1.10.5

June 8 ditto pd. Jo. Carter for Taxes £1.4.7
Carriage of Tobo & Expenses of ditto £0.16.7

Decmb. 12 Cash pd Sto. Turner per Taxes £0.13.6

1796
March 11 ditto pd Wm Vaughan for Taxes £0.12.5

March 13 ditto paid Hay for Subscribing £0.6.2

April 9 ditto pd. Saml. & D. Pannill £3.4.8

May 7 ditto pd. Thos. Anderson £0.16.9

May 16 ditto pd. Wm Smith £8.0.10

July 21 ditto pd. William Todd £10.13.7 3/4
Ditto pd. Griffith Dickerson £2.8.0
Ditto pd. Charges at Sale £1.0.0

Decm. 17 ditto pd Saml. & D. Pannill £19.0.1 ¾

1797 Mar 10 ditto pd Francis Irby £0.8.10

May 27 ditto pd. Wm Vaughan £6.14.5 1/2

1798 March 12 Ditto Isaac Clement £0.11.11
ditto pd. Fullington Johnson £0.18.4

June 6 ditto pd F. Johnson £1.9.6

1799 Jany 1 ditto pd. For Stamp paper £0.1.2 ½
Cash pd Betty Oaks £12.00

1804 Jany 1 ditto pd. John Jenkins £1.0.0
ditto pd. Ro. Miller for Crying Negroes £0.12.0
Cash Lent F Irby Sen in 1792 £3.10.0
Cash pd. Chain Carriers £ 1.0.0

1795 Feby Nathan Glenn £88.2.8
By Amt. Of Articles Bought at Sale £3.5.2
Edmund Tunstall for ditto £74.15.9
Abraham Irby for Ditto £15.6.10
Gilbert Hunt for Ditto £0.1.7
Vincent Shelton for Ditto £1.7.2
William Todd for Ditto £ 8.15.0

John Rowlin for Ditto £1.6.6
Griffith Dickerson for Ditto £2.3.9
William Dunning for Ditto 0.11.6
John Collins for Ditto £1.10.9
Jesse Rowlin for Ditto £1.2.4
John Grigory for Ditto £5.11.4
William Irby £23.16.4
John Ward for ditto £2.2.1
Samuel Hunt for ditto £0.15.7
Wyatt Shelton for ditto £1.7.4
Daniel Jenkins for ditto £0.14.0
Ambrose Doss for ditto £1.10.3
John Tunstall for ditto £0.8.3
James Mitchell for Ditto £3.3.0
Rebecak Irby for ditto £0.10.6
Jesse Sanders for ditto £0.6.0
William Lester for ditto £3.19.6
William Craddock for ditto £0.3.0
Allen Woodson for Ditto £1.4.6
Charles Callaway for ditto £14.10.2
John Craddock for Ditto £5.3.0
David Irby for Articles Bou't at Sale £1.1.9 ½
Samuel Irby for Ditto £3.19.4
Terry McHaney for Ditto £1.2.0
Leroy Shelton for Ditto £2.7.6
Henry Worsham for ditto £1.14.0
Vachel Clements for ditto £7.11.0
Nathan Glenn for ditto £1.6.0
James Lewis for ditto £0.11.0
John Patterson for ditto £0.2.6
Donald McNicholes for ditto £1.16.0
John Jenkins for ditto £3.5.0
Jeremiah Sanders for ditto £15.10.0
William Roper for ditto £19.2.0
Zacha. Irby for ditto £19.3.0

1796 Jany 1
John Ward for hire 1 negro £0.10.0
William Grigory for 6 geese £0.13.6
Nancy Pannill for Plank £1.16.3
William Roper for Rent Plantation £13.0.0
Edmund Tunstall for hire 1 negro £0.10.0

1797 Jany 1 William Roper for Plank £1.4.4
Robt. Goggings for hire 1 negro girl £8.0.0

1798 Jany 1 Edmund Tunstall for hire 2 ditto £12.0.0
Edmund Tunstall for " 1 Ditto £10.15.0
Robt. Goggings for " 1 Ditto £10.2.6
Richard Craddock for " 1 Ditto £4.11.0

1799 Jany 1 Edmund Tunstall for " 1 Ditto £12.0.0
William Lester for " 1 Ditto £13.13.0
Samuel Irby for " 1 Ditto £5.1.0
John Bruce for " 1 Ditto £2.1.0

1800 Jany 1 Robt. Goggins for hire 1 negro £11.1.6
Edmund Tunstall for 1 ditto £15.0.0
John Bruce for " 1 Ditto 3.10.0

1801 Jany 1 Robert Love for " 1 ditto £5.12.0
Edmund Tunstall for hire 1 negro £10.1.0
Robert Johns for 1 Ditto £11.10.0
William Martin for 1 Ditto £6.0.6

1807 Jany 1 Nathan Glenn for 1 Ditto £3.13.0
Jeremiah McCullock for 1 ditto £15.0.0
William Roper for 1 Ditto £15.0.0
Thomas Mustain for 1 Ditto £6.7.0

1803 Jany 1 Cary Whitehead for 1 Ditto £3.11.0
Nelson Tucker for 1 Ditto £3.3.0
Jerre. McCullock for 1 Ditto £11.1.0
Robt. Love for 1 Ditto £6.14.2

1804 Jany 2 Cary Whitehead for 1 ditto £6.2.0
William Roper for 1 Ditto £15.8.6
John Douglas for 1 ditto £14.2.0
Thomas Mustine for 1 Ditto £7.2.0

1805 Jany 1 Jere McCullock for 1 ditto £6.0.0
Drury Scruggs for 1 Ditto £13.0.0
Joseph Polley for 1 Ditto £10.0.0
John Douglas for 1 ditto £15.1.0
Samuel Irby for 1 ditto £4.11.0

1806 Jany 1 Francis Irby for 1 ditto £13.13.0
John Douglas for 1 ditto £10.4.0
David Irby for 1 Ditto £7.14.0
Wm R Irby for 1 ditto £3.0.0

1807 Jany 1 Francis Irby for 1 ditto £13.2.0
Peter Irby for 1 ditto £11.1.6
Thomas Mustain for 1 ditto £1.10.0

1808 Jany 1 Francis Irby for 1 ditto £9.15.0
Jere. McCullock for 1 ditto £9.10.6
Peter Irby for 1 ditto £3.3.6
Cash rec'd for tobo. £8.2.4
Cash rec'd of Legrands estate in June 1803 £120.4.0 1/2
4 Barrels Corn Rec'd of Legrand estate £4 1/2.10.0
Balance : 681.5.4 3/4

In obedience to an order of the Worshipful Court of Pittsylvania County to us directed for the Examination of the account Current of Nathan Glenn administrator of the Estate of Francis Irby, Deceased, we have proceeded to Examine the Said account and the Vouchers respecting the Same and do find a Balance due the Said Estate amounting to Six hundred and Eighty one pounds five shillings and four pence three farthings Exclusive of the interest on Said money which Said Interest we think it Reasonaable to allow the administrator for his Services Rendered the Said Estate. Given under our hands this 24th day of May 1809.
Vincent Shelton, Zachareas Lewis, Charles Bailey, Jno. Stone Jr.

Recorded: July 17, 1809

**AC Book 4, Page 213**                                               **Jas Love's Inventory**

In obedience to an order from the County Court of Pittsylvania we John Ward, jr., Jesse Keesee/Reesee, Avery Mustain and Thomas Simpson have met on the 24 June 1809 in the House of James Love Dec'd and after being Sworn as the law Directs, Viewed and appraised the personal Estate of the Said James Love, Dec'd that was to us produced as follows

One old Bay mare, 1 Sorrel Do, 11 head of Hoggs, 2 Sheep, 1 Cow, 2 feather Bed and furnature, Stead and Cord, 8 Chairs at 2/6 each, 1 Musket, 1 Table, 1 Chest, flat Irons, 1 Cotton Wheal, 1 Looking Glass, Sundery Glass Were, 2 Razer cases, Sundry Earthen Ware, 4 Basons, 5 plates and a Dish, 10 Forks, 3 knives, 1 pair sheep Shairs and pan handle, 1 Coffee pott, funnel and Coffee mill, 1 Straner, 5 Spoons, 1 pott and hook, 1 Iron Tea kittle, 1 Dutch oven and hooks, 1 Broken hoe, 1 tub and Runlett, 1 Water pitcher, 1 plow hoe, some small Irons

1 Cotter, 2 pair hames and 2 pair Iron Traces, 1 broad ax, 2 pole axes, 1 old poll ax, 2 Iron Wedges, 1 hand saw, 1 X cut Saw, 1 Jointer and Jack plane, 2 augers and 1 Drawing, 2 mattox, 1 Frow, 1 spade, hammer and bell, 5 old hoes and 1 Howel, 1 pair fire Tongs, 1 pair Coumpases, 1 Chessel, 1 pair pinchers and Gimblet, 1 loom and flax wheel, 1 Brass Wier Sifter
Total £45.15.6
John Ward Jesse Keesee/reesee, Thomas Simpson, Avery Mustain
Recorded: July 17, 1809

**AC Book 4, Page 215**                                               **Jas Crews' Invenory**

An Inventory and Apraisment of the Estate of James Crews Deceased

1 Mare and Colt, 3 Casks, 1 Bridle and Saddle, 1 Hair Trunk, 6 Chairs, 2 Flat Irons, 1 Hand Saw, 1 Rum Cock, 1 Screw auger, 2 Gimblets, 1 Shoe Hammer, 1 pair nippers, 1 Chisel, 1 Flesh fork, 1 Trumpet, 5 Case Knives and Six forks, 5 Table Spoons, 1 Tin Coffee Pot, 1 Tin cup and funnel, 1 Pitcher, 1 mug, 1 Dish and 10 plates, Small parcel Crockry Ware, 2 Water Pails, 1 Sugar box, 1 pepper box, 1 Case bottle,
1 Stone Jug, 1 pine Table, 1 pair Saddle bags, 1 pair Hames and Trace chains, 1 Plow and Colter, Swingletree and clevis, 1 Ax, 1 Ploe hoe, 2 hilling hoes, 1 pot, one oven and pot hooks, 1 Loom,
1 Bedstead and Cord, Bed & furnature
Total: £32.7.3
August 18, 1809
Agreeabe to an order of the worshipful Court of Pittsylvania to us Directed, we have proceeded to Value the estate of James Crews deceased as Stated above.
John Hunt, Georg Boyd, Reubin Hubbard
Recorded: August 22, 1809

**AC Book 4, Page 216**                                               **Jno Davis' Inventory**

In obefdience to an order of the County Court of Pittsylvania we the Subscribers being first Sworn as the Law directs do apprase the Estate of John Davis, Dec'd as followth to Wit:

19 Head of Hogs, 1 York Stier, 3 Cows and Calves, 6 Heffiers, 6 Head of Sheep, 13 Head of Shoats,
1 Sorrel Mare, 1 Bay mare, 1 Sorrel mare Coult, 1 Sorrel Horse, 1 Negro Man Harry, 1 negro man Carter,
1 negro man Tom, Sunderies of Plantation tools & two pair of chain, 5 axes, three grubbing hoes and 1 Mattock, 1 Spade, 1 Lock chain, 1 Cotton wheel, 8 Hoes, 1 Grind Stone and 3 bee Stands, 1 Cart, 1 Still,
1 Bed Sted bed and furnature, 1 Sack of Salt, 1 parcel of Tobacco, 1 Wheat Sifter, 1 Side Saddle, 1 Bed stead and Counterpin, 2 Cotton Wheels and one flax wheel, 1 Pot, 1 oven and 2 pair of hooks, 1 Skillet and 1 grid iron, 1 Loom, and one ax, 1 hand Saw, three augers, 1 chisel, Coopers adz., 1 Rifle gun, 1 Shot gun,
1 Table, Six pewter plates, 1 earthern do, 1 Set of Knives and forks, 2 Dishes and bason, 1 Coffy pot,
1 Hone and Sithe blade, 2 Jugs, 1 Steel trap and flat Iron

Will. Witcher, David Vance, Henry Atkenson

The foregoing is a true and perfect Inventory and appraisement of the personal Estate of John Davis dec'd Except twenty nine pounds fourteen shillings and nine pence Cash in hand.
Frankey Davis, Admr.
Recorded: July 17, 1809

### AC Book 4, Page 218                                                              Division of Waller's Estate

In obedience to an order of the Worshipful Court of Pittsylvania to us directed and here unto annexed, we have proceeded to lay off and allot to Rebeckah Waller, Widow and Relict of John Waller, Dec'd one third part of all the Estate of the Said Decedant real and personal in the following manner Viz:

We find by Survey made by James M Williams, D. Surveyer the 29th Day of March 1809 that there is 845 acres of land in the tract willed to Pleasant Waller out of which we have allotted to the Widow two hundred acres including the Mansion House, apple Orchard, and as one third part of her dower in Value in the Said Tract. Beginning at Mays Corner pine, thence the said Mays line South eighty degrees West ninety nine poles to pointers, Flippins line thence his lines North 22 Degrees East 78 poles to a pine South 84 degrees East 144 poles to a branch thence up the said branch as it meanders 74 poles to a fork of the Said Branch, thence the right hand fork as it meanders 72 poles to a Ash in Cornwell's line thence South 19 degrees East 12 poles to a White Oake, thence Slaydons line North 89 degrees 108 poles to pointers thence New lines South 10 degrees West 168 poles to a stake and thence in the field, thence West 180 poles to the Beginning.

We also find a plot made by the Said Williams from the original Survey of the Creek lands Wiled to John & Joel Waller that there is four hundred and thirty four acres out of which We have allotted to the Widow 144 acres as her dower in full of the Said Tract. Beginning at pointers in Stamp's line thence his line North 40 degrees east 22 poles to a red oak Corner in Simpsons line, Thence his line North 19 degrees West 78 poles to a pine in Cooks line, thence his line South 66 degrees West 122 poles to two pines North 65 degrees West 15 poles to a pine N 17 degrees West 176 poles to a pine Stump by the ridge path North 10 degrees West 38 poles to a pine Corner in Mayes line, thence his line South 47 degrees West 178 poles to two pines, thence the old patent line South 65 Degrees east 170 poles to a dividing line run here to fore between the Said John and Joel Waller thence the Said line South 34 degrees West 14 poles to pointers thence a new line South 75 degrees east 172 poles to the Beginning. Property Viz:

One yoke of oxen, One Brindle Cow and Calf, One Cow & yearling, One Hepher, One Bull, One Hepher, One red Hepher and one Black do, One Black horse, One horse, One colt, One wagon, One bed Sted in part,, One bed and furnature, 5 counterpins, 1 Cupbord, 1 Table, 11 Chiers, 1 Walnut Chest, 8 Knives and forks, 1 looking glass, Sundry earthern ware glass &c, Do do, Do do, Canister and Waiter, Phyals, Shovel, Tongs and fire Dogs

One Negro man named Cupet, One Negro woman named Silvey, One Negro man named Sye, One Negro boy named Peter, One Negro woman Named Reas?, One Negro girl named Mary, One third part of the Valuation of one Negro woman Named Hannah Will'd to Mrs. Boulter

One bee hive, One third part of the working tools, 1 Cutting knife 3 hhds, 2 Do, parcel of soap, Card and chirn, Loom and Geer, Large Oven, 1 Cotton wheel, 1 pott Hooks and Spice Morter, two old wheels, 1 Spotted Sow, 5 Hogs, 2 Sows and four pigs, 6 Bushels of Wheat, 1 Small Trunk, 1 Flax Wheel, a pr. Sad Irons, 2 pr. Scissors, 1 Lott in Cotton, 1 Do in potatoe Seed, 1 Do in Dryed fruit, 1 Do in flax, 23 blls and 4 Bushels of Corn, 300 bundles of Blads, 2 ½ bushels of Corn, 2 Tite Casks, 7 ¼ lb Tallow, parcel of oates, 13 ½ bushels of oats, Soap fatt, 1 Sack bag, 1 Tubb, 213 lb bacon, 1 Cow in Settlement with Pleasant, 1 pot of butter

4 head of Sheep, 1 hog from Lydea White's heirs, 1 Pott, 1 white Heipher, 1 Lott Hogsheads, 1 Jugg and whip Saw

We have further proceeded to allot to the legatees viz to the heirs of Lydia White born of her body
1 Sett of working Tools, 1 Chest and Case, 2 beds and furnature, 1 Knotted Counterpin, 2 Shoats, 2 Dear skins, 1 Lott of Hard Ware, 1 Lott of Smith tools, 1 Lock Chain, 1 muskett and old chest, 4 old hoes, 1 Pot Sack, 1 brass Tea Kittle, 2 hides, oven, 1 pistole, water vessel, 1 half Bushel Measure, 1 lott in Cotton, Do in potatoe Seed, 1 old Saddle, 1 pide hepher, 1 Red Cow and calf, 1 yoke of Steers, 1 Cow without horns, 1 yearling, 1 Blade Saw. 1 Spotted Sow, 7 piggs, 5 do, 15 lbs. And 4 bushels of Corn, 200 bundles of blades, ½ Barrel Corn, one Boor, 4 ¾ lb Tallow, Oates, soap fatt, 139 ½ lbs bacon, 1 Bag and tub, Oats to balance this Settlement

To John Waller one of the other legatees
To 1 Lott of Working Tools, 1 Shott gunn, 2 Beds and furnature, 1 Counter pin, 1 Sheat, 3 Deer Skins, 1 Lott of pewter, House Furnature, 1 Still, 1 mans Saddle, 1 Cotton Wheel, 1 hatchet, 3 pr cotton Cards, 1 Trevett, pott and hook, 1 hide, 1 bed stead and Cords, 1 piggon, pail, Tray and Water Vessel, Lott in Cotton, Do in Potatoe Seed, 1 Do in old Hhds. And Iron No 3, 1 cow and Calf, 1 yoke of oxen, 1 Cow, 1 do, 1 hepher, 1 yearling, 1 Sow, Do, Do, 6 pigs, 15 lbs and 4 bushels Corn, 1 Steal Trap, 200 bundles of blades, ½ Barrel of Corn, one Sow, 1 boar &c, 4 ¾ lb Tallow, parcel oats, Soap fatt, 139 ½ lbs bacon, 1 bag oats

Allotted to Pleasant one of the other legatees Viz:
1 Lott of Tools, 1 Walnut Table, 1 Dish and Feather Bed, 1 Knotted Counter pin, 1 check'd do, 1 Sheat Do, 1 Counterpin Do, 1 Do Do, 2 Deer Skins, 1 Lott of pewter, Household furnature, 8 Sheep, 1 Cow, 1 churn, 1 foot adz., 1 Bell, 1 Bedle? & Saddle, 1 Cotton wheel,, 1 pott and Hooks, 1 pr. New Cards,, 1 pr. Do Wool, kitchen Table, 1 Tub, 2 hides, 1 pr Steelyards, Water Vessels,, Lott in Cotton, Potatoe Seed, 15 Geese, 1 bee hive , 1 Lott and Hhd & Iron, 1 Cow and Calf, 2 Cows and yearlings, 1 yearling Hepher, 1 bull, 1 Sow, Do, one Sow, 5 piggs, 13 blls., 4 Bushels Corn, 1 Small Jugg, 200 Bundles Blades, 2 ½ bushel Corn, 1 Gilt Sow and boar, 43 ¼ lb tallow, Oats, Soap fatt & 141 lbs bacon, Lumber and bags, 1 pott Rack and Hooks

We have compared the above and Set our Signatures this 16th Day of June 1809
Creed Tanner, Sto. Turner, Joseph Flippin, Robert Walters
Recorded: August 21, 1809

## AC Book 4, Page 224                                                                                   Mease's Inv'y

An Inventory of the Estate of Philip Mease Sen. Deceased taken the 25th Day of August 1809 by William Witcher, Jno. Witcher, jr., Daniel C Edwards, and Henry Atkinson agreeable to an Order of July Pittsylvania Court Last have Procceded and appraised the sd. Estate after being first Sworn as follows to Wit:

1 yoke of oxen and Bell and Coller, 1 Cow and Calf, 1 Cow and Do & bell and Coller, 1 Cow & do do, 1 Cow and yearling, 1 Cow and Calf, 1 Cow, 1 Cow and Bell, 1 Hepher, 1 Ditto and Small Steer, 1 hepher, 1 Small Bull, 1 Large ditto, 6 head of sheep including a bell, 30 head of Small Hogs, 8 Sows and Barrows including 7 young pigs, 1 Barrow, 3 young Sows, 1 shoat, 1 Dark bay Stud horse, 1 Sorrel horse, 1 Cotton wheel, 1 spool wheel, 2 pair hind wagon geers, 1 old Trunk, a Parcel of old Waggon Geers, 4 old Tobo Hhdgs, 3 Boxes, 6 Sack bags, 3 Small Boxes, a parcel of old Iron, 3 old Tubs, 2 old Syth blades with 2 Blades, 1 old mans Saddle and cloth, 1 old flax brake, 3 pitch forks and 2 Shovels, 4 old hilling hoes, 1 foot Addz., 1 Mortering Ax, 2 Lock Chains, 1 Mortering Chezel formers, 2 Shovell plows, 2 Coulter plows with there Coulters to them, 13 old Reap hooks, 35 lbs. Bear Iron , 4 lb Croley Steel, 1 Jack Screw, 1 Hhds. Jointer, ¾ lb Blisted Steel, 2 Wedges, 1 frow, 1 Stone pick, 3 Screw Augers, 6 pole axes, 1 mattock and old Shovell plow hoe, 2 Drawing knives, 1 hand Saw, 1 Square made of Iron, 2 old Barrels, Augers & 1 old Chezil, a parcel of old churns, a parcel of Small Tools, 6 Trowels & 2 Stone hammers, 3 Baking pans, 3 Cow Chains, a parcel of old cliveses & other Irons, 1 old brass Sythe Blade, 7 House chairs, 1 Water can, 1 Bell, a parcel of old Irons, 1 old Syth Blade, 1 Rifle gun, shot, bag and horn, 1 Rifle, gun, Shot bag and horn, 1 old Coper kittle & 1 Iron Do, 2 Tubs, 1 Pipe Stove, 7 Bee Stands, 1 Bag and 11 lb Duck and Geese feathers

4 flax wheels, 2 flax Hackhels, 1 Bed bedstyd and furnature, 1 do do  do, 1 do  do do, 2  do do do, 1 house clock time piece, 1 Black Walnut Chest, 1 Pine Table, 1 P. Steelyards, 1 poplar Chest, 1 pare Saddle bags, 2 Cyphering Slates, 1 Large holy Dutch Bible, 1 Prair book and 3 Hymn books, 1 Looking glass, a parcel of old Spelling Books and others, 1 Real, a parcel of pewter eathen ware, tins &c, 1 frying pan and Skillet, 1 Grind Stone and Testament, 1 Roling Knife, 17 Crocks, 1 earthen Dish, 2 Jugs, 1 churn and 2 Tubs, 6 Casks and 2 Runlets, 3 Glasses and 3 Sweat  oil bottles, 2 Damaged pots and 1 Dutch oven, 1 quart bottle,, 1 flat Iron, 1 Tin bucket and Sundies other things, 4 old Hhgs., 1 Cutting box and knife, 1 old Waggon, 34 Ducks and 7 Geese, 1 Grass Sythe, hammer and anvill

Caty (herXmark) Muse, admrx.,   Will Witcher, John Witcher, Daniel C Edwards, Henry Atkinson
Recorded: September 18, 1809

**AC Book 4, Page 228**     **Smith's Inv'y**

Pittsylvania County Virgina the 4$^{th}$ of August 1809 in Obedience to an order of the Worshipful the Court of Pittsylvania  we whose names are under Signed, Being first qualified have attended to what is said to be the personal Estate of Edward Smith, Deceased and have apraised the Same as followeth to Wit:

1 bedstead, To 1 bed, 4$^{th}$ to 1 do, 1 bedstead and Bed Bord, 1 White Counter pin and Sheats, 2 Counter pins and 1 Sheat, 3 Little puter Basons and 2 puter plates,  2 puter Dishes,  5 Earthen plates, 1 jug and flat Iron and Tongues, 1 Dutch oven and Canister,  1 old Walnut Table,  1 old wallut chest, Watsons Body of Divinity, a book, 1 large but old Bible,  2 Small Books,  1 Decanter,, To 1 Cubbard
Given under our hands this day and year above mentioned.
Hezekiah Smith, John Still, James Fulton
Recorded: September 18, 1809

**AC Book 4, Page 229**     **Wynne's Inventory**

An Inventory of the Estate of Robert Wynne dec'd takin this  23 Day of July 1808

1 negro Boy Burwell, 1 gray Horse, 1 Chesnut Sorrel Do, 2 mens Saddles, 2 Trunks, 1 Bridle, 1 pr. Horse mans pistoles and Holsters, 2 plate Spurs, 1 umbrella, 1 Silver Watch, 1 Book, the Tutors Guide, 2 pair of gold Scales in Weight, 2 Setts of Razors and Cases, 2 Shaving Boxes, 2 Looking Glasses, 1 Dutch Blanket, 1 Ink Stand, 1 pr Saddle bags, 1 pistole
Total:  £174,9,0
Agreeable to the first above order,  being first Sworn, we have apprs'd the personal Estate of Robert Wynn Dec'd and find it to Stand as above Stated.
Thomas Stewart, Thomas Barnett, Daniel Sullivan
Recorded:  September 18, 1809

**AC Book 4, Page 230**     **Payne's Apr. Current**

The estate of Charles Payne Dec'd in acct. with William Dodson and Leana L/S Payne the administrators thereof:

1809
Cash paid James Colquhoun & Co, John and Nath'l Wilson, Majr. Tat? Soyers, Jas D. Patton Esq. Alex. Brown, Geo. Lampkin, Wm Yancey , Daniel Price, Ditto, William Bucy, Leven Downs, the Exor. Of F/T Fearn , Dec'd, the Estate Wm B. Burton pr acct & note, Exors. T Fearn Dec'd, Harris & Brown, Samuel Jorden, Thomas Gatewood, William Dodson, To the admirs. For their Trouble in Settlement of the Deceadents Estate

Cr By Amt. Of Sales of the deceasdants Estate pr acct here with filed £604.7.8 1/3
Regarding of Sales of the deceased and Estate acct her with filed £604.78 1/3
Bal. Due the admirs. £11.1.0 ¼
Wm Yancey, Nath Wilson, Thos. Stewart

Recorded: September 18, 1809

**AC Book 4, Page 231          Payne's Account Current Sales**

This account of Sales of the Estate of Charles Payne Dec'd March 24, 1808

Luannah? Payne
 4 Negroes Cretia and their children Abram, Hurt and John
Do 1 Bed and furnature, 2 do do, 1 walnut Cubboard and Queens Ware, 1 Walnut Desk, 9 Winsor chairs, 1 Folding Table and Toylett, 1 small Trunk , 1 parcel of Books, 1 Small Trunk, 1 parcel of Books, 1 Sorrel Horse and Bay Mare, 2 Decanters and 2 Brass Candle Sticks, 1 Pair of Hand Irons, 1 Saddle and Bridle, 2 Trunks and 1 Chest, 4 Butter potts and 1 Jug, 1 chim and Furkin, 1 Waiter, 1 Lot of Hoes, 2 pair of geers and plow hoes, 1 cutting Box, 2 pole axes, 3 potts, Sundry Pailes &c, 4 Head of Cattle, 1 Jugg
Total £537.83.0

Daniel Price 2 Bottles, 2 Tee Kites & 1 Tob. Hhds.

William Dodson 1 Pair of Wedges

James Richardson 1 Pair of hand Irons & 1 Cow

Selby Benson 1 Bed Stead, 1482 lbs. Of Daville Inspected Tobo.

Acct. on Edward Bucy for
Do on William Chapman
Pittsylvania County Sept. 14, 1809
We certify that the within is a true account of sales of the Estate of Charles Payne Dec'd . Given under our hands this day and date Written.
Leannah L Payne, William Dodson
Recorded: September 18, 1809

**AC Book 4, Page 232                                                                                        Smith's Inventory**

An Inventory and appraisement of the personal Estate of George Smith Dec'd Taken this 14th Day of September 1809

6 Cows and Calves, 6 Ditto, 5 Steers, 8 young Cattle, 2 ditto ditto, 1 Stear, 1 Bull, 1 Young Grey mare, 1 ditto ditto, 1 " Sorrel Ditto, 1 " " Horse, 1 Bay Colt, 1 Sorrel mare and Colt, 1 Sow and Six pigs, 1 Ditto and Six ditto, 4 Hogs, 2 Sows, Six Sheep

1 mans Saddle, 1 Ox Cart, 1 Harrow, 3 pair Iron traces and Hames, 1 Beir Shapre plough, 5 Shovel ploughs, 3 Colters, 3 pole axes, 3 mattocks, 6 hoes, 2 Spades, 1 Broad Ax

31 lb Box Iron, 1 pair Steelyards, 1 X Cut Saw, 1 pott and Oven, 1 pott and Skillett, 1 plough Shovel, 1 Lock chain, 2 Small Spinning Wheels, 1 Large do, 1 cutting Box, 7 Bee Stands, 1 Clock Ril, 1 Box Iron, 1 Hand Saw, 1 Screw Auger, 1 Drawing Knife, parcel Leather, parcel Do in tan, 4 Beds and furnature

1 Bedstead, 1 Case of Bottles, 1 folding Table, 1 Desk and Book Case, 1 Cupboard, 1 Looking Glass, 1 Chest, 1 Dito, 2 Small Tubs, 1 Jug, 1 pair fire Dogs, ½ Dozen Chairs, parcel of Books, Cradles Irons, 1 Negro Man Stephen, 1 ditto ditto Lymus, 1 Ditto ditto Rewbin, 2 ditto Womans Easter and her child, 2 ditto women Voilette and her child, 1 ditto girl Nance, 1 ditto ditto Jude, 1 ditto small Boy Dick, parcel pewter plates, ½ dozen E. plates, 5 Basons and Dish, 1 Pewter Basen, 1 Butter pot, 2 Coffee pots, 1 tea pot, 1 mug, Cups and Saucers, ½ doz.Tea Spoons, 1 Case Bottle and 1 wine glass, 1 Loom, 32 Yards linen, 1 Still
Wole amount £852.5.10

In obedience to an order of the worshipful Court of Pittsylvania We whose names are hereunto annexed have proceeded to Inventory and appraise the personal Estate of George Smith deceased shown us by the Executors.
William Atkinson, Joseph Reynolds, Alexander Mahan

1809 Octo. 16 The Within named William Atkinson, Joseph Reynolds and Alexander Mahan made Oath in open Court that the Within appraisement was made according to the best of their Judgment
Teste: Will Tunstall Clk.
Recorded: October 16, 1809

**AC Book 4, Page 235**                                                                                **Callaway's Inventory**

An Inventory and appraisment of the personal Estate of Doct. Henry G Callaway Dec'd Taken this 11$^{th}$ Day of Nov. 1809 Viz:

1 Cupboard and its Contents, 1 Map of Virginia, ½ doz. Windsor chairs, 7 ditto ditto, ½ doz. Flag Bottom'd Ditto, 2 Walnut Dressing Tables, 1 Desk and Book Case, Parcel of Books, 3 Beds, Bedsteads and furnature, 1 Curtain Ditto, 1 Check Reel, 2 Large Jett? Looking Glasses, 1 Womans Saddle,, 1 Flax wheel

8 Prints in Gilt Frames, 4 Larger Ditto, 1 Large folding Table, 1 Case Bottles, 1 Violin, 1 Ger. Flute, 2 figur'd Carpets, 1 Back Gammon Table, 2 Lar. Trunks, 4 Small ditto, 1 Candle Stand, 2 pr. Tongs, 2 shovels, 2 pokers, 1 painted Cribb, 1 Shott Gun, 1 Rifle Ditto, 1 Muslin Umbrella , 1 Negro Child Randolph, 1 Gegg and Harness, 2 Walnut Tables, 1 Nest Wooden Ware, 2 Spades and 1 Shovel, 1 Iron pott Rack, 2 pr. Pott Hooks, grid iron, 2 Large potts, 2 Sml. Ditto, 2 Dutch Ovens, 2 Skilletts, 2 pr. Hand Irons, 1 Tea Kittle, 1 spice mortor and pistle, 1 Tin Buckett, 1 hand axe, 1 Large Jug and 2 Butter potts, 1 Brass Kittle. 1 Sett Surgeons Instruments, 1 new Waggon, 1 Medicine press And contents, 1Tea Trunk, 3 pole axes
2 Grubing Hoes and 1 old Hilling Hoe, 1 Tool Chest and Contents, 1 Bay horse, one Bay ditto, 1 Grey mare, one Bay colt, 8 hogs, 43 Shoats, 3 Cows and yearlings, 4 Heifers and 2 Steers, 1 yearling, 1 yoke oxen Cart and Lock Chain, 2 Shovels plows and Gears, 1 pr. Chain traces, 3 pole axes, 2 mattocks, 3 Hilling Hoes, 1 pr. Iron wedges, cutting Box and knife, 1 hand saw, 1 Drawing Knife, 2 Augers, 2 chests, 1 Pr. Steelyards, Dutch Oven, 1 Ratt Trap, 1 Roan Mare, 1 Negro man Matt, 1 " Boy Sam, 1 " man Patrick, Creasy and her child Christian, 1 " Girl Sarah, 1 " Boy Harry, 1 " Woman Hannah, 1 " man George, 1 " woman Rachel, 1 " girl Susan, 1 " woman Dorcas, 1 Boy Daniel, 1 girl Lucy

In obedience to an Order of the Worshipful Court of Pittsylvania to us Directed we the undersigned Subscribers have proceeded to Inventory and appraise all the personal Estate of Doctr. Henry G Callaway, Dec'd agreeable to the foregoing Statement.
James Hopkins, William Walker, Caleb Hundley

1809 November 20$^{th}$ the above named James Hopkins, William Walker and Caleb Hundley made oath in open Court that the foregoing appraisement was made According to the best of Judgment.
Will Tunstall Co. C
Recorded: November 20, 1809

**AC Book 4, Page 238**                                                                                  **Patrick's Apo Current**

Dr. the Estate pf Davod F. Patrick In Account with Samuel Pannill Executor

1808
August 27 To 10 lb. Sugar
Spt. 3 2 lb putty, 16 paines Glass
Oct 3 Bailey Stout pr. Receipt
Oct 8 Cash paid David Ham Creek per Rect., 1 Sack Salt
Cash paid Thomas McCleland per Rect.

Oct 14 William Collins per Rect.

November 1  2 pieces napt cotton , ½ Bushel Salt, 1 Oven weighing 204 lbs, 1 pair fire dogs, 1 Candlestick, 1 paper pines, 1 Doz. Nedles, 1 Tumbler, 8 Childrens Knives, 1 nutmeg
Nov. 9 ½ quire Letter paper
Nov 15 22 ¾ Sole leather, To 1 Syde upper leather, 1 Rip skin

December 5 Cash paid Doctor A Johns per Rect.
Dec 21  Wm Worsham for 17 Barrels Corn Per Rect.
Dec 26 25 lbs Sugar, 6 lbs. Coffee, 1 almanack, Joseph Hayns P. Rect.
Dec. 28 John Marshall Per Rect, Amount paid William Whitlow Per Rect., 1 york oxen
Dec 30 1 pair Sad Irons
Dec 31 1 Cotton  wheel, 1 Empty Barrel

1809
 Jany 2 amount Smith's account for the year 1808
Jany 6 David Hornbrick Per Rect,
Jany 7 5 Knitting pins

Feb 10 Riche Pitts Per Rect
Feby 18 10 lb. Cotton

March 2 1 oven weighing 35 lbs
March 11 36 lb. Iron
March 21 Cash paid Clerk Pittsylvania Per Tickett
March 25 100 lb 10 dy. Cut nails, 5 lb  Blister Steel

1809
April 13 2 Gallons Molasses
April 29 25 lb. Sugar, 1 Bushel Salt

May 6 3 Yard Velvet Binding
May 13 1 Hat
May 22 1 lb. Chocolate, 1 paper pins
May 25 11 lb. Iron
May 30 Cash paid John Turner P. Rect.
May 31 Daniel Marshall per Rect.

June 22 Cash paid Andrew McHaney Per Rect.

July 10 1 pair Cotton Cards
July 11 50 lb 10 dy nails
July 25 200 lb  10 dy nails

August 5 100 lb 10 dy nails
August 15 Cash paid John Dabney per Rect.
August 26 Cash paid Sheriff Pittsylvania  Tax Per rect.
August 29 5 Per Cent Comms. Allowed on Collecting £377.9.45

Credits

1808
August 25 By Balance due 29th August 1809 per amount Settled and  Return'd  by Commissioners.

September 13 Amt. Rec'd of Ro. Alexander bal. due on Execu.

October 8 5 Barrels Corn
October 14 Over charge for Recording Power of attorney formerly

Novem. 23 Amt. Rec'd of Reubin Chirnhall?

December 15 William McCallesterr for Season of Mare
December 16 James Arnold Sen

1809
January 12 Amt Rec'd of Robert Alexander

March 6 Cash rec'd of Robert Alexander

April 3 Cash rec'd of Robert Alexander

June 8 2 Hhds. Lynchburg Tobo. 3137 lbs, Deduct Turning Up
June 12 amt Rec'd of Robert Alexander
June 27 amt rec'd for Mitchill M Gallions note ren'd

July 17 Cash of Andrew McHaney

August 14 Cash of Clack Stone in part his Bond
August 29 By Balance due Per Contra
Pittsylvania Count Acct.
In obedience to an order of the County Court of Pittsyl' bearing date June Court 1809 We Joshua Stone, William Smith and Philip L Grasty, three of the Comms. Named in the Said Order have State'd and adjusted the account of Sam'l. Pannill Exor. with the Estate of David F Patrick dec'd and after examining the exhibits produced before us, find a balance due the Said Estate of three Hundred and ten pounds 8/3 agreeable to the above Statement given under our hands thes 29th day of August 1809
Joshua Stone, Wm Smith, Philip L Grasty
Recorded:  November 21, 1809

**AC Book 4, Page 241**                                                                                  **Pannill's Apc. Currt**

Dr. The Estate of David Pannill Dec'd In acct. With Samuel Pannill Exor.

1809
March 13 To Cash paid West Dandridge atto. Per Rect.

Apl. 17 Paid Ro. Love for delivering 507 ½ lbs Bacon at Chalk Level P. S. Pannill &c Rect.
June 21 paid Sheriff Pittsylvania vs. Jesse Rowland as Rect., Ditto   ditto vs. Rowland do

Aug 15 ditto Jno. Dabney atto. Fee & Tax in suit vs. McNely Pwe Rect.
Aug 25 Paid Thomas B James Per Rect., Clerk Pittsylvania Per Tickett
Aug 29 5 Per Cent Commisson Collecting £235.3.11 ¼ , Cash paid Bethemea Pannill her 1/3 part of Nett amount rec'd Since 25 Aug 1808, Heirs of David Pannill dec'd for two Thirds of the Nett Balance due on the above acot.

CR
1808
Oct 19 By William Williams Waggo'

1809

Jany 4 Daniel Fisher rec'd of him
Jany 14 Joseph Leak

Mar 16 John Bruce w. Son? Per Sheriff's Statement, deduct Sheriff's Commis., Zacha. Irby for Cash, James Calloway Sen.

Apr 17 Samuel M. Scott, Robert Love for 507 ½ lb Bacon

May 27 Joshua Compton

June 21 Geo McNely, Jane Mitchell in full Memo. Acct.

Aug 14 David Hunt in full
Aug 28 Grasty and Pannill, Susanna Irby in full, William Martaine 21$^{st}$ Decr. Last, Robert Mitchell in full

Pittsylvania County
Agreeabe to an Order of Pittsylvania County Court bearing date June Court 1809, We Joshua Stone, William Smith and Philip L. Grasty , three of the Commissioners Mentioned in the Said Order, have examined the Accounts of Samuel Pannill, Exor of David Pannill, dec'd, With the exhibits and find the Account to be closed agreeable to the above Statement. Given under our hands this 27$^{st}$ day of August 1809. Joshua stone, Wm Smith, Philip L Grasty
Recorded: November 21. 1809

## AC Book 4, Page 243 — Pannill's gdn Account Current

The Heirs of David Pannill In account with Saml. Pannill, guar.

1808
August 25 By Balance due Pr. Return'd by Comms., Hire of Negro Dick due 1 Jany 1809, Ditto of negro Jack due Same time, Ditto of Negro Stephen due Same time

Septem. 21 Cash of William Dove

1809
Feby 21 Cash of Godfree Burnett

March 16 Saml. Pannill & Co for Cash of Charles Lewis

Aprl 19 Cash of Godfree Burnett, Ditto of George Davis
Apr. 24 amount Rec'd of Jesse Leftwich

May 29 Cash of Richard (Unreadable)

June 21 Cash of Jesse Leftwith

August 29 Cash of Saml. Pannill Exor for y part of nett amt.of his acct.since 25 August 1808
Interest on £1448.11.2 ½ since 25$^{th}$ August 1808
By Balance due as below £1808.3.2

Oct. 8, 1808 To William B Banks Per Rect.

Jany 17, 1809 Bethenia Pannill for Expenses to 31$^{st}$ December last Pr. Receipt

March 21 Cash paid Clerk of Pittsylvania Per Ticketts

Aprl. 15 1 pair children Shoes, 1 pair Ditto, Cash paid James L/S Vaughan per Rect.

August 26 Cash paid Sheriff Pittsa. Tax Per Rect.
August 29 5 Per Cent Comms. Allowed on 262.15.6
Balance due the Heirs of David Pannill Dec'd
Pittsylvania County
In bedience to an Order of the County Court of Pittsylvania bearing date June Court 1809 we Joshua Stone, William Smith and Philip L Grasty, three of the commis. Mentioned in Said Order, have examined the account of Samuel Pannill, Guardian, with the Heirs of David Pannill dec'd together with the exhibits produced before us, and we report the Balance due from the Guardian to the orphans of Eighteen Hundred and Eight pounds three Shillings and 2 3/4 agreeable to the Within account. Given under our hands this 29$^{th}$ Day of August 1809
Joshue Stone, Wm Smith, Philip L. Grasty
Recorded November 21, 1809

## AC Book 4, Page 244                                                                 Farmer's Inventory

We the appraisers appointed by the Worshipful Court of Pittsylvania do make the following Inventory and appraisement of the Estate of James Farmer Dec'd the 21 Day of September 1809

To one Negro man named Jesse, One do woman named Denes, One ditto Boy named Barnett, One ditto Boy named Anderson, One ditto Woman named Rachel

One Bed and furniture, One ditto, One ditto, One york of oxen and Cart, One mare, One Cow and Calf and Bell, One ditto, One ditto, One ditto, One lot of Iron tools, One pare of Steelyards, 6 axes, 2 plows and 2 pair of gear, one Saddle, 6 hoes and 3 grubbing hoes, 1 pair of Iron Wedges and frow, one cutting box and blade, one lot of kitchen Iron, furnature, one lot of kitchen Wooden furnature
one lot of pewter, one Jack Sale?, 2 Cotton wheel, 1 Flax wheel and 4 pair of Cards, one lot of knives & forks, one Safe and furnature

one chest and Small trunk, parcel of Books, 2 Tables, 6 Chairs, one looking Glass, To 5 Slays, To 1 loom One lot of Smoak house furnature, one lot of stone ware, To 37 head of Hogs, To 8 head of Sheep and Bell, To 1 Crosscut Saw, To 7 head of Geese, To 1 Shot gun, To 1 Coffee Mill, To 2 Hogsheads and 1 Barrel, To 1 Grind Stone, To 1 Lock chain

We whose names are hereunto Subscribed being first Sworn have appraised the personal Estate of James Farmer Deceased to the Sum of five hundred and fifty three pounds Eight Shillings and 7 ½ p. as above State't. Given under our hands this 21 day of September 1809
Willis Glass, William Rogers, Joseph Blanks
Recorded: November 20, 1809

## AC Book 4, Page 246                                                                 A. Martin's Inventory

An Inventory of the personal Estate of Abram Martin dec'd agreeable to Sale Per John
Martin, admr. Feby 11, 1808

Apr 6 Sales
Patsey Martin -one Negro girl Edith
Philip Thomas -one Negro woman Judith
John Martin - one Negro girl Easter, top fodder, pott Hooks, one Whip Saw, 3 Water vessels, cards, fire tongs, Table & bench, one meal log, a pail of corn, beacon, meal, one lid, one bead and furnature.

William Martin -one mare and Colt, a parcel of fodder, one Hogshead, one Kettle, one Jugg, one bed& counterpin

Luke Mathews - one cow and calf, one Chest, Sundry articles

Benjamin Burnett - one cow and calf, sundry articles, one water pale

Robert Adams - 2 Sheep, plow chains & swingletrees, 1 parcel Coopers tools, one cow hide

Abraham Fendly - a parcel of tobacco

John Thomas Sen.- A parcel hoggs, one tray and pales

Josiah Johnson - 3 axes, one chest, one be gum, 4 chares, corn, one bed

Thomas Matthews - one grind stone

William Morris Sen. - one Coulter, one pot & hooks

John Pigg - Sundry Iron tools

Samuel Armistead - one Cotton Wheel

Richard Parrish - one oven, one shoot gun, Iron fitters

William Beck - one cash, one tub, one Hogshead

James Emmerson - one bed stead, pewter knives and forks

John Quin - one testament

Agness Martin - one pr. Cards

James Dunn - one Gum, to one pr. Sheep shears, to corn, one bed, pot hooks

Elisha Williams - Cotton

Fountain Price - one bell

Thomas Dunn - rent of land

Total: £237.4.2 ½
Test; Saml. Beck C.S.
Recorded: November 20, 1809

**AC Book 4, Page 248**                                                                           **Towns' Acct Current**

DR The Estate of Halcott Towns Dec'd In Account with Ro. Payne

1809
Jany 2  paid James D Patton the amt. of 4 judgmn. Per Rect., Paid Jos. F? Green Per rect.
Cost of Sundry Exos. as per Voucher here with filed $26 57 cents

Balance as Per Contra
Credits
By Balance in my hands to collect on a former Settlement £165,14,2
By Balance due Ro. P. £2.13.71/2

Nov. 18, 1809
In obedience to the within order we have Settled the balance of the account Current of the Estate of Holcott Towns dec'd with Robert Payne his admrs. and find a balance due from the Estate to the Said admrs. of £2.13.7 ½
Given under our hands this day and date above written.
Wm Young, James D Patton, Nath'l Nelson
Recorded: November 22, 1809

**AC Book 4, Page 249**                                             **Wm Hardey Division of Estate**

Agreeable to an order of Court to us directed, we have met and agreed to give to John Williamson and Polly his wife all the land on the west Side of Pudding Creek Containing 133 1/3 Acres by estimation be the same more or less. Given under our hands the 21 Nov 1809.
Adin Gray, John Boling, Edm. Tompkins

At a Quarterly Court convened and held for Pittsy. County the 22$^{nd}$ Day of November 1809 This report of the allotment of the lands of William Hardy Dec'd to Polly Williamson wife of John Williamson and late widow of said William Hardy Dec'd was returned and by the Court ordered to be Recorded.
Teste.  Will Tunstall CC

**AC Book 4, Page 250**                                             **Wm Burton's Inventory**

In obedience to an order from the worshipful Court of Pittsylvania County to us directed, we have accordingly (after being first sworn) appraised the personal Estate of William Burton, dec'd in the following manner viz:

1809 May 17
1 Sow & 9 pigs, 1 ditto, 5 ditto, 9 Sows, 4 barrows, 27 Shoats, 1 Grey Mare, 1 Sorrel Horse, 1 yoak oxen & cart, 1 pided Cow and Calf, 2 Small Heifers, 1 Red Cow & Calf, 1 Cow & Calf, 1 large Still, Worm & tub, 1 Small ditto  " ditto, 10 mash Tubs, 2 half bushels, 2 barrels, 2 tubs, 2 buckets, 1 funnel & a half bushel, 9 Iron Hhd. Hoops, 2 bushels sheled Corn, 2 Tignt Casks, 2 Bushels Rye, 1 Loom, 3 old tubs, barrels Corn, parcel Cotton in the Seed, 1 flax wheel, 1 grind stone, 4 dutch plows, 8 chisels & 1 Gimblett, 1 mattock & 1 grubing hoe, 1 flacks Hackel & 2 Reap Hooks, old iron, Coopers Tools, 2 Clevesis Waggon, hamers & Frey Irons, 2 axes, 1 frow & 1 wedge

hilling hoes and 2 Colters, 1 bell, 1 pr. Sad Irons, 1 pr. Steel yards, 2 pr. Leading lines, 1 pr. Hames Traces & swingletree, 1 mouse Trap & Curry Comb, 2 bee Stands, 1 bay horse which was hired to William Robertson until Sept. next, 2 feather beds, 1 ditto furniture, 1 Cotton wheel, 1 Case & 9 bottles, 1 bead Steed, 1 doz. Pewter plates & 2 dishes, 6 basons, 1 dish, 1 Candle box, Tea Canister & 4 Tin measures, 1 pewter gallon Measure & half pt. Ditto, 1 Earthern dish & 2 plates, 2 Juggs & 1 butter potts, 1 cupboard, 1 Slay & Spools, 6 chares, 1 Table, 1 pr Fire dogs, 1 bread baker, 2 Iron potts, 3 pr. Hooks, 1 Dutch oven full of hogs lard & 1 pott full ditto, lb bacon, 1 box & shoe Tools, 1 Saddle & bridle & Saddle bags, 1 Sifter & Candle moulds, 1 gun & Shott bagg, 1 pr. Warpt Cotton, 1 Cask, 1 desk, 2 bottles & Contents 1 Iron bound Hhg., 1 Chest, 1 Cuting knife, 1 box, 1 rasp, 2 brass locks, 2 Sundials, Cash on hand, 1 brass barrel pistol, 1 umbrella
George Adams, Permecious Williams, William Murphey, David Rice, Apres.
Recorded: January 15, 1810

**AC Book 4, Page 252**                                             **D. Shelton's Estate Division**

Agreeable to an order of the County Court of Pittsylvania we have this 29$^{th}$ Dec 1809 valued the Slaves belonging to the estate of Daniel Shelton dec'd & allotted them to his four Sons Young, Roy, Daniel & Tunstall as follows-Viz:

Randolph £135 to Roy Shelton to receive

Isaac £150 to Young Shelton to pay
Matilda £90 to Daniel Shelton to receive
Bob £45 to      "              "
Cloe £66 to Tunstall Shelton to receive
Moses £60 to    "              "
Lucy £0.0.0.
And are of opinion that each of the above mentioned Sons pay to the children of Willis Shelton the sum of £27.6 subject to pay one fifth of the debts above the amt.of the sales of the personal Estate. Given under our hands the date above.
Thos. B Jones, Allen Womack, John Adams, Isaac Coles
Recorded: January 15, 1810

**AC Book 4, Page 252**                                                                 **M Tompkins Inventory**

Pittsylvania January the 8$^{th}$ 1810
In obedience to an order of Pittsylvania Court we the under sign'd have appraised the Estate of Mourning Tompkins dec'd in the following manner to Wit:

One Negro woman Named Easter & her child. Named Joseph, One Negro man Named Benjamin, One negro man Named Isaac, One Sorrel Horse, One feather Bed, Boulster & Bedsted, One cupboard, One Bedstead, One do, One folding Table, One Chest, One Do, One Flax Wheel, Eight Cheers, Seven Books, Two Hackels, Five Slays, One Mattock, a new grubbing hoes, one ax, One wedge, one lock chain, One pot, one oven, One Dish, one Bason, one Spice Morter, One pr. Stillards, Three Butter Potts, One Cut Saw, One tea kittle, One cow & yearling, 4 head sheep, Candle stick, snuffers & looking glass, One coffee mill, One wheel & pot hooks, One auger
Total: £277.5.0
Amount Brought over   £285.15.0
Done By us: James Hart, Jesse Hodges, John Bowling
Recorded: January 15, 1810

**AC Book 4, Page 254**                                                                 **Division of B Hardy's Estate**

In obedience to an order of the County Court of Pittsylvania bearing date January Court 1810 we have proceeded, allot'd and lay off to Nancy Hardy, Widow of Benjamin Hardy Dec'd, one third part of the real & personal Estate of the Said Dec'd as follows to Wit: from the amount of the Sale: thirty three pounds Seven Shillings and one penny half penny and from the value of the Negroes to wit: Rhodah a woman at the price of Eighty pounds and leaving a balance due her of eight pounds Six Shillings and one eight pence, also one hundred and thirty two acres of land including the mansion house. Beginning at a red oak in the pattant Line thence the said line of the Pattant North 32 Degrees East 63 poles to a white oak saplin, thence a new line South 70 degrees east one hundred and sixteen poles to a apple tree in the field , thence south 3 degrees west 152 poles to the back line of the patent, thence the same North 80 degees west 126 poles to a pine north 7 degree west 116 poles to the beginning this 5$^{th}$ Day of Feby 1810.
Washington Thompson, George Shelton, J M Williams, Robert Clopton

This is to certify that the balance appearing to be due from Nancy Hardy to the Estate of Benjamin Hardy, Dec'd from her purchase at the sale of dec'd is forty Shillings and six pence which we freely give to her this 5$^{th}$ day of Feby 1810.
Jesse Hardy, Reubin Hardy, John Hardy, Vincent Hardy, Lewis Hardy, Preston Hardy, Stephen Hardy, Soloman Hardy, Hezekiah Bennett, Sarah Lewis

At a Court held for Pittsylvania County the 19$^{th}$ day of Feby 1810. The within report of the allotment to Sarah Hardy, widow of Benjamin Hardy Deceased, one third part of the real and personal Estate of sd. Benjamin was returned and by the Court ordered to be reeorded.
Teste Will. Tunstall CC

**AC Book 4, Page 255**                                      **Division of Este of Glascock's Hiers**

Agreeable to an order of the worshipful court of Pittsylvania County to us directed, we have proceeded to divide the four Negroes mentioned in the said order of Court as follows to wit: Hannah & Nancy to the plaintiff for the use of the heirs of George Glascock, Dec'd & Lucy & Lindley to the Defend and for the use of the heirs of William Glascock, Dec'd and that the Defendant pay the plaintiff Three pounds six shillings & eight pence. Given under our hands this thirteenth Day of December 1809
Answorth Harrison, William Echols, John Jinkins
Recorded: January 15, 1810

**AC Book 4, Page 255**                                      **Lucy Tanner's Third of M. Tanner's Estate**

In obedience to an order of the worshipful Court of Pittsylvania County to us directed have this 23rd of February 1810 Convened at the late dwelling house of Mathew Tanner, Dec'd. We have proceeded to Lay off the third of the estate of the Dec'd to Lucy Tanner, Widow of the said Dec'd agreeable to the Will of the said Dec'd agreeable to the best of our Judgment which is as follows to wit:

4 Sheep, 1 Sorrel mare, 1 yoke of Stears, 1 Red heafer, 1 Read Cow, 1 Cow & Calf & bell, 1 Bull yearling 6 hogs, the third part of Plantation tools, 1 Pot, 1 oven, 1 Skillet, 1 flat Iron, 2 rack hooks, 1 grind stone, 1 cross cut Saw, 1 Tub, 2 poles and Vinigar barrel, 1 Bed and furniture, one do, 1 Cubbard, 2 mughs, 2 boles, 1 teapot, 2 Earthen pots, cups and Sausers, 1 decanter, 1 Caster, 1 Sugar dish, 6 Tablespoons & nine tea do, 1 Small table, 6 knives and forks, 1 Cotton wheel, 1 drinking glass, 1 black bottle, To one third part of Bacon & Lard.
The third part of Land was settled by Lucy Tanner and Creed Tanner by agreement.
Thomas Tanner, Silvany Gardnor, Samuel Walker

At a Court held for Pittsylvania County the 14th Day of March 1810 The within Report of the allotment to Lucy Tanner widow and Relict of Mathew Tanner Deceased her dower of the real and personal estate of said Matthew Tanner, Deceased was returned and by the Court ordered to be recorded.
Test  Will Tunstall CC

**AC Book 4, Page 256**                                      **Inventory Thomas Shelton's Est**

Agreeable and in Subscription to an orader of the worshipful Court of Pittsylvania County made July Court 1808. We the Subscribers being convened at the plantation and house of Thomas Shelton Deceased this 10th Day of September 1808 and after being sworn according as the Law directs, have appraised the personal Estate of the said Thomas Shelton Deceased in currant money and have taken and Inventory of the same as followth Viz:

1 white cow and calf, 1 black white faced Cow and Calf, 1 black Cow and Bull yearling, 1 pided Heifer, 1 yoke of oxen and Cart, 1 Cutting knife and box, 1 lock Chain, 1 bay horse, bay Colt blaze faced, 1 Bay mare, 5 head of Sheep, 5 grown hogs and 4 Shoats, 2 plows Coulter, 1 Clivis, 1 Swingletree and 1 Iron tooth Rake

1 pare of Iron ploug axes, 2 small rings and 1 pare of Rope plow gares, a parcel of old Iron, 3 axes, 1 Cross cut Saw, 1 pare of small Steelyard, and 2 bells & Collars, a parcel of old Iron trumpery and tub, 2 Iron wedges, 1 drawing knife, 1 Conk shel, 1 sett of flat Irons, 1 auger and a parcel of old Iron side lines, 1 sawrest, 3 files and 1 old stock lock, 1 mans Saddle, 1 womans Saddle, 1 bridle, 1 Shot gun, Shot bag and curreomb (sic), 1 sand sive, 1 Steal trap, 1 feather bed and furniture & bed Stead, 1 feather bed furniture & Stead, 1 feather bed & furniture, 1 bedstead, 1 black walnut chest, 1 Table and trunk, 1 pine box and 6 Chures

1 Cass of Bottles and old Slay, 1 Clock real & 20 Spools, a parcel of lumber, 3 old bags & a tub, 3 tubs, 2 Jugs, 3 baskets, 1 bag, 1 Cotton wheel, a pare of old cotton Cards and 1 pare of old shares

1 looking glass, 1 sugar box, 1 Candle mold, 1 old Cotton wheel, 12 pare of Cotton Cards, 1 old flax wheel, 1 pare Sheep Shares, a lot of Earthern ware, 1 pewter bason, 1 grind stone, a parcel of Kitchen furniture, 1 Jug, 1butter pot & 2 parcels of old Cards, a parcel of Tubs, a parcel of water vesels, a parcel of knives & forks, 2 reap hooks, a lot of pewter, lot of Earthen ware & an old hand saw, and old trumpery Iron

1 Table & six spoons, 1 funnel, 2 tumblers, 2 old hogsheads, 1 bee hive, 1 Churn, 1 tub, a lot of old hoes, broad ax, hand saw & hammer, 1 powdering tub & old Iron trumpery, 1 spice morter and old lumber, 1 bedstead & canm. & trays & 4 chares, 1 Table, 1 piggin & 1 water stand, 1 old Slay & 1 small cask, 1 old Tea Kettle, Sifter & Iron? Trumpery, 3 small sides of Leather, 1 Jug

a parcel of plank & small tub, a parcel of oats & fother, a parcel of corn, a parcel of wheat in the straw, 2 Iron pot racks, 1 old Hogshead, a parcel of wool, 6 gallons of Brandy
Total: £122.9.3
Appraised by us Geo. Dodson Sen, John Shelton, Thos. B. Holt
Recorded: October 17, 1808

**AC Book 4, Page 259**                                                            **Inventory of George Hardy's Est.**

An inventory of the Estate of George Hardy. Deceased taken the 27th Day of April 1808 and appraisers

One feather Bed, stead and furniture, One pine table, One water pale, 6 chairs, 1 Barrow, 1 sow, 5 pigs, ½ doz Table spoons, 1 pewter dish & 7 plates, 1 parcel old pewter, 1 pewter Bason, 4 Tin Cups, 1 Case Knives & forks, 1 old Cotton wheel

1 Iron Skillet, 1 Loom, 3 Shoes, 3 old Barrels, 2 pr. Cotton Chards, 1 parcel old Iron, 1 pr. Iron Wedges, 1 parcel shoe makers tools & 1 auger, 1 drawing Knife, 1 parcel old E. ware & 1 Case bottle, 1 pr. Old Stirrep Irons, 2 Tea Cannisters, 7 E. plates & one mug, 1 Case & Razors, 1 Bottle & Spirits turpentine, 1 parcel old Books, 1 looking Glass, 1 Cut reel, 1 Womans Saddle, 1 mans saddle, 1 Shott Gun, 2 axes, 1 Mattock & 2 hoes, 2 Plows & hoes, 2 old Sheep & 1 Lamb, 1 Candle molds, Candle Stick & 1 Ink Stand, 1 Small Hestay (sic), 1 old tool Bench & Table, 1 Bed cord & 1 old Bridle, 1 small Bell, 4 Geese, 1 Churn, 1 pot rack, three tubs, 2 hoes, 1 powdering Tub
Total: £23.5.0
In obedience to an order of the Worshipful Court of Pittsylvania baring date Apl Court 1808 We have proceeded to appraise the Estate of George Hardy, Dec'd and find it as stated above. Given under our Hands.
Robert Clopton Jr, Thos. Madding, William Lewis
Recorded: October 17, 1810

**AC Book 4, Page 261**                                                         **Geo. Hardy Dec'd Sales of Estate**

The Amount of the sale of George Hardy, dec'd
Rosanna Hardy      DR
1 feather Bed Sted & furniture, 1 do ", 6 Chairs, 1 pine table, 1 Waiter plate, 1 Lott Hoggs, ½ doz. Table spoons, 1 lott pewter, 4 tin Cups, 1 Case knives & forks, 1 old Cotton wheel, 1 Iron Skillott, 1 Loom, 3 old Barrels, 3 Slaes (sic), 2 pr. Old Cotton Chards, 1 parcel old Iron, 1 pr. Iron Wedges, 1 parcel Shoe makers tools, 1 auger 1 Drawing knife, 1 parcel old E ware, 1 Case Bottle

1 pr. Old Sturrip Irons, 2 Tea Cannisters, 7 E plates & 1 mug, 1 Case Razors, 1 Bottle Spirits Turpentine, 1 parcel old Books, 1 looking Glass, 1 Cut Reel, 1 Womans Saddle, 1 Man Saddle, 1 Shott Gun, 2 pole axes, 1 mattock, 2 hoes, 2 plows & hoes, 2 old Sheep & 1 Lamb, 1 Candle mold, Candle stick & 1 Ink Stand, 1 Small History, 1 old tool bench & Table, 1 Bed Cord & 1 old Bridle, 1 Small bell, 4 Geese, 1 Churn, 1 pot rack, 3 Tubs, 2 hoes, 1 Powdering tub
Total: £23.16.0
Recorded: October 17, 1808

**AC Book 4, Page 263**                                    **G. Hardy Acco. Currt.**

The Estate of George Hardy Dec'd To Rodah Hardy, Admr.     DR

1808 May 15 Paid Champ & Jere Terry Per bond
To Int on Do from 1 April 1805

Cr
By amount of Sales of the Estate
In obedience to an order of the worshipful court of Pittsylvania dated Sept Court 1808, We have settled the account Current of the estate of George Hardy Dec'd With Rhodah Hardy, the adminstratrix, and find a balance against the estate of two pounds twelve Shillings agreeable to the above Statement. Given under our hands this 14th Opct 1808.
J. W. Williams, Robert Clopton Jr, David Terry
Recorded: October 17, 1808

**AC Book 4, Page 263**                                    **John Hodnett's Account Current of Sales**

List of Propery belonging to the Estate of John Hodnett, Dec'd Sold the 6th February 1808

Lucy Hodnett                           DR
To 1 Bed, 1 Desk, Books, Coverlet, ½ Doz/ Winsor chairs, 1 Dish, Decanter & Glass, Lott of E. Ware, 1 pewter bason, Lott of pewter & pewter Bason, Fire dogs, Sand Sive, Flax Seed, 9 Bushels Wheat, 3 Barrels, 1 do, 1 Womans Saddlel, 1 Reel, 1 Walnut Chest, 1 Cotton Wheel, 1 Loom, 1 Slay, Walnut Table, 1 Bed &c, 1 Ditto, 1 Spice morter, 1 Coffee pot & Candle mould, Fire dogs, pork & Tub, 3 pots, Lard & Butter, Tubs & Chirns, Tray & Flax, Cotton Wheel, ¼ part G. Stone, Tray & Sifter, Haymes & Traces, 1 pr. Iron wedges, Lot of hoes, 2 plows, old Saddle, 2 Axes & Mattox, 1 sythe, parcel Flax, 10 Barrels, 20 ditto, 1 Roan mare, 1 Ditto Bay, 1 Sorrel Colt, Stack of oats, 1 Stack & Shucks, White Cow & Yearling, ditto Heifer, ditto pided Cow & yearling, ditto red Hefer, ditto yoak steers

6 Sheep 1st Choice, 1 stack fodder, ditto Tops, 14 gees, 1 meal tub, 2 Barrows & 1 Sow, 6 Shoats, pot & Skillet, pots & Hooks

James Hodnett                          DR
1 looking glass, 2 bed quilts, 1 water Stand, 1 pine Chest, 6 Chairs, heather, Fro & ax, a mans Saddle

Wilson Hodnett                         DR
1 Coverlett

Robert F White                         DR
1 walnut Table, walnut Vessels, oven, 1 Brown Cow, 4 ditto pided, 1 stack fodder

Miss Elizabeth Hodnett                 DR
1 Bed

Josiah Tyre                            DR
1 Hymn Book

Joseph Mottley-Son of David            DR
augur, hammer & D. knife

Anderson Barker                        DR
1 Bay filley

Freeman High                           DR

1 Bay Colt

Nathaniel Terry                              DR
R. pided Stear, ditto B. ditto, 6 2$^{nd}$ Choice Sheep

William Wimbish                          DR
1 Bull, 1 Ditto, Ditto Red Heifer

Ayres Hodnett                             DR
1 Shott Gun

Mrs. Lucy Hodnett                      DR
To amt. of a/c brought fow'd £120.12.9, ½ part in 1 pr Cart wheels
Total:£127.11.9
Lucy Hodnett Executrix
Recorded: October 17, 1808

**AC Book 4, Page 266**                                            **Inventory of the Est of Thompson Phillips**

An Inventory of the Estate of Thompson Phillips Dec'd Taken the 16$^{th}$ Day of July 1808.

1 feather Bed and furniture, Bedsted &c, 1 pine Table, Tray & meal sifter, 5 knives & forks, ½ Dozen pewter plates, 2 Basons, 3 spoons, Tin cup & pepper box, 1 Qt. Tin, 1 pr. Flat irons, 1 Case & 11 Black bottles, 1 pint Decanter, 1 Small pine chest4 old Chairs, 1 candle Stand, 2 water pales, 1 meal gum, 1 poll ax, 1 pott, 1 dutch oven & Hooks, 1 Cotton Wheel, a parcel of old Iron, 8 ¼ lb. Bare Iron , 2 Baskets, 1 pair cotton Cards, 1 bridle & Saddle, 1 Sack bag, 1 Meet Tub, 1 Small Do, 1 Small Runlet, 1 Cradle & scales, 1 Chest, 1 Bed & Furniture, 1 Pided Steer yearling, 2 sows, 1 spotted barer, 6 Shot, 1 White Sow & 5 pigs, 1 spotted sow & 6 pigs, 1 Sorrel mare, 1 Sorrel Colt
Total £50.7.9
In obedience to an order of the Court of Pittsylvania Dated June Court 1808. We have appraised the estate of Thompson Phillips, Dec'd agreeable to the Within Inventory. Given under our hands the 10$^{th}$ Day of July 1808.
Robert Easly, Jacob Anderson, N C Williams, John Shaw
Recorded: October 17, 1808.

**AC Book 4, Page 267**                                                   **Inventory of Theo. Haley's Este.**

Inventory of the Estate of Theophilus Haley dec'd taken the 29$^{th}$ November 1808

1 Black Sow & 3 Pigs, 1 blue Sow and 5 Shoats, 2 Cows, 1 yearling & 1 Calf & Bell, 1 Turners Lathe, 2 old Hads, 1 Bay mare, 1 Roan Colt, 1 pr. Iron spancets?, 1 Box old Irons, 1 Box Shoe makers Tools, 1 Hand Saw & adze, 4 old plains & 1 Bell, 1 Cooper addz, 4 old Chisels, 1 Hammer & 1 drawing knife 1 old straw knife, Steel & Screw, 1 pr.. Hinges & 2 trowels, 1 Basket & shoemakers Casts, 1 goard & Nails,, 1 pine chest, 1 Furkin & half Bushel & some clover Seed, 40 lb Seed Cotton, 1 Basket, 1 Coulter, Collar & Haymes, 1 Plow traces, Collar, Haymes, 1 swinngletree & clevis pin, 3 pole axes, 1 Broad ax & Hatchet, 4 Hilling hoes old, 2 Grubbing Hoes, 1 Froe & curry Comb, a parcel of old leather gear, 1 grind Stone, 1 pr. Saddle Bags, a small Bundle Leather, a parcel of pewter, Sundry Earthern ware & coffee mill, Butter pot, 1 Safe, 1 Brass Skattle (sic) & Trivet, 1 pr. Tongs & shovel, 1 spinning Wheel & pr. Cards, 1 pine Table, 1 Family bible, 2 Vols. Miltons Works, 2 small Historys & Law's Collections, 1 Case Razers, Shavg. Box, 1 Walnut Book Case & 1 Small pine Table, 1 Trussel

1 Mans Saddle, 1 Shot gun, powder Horn & Shot pouch, 6 Comme. Chairs, 1 Hair trunk, 1 do do, 1 Womans Saddle, 1 Pot & Hooks (large), 1 small pot, 1 oven & lid, 1 Skillet & lid, 1 Loom , 1 Harness, 1 Boxes, 1 Tub, 2 pails & 1 piggin, 1 Bred Tray, 1 Half Bushel, 1 Hive of bees, 1 Hammer, 1 griddle, 1 Cart Box, 1 Old flax Wheel, 2 meal tubs, 2 pickle tubs & 2 old Churns, 1 Runlet, 1 Jug, 1 old safe,

12 gallon Jug, 2 Slays, 1 Feather Bed & furniture, 1 do do do, 1 Larch & candle Stick, 1 piggen, 1 Keeler, Barrels Corn, 1 Stack top fidder & Shucks, a parcel of Blades, a parcel of wheat in the Cheaff, 1 Measuring Tub, Barrels onubbins?, 1 Sugar tub, 1 Straw Basket, 1 pr.sad irons, 1 Negro girl Ritter, 1 Negro Boy Bedford, 8 knives & 5 forks

Persuant to an order of the worshipful Court of Pittsylvania County to us directed, bearing date November Court 1808, We Philip L Grasty, Edward L. Douglass & John Douglass, three of the appraisers mentioned in said order, do appraise the estate of the said decedent as we then stated. Given under our Hands this 29th of November 1808.
Philip L Grasty, Edward Douglass, John Douglass, Wyatt Haley, Admr. of Theo, Haley, dec'd
Recorded: November 19, 1808

**AC Book 4, Page 270**                                              **Account Sales of Theo. Haley's Est.**

Account Sales of sundry property sold 10th Dec. 1808 as the property of Theo. Haley dec'd by his admrx. Wyatt Haley

James Doss - 3 Sheats, 3 pigs, 1calf, 1 box Shoe Makers Tools

Daniel Clement - 1 Blk Sow, 1 Blue Sow, 2 pole axes, 1 Lot old plains, 1 pewter Dish, 2 meal tubs, 1 Old Safe

Joseph Mays - 1 Sow Shoat, 1 ditto, 3 Hoes, 3 ditto, 1 pr. Iron Wedges, 1 pott

Wyatt Haley - 2 old Hhds, 1 cow, 1 Trussel

William Blake - 1 Cow & Bell

Robert Waller - 1 yearling, 50 ¼ lbs Seed Cotton

William Smith - 2 axes, 1 safe, 1 tub & runlet , pr. Shoe Brushes, 1 Tub & Hammer

Francis Irby - 1 plow & coulter, 1 grind stone

Shadrack Beal - 1 froe

Henry Wade - 1 pr. Iron spancels & curry comb

Joseph E Haley - 1 lot old Irons, 1 lot old tubs, 1 candle stick

John Rowland Sen - Hand saw & addze, 1 box old Irons, 1 lot plow gear

Edm'd Tunstall - 1 lot Coopers Tools, 1 Goard nails, 1 Lot old bridles, 1 pr.Bruching, 2 Tubs, 1 Basket, 1 Man Saddle, 5 lb. Fodder, parcel of Nubbins?, 1 Shot Gun, 1 Lea. Whip, 1 half Bushel

Henry R Shelton - 1 Bay mare, 1 Roan Coalt

Peter Irby - 1 Loom 1 flax wheel

Elish Burch - 1 small pot, 1 Stack of fodder, 6 chairs, 1 pine chest, 1 pine table, piggins & keeler, 4 4/5 Barrels Corn

Warfield Scruggs - 5 Barrels Corn, 5 ditto, 1 pale, 1 shovel & tongs, 11 ½ Bus. Wheat

Thomas Black - 1 Book Case & Table

Josiah Rice - Parcel of Leather

Thomas Anderson - 1 Jug

Mrs. Ann Haley - 1 Stand bees

John Mustain - 1 Turners Lathe

Mrs. Sarah Haley
1 spinning wheel, 1 tub, 1 Skillet, 1 kittle & Trivet, 1 oven, 1 pr. Spool frames, 1 Bed & furniture, 1 ditto, 1 sugar Tub, parcel of Books ,1 Trunk, 1 ditto, parcel of Ear. Ware & Pewter,1 pr. Saddle Bags & pr. cards, 1 Case razors & shav. Box, 1 Womans Saddle, 1 Powder horn & Shot pouch, 2 Slays, 1 Straw Basket, 1 Hatchett, 3 Basketts, 1 Griddle, 1 pr.sad irons, 8 knives & forks

Total: £24.6.7
Recorded: November 19, 1808

**AC Book 4, Page 273**                                              **Thomp. Philips' Account Current**

The Sale of the Estate of Thompson Philips dec'd Sold the 11th of July 1808

One Sow & six black pigs, three choice hogs, One Sow & Six ??, one boar & Sow, Tree spaid sows & 1 Barrow, One steer, one sorrel mare, One bridle, one sifter, one Case, One Decanter, one chest, one Table, One pail, one pigin, 4 chairs, One tray, one barrel, 6 plates, One bason, one bason & spoons, One plow hoe & hilling hoe, Knives & forks, 1 Iron hoes &c, One pair Cotton cards, 1 pr. Flax Irons, One bed, one wheel, one pepper box, One shoe knife, one basket, one do, One tin Jack, one tin cup, one pole ax, One Runtet, one gum, one powdering Tub, One Candle Stand, one mans Saddle, One pot, one oven & Hooks, One sack bag, one Sorrel Colt, One Bed, one Chest
Amount in full  £46.0.4 ½
Recorded:  December 19, 1808

**AC Book 4, Page 274**                                **Inventory of the Est. of Henry Bohannon**

In Complyance of the Worshipful Cort. Of Pittsylvania September 1808,  we have proceeded to appraise The Estate of  Henry Bohannon, Dec'd As Follows to wit:

11 Shoats, 11 large hogs, 4 Cows, 3 Yearlings, 2 Calves, 1 Sorrell mare, 3 Feather Beds, 1 gunn, 1 Sugar Box, 1 Table & Cloth, 1 Loom, 1 Chest, 1 Flax Wheel, 2 Tubs, 1 hand Saw, 1 Cotton wheal, 2 bottles, 2 Bred Trays, 4 Baskets, 1 Skillets, 1 Sack Bay, Sundry Water  Vessels, 4 pare pot hook, 1 Barrel, 1 Dutch oven, 4 pair of Cards, 1 pare Flat Irons, 1 Pair of Scissors

2 Sides of Leather, 1 Bed Stead, 2 Pair of Weving harnesses, 1 Tea Kettle, Sundreys

One Slay, 6 Chiers, 1 Pot, 1 oven, one trivet, 3 old pots, Sundry Pewter, Sundry Earthern ware, 1 Bee hive Sundry hoes, 3 axes, 1 pair of  Chain Traces, 1 Pair of Wedges Sundrys, 2 ploughs, Onepair Rope Traces, 1 colter, 1 Tub
Total: £67.14.6
October the 19th 1808
Timothy Stamps, Linen Carter, Noel Waddill
Recorded: January 16, 1809

**AC Book 4, Page 276**               **A Divison of Mr. Bates Estate ac to Hodnett & L H Bates**

In Obedience to an order of the Worshipful Court of Pittsylvania County bearing date December Court 1808, We have proceeded to Settle and adjust the accounts of David Nowlin, Guardian of the orphans of Mathew Bates, Dec'd and find the Balance in the hands of the said guardian to be £256.15.1/2 Including Interest to the first day of January 1809, also six Negroes to the Value of £447.10.0 out of which we have allotted to Lucy H Bates, one of the orphans, Silvey, a Negro girl at the Value of £30.00, also find her proportion of the other first sum mentioned in the hands of the said guardian to be £50.10.3, subject to this Day also allotted to Nancy K Hodnett, wife of Ayres Hodnett, one other of the said orphans, Primas, a Negro Lad at the Value of £120.0.0, also £54.16.3 as her proportion of the first said sum in the hands of the said guardian subject to a Credit of £41.19.6 as Settled to this Day.
Given under our Hands this 23rd day December 1808
J W Williams, Allen Womack, Edmond Fitzgerald, John Adams Jr
Recorded January 16, 1809

**AC Book 4, Page 276**                                      **Inventory of the Est. of James Strange**
January the 13 1809

A Inventory of the property of James Strange, Dec'd Lent to his Wife Susannah during her single life or widowhood.

To one Negroe Man named Stefiny, 2 horses, 4 head of Cattle, 23 head of hogs, 1 Bed and furniture, 1 Cubord, 1 Table, 1 Chest, 6 Chears, 1 Cotton wheel, 1 Flax Wheel, 3 Jugs, 1 looking glass, 2 powdering Tubs, 1wier wheat sive, pot & 2 pair of pot hooks, 1 oven, 1 puter Dish, 6 puter plates, 1 smoothing Iron, 2 axes, 1 plow, 1 Coalter, 1 matax, 2 Bee Stands, 3 water Vessels, 1 washing Tub, one Grinding Stone, one Reaping hook. 2 Bells, 2 pair Cotton cards, 1 Iron wedge, 6 knives & forks, 1 pair harness, one chain Trades, 1 churn, 1 Lock Chain, 1 Drawing knife, 1 Claw hammer, 1 Womans Sadle, one half Booshel, 1 Bason, 3 Slays, 2 pair harnesses
Josiah Morton, Thomas Harris

January 13th 1809
A Inventory of the property of Jame Strange Dec'd that is to be Sold at present

1 Negro man named Dick, 2 horses, 1 yoke of oxen, 2 head of Cattle, 1 mans Saddle, 1 Chest, 1 Comb, 1 hone, 1 case of Razors, a parcel of Books, 1 Sithe & Cradle, 1 foot adds, 1 froe, 1 hand Saw, 1auger chissil & a gouge, 3 cup hooks, 1plow, 1 stock lock, 1 Cask, 1 pr. Stillards, 1 ax, 1 pair Sheep Sheers, 6 Vials, 1 pair of Saddle Bags, 1 pair hames and Chain Traces
Josiah Morton, Thomas Harris
Recorded May 16, 1809

**AC Book 4, Page 279**                                      **Inventory of the Est. Of Geo. Lewis**

Inventory of the Estate of George Lewis, Dec'd Taken the 26 of February 1807

1 Sorrel Horse, 1 red & white heifer, 1 ditto Cow & yearling, 1 ditto Cow, 1 Sorrel mare, 1 ditto mare & colt, 4 Spotted Sow, 1 Cotton Wheel, 1 Flax wheel, 1 old Saddle, 1 Chirm, 1 small D. oven & Lid, 2 Pots & Hooks, 2 pole axes, 2 hoes and 1 matox, 2 old plows, 1 Colter, bell & shoe Hammer, 1 Skillet, 1 old tub & 2 piggins, 1 large Bible, parcel old Books, 1 pr Cotton & 1 pr Wool Cards, 2 pewter dishes,6 plates, 6 Basons, knives, forks, spoons and some old pewter, 1 Tub, clean oats, 1 Saddle & Bridle, 1 Side Saddle 1 Drawing knife, 1 large & 2 Small Jugs, 1 large pine Chest, 1 small ditto, 1 pr. Sad Irons & reap hook, 1 Bed & furniture, 1 ditto ditto, 1 poplar Bed stead, 1 Bed furniture & Stead, 4 old Chairs, 2 ews & 2 lambs, 1 old tub, Soal leather, 4 raw Hydes, 1 old Loom, 1 Sheep Skin, parcel flax, 100 lb bacon, 15 lbs Tallow, 1 Shot gun, 3 ½ barrels Corn, 1 Coffee pot, old Sifter tray & 4 phials, 1 old hand saw & Curry Comb, 1 Razor, 1 file & Gimblet, 50 lbs. seed Cotton
Total: £83.0..6
Agreeable to an order of the County Court of Pittsylvania directed we, being first sworn as the Law Directs, have appraised the foregoing estate as stated above. Given under our hands this 26th February 1807

Recorded January 16, 1809

**AC Book 4, Page 280**                                                                 James Strang's account of **Sales**

A List of the Auction of the property of James Strange Dec'd
February 9, 1809

Joel Dyer - one old red Heifer
Susanna Strange - 1 Brindle Cow
William Hule - one yoake of Steers
Jesse Strange - one Sorrel hors Colt
Jesse Strange - one Sorrel horse & colt
Peter M Harris - one pair of Steelyards
William Hawkins - one Negro man
Francis T? Strange - one walnut chest
Smith Strange - one Loom
William Hale -7 Viols
Isaiah Morton - one sythe & Cradle
John Davis - one pair of hames & traces
Robert Bullington jun - one sett of Razors & hone
Peter H. Harris - one pole ax & plow hoe
Taply Akin -one frow
James Green - 3 reap hooks
Isaiah Morton - one foot adzes
Jesse Arthur - one saw & Sundrys
Jeremiah Walker - 1 Saddle
Smith Strange - 1 pair saddle Bags
George Cook - one hogshead
Isaiah Morton - one pair sheep shares
Peter Harris - one stock Lock & Books
Taply Akin - one Book
David Beagerly one pair of money scales
The amount of the sale  £190.16.0
A true list of Taply Akin
Recorded February 20, 1809

**AC Book 4, Page 281**                                                                 Inventory of the Est. of John Muse

We the Subscribers, being first Sworn as the Law directs, In obedience to an order from the Worshipful Court of Cty have appraised the estate of John Muse Sen Dec'd as follows Viz:

38 head of hogs, 9 head of Horses, 2 Yoark of oxen, 10 Head of Cattle, 16 heads of Sheep, one Chart
A Quanity of Plantation tools & old Iron, 1 bed stead and 2 wheals, 150 barrels Corn, one shot gun,
1 pr. Of fire dogs,, 1 pr. of hand Irons, 2 bedsteads and 4 beds & furniture, 2 Cubboards & furniture & 2 tables, 3 Jugs, 1 Butter pot, a parcel of Pewter, 1 Desk bookcase & chest and flax wheel, a parcel of kitchen furniture, 3 axes, Candle moles, 10 hogshead, 11 Casks, 1 bag of wheat, Churn, Tongs and Shovel
1 apple mill, 1 Looking Glass, 3 Cow hides, Shoe makers Tools, 1 Negro Man Harry, 1 Negro Man Jack,
1 Negro woman & Child Winny, 1 Negro Woman Tarmar & Jerden, 1 Negro girl, 1 Negro boy Abram,
1 Negro Girl Lily, 1 Negro boy Peter
Will Adkison, Nath'l Kirby, Moses Kirby, Will. Witcher
Samuel A. Muse & Joel Muse, administrator of John Muse sen, Dec'd
Recorded: January 16, 1809

**AC Book 4, Page 282**                                                      **Shaws acco. Currents**

DR The Estate of Thomas Shaw, Dec'd  In account with Alexander Shaw, administrator

1805
Jany 7  To Cash paid Rodham Gilpin A/C, Lovelace Haley, Betsy Tate a/c, Jacob Farguson for fish, John Terry for Oats, Richard Jones for Coffin, George Dodson for 3 qts Brandy, 1 quire paper used of Sale, John Nash a/c

1806
Jany- omitted in Feby 1805, Champ. & Jerre. Terry a/c

March 10 Ditto  do in full, Mary Slate

April 19
Wm & Joseph Terry, pd the Clerkk of Pittsylvania Court, To the Sheriff for Tax Due for 1804

Oct. 12
To Sheriff for Tax Due 1805, Pd. Reves Higgenbothum & Co, Pd. John Stamps per note, Robert Shaw for wheat in my father's left me, Reubin Walrond, Rawley Dodson, James M Williams for Surveying &c, 5 Per C. for my  Services, Balance due the Estate

1804              Credit

Nov 23 By amount of Sale this Day which will be due 25$^{th}$ Decr. 1805

1805
Feby 14
Nathaniel Shaw for C. & J. Terry, Cash of Mary Wimbish, Wm Hall, John Henry for 16 Days work, John Motley, Daniel Motley, Samuel Gray, Elizabeth Terry, John Nash
Balance due from Pat Shaw to the Estate
Recorded: February 20,  1809

**AC Book 4, Page 284**                                      **John Wilson's acct. of Guardianship**

Peter Wilson orphan of  P. Wilson, Dec'd To Jno. Wilson, his Gdr.         DR

1806
Sept 2 - 3 ¼ yd Cotton Cassimere, 3 ¼ yds Striped Nankeen ?, ¾ yd Mersails Quiltin, 2 ½ yds Country Cloth, 21 Button moulds, 1 ½ doz. Ditto, 2 Hks Silk, 1 Stk. Twist, 6 Hks thread, 3 ¼ yds Country Cotton, 1 mans Hatt, 1 pr. Cotton Stockings, 1 pr Suspenders,  Bendanna Hankf., 1 gr. paper, 1 Ink Stand, 1 pen knife, 1 Scotts Sessons, 1 large Slate, 3 pencils

Dec 22 -  To Thomas Tiffon for making 2 pr. Briches & wais coat, 1 Spelling Book, 2 gr. paper

1807
Jany 3 - 3 ½ yds fancicord, 3 ½ yds  ditto, 1 ¼ yd Country Cotton, 2 Hks Silk & Twiat, 2 ½ doz. Buttons, 1 oz
 Col 'd thread, 1 pr. Shoes, 1 pr Wosted Stocking

Jany 24 - 2 yd Bro. Cloth, 1 ½ Doz Buttons, 2 Hks Silk, 1 Stick twist, 1 ½ yds Bro. Holland, 3 Hks

March 28 - 3 ½ yds Linnen, 4 Hks. Thread, 2 Doz Shirt Buttons, 1 yd Muslin, 1 pr. Indiv. Stockings, ¾ yds Tilonett, 2 Sticks Twist, 3 ½ thick set, 2 yds Country Cotton, 2 Hks Silk, 20 Quilt Buttons, 15 Do  Do, 3 Hks thread

March 31 - 1 fine Imported Hatt, 1 ½ yds Silk ferling

April 6 - To Thomas Tiffin for Tayloring

May 23 - 1 Glass tumbler, 1 gr. Paper

June 27 - 1 pr. Pankeenr, 3 ½ yds. Cotton Cassemere, 1 ½ yd Country Cloth, 2 hanks silk Twist, 2 Hks Col'd thread, 11 hone moulds, 11 Plated Buttons

July 6 - 6 ¼ yds cotton cassmere, 2 Hks silk, 1 Stick twist, 3 hks thread, 3/4 yd Home Spun, 1 pr mens shoes, 1 pr cotton stockings

July 30 - 1 pr mens Shoes, 1 pr Cotton Stockings, Robert Payne for Teaching P. Wilson from Sept 9th Till June 23 1807

Septr 6 - 3 ½ yds. Linnen, 3 Hks thread, ½ doz Shirt Buttons, Upper & Sole Leather for menn Shoes

Septr. 20 - 1 pr. Cotton Stockings
Oct 6 - 7 yd Cotton Cloth, 1 oz N. Thread, 1 ½ Doz Shirt Buttons, 3 ½ yds linen, 3 Hks N thread, 1 pr. Half Soles, ¼ yd cambrick

Dec 2 - 1 ½ yd Coating, 2 5/8 yds Horne spun, 1 Doz Buttons, 8 Ditto, 10 oz. Gold thread, 1 pr. suspenders, ¾ yds Cotton Patton Cord, 9 Quill Buttons, 2 Hks Silk, 1 pr. Stockings

1808
Janury 2 - 1 Knife, To bring of Peter Wilson's Negros on day of hiring pair Thomas Casey Jr

Feby 6 - To Thomas Tiffin for Tayloring acct.

Feby 20 - 1 pr. mens Shoes, 1 doz Buttons

Mar 4 - 1 Knife

Mar 5 – 3/4 yds Horne Spun, 17. Buttons, 3 Hks silk, 1 oz Gold thread, 1 Handkf, To Jno. & Nath. Wilson for March 27, 3 ½ yds. Fancicord, 1 oz. Gold thread

May 11 - 1 Danville Hatt, ¾ yds Velvett Ribbon
6 yds. Oznas, 1 Truck, 1 pr. Sleave buttons, 7 ¼ yds Callico for Sister, 1 Toille Shell Comb

June 1 - 1 ½ doz Buttons, ¾ yds. cotton Cassmere, 11 large Buttons, Silk & twist

June 25 - , 1 pr mens shoes, 1 pr cotton Stockings, 1 knife

August 6 - 1 ¾ yds Blk. Florentine, 1 Hk Silk, 16 Buttons, 1 ¼ yds. Linnen, 1 pr suspenders

August 12 Lent

Nov 21 - 2 yds Blue Bro. Cloth, 4 Hks. Silk, 1 Stick Twist, 2 ½ yds. Country Cloth, 2 ¾ yds Blue Cassmere,, 11 Guilt Buttons, 1 pr. Shoes, 1 Tip'o Bridle, 1 pr. Lambs Wool Stockings, 1 pr. Ladys open block'd Stockings

Nov 25 - 3 ½ yds Drable Cloth, 1 Doz. Large Buttons, 3/8 yds fancied Cord, 2 Hks Silk, 1 Slk Twist, 1 yd. Bro Holland, 1 oz. Col'd thread, 1 ½ yds Col'd home spun, ¾ yds. Blue plains, 2 ¼ yds lead flannel, 1 pocket Knife, 7 yds Home Spun, ½ Doz shirt Buttons

Dec 10 - 1 Danville Hatt, 1 Hatt Bans, 1 Dutch Blankett

Dec 20 - 1 yd Cambrick, 1 printed Handf. , 1 Hk Silk, 2 yds drab cloth, ¾ yds Home spun, 1 Black Bell

Feb 11- Clk. Pittsylva. For tickets

May 29 - 2 ¾ yds Country Cloth, 3 yds orgas., 1 Side Upper leather, 12 lb Sole, 1 pr Leather Slippers, 2 pr. cotton Stockings

June 16 - 7 yd. Linnen, ½ yds thread cambrick, ½ oz N thread, 4 Shirt Buttons

Augst 25 - 1 shott gun., 4 lb shott, 1 shag box, 1 lb powder, 1 pr nankeen, 1 pr. Suspenders, ½ doz gun Flints, 1 ¼ yds callico, 1 doble Blade Knife, Shoeing 1 Horse round

Sept 10 - 1 pr. mens shoes, 6 yds Callico

Octr 4 - 2 lbs Shott, 1 Blacking ball, 1 phial Essence of Peppermint

Octr 20- Cash

Nov 22 - 3 ½ yds Blk. Velett, 2 Hks Silk, 1 Doz Guilt Buttons, 2 Hks Col'd thread, 1 Doz mettle Buttons, 1 ¾ yds County Cloth, 1 Girth , 1 Hk Silk, ¾ oz. Bennetts Cord, 5 yds Callico, 1 pt. Brandy, 1 yd Country Cloth, 6 ¾ lb Sole Leather, 1 silk Shawl, paid John Dabney's Fees agt Ware & Williams

Dec 12 - 3 yds Country Cloth, 1 oz N thread, 100 6oz. nails

1810

Jany 1- 100 10dy nails, 1 Ink Stand, 1 pt. Brandy, John Worsham for Boarding Peter Wilson, Thomas Tiffin for Tayloring, 1 Bed & furniture, Bond on Nicholas Perkins & others

1808
Ditto on Conner & Thompson for the hire of Negro girl Lucy

1809
Ditto on Ditto for Ditto

1807
To bond on Obediah Owen & Geo. Adams for the hire of Negro Girl Lucy

1805
Bond on Churchel Brim & Wm Ware, John Dabney's Recipt for Bonds Pd in Suit agt Perminias Williams & Thomas Wortham & also William Ware & Geo Adams Amounting to £75.3.3, To account aloud by Commissioner for my services as gua'd for you £15
By amot Due you from me as yr Guardian pd acct. herewith filed £265.7.11 ½

DR By Bal. due the Guardian £78.9.3

In obedience to this order we have stated, Settled & ajusted the acct. Current of John Wilson with Peter Wilson orphan of Peter Wilson, Dec'd for whom he was Guardian & find a balance in favor of the Guardian of £70.6.3
Per acct. here with returned January 6th 1810
Wm Yancey, James D Patton, David Rice
Recorded: January 15, 1810

**AC Book 4, Page 289**                                    **Peter Wilson's acct of Guardianship**

John Wilson, Guardian, To Peter Wilson Jr.          DR

1806 - Cash Geo. Adams, Pole on Churchill Brim & William Ware

1807- Jany 1- To the Hire of a Negro Dick for 1 Year
To hire of a Negro Boy Rob to Anderson Tucker for 1 year
To hire of Negro Girl Lucy to Henry Perkins for 1 year

1808 - Jany 1 To the hire of Negro man Dick to William Linn, Hire of a Negro Boy Rob to Perminius Williams, hire of a Negro Girl Lucy to Obediah Owen

1809 - Jany 1 To the Hire a Negro Dick to Thomas Ragsdale, Hire Negro Boy Rob to William Murphy, Hire Negro Girl Lucy to John Conner, 1 feather bed & furniture
Total: £265.7.11 1/2
Recorded January 15, 1810


**AC Book 4, Page 290**                                              **Flemming Mays's Inventory**

February 9, 1810  An Inventory & appraisment of the Estate of Flemnen Mays, Dec'd

One Bed & furniture, One Do Do, One Table, One do, One Chest, one Cotton Wheel, Three Chairs, parcel pewter, Knives, Forks & Two tins, one wire Sifter, One Mans Saddle, one Raw hide, One Dutch oven, 1 hook, one hive of Bees, One plow & Geer, Two axes, Three hoes, One Loom, one Flax wheel, Two poles, one pot, Nine gees, one Horse, Two cows, one Hhd, A parcel of Tobo., one Stack of Blades, Stack tops, one Stack Oats
Total: £36.3.0

We do Certify that the above iks a true Inventory of the Estate of Flemmen Mays that was exhibited to us by the administrators & also the Value there of to the best of our Judgment.  Given under our hands the date above Written.
Henry Gosney, James G Keatts, Richard Keatts
Recorded:  February 19, 1810

**AC Book 4, Page 291**                                                        **M. Tanner's Inventory**

In obedience to an order of the worshipful Court of Pittsylvania County to us directed, we have this 2$^{nd}$ Day of January 1800 Conveaned at the late Dwelling house of Mathew Tanner, Dec'd and being first sworn, hath proceeded from time to time to Inventory and appraise all the personal Estate of the said Deceased that was brought before us by Creed Tanner, Executor which is as follows:

Negro Men:  Mingo, Abram, Peter, Robin, Ben
Negro Women:  Laney, Jude Viry
Negro Children, Zoe, Amy, Jancy, Tom

horses: 1 Sorrel Mare, 1 Do Do, 1 Do do, 1 Bay Mare Colt, 1 Mare Colt
Cattle: 1 yoak & Stears, 1 Cart, 1 Black pied Cow, 1white face red Cow, 1 Brown no horne Cow, 1 Brown pied Cow, 1 Red pied heifer, 1 White Speckled heifer, 1 Bull, 1 Brown heifer, 1 red heifter, 2 white face red heifers, 1 Speckled heifer, 1 Stear, 1 White face red Cow, 3 Calves, 1 Cow & calf & Bell, 12 sheep

Crop of Tobacco, Blade fodder, Top fodder, Shucks, Oats & straw, 3 hogheads, Crop of Corn, Corn box & Tub & tallens?, Grind stone, Sault Poark, Irish Potatoes, Sithe & Cradle, Plantation tools & gears, Cooper Tools & hand saw, Old Cutting knife & box, 2 wedges, 3 plow Stocks & lumber, 20 head of Hogs,

1 Copper Still, 1 hone & moner Scales, 1 Cross Cut Saw, 4 ovens & 2 Skillets, 2 pots & hooks, 2 flat Irons
& ladle & old Irons, 2 Cotton wheels, 4 pr. Cards, 2 linnin wheels, 1 loam & gears, 1 pr. Brass Scales,
1 Spice Morter, 1 pr. Cards, 2 Candlesticks & fleuns, 2 brushes & steel, 10 Baskets
Sheep Shares, 2 pr. sissers & cask Cock, 1 pine Table, 5 ½ Bushels wheat, 6 old Barrels & flower tub,
parcel Leather, parcel spun Toe, well Chane, 20 lbs flax, Bridle, LuseToe, Cotton, 1 Bridle, 4 cuphoks,
2 augors & other old Irons, stillards, 1 pan & Grid Iron, 1 Reel & 3 old Locks, Box & Sugar, 2 mugs & 2
pictures, 2 Boles, 1 tea pot & Dish, 4 Plates, 1 Cham. Pot, Cups & Causers, 1 Suger Dish, 1 Teapot, milk
pot, salt seller, 1 Caster & 1Decanter, 1 Drinking Glass, 6 Table spoons, 9 tea Do, 2 Black bottles, 3 Vials,
3 Butter pots & Butter, 1 Case of Bottles, 1 Cubbard, 1 Table, 1 Trunk, 5 old books, 14 Chars
6 Basons, 5 old spoons, Knives & forks, parcel tin, Old Cubbard, Wooding ware, 2 Chests, Box Taller &
bees wax, 1 Looking Glass, 1 Bed & sted, 1 cord & Furniture, 1 Bed do, 1 Bed do, 1 Bed do, 2 Chetes &
Countipin bed quilt,& 2 Table Cloths, 1 Table Cloth, 2 Towels, 1 pillow Case, 1 Paper Box, 1 Jug, 1 Gun,
1 pr. fire Dogs, 1 Coffee Mill, 1 Froe & 1 Caphack, 1 Grubing hoe & other old Tools, 1 Clevis, 1 pin &
ring, 18l bs Iron, 2 ½ lbs Steel, Old Jointer Iron, 1 Sithe blade
Thomas Tanner, Silveing Gardner, Samuel Walker
Recorded March 19, 1810

**AC Book 4, Page 295**                                                                                  **Fearn's ano. Current**

The Estate of Thomas Fearn, Dec'd In account with Js. D. Patton, Exeor.

1805 Decemb. 14 To postage 3 letters Lexington, Va., Cash advanced Thomas

1806- Jany To do do do
Jany 10 mTo do do Mitchel
Jany 13$^{th}$ To do for Paper, To Expenses Caswell C. House

Feb. 28 To ½ qeuire of Paper Miss Polly, To do do Estate

March 14 To Cash paid James Baxter

April 19 To Do paid Nat. Wilson
April 25 To do pd Silas Histen

May 17 to do for Paper
May 20 To do advance Thos. , Lex.Virginia

June To do do do do do, To do do Wm Beavers

Aug 14 To Cash paid Nathaniel Wilson
Aug 21$^{st}$ to Do Do William Clark
Aug 27$^{th}$ to do do Jno. Noble

Septr To do do Selby Benson

Octr To do do Wm Yancy, Jo. Cowan, To Black Jims Ferrage, To Cash paid Curri Barnett
Oct 14 To do advanced Thomas

Novr. To Do Do Heston for Miss Polly
Novr 20 To Do pd Clerk of Henry

Dec 13 To Do pd Js. Ferguson

1807
Jany 6 To cash paid Philip Cox Sen
Jany 13- To do Do Thomas Harrison, To Do Do Wm Clark

Fby 21 To Cash for the Sheriff for 1804, To do paid Js Ferguson, To do do do
Fby 23 To do do do Dix

March 18 To do do John Dabney
March 23 To do do Anthony D Haden, To do do Thos. Sutherlin

April 15 To do do  Jo Arnett
April 16  To do do Jno  Pat. Wilson
April 17 To do do Richard Goin
April 22 To do do Benj  Ratliff

July 18 To do do Ignatious Tennison, , Mr. Ast, postage as to letter
July 29 To do do Sheriff of Caswell

Sept 15$^{th}$ To do Jo. Payne

Oct 2  To Hammon & Dan'l

Nov 9$^{th}$ To do do Jas Burton

1808 To Do Woodson

1808  Aug 7 to do Mrs. Payne Exp.  J. C. H.?

Dec 10$^{th}$ To do Clerks Tickets, for Tax 1807,
To Balance on myBooks Dec 28 To Cash paid Wm C Payne
So much allowed James D Patton for paying& adjusting the foregoing Charge.

1809 Feby 10 To Cash pd H. Spilter Tuition Ro. & Geo.
To Cash pd Mrs. Gregory  do Polly Fearn

March 28- To cash paid Wm Caldwill Ro.
To Leop'd Mo Payne Bal of acct

May 4 th To Cash paid Mr. O'Kilby

Aug 15 To Cash pd Mr. Dodson, Tax Ticketts & orders
To cash pd John White Comm.

 June  20$^{th}$ To cash pd Mrs. Paynes Expences C.H.

July 28 To cash pd John Burnett
July 31 to cash pad Mrs. Paul

1807     Omitted
To Cash pd Ro Payne Tuition Ro. & Geo.

1809     To cash paid Ro Payne  do  do

August - To cash pd Pleasant Tucker  do  do  do
This amt. was applied to the credit of Ferne's acct.
To Cash pd Colquhoun for Fearn's Note
To amount of Crop Tobacco paid Colquhoun & Co after taking out ¼ for the overseer with which I am charg'd on the amt of.

To the overseers pd 1807
To the Interest 2y & 6 months on £36.18

1809 August 24th To Cash paid William Leigh E & I vs. Brown

1810 March 12 To James L Patton for his Services from Feby 16th 1809 to this day ( allowed by the commissioner)]To balance due on former Settlement
To Balance due the Estate

1805 - December  By cash of Dan'l Coleman
By do of Go. Damson

1806  Jany By Do of Isaac Hill
Jany 13 By Do of Daniel Price

Feb By do of Thomas Stewart
Feb 28- By Do of Jerry Hudson

March 14th By do of Jno. & Wm Travis

April 3 By Do of Wm Dix
April 12 By Do of Wm Gossage
April 19 By  Lewis Cox Do
April 28 by Do of Doctor Dabney

May 13 By do of Thomas Dix Jr
May 15 By do of Go. Leabrvson?
May 27th By  do of John Worsham
May 30th  By do of  Do Do

June 23rd By Do of Creed Taylor

July 4th By do of Jas. Gitton
By do of Andre Harrison Ex of Thos. Harrison, Dec'd
By cash of H Doss for Reg. Atkinson
By do of  Daniel Gossage

Augst 16th By Do of Tim Adams
Oct 3rd By Do of Heston for L Jordan
Feb 24th By do of Daniel Gossage
By D of Thos. Swann

Novm. 8th By Do of Thos. Baxter
Novm. 13th By do of John Winters

1807
January 6th By do of Philip Cox jun
January 13th By do of S/L Palmer
By do of  Dudley Gatewood

1807 January 13th By Cash of Sam'l Jorden
Feby 2nd By do of Larkin Dix
Feby 6th By do of Wm Chilton
Feby 9 By do of George Lumpkins
Feby 16th By do of Joel  McDonnald

By do of Elijah Sims
Feby 20th By do of John Payne though the hands of Gunn & Burton
By cash of Wm Ware  H C
Feby 25th By do of Joel McDonnald
By do of Ferd.Rowland

March 8th By do of Maj. Price
March 24th By do of Wm Wear H.C.

April 4th By do of John Lumpkins
By do of Go B Dawson

May 12th By do of Mrs. Ann Thompson

Septe. 26th By do   do do do

Novr. 9th By do of Jas Burton for Wm Burt
Novr. 21th By do of Hall Dixon

Decm. 17th By do of Alex. Lee

1808
Jany 20th By do of Edward Lewis

Feby 1 By do of   do do

April 30 By do of Joshua Jeffers

June 24 By do of Wm Richardson

Oct   By do of Sherward Goin

Novr. By do of Edward Bursey, By do of Severn Busey

1809
January  By Cash of Wm Linn, By Balance due Jas. D Patton, The Exor.

August 15th By Cash of Mrs. Dix By Mr Dodson, By cash of Mrs Wynn   do, By Cash of Mrs Dodson for old mill House, By amt. Due from Colquhoun &Co

1810
March 8th By Cash of old William Whit
In obedience to this order we have Settled the acco. Currant of the estate of Thomas Fearn, Dec'd  with the Executors of the said estate  and find a balance due to the estate of $191.13 which will appear from the foregoing Charges here with returned.  Given under our hands this 12 Day of March 1810.
Wm Yancy, Hezh. Puryear, Tho. Barnett
Recorded: March 19,  1810

**AC Book 4, Page 300**                                                                                                **Bleakley's acco. Currt.**
James Bleakley & Robert Devin, Executors of James Bleakley, Dec'd in Current with the Legatees of the aforesaid Bleakley, Dec'd.

To the total amount of the Sale, Debts due,  The Estate and Interest collected by them over paid which the Legatees is to refund back to the Executors.
James Blakely & Robert Devin

By Sundry accounts Receipt &c which do appear to be Established.
Due Lucy Morton £7.15.5
Due George Ward's Heirs £6.13.11

In obedience to an order of the worshipful Court of Pittsylvania County, we whose names are under Written have proceeded to examine & Settle the account Currant between the Legatees of James Blakely, dec'd & the the Executors of said Blakely, Dec'd and after having examined their Vouchers, do find that the executors to have over paid the Legatees the sum of Twenty two pounds and nine pence. After paying Lucy Morton £7.15.5 and the Heirs of George Ward £6.13.4 it appearing We have not yet paid thein Legaseys, Given under our hands this 19 Day of March 1810.
Jas. Hart, John Carter, Sam'l Callund
Recorded: May 19, 1810

**AC Book 4, Pagae 301**                                                      **Thoms Gdn. Acct.**
Nath'l P Thomas To Asa Thomas, Guardian

1807
Octr 1 To Balance due this pr. acct. rendered to Court
Novr 16 Pd John Hubbard as per. Rect.
Novr. 7 1 pr. Shoes
Dec 24 Tho. Gatewood & Co as per Rect., To Tos Do. Bouldin

1808
Jany 18 James Nelson for tuition
Feby 11 Thos. Bouldin as per Recpt.
Feby 27 To William Hudson for mending a pr. shoes

Apr 4 John Epperson acct. rendered as per Rect.

June 13 To David Bradford for a wool hat
William Hudson for mainga. Pr. Shoes
Anne Gillispee per one half of her Charge for Bringing Amy to Bed in July 1806
To William Eddings as per Rect.

Octr 1 Board from 1st Day of Oct. 1807, To Int. on £10.2.1 ½ for a balance due last year, To Services rendered last year

Decr. 10 To 1 pr. Coarse Shoes

1809
June 20 To pd. Jas.Stewart for a fur seal
Sept 30 to Thos Bouldins a/c as per Rect., Shiff. of Pittsva. One half of Clks. Tickets
Octr 1 Board from 1st Octr. 1808 to this day , Interest on £17.4.6 for 1 year, Services Rendered last year

CR

1807
Dec 24th By half the hire of Patience this year, Do amt. Of land to Roger Warf?

1808
Feb 11 Do amt. of Land to John Akin 1807

July 16 Do Hire of Abram last year
Interest     "     "          10/10

1809
By half the hire of Abraham for 1808 Including Interest

Apr 1  Cash Rec'd of Jesse Harper for half of the amt of Land last year, Half the hire of Amy & Children to John Holland for 1808

Octr 1  Do Patience and her Two Children to John Epperson for 1808, Do Amy to Calab Dodson for 1808 Interest 5/11
Balance due
In obedience to an order of the worshipful Court of Pittsylvania we have Examined the above acct. of Asa Thomas, Guaradian of Nath'l P. Thomas and find the above Balance of Twenty Pound Eleven Shillings. ½ Due him.  This 3rd Day of March 1810
Wm Stamps, Bazaleel Wier, Thos. Wilkinson
Recorded May 21, 1810

William Thomas To Asa Thomas Guardian DR

1807
Oct 1 To Balance due per a/c Rendered to Court
Novr 16 Pd John Hubbard as per Rect.
Novr. 28 1 pr. Shoes

Decr. 24  Pd Thomas Gatewood & Co per Rect.

1808
Do Thos. Bouldin

Jany 18 Jas Nelson for 1 years tuition

Feby 11 Thos. Bouldin as per Recipt
Feby 27 1 Spelling Book, bot of a Peddlers

Apr 5 John Epperson A/C. rendered as per Rect.

June 12 David Bradford for making a wool hat, William Hudson for making a pr. Shoes, Ann Gillispee one half of her Charge for Bringing Amy  to Bed, William Eddings as per Rect.

Oct 1
Board from 1st Day of Oct. 1807, Interest on £9.11.7 ½ balance due last year, Services rendered last year

Decr. 10 1 pr. Coarse Shoes

1809 Mar 27 1 pocket knife bought of Achilles Whitlock
June 20 Jas Stewart for a fur hat, pd Henry Mahon for a pr. Shoes as per Rect.
Sept 30 Thomas Bouldin per a/c & Rect., Shff of Pittsy for ½ -see file of Tickets

Octr 1 Board from 1st Oct 1806 to this day, Interest on £17.4.8 ½ for 1 year, Services Rendered last year

CR

1807
Dec 24 By half the hire of Patience this year
To do for Rent of Lnd to Roger Warf

1808

Feb 11 Do Do of Rent of Land to John Akin 1807

July 16 Do for Hire of Abram Last year Including Int. 10/0

Oct 1 Balance due

1809
By half the hire of Abram for 1808 & Interest

Apr 1 Cash Rec'd of Jesse Harper for half of the REnt of Land Last year
Half the hire of Amy & Children to John Holland 1806, Int.
Half the hire of Patience & her two children to John Epperson 1808
Do Patience and her two Children to John Epperson for 1808
Do for Amy to Caleb Dodson for 1808
Balance due

In obedience to an order of the worshipful court of Pittsylvania we have Examined the above account of Asa Thomas Guardian of William Thomas and find the above Balance of Twenty two Pounds Thirteen Shillings his Due 3rd Day of March 1810
Wm Stamps, Thos Wilkinson, Bazalul Wier Sen,
Recorded: May 22, 1810

## AC Book 4, page 304                                    Rich'd Bayne Act Current

DR The Estate of Richard Bayne Dec'd To Dan'l Coleman & Sto. Turner, admr. with the will annupt of Said Bayne.

1800
May 27 To Cash paid Samuel & David Pannill
June 30 Cash paid James Bruce per rect filed on the office of Halifax Court, Cash paid David Logan
July 22 Cash paid John Hagood, Cash paid John Carte a printer for advertisment
Aug 13 Cash paid Joshua Stone Esq.

1801
Jany 31 Cash paid Joseph Terry proved acct
Feby 17 Cash paid The Clerk Halifax
Apl 23 Cash paid Wm McCraw, Collector of the direct Tax
Augst Cash paid Wm M Watkins fee ads. Bruce

1802
June 22 Cash paid Nath'l H Claiborne for drawing Deed for Land conveyed to David Logan
Augst 23 Cash paid Samuel & David Pannill for Errer in the other Settlement

Paid James Lynn the amount of his Judj, Cash paid the Clerk Halifax , Cash from John Dabney fee ads Linn, Paid the clerk Pittsylvania fee ads Linn  , Paid Henry Barksdale proved acct., Allowance made D. B.Coleman and Ste. Turner admrs. for their personal Services

CR
1800
May 15th By sale of 344 ac. of Land in Halifax to D. Logan

1802
Jany 1 Cash rec'd of James Bruce, Cost of a Suit

1803

By sale of 400 acres ol Land in Pittsylvania to S. Turner, Brought forward, Amount of Debt
Balance due the Estate

Pittsylvania County To wit. By Virtue of an order of Pittsylvania Jany. Court 1801 We James M Williams, Answorth Harrison, Joshua Stone three of the Commissioners named in the said order above, Settled and adjusted the account of Daniel Coleman & Stokely Turner, admrs. with the will annex'd of Rich'd Bayne, Dec'd and find a Balance due from the admrs. Of £14.4.2 ½ in favor of the said Estate. Given under our hands the tenth day of June 1807.
J Williams, Answorth Harrison, Joshua Stone

At a quarterly Court Court held for Pittsylvania County the 20$^{th}$ day of August 1807 This Account Current of the Estate of Richard Bayne, Dec'd with Daniel Coleman & Stokely Turner his administraters was returned and James Yancy by his attorney filed Exception to the said account Current which are continued for argument And at another Court held for the said County the 22$^{th}$ Day of May 1810 the said James Yancy Withdrew his Exceptions and was ordered by the Courtt that the Said Accoount Current be Recorded.

**AC Book 4, Page 305**                                **Inventory & appraisement of Thos. F Bennett's Est.**

Inventory of the Personal estate of Thomas F? Bennett and administered by Eliza Bennett late adm'd, Dec'd Taken 22$^{nd}$ Jany. 1810 and apprais'd According to Law.

1 Negro Woman Chloe, a Do Do Vilett & child Jesse, 1 do do Dols, 1 Do do Man Harry, 1 Black Mare, 1 Do Horse, 1 Gray Horse, 1 Bay Mare, 8 Cows, 1 Red Calf, 9 Earlings, 22 Hogs, 9 Sheep, 1 Feather Bed & Furniture, Cord & bedstead, 1 do do, 1 do do, 1 do do, 1 do do, 215 lbs Seed Cotton, 3 pewter Dishes, 14 do plates, 2 pewter Basons, 2 tin Bucketts, 1 Coffee Pott, 2 tin pans, 3 Cups, 1 Iron tea Kettle, 1 Copper Spice morter & pestle, Sundry Earthen Glass ware, 2 pewter spoons, 9 Knives & 11 forks, 4 pots, 2 Dutch ovens, 4 pr. Hooks, hanger & flesh fork, 6 lb Feathers, 3 lbs Wool, Sundry Pieces of sole Leather, 1 Womans saddle, 4 Chests & 1 powdering Tub, 23 lb hoggs lard & Tub, Bees wax & Taller, 1 Walnut Chest & Table, 1 pr. Money Scales & Weights, 1 Small Trunk, 1 Sugar Box, 1 Stone pitcher & do Jug 3 Black Bottles, 1 Glass tickles, 5 Jugs & 2 pitchers, 1 Double Bolted pad lock, Six phials & 1 looking glass, 1 pr tin Candle molds, 1 pr flat irons, 1 flax hacker, 1 large Jug, Blades & Tops, 2 Stacks of Oats, Corn supposed to be 30 Barrells, 5 barrels Short Corn Supposed, 16 Bushels Wheat Suppos'd, 13 geese, 1 pr Steelyards, 3 Colters , 2 plow hoes, 1 pr. Iron Wedges, 2 pr. Iron Traces & hames, 1 pr. Rope Traces & hames, 7 pole axes, 1 frow, 1 grubbing hoe, 2 Singletrees, 2 Clevises pins & Lap rings, 1 Grind Stone, 5 Hilling hoes, 4 Casks, 3 powdering Tubs, pickle pork Sup'd to be 1000 lbs., 1 flax Brake, 2 Cotton wheels, 1 Tub, 1 pole & 3 piggins, 3 Stands of Bees, 1 Loom, 1 Flax wheel, 1 Do do, 1 Draw knife, 1 hand Saw, 2 augers, 5 Chairs, 2 Slays, 1 pr. Harness, 1 Shott Gun, 1 Walnut Table, 2 Table Clothes
Total: £460.19.10

The foregoing appraisment contains a true & perfect Inventory of the Estate of Thomas F Bennett, deceased which has come to our hands as his administrators.
James Bennett, Bartlet Bennett
Recorded: May 21, 1810

**AC Book 4, Page 308**                                                    **Inventroy of Richie Pitts**

An Inventory & appraisment of the Estate of Richie Pitts, Dec'd taken this 23$^{rd}$ Day of April 1810

Negroes: James, Lewis, Salley, Silvey, Mary
Horses: 1 Gray Mare, one Gray filley, One young Bay Mare, one Bay Mare
One yoke of Steers, fifteen head Cattle, Twenty seven Head hogs, Eight Sheep, One Waggon, one ox cart, One grind Stone, three Axes, Six hilling hoes, one spade, two mattox, Five Coulters, three Dutch plow hoes, Two Swingletrees & clevises, two Sets Gier, One feather Bed, a parcel tools, gun, One barrel Cotton, one Cupboard, Three Beadsteads, 1 Cord, one Flax Wheel, Coffey mill, flat iron, Barrell flax

One chest, 1 Table, two sythes & Cradles, One Cuting knife, one slate, 1 Roul, One Sythe Blade & two Wedges, three Chairs, One cotton wheel, two Basons, one Dish, Coffey pot, One Saddle, reap hook, one

Churn & Water paddle, Three casks, foooour butter pots, four Jugs, One dimmey John, one Jointer, Three pots, one oven, one Skillet, Bread hoe, A Parcel Corn, parcel small Grain, Two Basons, one Dish, four plates, Candle mole, Two Bells. One Bason & one plate, One womans Saddle, 10 Cups & Saucers, Bottle, One shot gun, one Clock Reel, Three Slays, one flax wheel, Cotton wheel, Two feather Beds & furniture, Steads & Cords, One Chest, Two do, one feather Bed, Wheat Sive, one Small Trunk, One flat Iron, four Books, two axes, One looking glass, parcel Cotton & Wool, Parcel salt, two pr. hames, loom
Total   £585.9.10

In obedience to an order of the worshipful Court of Pittsylvania to us directed bearing date March Court 1810. We have proceeded to Value the personal Estate of Richie Pitts Dec'd that was exhibited to us by the admin. To what we believe the Value thereof to in Current Money to the best of our Judgments & I have made a true Inventory thereof & we do Certify that the above is a true Memorandum of the Same. Given under our hands this Day & Date above Written.
N. Tucker, George West, George Dejurnete
Recorded: May 21, 1810

### AC Book 4, Page 310 — Inventory & appriasement of the est. of Mary Markhum

An Inventory and appraisment of the estate of Mary Markhan, Dec'd Taken this 31$^{st}$ day of October 1819?
1 Bay horse, 1 Studd Colt, , 3 Cows and Calves, 2 Red Steers, 1 Barren Cow, a parcel of old Iron viz: hoes, axes, hoops, Chisels, locks &c. and 1 hand saw amd 1 old pot, 3 unmarked Shoats, 1 press, 4 Chairs & 1 Case, 3 Feather Beds & furniture, 1 Curtain bedsted, 1 Cord, 22 hogs, 10 ditto, 21 geese, 14 Turkeys, 1 Loom, 3 Slays, 1 Cotton Wheel & 2 pair Cards, 2 flax wheels, 1 pitcher, 1 small butter pott, 1 bag of feathers, 2 Tables, 1 Side Saddle, 2 Sides of leather, 1 bybe? Tar & 1 pistol, a parcel of lumber, a parcel of earthen Ware & 1 Coffee pott, a parcel of Pewter & knives & forks, 1 Bible, 1 tea kettle, hoe and Trivet &c 1 pail & tubb, 1 Tray, 1 paiaar fire Irons & 1 Candle Stick, 1 pair of hames, Traces & Collar, 1 Dutch oven, 1 pott & pott hooks, 1 flax brake, 1 looking glass, 1 Negro Woman Named Milley & her child, 1 powdering Tub & 1 Raw hide, a parcel of unbrake flax, 4 Stacks of blade fodder &1 of Tops, 1 sack bag &1 barrel, 6 ½ barrels of Corn
Total: £218.3.4 1/2

Pursuant to an order of Court bearing date October Court 1809 We the Subscribers being first Sworn have appraised the estate of Mary Markham, Dec'd as above expressed.
Jos. E Haley, Thos Anderson, Allen Womack
Recorded: April 16, 1810

### AC Book 4, Page 312 — Inventory of Charles Yates, Dec'd

An Inventory and appraisment of the Estate of Elijah Yates, Dec'd Viz:
1 White Cow & Calf, 1 Shott gunn, 1 Bed & bed quilt, 1 Pewter Bason, 1 Pewter dish, 3 plates, 1 Silver Watch, 1 Inch augur, 1 Frying pan, 1 Curl Bridle, 1 Snaffle ditto, 1 pr. money Scales, a parcel of Flax, 3 Chains, 1 Walnut Chest, 1 Big Swingletree & 1 Small ditto, 1 pided Steer, 1 ditto Heifer, 1 Pied Cow, 1 Black ditto & yearling, 1 Red pided heifer, 1 Sow and 4 Shoats
Total: £22.6.0

Pursuant to an order of the Court of Pittsylvania, we the Subscribers, do certify that we have this day appraised such of the Personal Estate of Elijah Yates, dec'd, as has been shown us by George Yates the administrator, as appears by the above list amounting to twenty two pounds, Six shillings. Given under our hands this 20$^{th}$ day of October 1809.
William Ware, Charles Williams, Thos. Elliott
Recorded: June 18, 1810

### AC Book 4, Page 313 — Thos. Fearns acco. Sales

Feb. 4$^{th}$ 1806
An account of Sales of the Estate of Thos. Fearn Dec'd
Fendal Rowling 1 ax & 1 hatchet
Joel McDannald 2 pole axes

Daniel Chandler 2 pole axrs
William Richardson 2 pole axes
Greenberry Voss 3 plough hoes & 1 grubing hoe
Pressley Carter one set of Black Smiths tools
Thomas Sutherlin 1B. Smiths Vice
Joel McDonnald  Old Irons
Greenberry Voss 2 plough hoes and some old Iron
Joel McDonnald  1 lot of Irons
Thomas Harrison  1 Rifle Barrel
Jno. Pistole  1 Rifle Barrel
Joel McDonnald lot of Irons
Joel McDonnald 1 Do do
Joel McDonnald 1 Do do
Joel McDonald  1 Do do
Joel McDonnald 1 Do do
Peter Smith  2 wedges & 1 froe
Joel McDonnald 3 harrow hoes, 1 froe
Major Price  1 lot of planes
Thos Sutherlin  1 lot of augers & Chissils
Sherwood Goin  1 Grind Stone
Mary Fearn  1 Cutting Box and 5 hoes
Greenberry Voss  2 grubing hoes
Greenberry Voss 2  do
Richard Saunders  1 Waggon
Andu. Harrison Jun 1 old Waggon
Zero Guinn  1 Black horse
Henry Dixon 1 gray mare
William Wear one Bay horse
Joseph Barnett the loan   Mare
John Hudson the old Roan Mares
Thomas Baxter the black Mare
Ignatious Tennison  1 Colt the roan mare
Jim      old Buck
Levin Dowris?  one Bay mare
Sylvanus Stokes one Sorrel Colt
Peter Smith one bay Colt
William Anderson one Dark bay Colt
James Pistole  1 Bay Colt
Richard Goin  1 Sorrel Colt
Charles Payne 1 no horned cow
Epp. Stone  1 Black Cow
Charles   1 pyed Ccow
Ro. Glascock  1 Red cow with spots
Mary Feearn  5 head of horses & 1 colt
Mary Fearn 6 Cows & 6 yearlins
Mary Fearn 1 Lot of Sheep
Mary Fearn 1 Lot of B. Smiths tools & 1800 owt.? of Iron
Mary Fearn 1 Waggon , 1 grind stone
Mary Fearn1 lot of hogs head staves
Mary Fearn 100 Barrels of Corn
Charles Payne 1 No horned cow
Robert Farguson 1 Red cow
Epp. Stone 1 pyed no horned Cow
Dudly Gatewood   6 heifers
Edward Busey 1 Black heifer

Benj. Ratliff 1 pyed Cow
David Michell 1 Lot Hogs, 1 Choice
Daniel S Farley 1 lot do 2  do 4
Daniel S Farley  1 lot do 3  do 4
William Liken 1 lot do 4   do 5
James Gatewood 1 lot of hogs, 5$^{th}$ Choice 5
William Linn 8 Shots 1$^{st}$ Choice
Jas. Gatewood  18 do,  2 do
Jo. Farguson  2 sows, 10 pigs on H. Creek
James Gatewood 1 sow and 5 pigs 1$^{st}$ Choice
William Linn 1 do   1 do 2$^{nd}$ Do
James Gatewood  1  do & do 3$^{rd}$ do
Edw'd Busey 1 do & do 4$^{th}$ do
Jas. Gatewood 1  do  &  do  5$^{th}$ do
Thos. Sutherlin 4 Sheep 1$^{st}$ Choice
Thomas Sutherlin   4 do  2$^{nd}$ Do
Francis Ray  4  do  3$^{rd}$ Choice
Thos. Sutherlin  4  do   4$^{th}$ Choice
William Wilkinson  1 Chair & harness
Geo. B Dawson 1 Dark Cow
Covington Farguson  1 Red heifer
Edward Busey  1 Cow and Yearling
Robert West 1 no horned Cow
Benj. Humfreys  1 Bull
Robert West   1 red heifer
Mathew Terry  1 Pyed Cow
Mathew Terry  1 Red heifer
Pampy     1 Dark heifer
Daniel Worsham 1 no horned heifer
Epp. Stone 10 Barrels of Corn 1 lot
Epp. Stone 10  do   do   2 do
Epp. Stone  10  do   do 3 do
Epp. Stone 10  do   do 4  do
John Baxter 10 do    do   5 do
Epp. Stone 10 barrels of Corn  6$^{th}$ Choice
James Robertson  10 barels of Corn 7$^{th}$ Choice
Epp. Stone  10  do   do 8$^{th}$  Do
Richard Jones  5  do of corn  9$^{th}$  do
Richard Jones  5   do of  do 10$^{th}$ do
Jno. Dix sen  5  do of  do 11$^{th}$   do
Jno. Dix Sen  5  do   of do  12$^{th}$  do
William Ware  1 Still and Worm
William Linn 1 Kettle and old Copper
Joel McDannald  1 old  sates?
Thomas Sutherlin  1 Whip saw
Joel McDannald 1 plough and colter
Merideth Price  1 plough 1 ox
Charles Payne  Hennings Justice
Meridith Price 1 Plough
Thomas Baxter  1  do
Joel McDannald  1 plough
Peter Smith 1 pr traces
Meredith Price 1 Colter and Stock
Joel McDannald  3 hoes
Joel McDannald   2 do

William Wilkinson 1 pr. Chain traces
Jas D Patton Latin and Greek school Books
James D Patton Dictionary of arts and sciences
Currie Barnett 1 Gazeeteer
Jas. D Patton 1 lot 2 Books
Jas D Patton 1 Domestic medicine
Jas D Patton 1 lot of Books
Jas D Patton 1 Lot pamphlets
Mary Fearn 1 Book case & chest Drawers
Mary Fearn Buffet & Furniture
Mary Fearn 2 large looking Glasses
Mary Fearn 2 Tables
Mary Fearn 1 Doz Cheirs
Mary Fearn 4 Bedsteds, Beds and Furniture & 1 Trunk bed
Mary Fearn 1 Still
Mary Fearn ½ Doz split Bottom Chairs
Mary Fearn 1 pr. fire dogs
Mary Fearn 4 Cotton wheels, 2 flax wh., 1 loom with all its apparates
Mary Fearn Sundry Kitchen Furniture pots & ovens &c
Mary Fearn 20 hogs, 30 pigs at the mill
Mary Fearn 2 night glasses
Mary Fearn 2 trunks & chest
Mary Fearn 1 stack of Tops
Mary Fearn 3000 dwt.? oats 1$^{st}$ Choice
Mary Fearn 3000 dwt. Blades 1$^{st}$ Choice
Charles Payne 1000 do oats 2$^{nd}$ choice
Charles Payne 10000 " 3$^{rd}$ do
Samuel Jordan 1000 do do 4$^{th}$ do
Isaac Hill 1000 do do 5$^{th}$ do
Charles Payne 1000 do 6$^{th}$ do
Sam'l Jordan 1000 do do 7$^{th}$ do
Sam'l Jordan 1000 do do 8$^{th}$ do
Isaac Hill 1000 do do 9$^{th}$ do
Charles Payne 1000 dodo 10$^{th}$ do
Charles Payne 2 stacks of Damaged blades
Edw. Busey 1 Stack of Tops
Jo. Furguson 1 Lot tops
Charles Payne 1 Sythe and Cradle
Major Price 1 do and cradle
Lewis Cox 1 do do
Lewis Cox 1 Cutting bar and knife
Philip Cox 1 stone jug
Robert Lorton 1 scene?
James Burton 1 Desk and Book Case
James Burton 1 Rum case
Ludwell Worsham 1 W. Table
William Towns 6 winzer chairs
James Burton 1 square Wal. Table
Jas. Dalton 1 feather bed and bolster
Jas. Burton 1 Fether Bed, 1 Bolster
Jas D Patton 1 Do do Mr. Mitchel
James D Patton 1 Bed and furniture Thomas
Mary Fearn Do do do
James D Patton Do do Do Polly
James D Patton 1 pine Chest Thomas

Sherwood Goin one mans Saddle
Robert Lerton one shot gun
Mary Fearn six painted cheirs
Lewis B. Allen one Canoe
William Towns one Dutch oven and Cap
Jo. Farguson one pot
Daniel Price one Dutch oven
Peter Black one oven and pot
Philip Cox sen one dutch oven
William Anderson one do do
Mary Fearn 1 Kittle
John Worsham 12 bushels of Rye
John Worsham 12 do do
Mary Fearn 6 Be hives
Mary Fearn Pewter &c
William Linn 1 Rum Hogshead
Mary Fearn 1 Cask
Benj. Humphries 1 Cask
Philip Cox Sen 1 Cask
Mary Fearn 10 Casks
Robert Lorton 1 Cuting Knife & adze
Richard Jones 1 doz. Han saw files
Richard Jones 1 do do do
William Dodson 9 files
Mathew Terry 20 files
Jas Burton 1 do do
Philip Cox sen 1 meal sifter
Mary Fearn old files &c
Jas Burton 20 saw plates for Cotton machine
Mary Fearn 1 sythe & Cradle
Mary Fearn 1 do do
Jas D Patton 2 Keggs W. Lid
Epp. Stone 5 Barrels of Corn
Robert Lorton 5 do do
Robert Lorton 6 do do
Robert Lorton 5 Bushels of Wheat
Robert Lorton 5 do do
Daniel S Farley 5 do do
John Dix 5 do do
Daniel S Farley 5 do do
Thos Lumpkins 5 do do
Daniel S Farley 5 do do
L. B. Allen 5 do do
Leanna L? Payne 5 do do
John Dix 5 do do
Daniel S Farley 5 do do
Merideth Price 3 Bushels Wheat
Mary Fearn 4 Raw hides
Mary Fearn 1 Tan Mill
Mary Fearn 1 H. heads & 5 Barrels
Mary Fearn 1 pr. Steelyards
Mary Fearn 1 hand Saw at the mill
Mary Fearn 41 Geese
Mary Fearn 2000 dwt.?oats
Jas Gatewood 1000 dwt.? Oats 4th lot

Thomas Lumpkins 1000 dwt. oats
Robert Lorton 1000 oats
Mary Fearn 3 mens Saddles
Mary Fearn 1 Grid Iron, & flesh fork
Mary Fearn 1 funnel
Mary Fearn 1 Cut saw
Mary Fearn 1 sett shovel and tongs
Mary Fearn 2 spades
Mary Fearn 3 Jugs
Mary Fearn 1 old side saddle
Jas D Patton 1000 dwt. oats
Jas Richardson 2271 do
Jas Colquhoun & Co. for Crop Tobacco after paying The overseer his part
Deduct for so much allowed to Doctor James D Patton for his Trouble &c in collecting the above sums by us.
Total: £ 655.14.3 ¼
Wm Yancey, Hez. Puryear, Wm Beavers
We certify the foregoing to be a true acct. of the sales of the Estate of Thomas Fearn, dec'd. Given under our hands this 12th day of March 1810.
James D Patton Esq., William Dodson
Recorded: June 18, 1810

## AC Book 4, Page 321                                                              G. Sheltons Est.

Account Current of Gabriel Shelton Deceas'd With Armistead Shelton, Admr.
1804
To Cash paid for 1 Mare furnished The Widow , Ditto paid Samuel Pannill Exor. Of D. P. Dec'd, Do   "   ", Jacob Saunders, John Lewis, Vincent Shelton Sheriff for 1802, Crispin Shelton   " for 1803, Will. Tunstall for recording Will &c., Printer at Lynchburg, Ditto for recording power of attorney, Beverly Shelton & Vincent Shelton Exors. of Crispin Shelton, Dec'd

Cash paid E Sydner on account of James Murdock
Bonds assigned to James Taylor for his Wife Jane's Legacy in sd. Decd Estate
Bond assigned Giles Payne for his Wife Catherines Legacy in said Dec'd Estate
Cash paid Wiatt Shelton for his legacy, Do   " for advice of a lawyer, Do   " for Copy of a Will
Beverly Shelton jr for his part of the Crop of Tobacco , Will. Tunstall for recording balance of an Inventory &c., Cash for Cryers Fee, Sundries furnished the Estate- Viz: 9 ½ yds. Aznuburg, 11 ½ yd Negro Cotton, 5 ½ Gallons brandy, 3 yds Plains, 1 ½ yds Negro Cotton, 200 8d nails, 3 pr. Stockings, Carriage 2 hh'ds Tobo. And finding to Lynchburg Warehouse expense &c
Cash paid for making Clothes & shoes for Negroes, To ½ Bushel Salt, Gabriel Shelton for his services rendered, My Services as administrator to the estate of Gabriel Shelton Dec'd, An Error in a bond taken Mgr. Vincent Shelton the dec'd being Security for Case per Mease
Total: £603.10.11 ¼

Centra

1803
Octr 20 By amount of Property Sold and Bonds taken , Interest on Bonds & Cash
Balance due the Administrators
June 9th 1810
Pursuant to an order of the Worshipful Court of Pittsylvania to us directed bearing date May Court 1810 . We have proceeded toexamine the accompts Current of Gabriel Shelton, Dec'd Kept by Armistead Shelton the administrator with the will annexed & find them correct agreeable to our Judgment. Given under our hands this date above Written.
N. Tucker, John Lewis, Thompson Robertson, Henry Kay

Recorded: June 10, 1810

**AC Book 4, Page 323**                                      **William Wilkinson's Inven'y**

In obedience to an order of the Worshipful Court of Pittsylvania County we do appraise the estate of William Wilkinson, Dec'd as follows Viz:

1 Negro man Gill, 1 " Ditto Cupid, 1 " Ditto Isham, 1 " Boy Wright, 1 " Ditto Stephen, 1 " Do Patrick, 1 " Do Abraham, 1 " Womans Milly & Child Charles, 1 " Girl Jeanil, 1 Child Peter, 1 " Do Pheobe, 1 " man Will

1 Chest Drawers, 1 Winsor Chairs, 1 cupboard, 1 folding Table, Sundries in Cupboard, 1 looking Glass, 1 Sugar box, 1 Waiter, 5 pictures with frames, 1 Desk, 17 Books, 1 Tea Tray, 11 Chairs, 1 Ink Stand, 2 Chests, 1 Bed, Bed Steed & furniture, 1 " " Ditto, 1 Flax wheel, 1 Clock Reel, 1 Jug, 1 piece Leather,, Bed Steed & Cord, 1 pr. Steelyards, bed steed and Cord, Gear Harnes Traces & 2 Collars, 1 Saddle, 1 Loom, 3 Cotton Wheels, 1 old gun, 2 sad Irons, 2 pewter basons, 1 spice morter & Saddle, 1 Roaster tribit & flesh fork, 1 oven & lid, 1 knife box &sett knives & forks, 1 Waiter & tin pan, 2 pots and pot hooks, 3 pails & churn, 6 Casks, 1 Chest , 1 Cotton Machine, 1 yoke Steers, 1 Work bull 3 Cows & Calves, 2 year old Bull, 1 Calf, 6 Sheep, &1 lamb, 1 Waggon & lock Chain, 3 Seythes & Cradles, 5 hoes, 1 Colter, 3 plows, 3 hides, 3 axes, 1 spade, 1 harrow, 2 mattox, 1 Bare share, 1 pr. Wedges 1 Clevis & 5 Frisons?, 1 Billows, 1 Lantorn, 1 Gouge & Chissel, 1 Saddle, 1 Cooper adze, 1 anvelle, 2 Cutting knives, 1 Bay mare, 1 Sow, 7 Pigs, 1 saw & 5 pigs, 2 Sows & 11 pigs, 39 geese, parcel Tobo., 1 Hilling hoe, 1 Sow and 9 pigs, 1 boar Shoat, 1 Jug, 1 Grid Iron

W. Beavers, Alex. Brown, Henry Wilson
Recorded: June 18, 1810

**AC Book 4, Page 325**                                      **Tho. Davis's Inventory**

An Inventory of the appraisment of the Estate of Thomas Davis, dec'd appraised by William Dews, Nathaniel Lovelace, William M Mitchell and Thomas Lovelace of the County of Pittsylvania on oath

1 Negro man Toby, 1 Negro man Joseph, 1 Negro Man Federick

1 Bay Mair & Colt, 1 Black Mair, 1 Stock of Cattle, 1 Stock of Hoggs, 1 Cart and Steers, 1 Stock of Sheep, 7 old Casks, 7 old hogsheads, 1 old Chest & Ginn, 1 Cask, 2 parcel old Wooding Lumber, 2 tubbs & 3 Pailes, 1 old table, 2 Potts & hooks & 1 old hoe, 1 Dutch oven, 1 Frying Pann, 1 X Cut Saw, 1 Sythe & Cradle, 6 axes, 4 grubing hoes, 3 coulters, a parcel of old Iron, 2 pair of horse Geer,2 plows, 6 Juggs & 2 Bottles, 1 Cann, 6 Basketts, 1 old Chest, 4 old Chairs, 1 Flat Iron, 1 Pair Pockett Steelyards, 4 Slays, 1 Pair of hinges & Sundrys, 1 Glass, 6 Books, 1 Desk, 1 Bed & furniture, 1 ditto & furniture, 2 wheels, &2 pair of Cards, 2 Seives, 1 hackle, 1 Candle mould, 1 Safe, 1 skillett & 1 Kittle, 1 pint Pott, 1 Jill Pott, a parcel of Pewter, 3 butter Potts, 3 hilling hoes & Sundries, Cash, 1 Hhhg of Tobacco
Total: £437.16.3

We the Subscribers being appointed by the Worshipful Court of Pittsylvania County and sworn according to Law for to appraise the personal estate of Thomas Davis, Dec'd have this day met and appraised the same unto £437.16.3 Current money as above stated. Given under our hands this 14 Day of June 1810
William Dues, Nath'l Lovelace, W C Mitchell, Tho. Lovelace
Pittsylvania
I do hereby that Wm Dues, Nathaniel Lovelace, Wm C Mitchell & Thomas Lovelace was sworn before me a Justice of Peace for the said County to appraise the personal Estate of Thomas Davis dec'd accouring to Law. Given under my hand thie 14 Day of June 1810
Ben. Lankford
Recorded June 12, 1810

**AC Book 4, Page 328**                                      **Stone &c of Morgan a/c Curn't**

The Estate of Haynes Morgan Deceased in acct Current with Joshua Stone, Exor.& Mary Morgan, Executrix

1795 the 16 June Paid Stookley Turner DS for Tax Rect. & parish Levies Clarks ano. Sheriffs Tickets for 1794.
Aug't 7 To paid S & D Pannills for a quart of Whiskey at an arbitration with John Buckley
Sept. 21st To paid Wm McCraw Riding Chear tax
Octr. 17th paid S & D Pannills as per their Rect.
Nov 5th Pd Thos. F Patrick Attorney for William Call
Nov 19 pd John Cox Clerk of Henry as per his rect.

1796
April 7th  Pd S & D Pannills Charles Lewis's  Replevy Bond
April 19 Pd Richard Anderson Wm Jones Sette'd acct.

1795
Aprl 20 Pd Joseph E Hailey per acct.
May 20 Pd Sam'l K/H Jennings as per rect., Mrs. McDaniel for Services, Miss Cloe Faris for her Services, David Pannill per John Pannill and in full for Sam'l & Pannills acct as per Rect., J Stone for Shoemaking, Thomas Anderson for Smiths Work,  Crispin Shelton Exor per bond & Interest, Colo. David Hunt per acct, fee for Writs, Jno. Buckley his award for Cutting his Mill

Nov 5th Pd Thos F Patrick for Field & Call as per Rect, Walter Lamb, John Browns Judgment agt Edward Lewis as per his receipt., Hart Brown & Co as per Rect, William Doss for his acct

1796
Pd Wm Lester for his acct., Tho. B McRoberts for fees, Richard Johnson his acct., Walter Lamb for Gordans order, Wm Phelps for his Clame, John Cox per his acct and Receipt, Walter Lamb per his account

1796
 To Cash paid Charles Lewis per acct.,  Joseph Akin, ditto James Bruce

1797
ditto pd McRoberts, Josiah Griggory, Sam'l & David Pannill for Jno. Cox's attendance as a witness at N. Landon vs Dillard, James Stewart Attorney for advise,  Jno. Dabney attorney for services, Mrs. Farris  for services

June- Paid Christopher Clark a British Debt

1801
 Ditto on the Score as per Receipt, Cash paid John Doss as per acct & Receipt., Doctor White for his acct., Mrs. Jenkins for her service

1798
Paid Benj. Hale for acct & Rect., Mrs. Farris for her sevices, Wm Munford ,ditto McRoberts, James Henderson senr per Bond & Interest, James T/F Johnson for Browns Judgment, Mrs Jenkins for service, Pd for stamp paper, Wm Hunt , ditto F/T Lester for Schooling

1799
 Pd Nicholas Perkins for a bond given P. Perkins, Jessee Dupuy for Betseys Schooling, Benjamin Hamrick for 1800

1800 Pd. Doctor White for services

1801 Pd. Doctor Walker for services, Chumley for the Cost of a warrant

1802 Pd for Betseys Schooling at the Springs., Wm Ward for Betseys Board, John Dabney for Services

1803 Pd Byrd Prewit per his acct.

1804 Pd the Sheriff Wallingtons Execution, John Emmerson for his Claim, Clerk and Sheriffs Tickets, The Sheriff for Taxes from 17795 to 1804, Cash deducted from 3 bonds for Interest in the payment of a British debt to C. Clark

1806 Paid Doctor White for services before the devision of the estate, Joseph Carter Omited in 1798
Credit the Estate of Haynes Morgan, Dec'd

1795
By Cash Received of James Ridgway, G. Hunt, William Clark, Beverly Shelton, Jno. Royal , V Shelton, Arms'd Shelton, William Devin, John White, Edward Nunnilee, Jno. F Patrick, D Hunt, Wm Levin, James Wooden, Jno. F. Patrick, D. Hunt, Wm Devin, James Woodin, T H Wooding

1796
By do of Wm Smith for H Richards, Colo. John Wilson, Luke Kent, Colo.Wm Clark, David Boyd, Colo. Wm Terry, Thomas Devenport, William Brown, David Hunt for Nath'l Hunts Estate at 3 or 4 times

1797
By ditto of Moses Hurt, Cash Rec'd of Robert Mann for the Jno.George Tract of Land in 3 payments
By Cost of the above, Cash of Thomas Hoskins by Judgment, bonds Rec'd of John B Scott & Wm Wms Amt. of John Williams dec'd in part of a debt, Cash Rec'd of James Dejarnett, the Sheriff for Moses Fuquay exor., In full of a Second execution, Received of Isaac Coles, Stookley Turner in full of Joseph Williams, exor., Jona. Dawson for Rent

1798
By Cash Received of Dan'l Shelton, A McCraw D.S. in full of an Execution against Wm Thompson,
By ditto for Mannings Execution, Geo Harston Cost of Dillards Suit

1800 By ditto in full by the hands of Joshua Stone

1803
By Ditto of Jno. B Scott & Will Williams admr of John Williams, dec'd in full of the estate claim agst him

1806
By Cash rec'd of Jno Buckley in part of an execution against him

Credit by Joshua Stone Executor

June 16$^{th}$ 1795 By Stockley Turner for his atto. Claim for Exeficia Services &c

Octo 13$^{rd}$ By cash of Blanks Moody for the old roan horse
Feb 27$^{th}$ 1796 By Ditto for the old Sorrel Mare

Feby 21$^{st}$ By Cash a Balance of McHaneys debt, Chas. Lewis Replevy Bond, Cash rec'd of Obediah Ham, Security of Wm Jones omitted the 7$^{th}$ day May 1795, amount of Cr Brot. forward
Amount of Debt £739.7.5 ½
DO of Credit £721.4.3
In pursuance of an order of the Worshipful Court of Pittsy. County bearing date April Court 1806 we have proceeded to exanine the account current of Haynes Morgan Dec'd with the executor and executrix & find a balance due the Executro & Executrix of Seventeen pounds, Eighteen Shillings, p 2 ½. Given under our hands this 14$^{th}$ day of July 1810.
Phil S/L Grasty, Jon. B Dawson, Nath'l Crenshaw, Wm Smith
Recorded July 16, 1810

**AC Book 4, Page 333**                                                   **H. Cooks Invedntory & appraisment**

In obedience to an order of the Worshipful Court of Pittsylvania to us directed, We whose names are hereunto annexed, being first sworn, do Inventory and appraise the personal Estate of Harmon Cook Dec'd as follows. Viz:

1300 feet Walnut plank & Santling (sic), 290 feet Cherry plank, 1350 Do Oak plank & Santling, 750 do quarter pine plank , 250 do bastard do, 618 Head of Hogs, little and big, 1 old lumbrel Cart, 1 ax Waggon & lock Chain, 1 Iron toothed harrow, 1 Road Waggon & hind geer, 1 Jack Screw, 1 Stone, 1 Yoke young Steers & yoke, 1 Do Bell and Do do, 1 Do do do, 1 Do white do do, 1 Cow and Calf, 1 do & calf, 1 Do Do, 1 Do do, 1 Do & Bell, one red do, 1 Pyded Bull, 1 Cow & bull, 1 Cow,1 Cow & bell, 1 Red Cow, 1 Brindle ox, 1 Do do, 1 Steer & heifer, 1 heifer & steer, 1 do do , 6 head of young Cattle, 3 Mill Stones 2 Stills, Caps and Worrns, 9 Marsh Tubs, 3 Casks, 59 head of Sheep, one small Cask, 1 Tobo. Hhd., 5 flour barrels

1 old Negro Woman Catey, 1 lad do Harry, 1 Negro Man Lewis, 1 do woman Betty, 1 gray Roan Horse, 1 young Bey Horse, 1 Strawberry Roan Horse, 1 Bay Roane do, one Bay Mare, 1 Dark Bay Mare, one Sorrel Do, 1 Sorrel mare Colt, 1 Bellows, anvil, Vice & Tools attached, 1 pr. of Cart Wheels not tired, 1 Iron toothed Harrow, one Walnut Chest, 1 Clock and case, one Walnut Table, 1 Walnut cupboard & its contents, 1 Looking Glass, one pewter Gallon pot, 1 Quart pott, 1flask & Mustard pott, 1 pint pott, 1 quart pott, 1 Spice Morter and Pestle, 8 Tablespoons, three Tea Do, 38 lb. Old Pewter, Candle Moulds and other old tin, 2 tin Coffee pott, one Coffee Mill, 1 pr. Small Steelyards, 10 Knives and 10 forks, 4 dripping pans, 2 Lamps, Sniffers &c, 3 Slays, 3 pr. of Harness, 1 long Table, 1 Trunk, 22 Chairs, 1 Rule Snuffers and Slate, 1 Feather Bed under Bed furniture & Stead, 1 Do do do do , 1 do do do do, 1do furniture & Stead, 1 covering feather bed, 1 Check Reel, 1 flax Wheel, 1 Walnut bed Stead, 2 Shott Guns, 1 Mans Riding Saddle, 2 do, 2 flour Barrels, a parcel bed Clothes, Table Cloths &c, 3 old Books, one Tea Table, 6 flour Barrels, 2 plank Boxes beans, 1 old box, old writing Desk, 2 Keggs, 2 Barrels, 1 candle Stand, a quanity of oil cakes

10 Barrels of Corn, 5 Raw hides, Two sows in the pen, 1 Large Iron kittle, 2 Dutch Ovens & Lids, 1 Small D. Oven, one do & old lid, 1 small pott, 1 Skillet, 1 Tea Kettle, 1 Chopping knife, 1 frying pan & Sawsage knfie, 2 potts, 1 skillet, a parcel Water Vessels, 6 Straw Baskets, one Small pott, a parcel tin ware, 1 flat Iron, 2 Juggs, 1 pitcher & 1 butter Crock, 1 loom, 1 old stove, 1 Cotton Wheel, 1 grind Stone, 1 old pott, 1 old Chest, 2 Crocks & 1 pot, 1 Churn, 1 Tub, 2 tar Bucketts, 1 hogshead, one tub, 10 Casks and a parcel of tubs, 1 Copper Kettle, 1 Demi John & oil, 1 Churn and parcel of old tin ware, 3 leather Collars, 3 pair Hames & Traces, 3 D. plows, 4 Bar Shear, Do Clevises, 3 axes, 10 Shovels & spaids, 8 weeding hoes, 3 pitch forks, 2 Mattocks and 3 grubing hoes, 2 old Cross cut axes & 1 Rake, 2 Stone picks, 1 barskin, 1 Shovel & plow hoe

3 lock Chains, 4 Yearlings, 1 apple mill, 1 Cutting Machine, 1Cutting knife & box, a parcel unbrake flax, 1 Wheat fann, a parcel of brok flax & 1 small Reel, 3 Grass Sythes, blades & 1 Kutting knife, 1 old course Table, 23 Bushels allum Salt, 10 peaces upper Leather, 165 Gallons Whiskey, 7 light Casks, 3 Screw augers, 2 old hand saws, 1 P. knife & adgt., 3 old Saw mill Saws, 4 Iron Candlesticks, one barrel one parcel hemp, 1 Skillet Cutting Knife, frow, 2 leather Collars, 2 pr. Hames & Chains, 1 pr. Saddle bags, 1 Riddle & 1 old Sword, 1 Tounging plain & 1 Jointer, 35 Iron Shovels, 1 barsheer & clevis, 1 Mill Gudgeon, 1 Iron Toothed Rake, 112 lb Wool in the Dirt, 1 Lott of Augers & Chissels, 3 axes, 1 grubbing hoe & 5 bells, 1 Cornice plain & a parcel of old Iron, 8 Reap hooks, 5 brace cocks, 9 Seythe Blades, 5 pr. Cotton Cards, 1 Demi John, 3 plains & Scuffing Knife

Some old tin & 2 brushes, 1 tin of nails, 1 pr. money Scales & weights, a parcel of olde lumber, 2 hoes, 1 chisse, 7 cow chains, 3 Jugs, 2 Gallons oil & butter pot, a parcel new tin pans & funnels, 49 lbs new pewter dishes, basons &c, 2220 lb Bacon, 5 pain window glass, 2 pr. Stirrup leathers, 7 Whip staves, 1 leather apron, 10 yds cotton & Tol? Linen, 20 yds. do , 18 lb Sole leather, 1 pistol, Moulds & powder horn, 1 Sack bag & Cotton, 1 old bag & do, 6 lb spun yarn, Rings for briching, 1 paper box and it contents,

1 pair Scales and Weights, 3 pr Shoes, 3 large tins with all spice & peper, 2 Cannisters, 3 Gimblets, Ginger & paint, 1 Bottle Caster oil, part of a bottle of spr. Turpentine, 1 Case & some bottles, 2 lb Wire, 1 mans Hatt, 1 Dressed buckskin, 2 qt. Tins, one small Jug & bottle, 1 Chest, 250 lb Brown Surar, 6 ½ yds Callico, a parcel Buttons &c, 105 Bushels of Salt, 1 Small Cask &1 Iron Wash bowl, 2 pott Racks, 1 Cabbage Machine, 1 Iron Rule & a parcel Cradle Irons, 4 Trum frame, 1 Dble. Tree, 1 Steel for cutting box, one Sythe blade &c, 1 Carry logg, 1 pr. Fire dogs, 1 hemp brake, 1 work bench & a parcel of pine & walnut plank, a barrel of unbroke hemp & flax, a parcel of Hd'd & Cask Staves, 1 Cotton Machine, 1 pair old hand Irons, 1 Waggon Sheat, 1 side of leather, 75 lb Tobo., 25 lb lard, 1 garden hoe
Total   £1026.9.5
Signed by us
Jas Hurt, Thos. Muse, Alexander Mahan
Recorded   July 16, 1810

**AC Book 4, Page 339**                                                                 **David F Patrick's Acct. Current**
The Estate of David F. Patrick In acct. with Sam'l Pannill Exor.

1809
Septr. 11 To 10 lb Sugar, 1 lb Coffee, 1 lb Chocolate, 1 Sett Knives and forks, 1 Doz. Needles, 1 lb Copperas, 1 Tumbler, 1 Mustard Pott

October 17 9 ½ Quire paper, 1 lb ushell Salt
October 23 Daniel Marshall for 1 Loom per Rect.
October 26 10dy Nails
October 31 Cash paid Doctor T/F. Slaughter per Rect.

Nov 6 3 pocket Hankfs., 5 ½ yards Divinity, 1 Dozen Needles, 1/3 lb Ginger, 1 pair Scissors, 1 Nutmeg, 1 lb pins, 1 Bowl, 4 ½ lb loaf Sugar, 1 Sett China Cups & Saucers, 1 piece N. Cotton, 6 yards Do
Nov 9 3 Bushels Salt, 1 Wire Sifter, 5 ¾ lb Cheese, 2 yards Ribbon
Nov 11 25 lb Sugar, 2 Yards Ribbon
Nov 14 1 Chamber Pott\

Dec 1 Cash paid Mrs Smith for Dying per Rect.
Dec 8 Cash paid Clerk of Campbell ticket in Case of Leverston, Sherif Land tax per Rect.
Dec 9 1 Wheat Sieve, pr. Enock Organ
Dec 18 1 Stock Lock

Novr 30 ½ lb pepper
Novr 23 100 dy Cut Nails, 5 ½ lbs Crawley Steele
Novr 26 Sam'l Nowlin for his Acct per rect.

1810
Jany 1 To 1 Hatt for Negro Baccus, 1 paste Board, Amount your Smiths Account for the year 1809
Jany 6 1 pair Cotton Cards, 1 Bay Mare 4 Years old Last Spring
Jany 13 37 lb Iron
Jany 23 34 lb Sugar, Vial Tallop, 1 Ditto Callomill

Feby 1 Wm Worsham for his part of Tobo. Made in 1809, Ditto for his part of A trial was
Feby 3 70 lbs Seed Cotton, 1 1/2 lb Crawley Steel, 1400 6dy cut nails
Feby 27 33 lb Iron, 1 Barrel S. F. Flower

March 7 800 6dy cut nails
March 26 200 6dy Cut Nails, 100 4dy wrought ditto, 50 20dy wrought ditto, ½ doz. E. Plates, 1 Ticklar, 1 mug, 1 Jug, 2 lb coffee, 2 Gallons Molasses, 1 hatt, 1 lb Chocolate, 1 Thimble, Comb g'd , Ivory Comb

April 11 37 lb Iron

May 1 Ferrage 3 Hhds Tobo., Edward Douglass for halling 3 Hhds. Tobo. To Lynchburg per Rect.
May 25 Cash paid Woodson Johnson for Corn per Rect.

June 4  100 8dy Cut Nails, 200 6dy Cut Ditto, 1 pair Wool Cards, 1 pair Wool Cards, 3 Doz B. molds, Cash, 1 Bunch Wiring, ½ yd Line Muslin, ½ yd Do do, 3 Yards Cambrick, oz Bluing, 1 Gimblet, 1 do 1 Bushel Salt, 4 Pocket Hankfs, 1 ½ yards Ribbon, 3 yards ditto, 1 ½ yards ditto, 20lb Sugar, 38 ½ lbs Seed Cotton, ½ lb G. Salts, 2 quarts whisky
June 6 John Collins Senr for your Crier
June 10 2 Sythes Blades, 2 Gallons Whisky, ¼ lb Alspice, 6 Doz Harrins

Augt 18 ½ quire paper pr. Enoch Organ

Septr 4  Commission on £270.19.10 being amount Received Since Setlement 29th August 1809 at 5 p. Cent Balance due the Estate of David F Patrick

1809
Augst 29 By Balance due per acct Settled & returned by the Commissioners

Oct 31  21 14/60  lb. Broken Wheat

Nov 2 22 34/60  lb  ditto ditto, 23 58/60  ditto ditto
Nov 7 22 34/60 ditto ditto
Nov 8  24 32/64 ditto ditto
Nov 9  23 46/65 ditto ditto
Nov 10 25 24/66 ditto ditto
Nov 11 24 15/60 ditto ditto
Nov 14 26 55/60 ditto ditto
Sam'l Pannill & Co for Balance due at Clack Stones note & Int.

Dec 18 James Pemberton for assumt. on acct. of Robert Alexander's Debt pd Rect. 1st Nov last
Dec 8 Amount rec'd of Robert Alexander In full his Debt Cost & Interest, James Pemberton for Error in Calculation. Int on Execution vs. Robt. Alexander
Dec 30 Amount rec'd of Wm Raine in part of Rent for 1809

1810
Feby 27 Cash rec'd of George Pannill Eor of Wm Pannill for Jere Pannill in part your part of Estate of Said Wm Pannill

April 26 2 Hhds. Lynchburg Tobo.weighing nett 2775 lbs., Deduct turning up

May 4 1 Hhd. Lynchburg Tobo. Weighing  nett 1392 lb., Deduct turning up

July 19  560 lb tobo prised in With Shadrack Barber, Deduct Carriage

Septr 4 Interest on £310.8.3 being former Balance 29th August 1809 till this Day.

By Balaance due as per Contra
Pittsylvania County
Pursuant to an order of the County Court of Pittsylvania to us directed bearing date June Court 1810 We Samuel Stone, William Smith and Joshua Stone Sen three of Commissioners named in the said order have examined and Settled the account of the Estate of David F Patrick, Dec'd with Samuel Pannill, the Exor as Stated above With the Vouchers Showing there is a balance due of four hundred and Thirty two Pounds, twelve Shillings & 14p on the said accat at this time as above stated.
Given under our hands this 4th day of September 1810

Sam'l Stone, Wm Smith, Joshua Stone Sr.
Recorded September 17, 1810

**AC Book 4, Page 343**                S. Pannill's Gdn A/C of D. Pannill's orphans

The heirs of David Pannill In account with Sam'l Pannill Guardian

1809
Septr. 16  To 1 pair Calf Skin Shoes for Elizabeth S/L Pannill

Novr. 1  Amount paid Sheriff of Hallifax per Ticket
Novr. 25  1 Hatt for Negro Dick

Decr. 6  Cash paid Clerks Halifax
Decr. 13 Samuel Pannill & Co for Amount paid James Mitchill per Rect.
Decr. 25 1 Blanket for Negro Dick

1810
Janury 3 Bathena Pannill for Board & Clothing &c per Rect.
Janury 13 1 Blanket furnished Jack

Feby 22 pair Children's Shoes (Calf Skin)
Feby 14 Charles Lewis for Tax paid Tax of Land in Patrick for 1805 & 1806 per Sheriffs Rects.
Ditto for Interest
Ditto for Tax for 1807 per ditto
Interest on Ditto from 1806

Septemb. 4 My Comm. on £365.1.10 amount received Since 20$^{th}$ August 1809
Balance due the Heirs of D Pannill Dec'd this day

CR

1809
August 28 By Balance per Acct Settled & returned By Commissioners

Septr. 19 Frederick Shelton for Rent for 1807, Int till 1$^{st}$ January 1809, Sheriffs Cost for Distress per Statement & Rect from Wm Clark, Rent for 1808

Decr. 16 Samuel Nowlin for hire of Negro Vanny the present year
Decr. 22 Bailey Street for hire Negro Sucky for one year from 30$^{th}$ this month till 30$^{th}$ December 1810
Decr. 28 By Cash rec'd of Paul Street

1810
Jany 6  Cash Received of Anderson Chick

Apil 14 Charles Lewis for Balance of Rent Cost and Interest for the years 1807 & 1808 per Replevy Bond & filed with my Rects., Ditto for rent for 1809, Int. on ditto till 21$^{st}$ Feby 1810

Apr 17 Sam'l Pannills & Co for Balance of Wm Doves Note and Int for hire of Negroes for 1808

June 20 ditto for Rent rec'd of John Lewis for 1809, Ditto for Int of ditto, By Sam'l Pannill & Co for Cash rec'd of Wm Dove the 14$^{th}$ Sept 1809

Sept 4 Ditto for Cash Rec'd of Wm Dove in Septr. 1809 for hire of Negroes for 1808 heretofore omitted
Estate of David Pannill for two thirds of £272.18.8 nett amount Received Since 20$^{th}$ August 1809

1806
Interest on £1.3.2 ½ from 20th August 1809 being the balance due by me that day
By balance due per Contra
Pittsylvania County
In conformity to an order of the County Court of Pittsylvania to us directed bearing date June Court 1810 we Samuel Stone, William Smith and Joshua Stone Sen three of the Commissioners named in the said order have examined, adjusted & Settled the account of Samuel Pannill Guardian of the orphans of David Pannill dec'd and after having examined the Vouchers charged in the said acct find a balance of twenty one hundred and Eleven pounds 19/p due from Samuel Pannill Guardian to the said orphans as Stated in the Within acct.
Given under our hands this 4th day of September 1810
Samuel Stone, Wm Smith, Joshua Stone Sen
Recorded September 17, 1810

**AC Book 4, Page 345**                                                         **David Pannill acct Current**
The Estate of David Pannill In account with Sam'l Pannill, Exor.

1809
Oct 25 To Cash paid Clerk of Richmond District Court per Ticket
Nov 22 Cash paid Clerks Ticket from Henry
Sam'l Pannill for ditto paid ditto of Patrick
Dec 10 Cash Paid Clerks Ticket Campbell

1810
March 22 Cash paid B. W. Leigh fee in Cases of Ball per Rect.
April 20 William Smith for his attendance as witness in Suit vs Irvine per Ticket
Cash paid Clerk of Patrick for Ticket
July 24 James Pemberton for amount Clerks Tickets from Hallifax
July 27 Cash paid Berriman Green Admr. Of John H. Faulks Atto. Per Rect., Ditto for ditto from Franklin, Ditto for ditto from ditto
Septr 4 Samul Pannill & Co for Cash they paid for Carriage of Bacon from Robert Loves to Chalk Level per Rect for 1809 & 1810

1809
Sept 6  By Cash rec'd pf Elizabeth Mays
Sept 19 Cash rec'd of Spencer Pace
Decr. 22 Sam'l Pannill & Co for amt Halling 1 Load goose by Wm Williams Waggoner in 1807 on acct Said Williams Debt
Cash rec'd of George McNeley per Wm Clark Sheriff

1810
Jany 3 Cash rec'd of Daniel Fisher
Septr. 4 5 per Cent Commis. Allow'd on Collecting £307.8.10 ½ Since Settlement in August 1809
Heirs of David Pannill for 2/3 of the Bal due on this Account transferred to them this day
Bethenia Pannill pd her 1/3 part per Rect.

Jany 16 Cash Received of James Linn per William Wimbish Acct per Rect., Sam'l Pannill & Co for 5 ½ Barrels corn from Robert Dove, Ditto for Assumset for George Martin Sr Dec'd 3rd Instant
Jany 20 Cash acct of John West

Feby 21 Cash Rec'd of Henson Spurling, Ditto Rects of Nathan Frissel

March 10 Cash Rect John Murphy

April 14 Charles Lewis for amt his Judgment, Bond dated 27$^{th}$ April 1809, Ditto for Int.on ditto till 21$^{st}$ Feb 1810
April 20 Cash rec'd of Nathan Frissel

May 22 Cash Rec'd of John West 19$^{th}$ Inst.
May 26 Cash rec'd of Gabriel Penn per Peaches Gilmore atts.
Deduct atto. Fee on Injunction in Suit vs. Penn. Deduct atto. Commission on the above

June 7 Grasty & Pannill for half of amt rec'd by me since 28$^{th}$ August last
June 20 Cash rec'd of Mcmillon per P. R. Gilmore in Henry

July 7 411 lb Bacon rec'd of Robt. Love

Pittsylvania County
Pursuant to an order of the County Court of Pittsylvania to us directed bearing date June Court 1810, We Samuel Stone, William Smith and Joshua Stone Senr, three of the Comsr. named in the said order have examined and Settled the account of the estate of David Pannill dec'd with Samuel Pannill the exor. as stated above with the Vouchers showing there is no balance on the said account at this time. Given under our hands this 4$^{th}$ day of Septr. 1810
Samuel Stone, Wm Smith, Joshua Stone Sen
Recorded September 17, 1810

**AC Book 4, Page 347                                                                      Benj. Lankfords Inventory**
An Inventory of the Estate of Colo. Benjamin Lankford Dec'd Taken the 25$^{th}$ day of August 1810

10 Negroes Viz: Simmons, Humfrey, Alley, Rachel, Edmund, Frances, Coleman, Little Humfrey, Jack, and Edy
One horse, one Yoke of Steers & cart, 3 cows 2 Yearlings and Calf
3 Beds & Furniture, 2 Desks, 2 Tables, 2 Cupboards, one Candle Stand, 2 Brass Candle Sticks & one pair of Snuffers, one looking glass,, 5 pewter Plates, one Sett of Knives & forks, one Pewter Dish, 5 earthen plates, ½ dozen Tea spoons, 4 Saucers, 3 Cups, 1 Butter plate, 1 Salt Sellar, 1 Copper Coffee Pott, 1 Small water, 1 mug,, 1 Tea Cannister & Funnel, 2 flax wheels, 2 Cotton Wheels, 3 pair Cards, 1 Loom, 1 pair harness, 1 Slay, 5 Chares, 1 large Cask, 1 Hogs head, 1 flax hackle, one grind stone, 3 pots, one oven & lid, 3 pair pot hooks, 1 Skillet, 2 pair of horse geer, 2 plow hoes, 2 Clevises & pins, 2 Swingle trees Irons, 4 hilling hoes, one weeding hoe, 2 Grubbing hoes, one Coulter, one froe, 3 pole axes, one foot adze & one howel, 2 Drawing Knives, one auger gouge, 1 nippers, one curry Comb, 2 Smoothing Irons, one Bett, 2 Sithes & Cradles, 3 reep Hooks, 1 Tub, 2 Water Piggins, one pale, one half Bushel measure one parcel of Flax, one Parcel of Oats Supposed to be 25 Bushels of wheat, one bulk of rye supposed to be 35 Bushels, one Cutting Knife and Box
This Inventory taken By me Benja. Stone
Recorded September 17, 1810

**AC Book 4, Page 348                                                                               B W Nowlins' Inventory**
An Inventory of the estate of Bryan W. Nowlin Dec'd taken the 23$^{rd}$ day of July 1810 by Peyton Graves, Abraham Rorer & John Keesee

1 Bed & Furniture bedstead & Cord, 1 do do, 1 do do, 1 do do, 2 yarn flowred bed leaves, 2 Blankets, 1 bed quilt & sheat, 1 large pine Chest, 1 Small Do do, 1 Black Walnut Do, 1 Pine Corner Cupboard & furniture, 1 Black Walnut Desk, 2 Black walnut tables, 14 Chairs, 1 looking glass, 1 Shot gun & powder horn, 1 pr large Steelyards, 1 pr. Tongs and Shovel, 2 pr. sad Irons, 1 tin lanturn, 2 Candle Sticks & 1 pr. Snuffers, 1 Tea Kettle and trivet, 1 Empty Case, 1 Slate, 2 Cotton Wheels & 4 pr. Cards, 2 Flax Do, 1 pr. Sheep Sheers & 2 pr. Scissors, 1 Pr Sad Irons, 1 set Knives and forks, 1 Knife Box, 2 Table Cloths, 2 Razor Strap Box & glass, 3 Brushes Stock , 1 lock, wafer box and lancet, 1 large bible, 1 Small Bible & Sundry other books, 1 Revis'd cpde amd Several acts of assembly, 3 dishes , 3 basons, ½ doz. Plates & 1 large

Spoon, 2 tubs & 2 piggins, 1 ½ Bushel measure, 2 Churns, 2 Kitchen tables, 1 Small pot and hooks, frying pan & 2 Skillets, 2 Large pools oven & lid, 1 pr R. Hooks

2 Iron pot Racks, 1 Hhs. , 1fish Barrel & meat tub, 1 Cloth loom, 1 pr tembles, 6 stays, 1 Side Saddle, 2 mens saddles, 1 Flax hackle & 6 Reaping hooks, 1 lock chain, 2 pr azes & wedges, 3 pr Hames traces , back bands, 2 clevices & double Swingle tree, 4 plow hoes, 2 plains, 1 Drawing knife & Chisels, Sundry old Irons, 1 pr. bare Iron, 2 pole axes, 1 Bell, 1 Wheat Sive, 1 Riddle & fann , 1 Hhds. Jointer & Crose, 1 Choping ax, 6 lite Casks, 1 Still Cup and Worm, 7 lb Wool, 2 open Casks, 4 Sack bags, 2 Sides S Leather, 3 Chamber Potts, 2 Seythes & Cradles, 1 bare Shear Plow, 1 pr. Hames & Rope Traces &c., 5 Stands Bees, 1 Grinding Stone, 8 hilling hoes, 1 White horse, 1 Bay mare, 1 Roan mare, 1 Roan Fillie, 4 Hhd., 1 ox Colter, 1 Grey Colt, Sorrel do, 1 black horse, 7 geese & 4 Goslins, 12 head of Sheep, 1 Yoke young Steirs, 1 White heifer, 1 white Bool, 1 Red Heifer Yearling, 1 White Cow & Calf, 1 White do, 1 Pided do, 1 speckled do, 2 White Cows & Calves, 26 head hogs, 2 Do Do, 1 Coffee mill, 2 grubbing hoes, pot

Easter Pats Daughter, Lucy, Levina, Fillis, Candice, Lina, Anna, Braneer, Carter, Davy , Wheler, Old June, Easter, Isaac, Mary, Juno, Lucretia, Ben, Asa, Phil

1 ox Cart
1 yoke oxen
1 ox yoke
In obedience to an order from the Worshipful Court of Pittsylvania County bearing date July 1810 We have proceeded to appraise the estate of Bryan W Nowlin dec'd so far as Can be ascertained at present. Given under our Hands This 23rd Day 1810.
Peyton Graves, Abraham Rorer, John Keesee

To a parcel of fodder tops & blades, 160 Barrels of Corn Supposed to be , Parcel of Green Tobo., Parcel of Flax unbroken, A parcel of wheat uncleaned, Two plains frow & Chisel, 1 Book & 1 pair of Saddle Bags, 1 Bridle, Parcel of Rye in the Stack, Two parcels of Cotton in the patches, 3 Stacks of Hay, a parcel of brandy Judged to be worth
Peyton Graves, John Keesee, Abraham Rorer
Recorded October 15, 1810

**AC Book 4, Page 352**                                                                 **Plst. Hardwick's acct. Current**

DR
The Estate of Pleasant Hardwick Dec'd in acct. current with William Sutherlin admis.

1810
Sept 17 To Cash paid an execution in favor of Hickman Spiller per Rect.
Sept 7- Cash paid and execution in favor of William Spiller per Rect.

1808
Augst 31 Cash pd Figg & Mickleborough per do

Aug 21 1810 Ditto do John Dabney per Rect., Gidean Mitchell per do, Cost vs Isaac Hill
Sept 29 ditto do John Mattock D. Shff per Rect.

1809
Novm. Ditto do Gidian Mitchill for his attendance in Court as a Witness, William Yancey as per his Credit folled and Recipted
a balance you over pd in a former Settlemnet per the Clerks Certificate
this sum allowed him for his services as an administrator
Clerks and Sheriffs tickets
Cash pd George Lumpkin per Rect.

Ditto pd Wm Linn per Rect, Robert White per Rect.
To balance due the Estate of Pleasant Hardwick

1810 Augt. 14 By Cash Rec'd on an execution against Isaac Hill , Richard Allen and Lewis B Alllen per Rect. From Benjamin Shippard Dpy. for G Stone S. H. C.
By 1 Gigg & Harness
In obedience to the annexed order we have Stated and Settled the foregoing account Current of the Estate of Pleasant Hardwick Dec'd with William Sutherlin his adminr. & find a balance due from him of sixty one pounds 1/p. Given under our hands the 6th of October 1810.
Nath Wilson, Hezh. Puryear, Bezaleel Ware
Recorded October 15, 1810

**AC Book 4, Page 353**                          **Jno. Wilson's accpt. Current**

The Estate of John Wilson Dec'd In account Current with James Wilson & Henry Wilson , Exors.

1807
Cash paid Thomas Wilkinson Senr the amt. His acct., Ditto paid William Beavers, Ditto paid Aabner Lynch, Ditto paid Dandrige Burch, Ditto paid Israel Matherley, Ditto paid James Colquhoun & Co, Ditto paid Josiah Baron, Ditto paid Henry Wilson, Ditto paid Martin Wilson for Maj Sawyers, Ditto paid ditto for Judgment obtained, Ditto paid John & Nathaniel Wilson, Ditto paid Will. Yancey Sheriff, Ditto paid John Lawless, Cash paid Abraham Pistole, Ditto paid Francis Cornwell, Ditto paid James D Patton, Ditto paid Will. Linn, Ditto paid Jessee Leftwich, Ditto paid Harris & Brown, Ditto paid Thomas Wilson, Ditto paid Peyton King, Ditto paid Johnson Lansdoun, Ditto paid Will Tunstall per Tickett, Ditto paid John Wilson Jun, Ditto paid Nathaniel Wilson for Samuel Walker, Ditto paid Rev Moore & Atkinson for attending funl., Ditto paid Henry Wilson asse. Philt. Payne per Statement, Ditto paid Will Tunstall for recording Mrs. Payne relinquishment of Dower, Ditto paid Philimon Payne per rect, Ditto for William Wilson by Will principal
Interest on the same &  7 years & 9 mo.
Ditto paid Nathaniel H. Clabourn a fee

Deduct a fee charged by Claiborne Stated in the other side
By amount sale property & tobacco
By cash received of the Estate James Wilson Dec'd
By Cash rec'd the Bal. for Building meetin house
By Int. on Sundry Bonds collected, say in all
Nov 12th 1810
After examining The above account we find the balance due by the Executors to the estate to be seventy one pounds 19/
Deduct for the Services of the Executors
Balance due by the Executors
Given under our hands the Date above
Wm White, Alexander Brown, Thos. Tanner
Recorded November 19, 1810

**AC Book 4, Page 355**                          **Haley of Haley Acct Current**

DR The Estate of Theoplolous Haley Dec'd In acct.

1809
Dec 19 Cash paid Taxes for 1807 per Rect., Cash paid S. Pannill for yr. Replevy bond taken in

June 19 Jas Hillyer atto. Fee per Rect.

Feb 21 Pd tax fror one Negro Girl which was included in my list of Taxable property, Paid the Clerk of Pittsylvania per Ticketts

Aug 26 paid Sam'l K Jennings on act. Per Rect.

Sep 24 pd do do ditto
Octr 9 paid ditto in full per rect.

1804
Jany 22 paid P. L. Grasty per acct. & rect., paid Samuel Pannill * co in full their acct. per rect.

May 5 paid F/T Chumbley Const. For cost of Wrrant against E Burch per Rect.
May 28 paid ditto ditto against Edmund Tunstall per Rect.
July 18 paid Clk. Pittsylvania per Tickett
Aug paid Wm Rice for his acct per his order & P. L/S Grasty's Rect.
Novr. Cash paid Jno Dabney per Rect., ditto paid Thomas Anderson for so much he paid N. Tucker for making coffin for the decedent per said Anderson's Recipt.

Amount of your Admr. Acct.
Dec 13 To Commission of 5 per Cent allowed on £303.3.11
Balance due the estate
Current with Wyatt Haley, administrator

1808
Decr. 10 Cash rec'd of Henry Wade for his purchase at sale, Ditto rec'd of Jos. E Haley, Shadrack Beal, Josiah Rice, John Mustain, Thomas Anderson, Mrs. Ann Haley

1809
Aug 24 ditto Thomas Anderson in pt. His bond, Peter Irby for his Note

Septr 29 ditto William Smith ditto
Dec 22 ditto Langhorn Scruggs & W Scrugg's Note

1810
Jany 17 ditto Daniel Clement
Jany 22 ditto James Doss
Jany 26 ditto Robert Waller, ditto Blake p. Edwd. Robertson Jr

Feby 9 ditto J Rowland
Feby 26 ditto Thos. Anderson, amt yr. Admis. Purchase at sale

Mar 5 Cash Received of Jos. Mayes
Apl 18 Ditto Thomas Black in full
May 5 ditto of Elisha Burch in full , Edm. Tunstall ditto ditto, Mrs. M Morgan, Rect. Of Thomas Anderson for balance due on his bond and Interest, By Henry R Shelton's Bond with Interest from 10th December 1809
Decr. 13 Sale of one Negro Boy Bedford , Ditto 1 " girl Ritter
Due 10th July 1810

By balance due per Contra
Pittsylvania County
In conformity to an order of the County Court of Pittsylvania we William Smith, Philip L Grasty and Joshua Stone Sen named in the said order hereto annexed, have stated and settled the account current of Wyatt Haley, admrs. With the estate of Theoplulous Haley, dec'd, agreeable to the Vouchers produced before us

and find a balance due the said Estae of two hundred and forty one pounds, three shillings, four half penny agreeable to the written Statement. Given under our hands this 13th day of December 1810
Wm Smith, Philip L Grasty, Joshua Stone Jr
Recorded December 17, 1810

**AC Book 4, Page 357**                        **Francis Henry's Appr Est**

We the appraisers of the Estate of Francis Henry, Dec'd being first sworn makes the following Inventory

1810 Oct 18
One set of B. Smiths tools, Two plains, 2 pr of Wedges, One cerring Knife, one pair of hames, One sawing kinfe, Three augers & two Chissels, Three Scythes blades, Old Iron, Frow, two Coalters & two plows, One Iron Winless, Hhds & two mattox, Five Reaphooks, frac augur & Swingletree, Two bells and bridle, arre ax, Six hogsheads and Sundries of Barrels, Eight head of Cattle, Six head of Sheap, Six head of horses, Four head of hogs, One flax wheel and Chest, Three feather beds, Two cubboards and Table, Eight Chears, flax wheel & Real, Kitchen furniture, One Loom, one pr. of hand Irons, Sifter, Sugar dish, cups & saucers, knives & forks and old bottle, one pr. of Stillards, two pr. of Hames & traces, one Cow bell, One bason, one L. Glass, one old same, Three Calf Skins, One swingletree and hand saw
Appraisers of Estate Nathaniel Kirby, William Thompson, John Muse
Recorded January 21, 1811

**AC Book 4, Page 358**                        **Keziah Sparks's Inventory**

An Inventory of the Estate of Keziah Sparks Dec'd

Six barrels of Corn, one Stack of Tops, Thirty feet long half full of shucks, Two plade? Stacks, One Cow and Yearling, two young sows and one share (sic) barrow, one red cow, six gees, three turkeys, And six pigs, one Speller sow and five pigs, five fatten hogs in the pen, Seven Mobby starids, two cider Casks, twenty one Gallons of brandy in a cask belong thereto, two beads, two bead quilts & two Counterpins, one pine Cupboard, one walnut table, two bead steads, Two Cotton wheels, one flax wheel, one Iron pott & Hooks, one Dutch oven, , 4 Hooks, one loom, one chearn, one skillet, two flat Irons, one of them is broken, two piggins, one looking glass, one six hundred slay, two pewter dishes, two pewter basons, eight pewter plates, six spoons, one sugar box, two candle sticks, four Chairs, two tea pots, one of them broken, two Jugs one of them broken, one large bottle, one Cullenter, one woman's saddle, four old books Sundries old recipts &c, one nutmeg Gratewr, one plow hoe, one ax, one hoe, one hand saw, one draw nife, one Iron wedge, one tower hock, one Iron & Spice mortar, one hackle, three Ducks, one bread tray, one pair of shears, two small augers, three old barrels, one pr. of Iron traces &c, one old sythe blade, one pair of cotton Cards, one bell, twelve pounds of Cotton, two frig. Irons, one open ring, two fish gigs, part of a soop spoon
Adams Sutterlin
Recorded January 21, 1811

**AC Book 4, Page 359**                        **Jno. Snoddy's Inventory**
In compliance with an order of the Worshipful Court of Pittsylvania County at November Term 1810 to us directed we have on the 29th November 1810 Convened together at the Late dwelling house of John Snoddy Dec'd and appraised his personal estate as follows.

1 Negro Boy Sam, 1 Negro Woman Cloe, 1 Feather Bed and Furniture, ditto, , 1 Table, 1 Cotton wheal, 1 Flax wheel, 1 Bed Sted & Casks, 1 Whip saw, 1 Table & Cotton, 1 Cask, 1 Gum & Onions, Dried fruit 1 pr flat Irons, 1 Jug, pewter, 2 Glasses &c, Knives & forks, 2 Chairs, 1 Box Razor & spectacles, 1 candle stick, Books, Box and Salt, Baskett & Toe, 1 Trumpett, panhand, 2 plows and Collars, 1 Bell and Shears, 2 axes, 1 Sythe & Cradle, 3 pr. Traces, Collar, hames & line, 2 Clevises & Swingle tree, 3 Augers, 2 wedges, 1 Saw Drawing knife & hammer, 1 Steel trap, 4 hoes & mattock, 6 piggin & Lumber, 1 Churn, Tub meat and fat, 1 loom , barrel of potatoe Seed, 1 Oven & hooks, 1 bread baker, 1 pair hooks & lathe,
1 pale, parcel Corn, 1 heiffer & Calf, 1 Cow & Yearling , 1 horse, 1 Ditto, 35 parcell Shingles, 1 Top Stack & shucks, 2 Wheat Stacks, 1 Blade Stack, flax Stack, Straw g'd, Flax, 4 Hhgs,. Toboacco, 1 Bull, 3 Sows,

1 Barrow, 2 Sows & pigs, 2 Cows & 1 heffer, part of 1 grind stone, 1 hide, 3 Stays, Fodder
Given under our hands & seals this 29th Day of November 1810
Joseph Flippin, Creed Tanner, William Simpson, Jackson Walters
Recorded February 18, 1811

**AC Book 4, Page 360**                          **John Owen's Inventory**

1811 February 2nd, We Willis Glass, Hubbard Farmer, Obediah Ham, William Whitlock being first sworn do appraise the Estate of John Owen, Deceased agreeable to Order and make Report thereon to Court

First To:
1 Feather Bed & Furniture, & Steads, 1 Ditto & furrniture & Stead, 1 Ditto & furniture & Stead, 1 pine Chest, 1 Ditto, 1 Ditto, one Case, 1 Table and Seven Chairs, 1 Cubboard with furniture, 3 Butter pots & pitcher, 1 Sheep Sheers & reap hook, 1 Looking glass & two Juggs, eight Barrels, The kitchen Iron furniture, The wood in kitchen furniture, Three wheels, one C. Reel, 4 pare C. Chaires, 1 Lamb & four Slays & harness, 1 parcel of pewter, 4 Baskets, 1 knife Box & knives & forks, 2 Sows, Six Shotes, 6 hilling hoes, 1 plow Froe, & froe, 2 augers & gauge & 1 Chisel & 2 bells, 2 Drawing knives, 1 Saw hammer, 1 cock Chain, 1 colter & 4 plow hoes, 2 Cows & 3 yearlings, 1 horse, 1 coulter, 2 hogshead & Cutting Knife & box, four bridles, 7 Head Sheep
The amount of the appraisment by us
Total $243.10
Willis Glass, Hubbard Farmer, Obediah Ham, William Whitlock
Recorded February 18, 1811

**AC Book 4, Page 364**                          **Will. Waller's Acct Curnt**

The Estate of William Waller Dec'd In acct. with Jane Waller, administratrix, with the will annexed

1807
Paid Jesse Leftwich Due per acct., Clerk of Pittsyva. Per Ticket, James Taylor per acct., Obediah Taylor per bond, Interest and Cost of Taylor's bond, James Harris per acct., the Sheriff of Pittsy. 1804 Tax, Shelton's Execution per Note, Dyers Execution, Jesse Hatton per Acct., Robert Loves Execution, John Parson per acct., Lynn's administrator per acct., Patrick Syms per acct., Thomas Turly per acct, Sheriff of Pittsa. Per his acct., Parnill Exor due per Note, Commissioner of Revenue per T, the Clerk of Pittsylvania per Ticket, Jacob Saunders per acct, William Parsons, Rich'd Bennettbal. of a Bond, Pay'd for Schooling of Children, For this Item there is no voucher

CR
By amount for 1 Negro Boy sold to pay the above Debts
The annexed acct. contains the Debits and Credits which Jane Waller, administratrix of William Waller, Dec'd, exhibited to the Commissiors appointed to Settle her acct Current. There is some uncertainty as to the particular time when some of the payments were made. The commissioners have therefore numbered the Vouchers on which the payments, not corresponding with the numbers, on each entry in the Debts all of which are herewith submitted. It appears to your Commissioners from the last Will of William Waller Dec'd, That after the payment of his debts, Jane Walle,r his widow, has the possession of the whole of his estate, real and personal, during her Widowhood or life" They therefore consider it improper to carry any part of the profits arising from his Estate into the acct. Current of his administratrix in as much as she holds after paying his Debts, the estate real and personal by devise and not mearly as administratrix. Jane Waller, the administratrix, States to your Commissioners that She knows of no Debts due from her Deceased Husband except a Debt of eleven pounds due to his Brother Hamton Waller which she has no reason to believe the said Hamlon intends to collect. A Debt of £700.8 to Jesse Hatton which She supposes is staid by the order of your Court and a Small amt to John Waller for a few days Sowing.
18th February 1811
Tho. H Wooding, Wm Rawlins, Thompson Robertson
Recorded February 18, 1811

**AC Book 4, page 363** — **Gilbert Deer's Inventory**

We the under Subscribers qualified before Thomas Garrett Esq. Hath this day appraised the remaining Estate of Gilbert Deer, Dec'd in obedience to an order of the County Court of Pittsylvania to us directed.
The following Property Viz:
One Negro woman & Child Silvy and Nancy
One ditto Boy named Bill
One ditto girl named Rutha
One do Boy named Bobb
One Do Girl named Sal
Given under our hands this 23rd January 1811
Abraham Parrish, Davis Petty, Christopher Robertson
Recorded February 18, 1811

**AC Book 4, Page 363** — **Jas. Nelson's Acct Curt.**

The Estate of James Nelson Dec'd In acct Current with Joseph Flippin, the Executor

Paid Ben Watkins his proven acct., Thomas Wilkinson Ditto, Carter Mickleburrough do, Henry Pell proven acct, Wm B Banks fee, Tho. Brown per Clerks Tickets, Sheriff & their Tickett, James Colquhoun & Co per proven acct, Wm B Banks fee & Barnett, Evans Shaw per Clerks Ticket, Ditto do do per do do Ditto the Clerk of Pittsy. Court per Ticket, do do, Henry Pell per Clerks Ticket, Wm Clerk paid him per ticket, Mrs. Conwell per proven acct, Clerk of Pittsy. Per his ticket, do ditto per ditto. Charles Shaw proven acct, Samuel Walker proven acct, Samuel Conwell per proven acct, Paid John Wilson per Do, Paid John & Nath'l Wilson per ditto
Paid John Madding Per Justice peace Judg.
Paid Shf Yancey Tax Year 1807 Paid Prattin per Clerks order
Paid Brown &Hams per proven acct. & Rect.
Whereas Abigail Twidle, mother of the widow Nelson, it appearing to us from the information of said widow and Some of the Children that the said Twidle Claimed Aconsiderable Sum on which a Suit & a dispute likely to insue and it being agreed on all sides that the Executor allow and compromise with her by allowing her which its appeased that be has paid the the sum of
To Cash paid Mrs. Nelson per her acknowledged
To amt. Geo. Cook proven acct. in payment of his bond
To amt which Mrs. Nelson being present & acko. that She received of the Executor by way sale money in bonds.

CR
By amt due from Henry Pell
By amt Due from Geo. Cook per Bond Subject each of the above to the amt. Of their proven acct paid in the life time of said Nelson.
By amt. Sold at the Sale
By amt Mrs. Nelson pd Charles Shaw
Account found in tavern the executor
We allow Jo. Flippin the Executor 5 per Cent on £336.0.0 which it appears he has collected & paid out to that amt.
We allow him a further sum of Six Shillings per Day for 15 Days which it appears he lost in attending to a law suit in the suit Barnett agt. Him as Executor.

Agreeable to an order of Pittsylvania Court we have examined and adjusted the acct. Current of Joseph Flippin Executor of James Nelson, Dec'd and find that he has paid away the sum of £4,0.9 more than is in his hands& have all'd him for his Trouble the sum of Sixteen pounds, six shillings amounting in his favor the the sum of £20.6.9.
Given under our hands this 13th March 1811
Ben Watkins, Ro.. Walter, Creed Tanner

Recorded March 18, 1811

## AC Book 4, Page 365 — Peter Wilson's Guardian acct.

DR Meade Wilson, (Ward) in acct Current with Peter Wilson, Guardian

**1806**
Bond on Geo. Adams taken in Exchange of Wm Cablers Bond given for the hire of Negroe fellow Isaac given to said Adams 1st January 1806 due 1st Jany 1807 & taken on sd Adams 1st Feby 1808 on Demand.

**1807**
Jany 2 Bond on James Sawyers & Samuel Thompson given P. Wilson's for hire of Isaact 2nd January 1807 due 2nd Jany 1808
Bond on Laban Gresham & Ellis Wilson given P. Wilson for hire Betty 2nd January 1807 due 2nd January 1808.

1808 Jany 2 Bond of James Sawyers & Geo. Robertson given P. Wilson for hire Isaac 2nd Jany 1808 due 1st Jany 1809
Bond Jesse Leftwich & Samuel Thompson given P. Wilson for hire Betty 2nd January 1808 due 1st Jany 1809.

Jany 2 Bond of James Sawyers & Thos. Ragsdale given P. Wilson for hire Isaac 2 January 1809 due 1 Jany 1810

Jany 1 Bond on James Sawyers & Juduthun Carter given 1st January 1810 due 1st Jany 1811
Bond on Henry Hall & Wm Sawyers given Peter Wilson for hire Isaac 1st Jany 1811 due 1st Jany 1812
Interest on James Sawyers Bond Collected 2nd June 1809
Interest on Greshams Bond coll'd
Cash

Contra
By bond on George Adams with Int from 5th Feby 1808
Bond on James Sawyers & Geo. Robertson with Interest from 1st January 1809
Bond Jesse Leftwich & Samuel Thompson with Interest from 1st January 1809
Bond on James Sawyers and Thos Ragsdale with Interest from 1st January 1810
Bond on James Sawyers and Juduthan Carter with Interest fro 1st Jany 1811
Bond on Henry Hall & William Sawyers with Interest from 1st January 1812
John Wilson & Geo. Adams Bond being ½ of bond given Wm & Meade with Interest from 29th October 1808
Wm Ware & Robert Harris on bond being ½ of a bond given Mead with Interest from 17th Jany 1810

**1806**
Sept 11 Paid Wm Tunstall per Tickett
Decr. 1 1 pair leather Shoes

**1807** 2 pair Socks
March 1 1 pair leather Shoes
Apr 1 6 yds Country Cotton, Making 2 Shirts at 3/, Making 2 pr pantaloons at 1/6
Novr. 1 1 pr. Leather Shoes

**1808**
3 pr. Socks, paid Thos. Tiffin for making Clothes Dec. 26th 1806 as per acct & Rect.

Feby 1 pr Leather Shes

Apl 1 Making 2 Shirts, Making 2 pr pantaloons, Thos Tiffin for making cloths as per acct & recipt, John & Nath'l Wilson, 4 yds ogn. As per Rect. , James Nance for Schooling 1 Year 1807 as per recipt, John Wilson for Sundry goods as per Acct & Recipt, Thomas Casey jun at the hiring of Negroes Board From the 1st Nove 1806 until the 1st January 10 1809 including washing & minding, 2 years and 2 months

Paid Thomas Swan for board while going to School to Robert Payne Esq from 1st Januy 1809 until 22th Sept @$40 per year as per rect., Paid Thomas Swan for finding 1 hatt per rect., Paid Do for making 2 pr. pantaloons per rect., Paid Robert Payne for Tuition as per Recipt
Nov 1 1 pair leather Shoes

1809 3 pr. Socks
Feby making 2 Shirts, 1 pr. leather Shoes

1810 paid James Nance for Tuition 8 months as per acct & rect.
Augt. Making 2 Shirts, 4 yds Country Cloth, making 2 pr. pantaloons, 3 pr. Socks, 1 pr leather Shoes, 1 pr leather Shoes, Board from 22nd Sept 1809 until 1st Feby 1811 1 Year & 4 monthsat $40 per year Including Washing, mending, Paid William Harrison for tuition 5/2 months as per Rect., Anne Walton as per Rect, Will. Harrison as per Rect. for tuition 9 months, Do for making Clothes as per Rect., John & Nath'l Wilson for Sundry goodsas per acct & rect., Thomas Tiffin for making Clothes as per rect., John Wilson as per acct & Rect. For sumdry goods

To my services as Guardian
By Cash
To amt of Debit brot forward
1 Negro man Isaac, 1 Woman Betty & 3 Children 1 of which is named Christiana, 1 Bed and furniture which is delivered to Mr. Jno. Watkins the present Guardian together with the aforesaid Negroes
In obedience to a Commission to us directed from the Worshipful Court of Pittstylania, we have proceeded to settle the Guardianship acct. of Peter Wilson as Guardian of Mead Wilson one of the orphan Children of Peter Wilson, Dec'd as per Statement hereto annexed. Given under our hands this 16 Feburary 1811.
Geo. Adams, Ro. Harrison, David Rice, Mathew Daniel, comms.
Recorded: March 19, 1811

**AC Book 4, Page 369**                                                                                          **P. Wilson's Gdn acct**
DR William Wison (Ward) in acct. Current with Peter Wilson, Guardian

1806
Jany 1st Bond on Wm Lynn & Doctor James Patton given Geo. Adams for hire of Harry Jany 1st 1806 due January 1st 1807, Bond on Robert Norman & Wm Cabbler given George Adams for hire Eddy Jany 1st 1806 due Jany 1st 1807

 1807 Jany 2 Bond on Reubin Curtis & Abraham Perkins given P. Wilson for hireof Harry Jany 2 1807 due Jany 2, 1808, Bond on Ellis Wilson & Nath'l Wilson given P. Wilson for hire of Osburn Jany 2, 1807 due Jany 2, 1808, Bond on John Scruggs & John Wilson given P. Wilson for hire of Eddy.

1808 Jany 2 Bond on Jesse Leftwich & Sam'l Thompson given P. Wilson for hire of Harry Jany 2, 1808 due Jany 1, 1809, Bond on Samuel Thompson & James Sawyers given P. Wilson for hire of Ozburn Jany 2, 1808 due Jany 2, 1809, Bond on John Scruggs & John Wilson given P. Wilson for hire of Eddy Jany 2 1808 due Jany 2, 1809

1809 Jany 2 Sibert Hail & Henry Hall bond given Peter Wilson for hire of Harry Jany 2nd 1809due Jany 2nd 1810, Bond on Sam'l Thompson & John Conner given P. Wilson for hire of Ozburn Jany 2nd 1809due Jany 2 1810, Bond on James Astin given P. Wilson for hire of Eddy Jany 2, 1809 due Jany 2, 1810

1810 Jany 1

Bond on Wm Sawyers and James Sawyers given P Wilson for hire of Harry 1 Jany 1810 due 1st Jany 1811,
Bond on Wm Rawlins and Thos Ragsdale given P Wilson for hire Osburn 1st Jany 1810 due Jany 1st 1811
Bond on Abraham Findley & Leroy Shelton given Peter Wilson for hire Eddy 1st Jany 1811 due Jany 1 1811

1811 Jany Bond on Wm Sawyers & James Sawyers given P Wilson for hire Harry Jany 1 1811due 1st Jany 1812, Bond on Samuel Thompson & James Sawyers given Peter Wilson for hire Osburn 1st Jany 1811 due 1s Jany 1812, Bond on John Conner & Harry Hall given P Wilson for hire of Eddy 1st Jany 1811 due Jany 1812., Interest on Lynns Bond Collected, Interest on Normans Bond Collected, Cash

Contra

By Balance Reubin Curtis & Abrn. P with Interest from 2nd Jany 1808
Wm Harrison Jr & Wm Ware Bd. Interest from 18th June 1810, Rich'd Watson & Wm Ware Bd. Interest from 28th May 1810, Ellis & Nath'l Wilson Bond with Interest from 2nd January 1808, Jesse Leftwich & Samuel Thompson ;with Interest from 1st Jany 1808, John Scruggs & John Wilson with Interest from 1st Jany 1809, Sebert Hall & Henry Hall bd. With interest from 2nd Jany 1810, Wm Rawlins & Thomas Ragsdale Bd. With Interest from 1st Jany 1811, Abraham Findley & Leroy Shelton Interst from 1st Jany 1811, Wm & James Sawyers bond Interest from 1st Jany 1811, Samuel Thompson & James Sawyers bd. Due 1st Jany 1812, John Conner & Harry Hall bd. Due 1st Jany 1812, Wm & James Sawyers Bd. Due 1st Jany 1812, John Wilson & Geo. Adams Bd. Being ½ of a bondgiven wm J Mead with Interest from 20th Oct 1808, William Ware & Robert Harrison bond being ½ of a bd. Given Wm J Mead with Interest from 17th Jany 1810.

1806
Sept. paid Wm Tunstall see Ticket
Dec, 1 1 pr Leather Shoes

1807
2 pr. Socks
March 1 1 pr. Leather Shoes
Aprl 1 6 yds Country Cotton, Making 2 Shirts, Making 2 pr pantaloons
Nov 1 1 pr. Leather Shoes, 3 pr. Socks, paid Thomas Tiffin for making Cotton December 26 1806 as per acct, & Rect.
Feby 1 pr Leather Shoes
Apl 1 Making 2 Shirts, making two pr. pantaloons, Paid Thomas Tiftin for making Clothes as per acct and rect., Paid John & Nath'l Wilson 4 yds. Ogna. As per Rect., James Nance for teaching 1 year 1807 as per Rect., John Wilson for for Sundry goods as per Acct. & Rect., Thomas Casey jr as Cryer at the Hiring of Negroes
Board from 1st Nov 1806 until the 1st Jany 1809 Including Washing & Mending 2 Years and 2 months at $40 per year
Paid Thomas Swan for board while going to school to Ro. Payne Esq. From 1 Jany 1809 until 22nd Sept @ $40 per year as per rect., Thomas Swan for finding 1 hat per Rect., Paid do for making 2 pr. pantaloons as per Rect., Ro Payne for tuition as per Rect

1808
Novr 1 1 pair Leather Shoes

1809
3 pr. Socks
Feby 1 Making 2 Shirts, 1 pr leather Shoes, Paid James Nance for tuition 8 months as per acct & Rect.
Augt 10 Making 2 Shirts, 4 yds Country Cloth, making 2 pr pantaloons, 3 pr Socks
Novr. 1 1 pr. leather Shoes

1811

Jany 1   1 pr do do
Board from 22nd Sept. 1809 until Feb. 1811 1 year and 4 months at 40 per year including washing &c., Paid William Harrison for Tuition 5 ½ months as per Rect., Paid Do for do as per Recipt 9 months, Paid Do for making do a suit of clothes as per Rect., Paid John & Nath'l Wilson for Sundry goods as per acct. & Rect., Paid Thomas Tiffin for making clothes as per Rect, Paid John Wilson for Sundry goods as per acct. & Rect., To my Services as Guardian
By Cash
To amt. Of Debit brot forward
1 Negro man Harry, 1 boy Osburn, 1 girl Eddy, 1 bed & furniture which is Delivered to Mr. John Watkins, the present Guardian together with the above Negroes.

In obedience to a Commission to us directed from the Worshipful Court of Pittsylvania we have proceeded to Settle the guardian Ship account of Peter Wilson as Guardian of William Wilson one of the orphan Children of Peter Wilson dec'd as per Statement hereto annexed. Given under our hands this 16th Feby 1811
Geo Adams, Ro. Harrison, Commissioners
David Rice, Mathew Daniel
Recorded March 19, 1811

**AC Book 4, Page 373**                                                         **Thos. Madding's Inventory**

In Complyance with an order of the worshipful Court of Pittsylvania County made September Court 1810 and to us directed we the Subscribers being Conveined together at the house and plantation of Thomas Madding deceased this 26th of October 1810 and being first Sworn according to your order have proceeded to appraise the Estate of the said Thomas Madding deceased and have Taken an Inventory thereof as follows;
1 Negro Woman Called Letty, 1 Negro Boy called Lawson, 1 Negro Girl called Sarah, 1 Negro Girl called Lucy, 1 Negro Boy called John, 1 Negro Boy called Anthony, 1 Sorrel Mare, 1 young White horse, 1 Yoke of Steer, 1 old Cow & Calf, 1 young Cow, 1 Cow & Calf, a parcel of hogs, a parcel of Sheep, 1 pair of old Cart wheels, 6 old hoes, 2 plow hoes, 3 Mattocks, 1 Spade, 2 pare of horse Gears, 3 Clevis Irons, 1 Set of Iron Wedges, 1 foot adds, drawing knife & ox ring, 2 pole axes, 1 feather Bed and furniture, 1 Ditto & Stead, 1 Ditto & Stead,1 Ditto, 1 Bed & furniture, 1 Cupboard, 2 Cotton Wheels, 2 flax wheels, 1 Clock Reel and one old Churn

1 Mans saddle, 1 womans ditto, 1 Skillet, 2 flat Irons, 1 Dutchoven & Hooks, 1 flax Kacklee, 1 hand Saw, 1 weaving loom, Slay & Gare, 1 old tub, 1 bread tray & meat barrel, a parcel of Earthern Ware, a parcel of Tin ware, 1 Salt Tub, 1 old big pot, 1 Chest, 1 Ditto, a panel of walnut planks, 1 parcel of Chairs, 1 Table, 1 Stone Jug, 1 Butter Pot, 1 Case of Bottles, 1 Coffee pot & bucket, a parcel of Books, a Case of Razors and old Cumposes, 28 Geese, a parcel of pewter, 1 cupboard, 1 Large pot and hooks, 1 Skillet and Jug , 1 Coulter & frow, a parcel of fodder, a parcel of Corn being 28 barrels in the whole

Sum Total: £450.19.3
Thomas Shelton, Geo. Dodson, Robert Clopton, John Lewis
Recorded March 19, 1811

**AC Book 4, Page 375**                                                         **Thos. Shelton Sr's Inventory**

DR The Estate of Thomas Shelton Senr Dec'd

Apr Cash paid Francis Dilley for making Coffin, Benj Watkins for note with Int, the Clerk Pittsylva., Charales Colley, Rawley White, Wm Dodson, Thoms Shelton Jr the amt of his proved acct. , the tax of 1808, amount of my Acct., Sum paid John Shelton
Holts & Turners bond for which is to be consent of parties divided amongst the distributies
James Shelton's Bond who is alegalee for William Johnson who is a legatee bond for
James Johnson bond for Archibald Walters' Bond Rec'd by T. S.

Paid Thomas Shelton Jr. legatee
Paid James Shelton Senr Do
My purchase at the sale
This Sum part Lucy Slayton a legatee
Paid Wm Shelton a legatee
This Sum paid John Madding for crying property at the sale.
To an allowance for manging the Estate
Due the Executor
In Account Current with William Shelton , Execor.   C.R.
1809 By Cash rec'd of William Ragland
By a list of Sales made on from the Estate
Also the sum of
In obedience to an order of the worshipful Court of the County of Pittsylvania to us directed we have proceeded to Examine the accounts of William Shelton Exor. Of Thomas Shelton Dec'd and find them as the law directs leaving a balance in favor of the Executor of £9.19.3 ½  Given under our Hands this 16 Day of March 1811.
Geo. Dodson, Sen.  John Shelton, John Ford, Sto. Turner
Recorded March 18, 1811

**AC Book 4, Page 376**                                                                                          **Champns Napier Inventory**

In obedience to an order to us directed by the Worshipful Court of Pittsylvania County we whose names are herewith assigned, being first sworn now proceed to appraise the personal estate of Champion Napier deceased as follows

1 Negro Man by the name of Robert, 1 By the name of Lewis, 1 Still & Cap, a parcel of unprised Tobacco
12 head of Cattle, 21 head of hogs, 28 Geese, 1 Bellus, a few tools & some old Waggon Iron &c, 1 Skillet & hooks and a parcel of pots, 1 apple mill, a parcel of hogsheads Casks, 1 loom and 2 Spinning wheels
1 flax wheel, 1 Desk & 2 tables, 6 Chairs, 1 Cupboard & furniture, 1 Curtain bedsted bead & furniture
1 do & furniture, 1 Bedsted & Cord, 2 beds & furniture, 1 Chest, a frow & grind Stone, 2 wedges, shovel, tongs & spice morter, 1 looking glass & 2 stays, 2 axes & 2 Bustands, 2 axes, 2 plows Chains &c,
2 grubing hoes
Total £ 371.19.0
James Fulton, Reubin Curtis, A Goolsby
Recorded April 16,  1811

**AC Book 4, Page 377**                                                     **Will. Patterson's Inventory**

In obedience to an order made by the worshipful Court of Pittsylvania County to us directed  to appraise the estate of William Patterson Dec'd, we proceeded as followth to wit:
2$^{nd}$ April 1811

1 Feather Bed & furniture & bed stock, 1 Bed stock, 1 pine table, 1 Cotton Wheel & p. Cotton Cards ,
5 Sitting Chairs, 1 set of cups & saucers, 3 books, 1 pepper box, 2 pewter dishes, 1 bason, 5 plaites & spoons , 2 water pails, 1 tin bucket, 1 dividing spoon, 1 tin Cup, 1 churn, 1 Sad Iron, 1 Salt seller, 1 Meal Barrel, 1 wire Sifter, 1 bread tray, 1 washing tub, 1 Black walnut Chest, 1 pare of chain traces, 1 p. Hames, 1 Swingletree & Clevis, 1 Mattox & plow, 1 hilling hoe, 1 screw auger, 1 Iron Pot, 1 Dutch oven, 1 pr Pot Hooks, 1 gimblet, 1 ax, 1 old hilling hoe, 1 Sow & 4 Shoats, 1 Bay mare & young Colt
Nathan Glenn, Griffith Dickenson, Zacharias Lewis
Recorded April 16, 1811

**AC Book 4, Page 378**                           **Robert Johns' Inventry**

An Inventory & appraisement of the Estate of  Robert Johns Dec'd Taken this 30$^{th}$ day of March 1811
Viz:

One red Heifer, One Dark pided Cow, 1 Yallow Do white face, 3 Yearlings, 10 bear Stops, 1 Sorrel Colt, Bay mare, 1 large Iron pot, 1 small do & hooks, 1 small oven & hooks, 1 Iron pot rack, Shovel & tongs, 1 large oven, 3 Sad Irons, a parcel of pewter, Parcel earthern ware, 6 knives & forks, 1 Loom, 1 wheat sive 1 Mans Saddle, 2 meal Sifters, Parcel Water Vessels, 2 Cotton wheels, 2 Flax wheels, 1 parcel old tubs, 2 Butter pots, 2 Jugs, 2 quart bottles, 1 coffee mill, parcel tin ware, 1 cupboard, 1 looking glass, 1 Slate, 2 Stays, parcel Books., Case Razors &c., 6 Chairs, 4 Phials, 3 Chests, 2 tables, 3 Beds, bedsteads & furniture, 2 Bee hives, 3 Empty do, 5 Hhds., 4 plows, 1 Cask, 2 tubs, 3 sythes & Cradles, 4 hilling hoes 3 grubbing hoes, 1 spaid, 2 P. Axes, 2 Sets Gare, 1 X Cut Saw, 12 Wedges, 2 Screw augers, Drawing Knife, parcel old Smith's tools, hand saw, cutting knife, iron, 1 small lite Cask, 1 pr. Steelyards
Total: £103.12.0
N. Tucker
We do certify that we have met at the Dwelling house of Robert Johns, Dec'd, pursuant to an order of the Worshipful Court of Pittsylvania to us directed and the within is a true list of the Decedents Estate as far as was to us exhibited and that the said prices is the true value thereof agreeable to our Judgment. Given under our hands this 30$^{th}$ Day of March 1811
Sam'l Nowlin, George Dejarnett, Andrew McHaney
Recorded May 20, 1811

<u>AC Book 4, Pge 379</u>                                                                                     <u>Will. Hayme's Inventory</u>

An Inventory of the personal estate of William Haymes Dec'd talen by us according to an order of the honorable Court of Pittsylvania to us directed April Court 1811.

14 Head of Sheep, 2 Yearlings, 1 Yoke of Steers, 1 old work Ditto, 1 Brindle Bull, 1 pied Cow & calf, 1 red pied Cow, 1 pied heifer Yearling, 1 Red Cow Ditto, 1 Do do do, 1 Black Steer, 1 pied Cow & Calf, I Do Do & Do, 1 Do Do & Do, I Do do & do & Bell, 12 head of hogs, 8 Shoats, 1Young bay mare, 1 gray mare, 1 grey horse, 2 coulters, 7 hilling hoes, 2 mattox, 2 pr geers with hames & collars, 3 swingletrees, Irons & Clevices, 1 pr Hames & traces, Irons belonging to half shares, 1 pr. Iron wedges, 1 Frow, 7 axes

1 pr. Stillards, 23 lb bar Iron, 4 plow hoes, 6 Saucers, 2 Cups & 1 nutmeg grater, 6 Saucers and 5 Cups, 1 Sugar Dish & 2 Cream pots, 6 Table and four Tea spoons, 1 old Jug, 3 Tin Cups, 1 Sugar Canister & Sugar Dish, 1 Tin Ladle, 1 Turene and 1 Coffee pot, 5 quart Botles, 1 Earthren Jug, 1 earthern pot, Sugar Cannister & pewter bason, 1 Sand Sieve & 1 looking glass, 1 Trunk, 1 Razor and Strap, 1 pine Table, 1 walnut Ditto , 1 water pail, 1 pine chest, 1 Bead Stead and furniture, 1 Ditto Ditto & Ditto, 1 do do & do, 1 arm chair, 1 old chair frame, 1 old base, 1 pot and skillet, 2 spinning wheels & 2 pr. Cards, 1 Loom & Geer, 1 Shot gun, 10 chairs, 1 side saddle, 9 books

2 Jugs, 2 quart pots & 1 Jill Pot, 12 pr. cards, 1 bell, mettle spice mortor, 1 Box knives and forks, 1 shovel & tongs, , 1 pr. flat Irons, 1 Bap kettle & trivet, 1 Bread waiter, 2 old tin coffee pots, 1 Lantern, candle mould & box, 3 Candle sticks, 1 pepper box & 1 nutmeg grater, 1 pr fire Dogs, ½ doz. New Earthen plates, 3 Earthen Dishes, 11 old Earthern plates, 1 Cupboard, 2 half pint Decanters, 2 small Con bottles, snuff bottles, 1 Caster, 8 Earthen bowls, 2 Salt Stands & 1 waiter, 7 glass Tumblers

1 Negro girl Hannah, 1 Ditto Woman Grace , 1 do do  Tabby, 1  do Boy John, 1 do do Henry, 1 do Child Sylva, 1 do do Joel, 1 do Woman Sarah, 1 do do Wining, 1 do child Grace, 1 do boy Garland, 1 do man James, 1 d do Jerry, 1 do do Beasau

1 tootaddz & Hackle, 2 small Casks, 1 pint bason, 1  flax wheel, 2 rum hogsheads, 5 small Casks, 2 large jugs,, Parcel of leather, 3 loose tubs, 3 Small barrels, 1200 lbs Tobo, 2 butter pots, 2 bottles, 1 tin Sugar boc & 1 candle stick, 1 open rum hogshead, 1 large pine table, 200 lb of Cotton, A parcel of Soap, 2 old boxes, a parcel of Wool, 4 hogshead & 3 Casks

A parcel of flax, 1 ox Cart, 2 Rum Hogsheads, 1 Flax Break, 1 Cutting box and knife, 3 bee Stands

4 Barrels & 1 hogshead, ,1 old Sadle & Bridle, I Cross cut saw, old hinges Ring, auger & Reap hook, 5 bells, 1 hand saw, drawing knife & hammer, 1 howel & craws, 4 augers & 1 pr. Fire dogs, 1 Skillet & 1 small pot, 2 Dutch ovens & hook, 2 potts, 1 Skillet & baker, 2 washing tubs, 5 water pails & 1 Tub, 1 Churn & 2 Trays, parcel of Tinware, 6 pewter Basons, 4 pewter Dishes, 18 pewter plates, 1 pewter pent pot, 1 Frying Pan & coffee mill, old Hooks and saddle, 1 biderprep? & plat form, 8 mash Tubs, 4 hogsheads, 1 Rum hogshead & 3 small casks, 1 Sythe & bindle, 2 wooden Buckets, 1 Funnel, 1 Still and warm tub, 1 Hhs. Tobo. Susposed to be 1400 lbs, 1 open Hds, 2 Jarrs, 2 pitchers, 1 Butter Pot, 1 Powdering Tub & 1 small barrel, 1 old hogshead, 1 kettle, trivet & hooks, 2 Shoats & 1 Barrel, 70 Gallons Brandy, 8 Bushel Wheat, 35 Barrels Corn, 40 lbs hogs lard, 700 lbs Bacon, 1 Double tree, 1 old grind Stone, 7 Shoats, 4 Large Hogs

Total: £1412.16.1

Jasper Hatchett, William Payne, Thomas Moore

Recorded May 20, 1811

**AC Book 4, Page 383**                  **Jos. Austin's Inventory**

Inventory of the Estate of Joseph Austin Dec'd taken this 20$^{th}$ Day of April 1811

17 head of hogs, 8 head of Sheep, 2 Steers, 2 Cows & 2 yearlings & bell, 1 Cow, 1 Calf, 2 Steers, 1 Sorrel mare, 1 grey Colt, 1 Sorrel horse, 7 old hoes, 2 plows Swingletrees hames & Clevis, 1 Bar Share plough, 2 pots & hooks, 7 bands & Sundry Iron, 3 Iron Wedges, 1 Spice Morter & pessel & Sundry Irons, 5 Waggon Botts & Sundry Irons, 1 pair Stillards, 1 steel cutting knife & Sundry Iron, 2 axes, 3 old bells, old Traces, buckets &c, 1 oven, 1 Kopper Kettle, Shovel, Tongs and pan handle, 3 Chisels, 2 flat Irons, 1 Lock Chain, Swingletrees & Sundry Irons, 1 man's saddle, leather, crock & pitcher, 5 waggon hubs, 4 locks & cock, trivet & screws, 1 hackle, 6 Reap hooks, 2 old saws, 1 auger, Crows &c, 3 flax wheels, 3 cotton ditto

1 Whip saw, 7 pewter Basons, 5 plates & spoons, 1 set knives & forks, 1 candle stand, shares and snuffers, 1 candle mould, & coffee pott, 1 copper coffee pott, 2 funnels & Lantron, 8 Stays and 6 pair Harness, 1 churn and Buckett, 1 hub auger, 2 feather beds and furnature, 2 ditto, 2 Sheats and Feathers, 1 Desk and money Scales, old books, 8 Chirs, 1 loom, Cubbard & furniture, 1 Table, 1 Jugg, 1 Dish and bason, 1 Chest and box, fire Dogs, 1 Womans saddle, 3 old wagon wheels, 5 hogsheads, 2 hogshead & 3 barrels, 4 old barrels, 4 lite Casks, 1 powdering tub

1 Negro girl Hester, 1 Negro man Tom, one " woman Pegg, 1 Negro man Cango, 1 Negro Woman Rachel, 1 Negro Girl Viney, 1 boy Lewis, 1 Boy Jack, 1 Negro Man George, 1 boy Sam, 1 woman Edith

In obedience to the worshipful Court of Pittsylvania in an order to us directed we have proceeded to appraise the Estate of Joseph Austin, Died Intestate. Given under our hands this Day & Date above written.

Mathew Wills, James Edwards, James Blakely

Recorded May 20, 1811

**A/C Book 4, page 385**         **Edw'd Nunnilee acct Curt.**

Edward Nunmilee To the Estate of Thomas Johns, Deceased
January 1$^{st}$ 1807 - Rent of the plantation to Jno Parrish
1808 - To the rent of the Do Do
1809 - To the rent of the Do Do  W. Parrish
1810 - To the rent of the Do to Joseph Austin.

CR

1805 By Cash paid William Yancey as balance per his account
July 11, 1802 To Cash Paid Jacob Johns as per his Rect., To my Expenses in Defending to suit Lyle vs Johns Det., To my apumset to Mr. Claborn.

1810

April 22, 1810 - To Cash paid Mr. Gilmore for tax on suit vs James Lanier at the suit of Charles Lewis.
August 2 To 2 days attendance at the suit of Lyle

November Cash to 2 Days attendance at the same
By Balance due to this date

April 3, 1809 To Clerks Tickets to the amount of paid Wm Yansee per my note.
To balance due
To Interest on the same till this date
To balance Due Nunnilee

In obedience to the order of the worshipful Court of Pittsylvania to us directed, we have proceeded to examine the papers of Thomas Johns, Dec'd and Judith Johns, orphan if said John Edward Nunnilee Guardian for the same. Given under our hands this 18th Day of May 1811
John Garrett, Mathew Wells, George Aarn
Recorded: May 21, 1811

## AC Book 4 Page 386          Edward Nunnilee Gdn. account

January 1st 1806 Edward Nunnilee Guardian of Judith Johns infant of Thomas Johns, deceased.
1806 Jany 1st to the hier of Mary a Negro girl to William Gravley for one year.
1807 To the hier of said Girl to Gravley
1808 To the hier of said Girl to Gravley
1809 To the hier of said Girl to Gravley

Contract CR

1807
Jany By 200 lbs pork, To Keeping your Negro woman Children, To 4 Barrels Corn

July 15 To medecin (sic) for your Negro in the flux


1808
July 19 - To medeon (sic) when your negro woman was wounded, To keeping your Negro woman and children form the 19th of July until 9th of October the same Date. To 21 yards of cloth
Balance due δ5.18.6
John Garrett, Mathew Wells, George Aarn
Recorded May 21, 1811

## A/C Book 4, Page 387                    Stephen Neal's Inventory

We, Stephen Coleman, Answorth Harrison & Hanes Morgan, Being first Sworn, have proceeded to View and appraise the Estate of Stephen Neal, Deceased, according to order and make Report thereon to the Court.

1 Bed & Counterpin, 1 Do with Bedstead & Cord, 1 Do with Counterpin, Bolster and Beadstead, 1 Chest and Table, 6 Sitting Chairs, 1 Iron pot, 1 Do Oven with lid, 1 Frying pan & Tea Kettle, 1 pair of Iron Wedges, 3 hilling hoes & 1 plow Do, 2 pole axes, 2 Augers, 1 Pair Iron traces, two frising?, one Clevis, one hook & gouge, 1 Grind Stone, 1 Loom & 1 Cotton wheel, 2 Grubbing hoes & three hilling Do, 2 plow hoes, Coalter and frow, 1 pair Iron Traces and Swingle tree, 1 Sythe Blade & Irons1 Pair of Chart (sic) Wheels, 5 Sheep, one Lamb, 1 oven and lid, a parcel of Corn, a parcel of Blades, 1 oneTop Stack with some Shucks, 3 Raw hides, 1 Red Cow, a parcel of Cooppers tools, 3 large Iron Bands, Spice Morter
Jany 30, 1811
Step. Coleman, Answorth Harrison, Haynes Morgan

1 pair Sad Irons, 2 slays, 2 Skillets &c, 1 looking glass, 2 Jugs, 2 pr. Cotton Cards, 1 Candle Stick, 2 Earthen Dishes, 1 Set of knives & forks, pepper Box
Answorth Harrison, Step. Coleman
Recorded: May 21, 1811

**A/C Book 4, Page 388                    Mary Henry Allotment of Dower**

In obedience to an order of the worshipful Court of Pittsylvania to us Directed, we whose names are hereunto Subscribed Did on Wednesday the 27th February 1811 proceed to lay off and allot to Mary Henry, widow of Francis Henry, Dec'd, her Dower of the land belonging to her said Husband viz: One hundred and ninety four acres including the plantation and Mansion house & bounded as followeth: Beginning at a post Oak on the road thence with Kerby's line S. 58° W 115 poles to a small red oak Saplin and pointers, thence new dividing lines S 20° E 150 poles to an ash on a branch, N 85°E 225 poles to a Dead pine, thence with Lepard's line N 32°W 168 poles to a white oak, thence with Kirbey's lines S 54°W 50 poles to the Pigg River old road and thence along the said Road to the Beginning.
Jas Hopkins, Nath'l Kirby, William Thompson, Comsr.
Recorded: May 20, 1811

**A/C Book 4, Page 388                    Rich Pitts' Inventory**

This additional Inventory is annexed to the former one.
Part of the Estate of Richie Pitts, Deceased
One grey Horse, One saddle, One pair Saddle Bags
Total: δ16.4.0
The above property was produced to us by John Brown, the administrator, which property at the time of the appraisment was in the Weston county cou'd not be come at till now & we believe the above prices to be the value thereof.
N. Tucker, George Dejarnett, George West
N. B. Mr. Brown wishes the same to be annexed to the former Inventory
Recorded: May 20, 1811

**A/C Book 4, Page 389                    Thos. Pistole's Inventory**

Pittsylvania County Va a list of Thomas Pistole's Sr property taken by Thomas Pistole Jr & Henry E Wilkinson, Executors

1 Negro man, 1 bay mare, 1 Gray Ditto, 1 Gray Colt, 1 Old Bay Mare, 1 Yoke Stears, 1 Cow and Yearling, 1 Cow & Yearling ditto, 1 Cow and Yearling ditto, 1 small hiefer, 1 Small Yearling, 1 Stear ditto, 8 hogs, 7 head Sheep, 1 Sythe & Cradle, 4 hoes ditto, 1 plow hoe & Colter, 3 Plow hoes ditto, 2 Wedges and a plow hoe, 4 bells, 1 hackle, 4 axes, parcel old tools, 3 bee hives, parcel Shoe tools, 1 Flax wheel, 1 Cotton wheel ditto, 6 Books, 1 peace?, 1 Chest, 50 Gallons brandy, 1 pair Stilyards, 4 Casks, 1 hogshead, 1 bed & furniture & Steads, 1 peace Sole Leather, 1 bed & furniture, 1 bed ditto, 1 large walnut Chest, 1 Cubbard, 1 Chest Drawers, 1 large Jug

1 Butter pot & Jug, 1 Walnut table, 1 Tea Kettle, 1 pine Table, 1 earthern dish, 5 Hogsheads, 3 Tubs, 120 Gallons Cider, 1 Cutting box, 1 Cotton wheel, 1 wash doc?, 2 pare traces & 1 Collar, 1 mans Saddle, 1 Cow hide, a parcel old pewter, 4 earthern plates, 1 coffee pot and 1 gritter (sic), 2 Dutch ovens, 1 pot and hooks, 3 Skillets, 1 big pot, 1 Sow & pigs, 1200 lbs Tobacco, 1 Cow & Calf, a parcel old water Vessels, 3 pare pot hooks, 1 pewter Candle mole, 1 pare Sheep Shares & Candle mold, 1 Small looking glass, ½ Dozen Chairs
Total: δ273.14.3
Bazabil Wier Senr, Thomas Worsham, Thomas Brown, Thos. Wilkinson, appraisers
The above is a true and perfect Inventory of the property which has Come to our hands.
Teste Thomas Pistole, Henry E Wilkinson
Recorded: June 27, 1811

**A/C Book 4, Page 391**                          **Rich'd Reynolds acct. Curt.**

The Estate of Richard Reynolds, DR To John Bennett, Exor.

1807 Nov. Cash paid Philip Cox Sr, James Watson, Samuel Walker, William Burgess, Richard & Samuel by John Stamps, Asa Thomas, John Holland, James D Patton, Morice? Shackleford, Sto. Turner, Robt Wynne (D S/L), Charles Thomas, James Dix, Thomas Gatewood & Co, Thomas Pistole, Clerk's Ticket, John White Coms., Samuel Dabney, John McCadin?, Thomas Burnett, Thomas Adkinson, Thomas Gatewood &Co, Geo Dabney for Thomas Gatewood & Co, Clerk's Ticket, Ro. Wynne on Execution, Geo Dabney for Thos Gatewood & Co, Ro Wynne on Execution, Thomas Gatewood & Co, Jno & Nat. Wilson, Clerk's Ticket, Negro Bob for making Coffin & too Tobo Hhds.
By amount of Sales, Sale of Tobo, Cash, Sale of Tobo
Total: δ178.8.1
In obedience to an order of the worshipful Court of Pittsylvania bearing date April Court 1807 we have this 8$^{th}$ Day of February 1808 stated, settled & adjusted the account Current of John Burnett, Executor of Richard Reynolds, Dec'd as above Stated. Given under our hands
Richard Jones, George Spratten, James S Wright
Recorded: June 17, 1811

**A/C Book 4, Page 392**                          **John Dupuy's Division Est.**

In obedience to an order of the worshipful Court of Pittsylvania County bearing date July Court 1810 we have divided the personal property of John Dupuy Dec'd between Caleb Anglin and Polly Dupuy both legatees of John Dupuy, Dec'd & after Valuing the property, settling all accounts &c, do find Caleb Anglin Indebted to said Polly Dupuy the sum of thirteen pounds, 5/6 ¾. Given under our hands the 29$^{th}$ Day of September 1810.
W. Beavers, Washington Thompson, James Soyers
Recorded: June 17, 1811

**A/C Book 4, Page 393**                          **Hez. Sparks acct of Sales**
Account of Sales of Keziah Sparks, Dec'd personal Estate

Blade fodder Stack, top fodder Stacks & Shucks, blades 2 of 106 lbs, Too moby Stands, too ditto mobby Stands, too ditto ditto m. Stands., Three Barrels of Corn, Eight Gallons of Brandy, Cask, three Chairs, culingder, one bell and Candle Stick, Fore pewter plates and bason, too old flat irons, One plow hoe, one hackle, 1 pr Shears, botel, One flax wheel, one hoe, Cotton wheel, One feather bead, Sow & pigs, One Sow and pigs, three Shoats, one Jugg, Six geese, hand saw, pigen, feather bead &c, Candle Stick, Sugar box, one 600 Sley, Old Sythe blade and Swingletree, two dishes, Remnant of old pewter, too geggs, old pr Cards, too augers, too old tea pots, one ax, Iron pott, Old Hand saw, one Shilling Tomhock, Dutch oven, Cotton wheel, Skillet, Cupboard, Side Saddle, tolet (sic), Bead sted, one ditto bed stead, Chear, Three old barels, Chern (sic), looking glass, Loom, Cow & calf, 145 lbs of poark, 12 lbs of Cotton, Spice Morter, Scrap of Iron
Total: 28.19.11.1 1/5
Larkin Ford, Admrs.
Recorded: July 15, 1811

**A/C Book 4 Page 394**                          **Sam'l Harris Inventory**

In obedience to an order from the worshipful Court of Pittsylvania to us Directed, we whose names are under written, did appraise the personal estate of Samuel Harris, deceased, as much thereof as was presented to our view as followeth. (Viz☺
1811 June 3$^{rd}$

13 Sheep, 11 head of Cattle, 9 hogs, 4 head of horses, 1 Cubbord and furniture, 1 Candle box & looking Glass, 1 Chest, 4 beds Steds & furniture, 1 Table, 2 Small trunks, 1 Coffee mill, 3 Juggs and Sundres, 8 Chairs, 2 Blankets & Counterpins, 1 Shot Gun, 1 Slay, 1 hammer, 1 Cross Cut Saw, hand Saw & Drawn, 2 flat Irons, 1 Can and Tumbler, 1 Loom, 2 Spinning wheels & real, parcel of Kitchen furniture, 1 Chest and warping bares, 3 plows & one Coulter, plowing gheers, 5 hilling hows (sic) & 2 grubing hoes, 3 axes, 2 wedges, Sundres old hogshhd &c, 1 ox cart & fixings, a parcel of Tobo, 1 Saddle, Sise and Cradle

1 Negro woman named Leah, 1 Negro woman named Shato, 1 Negro girl named Agg, 1 Negro girl named Lucy, 1 Negro boy named Harry, 1 Negro girl named Liza, 1 Negro Man named Isaac, 1 Negro Boy named Tom

Total: ẟ659.6.10 1/2

    her
Nancy (X) Harris, Administratrix of Samuel Harris, Dec'd
    mark

Shadrack Boaz, James Fulton, Thomas Garrett
Recorded: July 15, 1811

### A/C Book 4, Page 395            Keziah Sparks Inventory

An Inventory of the Estate of Keziah Sparks, Dec'd
1811 February
1 Stack blades, 1 Ditto tops, 6 hogsheads, 106 lb Blades, 2 sows & 10 pigs, 3 Shoats, 4 plates, 1 Bason 1 Plow hoe, 1 Bed & furniture, 3 Casks, 1 Spinning wheel, 1 flax ditto, 1 Jugg, 1 hackle, 1 Cullender, 1 Cannister, 1 hilling hoe, 3 Barrels Corn, 8 Gallons, 1 Cask, 2 Sad Irons & old bell, 1 pr. Shears, 1 large bottle, 2 Dishes, 1 Bason, 3 plates, 6 Spoons and one ladle, 2 augers, 2 hand saws, 1 hatchett, Candle stick, 2 giggs, 1 Sugar Cannister, 1 pr. Cards, 1 Bassket & old Irons, old books, 1 Pott, 1 oven and hooks, old Sythe blade & 2 staples, 1 Woman's Saddle, 1 Slay, 1 Cow and Yearling, 1 Ax, 1 old table, 1 Cupboard, 1 Wheel, 1 Bedstead, 1 Bedstead, 1 Piggin, 2 old tea potts, 6 Geese, 1 bed, 1 curn (sic), 3 old Barrels, 1 Chair, 1 Loom, 1 looking glass, 1 Skillet, 146 lbs pork, 12 lbs Seed Cotton
Total: ẟ27.5.8
In obedience to an order from the Worshipful Court of Pittsylvania to us Directed, we have accordingly appraised the Estate of the above Keziah Spark and find the amount to be twenty seven pounds, five shillings and eight pence. Given under our hands this 1st Day of March 1811
Wm Ware, Geo Dodson, Drury Pulliam
Recorded: August 19, 1811

### A/C Book 4, Page 396            Mays acct Curt.

DR The Estate of Fleming Mayes, Dec'd In acct Current with Joseph Mayes, Admr.
1811
Feby 9th To paid John Keatts for bala. your note & Int per note taken in
March 3 Paid Samuel Pannill & Co for two notes & Int. per notes & Rects.
May 8 Paid Nathl. Farris per note & Int per Rect.
June 15 Paid Thomas Simpson per note & Rect., paid ditto ditto per ditto, paid F Chumbley, Const. for balance owe on Replevy bond per Rect., Paid William Clark, Sheriff no Voucher
Bala. your note & Int due your admr.
So much allowed for Comms. and trouble of Funeral Expenses.
Total: £48.1.7

CR

1811
Feby 17 By amount of Sales due this day, amount received of Thomas Richardson for his bond.,
Do do do for interest, Amt rec'd of Vincent Walker per acct., Amt rec'd of Robert Walker per acct, Amt Rec'd of Drury Mustaine per note

Balance due J/L Mayes
Total: $48.1.7
Pittsylvania Courty
In obedience to an order of the County Court of Pittsylvania bearing date June Court 1811, we Isaac Coles, Willliam Smith & Samuel Stone named in said Order have Settled the account Current of the Estate of Flemming Mayes, Dec'd with Jos. Mayes the admr. agreeable to the within Statement and report a balance of one pound, two Shillings and 3/due said Admr. Given under our hands this 16$^{th}$ day of August 1811.
Isaac Coles, Wm Smith, Sam'l Stone
Recorded: August 19, 1811

**A/C Book 4, Page 397                    Summerbay's acct. Curt.**

The Estate of Robert W Summerhays To Benjamin Ratcliff   DR
To trouble at my house when sick, burying & expense of a funeral &c
CR
By the amount of Sale
By Cash rec'd of Sundry people who owed said Summerhay before he deceased.
Balance due the Estate of Robert W Summerhays after deducting the Clerks fee &c which I cannot assertain at this time.
Recorded: August 19, 1811

**A/C Book 4, Page 397                    Benjamin Lankford's Est. apprst**

The following is a list of property shown to be appraised as the property of Benja. Lankford, Dec'd by the Exor.

1 Negro man Humphrey, 1 do do Simmons, 1 Woman Alley, 1 do Rachel &, her Child Eady, 1 Negro boy Edmund, 1 Girl Francis, 1 Boy Humphey, 1 do Coleman, 1 do Jack

1 Sorrel Horse, 1 Sow, 1 Yoke of Oxen, 1 Cart and yoke, 1 Red Cow, 1 Black do, 1 yellow do, 1 Bull, 1 Calf, 1 Bed and furniture, 1 Ditto ditto, 1 Bed Sheet, blanket & quilt, 2 Barrels & feathers, 1 Flax wheel, 1 ditto do, 1 Mans Saddle, 1 Square foulding table (walnut), 1 Round ditto, 1 Candle Stand, 1 Desk, 1 Small Cupboard, 1 Desk (old), 1 old pine Cupboard, 1 Cotton wheel, 2 pr Cotton Card, 1 pr wool ditto, 1 Hackle, 1 pr Sad Irons, 1 Loom, Slay and harness & Shuttle, 1 Iron pot and hooks, 1 do do do, 1 Dutch oven & Hooks, 1 Grind Stone, 2 Sythes & Cradles, 3 Reap hooks, 4 hilling & 1 weeding hoe, 2 grubing hoes & 1 Coulter, 3 old axes, 1 auger, Gouge, Drawing Knife, foot addze, shovel & froe, 2 plow hoes, 2 Swingle trees & Clevises & pinns, 2 pr Haymes, Collars, 4 old rope traces, 1 scales beame?, 1 pr Sheep Shears, 1 Curry Comb & pewter Candle mould, 1 jointer & Irons, 1 Straw knife & box, 1 Raw hide, 1 Stack of Rye,, 1 tub, pail & 2 piggins, 5 Cornsul Chairs, 1 Looking glass, 1 horse, 1 pr brass Candle Sticks, tray, and Snuffers and waiter, 5 pewter plates, 1 dish & Bason & 3 Spoons, 6 Knives & 5 forks, 5 Earthen plates 1 Copper Coffee pot, 1 Caster Stand, 2 Cannisters, 4 Saucers, 3 Cups, 1 small plate, 4 Commo. & 1 Silver tea spoon, 1 funel & Bowl, 9 Geese
Total: $685.2.3
Pittsylvaina
Pursuant to an order of the County Court of Pittsylvania, bearing date Sept Court 1810, We William Smith, Philip L Grasty & Joshua Stone, named in the said Commission, have appraised the personal Estate of Benj. Lankford, dec'd agreeable to the preceeding list which amounts to the sum of Six hundred and eighty five pounds, two shillings & three pence. Given under our hands this 12$^{th}$ day of October 1810
Wm Smith, Philip L Grasty, Joshua Stone
Recorded: September 16, 1811

**A/C Book 4, Page 399                    Chloe Coleman Gdn acct**

Polly W Coleman Orphan of William Coleman, dec'd in acco. with Chloe Coleman her Guardian.  DR
1810 Jany 1$^{st}$ To your board up to 1$^{st}$ Sept 1811

Cash paid Permelia to make her proportion equal with the rest of the heirs of William Coleman, dec'd
Ditto paid Johnson for ditto
    Credit
By amount of hire of your Negro man Jacob 1810
Ditto for 1811
Balance due from Sally δ9.13.4

Lucy Coleman orphan of William Coleman, Dec'd in acco. with Chloe Coleman ber Guardian
1810 Jany 1ˢᵗ To your board up to 1ˢᵗ of September 1811
Cash paid William Colemam to make his proportion of the Estate of William Coleman, Dec'd Equal with the rest of his heirs.
Ditto paid Spilsby for ditto
Ditto paid Stephen for ditto
Ditto paid Chloe for ditto
Credit
By the hire of Peter your Negro man 1810
Ditto for 1811
Due to Lucy δ0.13.8

Johnson Coleman Orphan of William Coleman dec'd In acct with Chloe Coleman his Guardian
To your board up to 1ˢᵗ September 1811 after including a Credit for your Labour.
Balance Due from Sally δ9.13.4
Credit
By the hire of your Negro Boy Ted for 1811

Polly Coleman Orphan of William Coleman dec'd in acco. with Chloe Coleman her Guardian.
1810 Jany 1 To board up to 1ˢᵗ of September 1811
Cash paid Betsy to make he proprtion equal with the rest of the heirs of William Coleman, dec'd.
Ditto paid Permelia for Ditto
Credit
By the hire of your Negro man Jesse for 1810 & Ditto for 1811

Joel Coleman Orphan of William Coleman dec'd In acct. with Chloe Coleman his Guardian
1810 Jany 1 To board up to 1ˢᵗ Sept 1811 including so much for my trouble with an Negro Woman belonging to you while she was in a State of pregancy.
Cash paid Chloe to make her proportion equal with the rest of the heirs of William Coleman, dec'd
Ditto paid Betsy for Ditto
Credit
By the hire of your Negro Lucy 1810 & Ditto 1811
Bal. due Joel £2.13.2

Chloe Coleman Orphan of William Coleman dec'd in acct with Chloe Coleman her Guardian
1810 Jany 1To your board and Clothing up to 1 Sept 1811
Credit
By the hire of your Negro Tom 1810
Ditto 1811
So much to be paid to you by me for Joel & Lucy to make your proportion equal with the rest of the heirs of William Coleman dec'd
Due to Chloe δ1.13.8

Spilsby Coleman Orphan of William Coleman Dec'd In acct with Chloe Coleman his Guardian.
1810 Jany To board & clothing of you up to 1 Sept 1811 @ $20 per year.
Credit
By the hire of your Negro Joe 1810

Ditto 1811
So much I am to pay you for Lucy to make your proportion equal with the rest of the heirs of William Coleman, dec'd
Due from Spilsby Coleman δ2.1.10 1/2

Mrs Chloe Coleman, Guardian of the Orphans of William Coleman, Deceased in acct with Sundries of them DR
1811 Aug 30 To Chloe
To Joel
To Lucy
The Sundry Orphans of William Coleman, dec'd who fell in Debt on a Settlement To Chloe Coleman, their Guardian.
August 30, 1811
To balance due from Spilsby
Ditto from Polley
Ditto from Salley
In obedience to the annexed order of Pittsylvania County Court we have Stated and Settled the acct of the Sundry orphans of William Coleman, dec'd who have not come of age with Chloe Coleman, their Guardian and find the balance to stand in favor and against the Guardian agreeable to this acco. herewith Return'd.
Given under our hands this 30 Day of August 1811
Wm Young, Hez. Puryear, James Soyars
Recorded: September 16, 1811

### A/C Book 4, Page 402        Thos Pullin's Inventory

In obedience to an Order from the worshipful Court of Pittsylvania to us Directed we have proceeded to view and appraise the personal estate of Thomas Pullin, Deceased as follows to wit:
One Negro man Adam, One Negro woman Beck, One feather Bed, furniture & Stead, One Trunnel Bed, furniture and Stead, One Feather bed, furniture & Sted, One walnut desk, One still and worm. One ox Cart & Chain, One yoke of oxen, One horse. One pine Chest, One flax wheel, One pair Steelyards, One Walnut Candle Stand, One frying pan and iron tea kittle, Three Jugs & one butter pot, One large puter dish, one small do, Seven plates and two basons and one quart pot, One copper coffee pot, One earthen bowl and three earthen plaits, One Stone pitcher & one tea pot, One iron Spice morter & pistle, One Candle lanthurn, One flax hackle, One large Bible & one Dictionary, Five small books, Three small books

One pair fire dogs, One money Scale, One looking glass & towel, Two butter pots, Old crockery wear & two phials, One Cupboard, plantation & Carpenters tools, Cross Cut saw, Two Cotton wheels, one flax do, Five chairs, One Iron plate, Dirt pitcher and bowl, One kettle, shovel and one tongs, One pot oven and iron bason, One tub, pail, one piggin, One baker, One walnut table, One loom, one Stey & spools, Two bags and hamper basket, One side Saddle, One trunk, One grind Stone, One old barrel, one cask, One tub,
One auger, two bells & one ax, One hackle, Two hogs, One sow and eight pigs, One no horned Cow, One Cow and Calf, Four hoes & two Coulters, Two Cow hides, One cutting box and knife, One slay, Six head of hogs, One clock reel
4$^{th}$ November 1811
Richard Bennett, Mark Anthony, Joeb T/L Adams
Recorded November 18, 1811

### A/C Book 4, Page 404     Jno Mottley's Inventory

We the under Subscribers being Sworn, as the law directs, appraised the estate of John Mottley Dec'd as follows the 6$^{th}$ of January 1811

1 Negro man Sam, 1 Negro woman Anaby, 1 Negro woman Jinney, 1 Negro girl Ailsey, 1 Negro Boy Abraham, 1 Yoke Steers, 9 head of Cattle, 15 Sheep, 1 ox Cart, 1 Sorrel mare, 1 Bay ditto, 1 Black ditto,

1 bay filly, a parcel Tobacco 3400 lbs., 45 Barrels of Corn, 1 Grind Stone, 1 pair iron traces, 1 pair iron wedges, 6 hilling hoes, 3 Plough hoes & 2 Colters, 3 Sows and pigs, 4 Shoats, Half X Cut Saw, 1 Cutting box and knife, 1 parcel Books, , Candle moulds, brushes &c, 3 Jugs, 1 parcel Shoe tools, 1 pr flat Irons, 1 parcel tools, 50 Gallons brandy, 6 Casks, 1 lamb, 2 Cotton wheels, 2 potts, oven &c, 3 tubs & two pails, 1 Claw hammer, 1 parcel pewter, knives & forks, 2 grubing hoes, 4 pole axes, 24 geese, 1 parcel fodder, 1 pair Steelyards, 6 feather beds , 35 pr new feathers, 6 windsor chairs, 9 common ditto, 3 ditto ditto, 1 Desk, 1 Walnut table, 1 walnut Chest, 1 pine ditto, 1 Flax wheel, 1 parcel seed Cotton, 1 Walnut Cupboard & Contents, 1 Sythe and Cradle, 1 Shott gun and Shott bag, 1 pair fire dogs, 1 Shovel &c, 1 looking glass, 1 pine table, 1 pine cupboard &c, 1 Bay filley
Total: £515.7.9
Champness Terry, Edm. Fitzgerald, John Adams
Recorded: October 21, 1811

### A/C Book 4, Page 406 — Waddill's Inventory

Inventory and appraisment of the Estate of John Waddill, Dec'd

1 Negro Woman named Silvy, 1 Negro woman named Betty and Child, 1 Horse, 1 Bed with a bedstead, a Counterpin, a Sheat, a Cord and Stead, 1 bed & Blankett, 1 quilt, 1 sheat, Stead & Cord, a parcel of Earthen ware, 1 Square table, 1 pine Chest, 1 Ditto ditto, 1 butter pot, 2 Table Clothes & Sheat, 2 Water pails, 15 Barrels of Corn, a parcel of Shucks and Top Fodder, 2 stacks of Blades, 1 Iron pot & pot hooks, 1 Skittle & parcel of old Iron, 2 large axes, a hatchett & a bell, 7 old hoes, 1 Flat Iron, Drawing knife and a Curry Comb, 1 Plow and traces, 1 wire Sifter, 2 saddles, 1 Spinning wheel, 1 Raw hide, 1 Loom, 2 Sack bags, The crop of Tobacco
Total δ819.2 1/3.0
In obedience to an order of the worshipful Court of Pittsylvania County, we have this 15$^{th}$ day of November 1811 Viewed and appraised the Estate of John Waddill, Dec'd as above stated. Given under our hands
Rich'd Jones, Thos. Bennett, John Bennett
Recorded: November 18, 1811

### A/C Book 4, Page 407 — Hampton's acct. Currt

This Estate of Thomas Hampton, Dec'd DR In acct Current with John Hampton, Executor. CR

Octo. 10$^{th}$ 1797 To cash paid Geo Burnett as per prc.acct., Colo.Wilson as pr Do, Charles Cox as per Do, John Oldam as per do, John Macan as per do, Wm Sneed as per do, Joseph Parks as per do, Wm McCraw as per do, May Lin Harris as per do, Mayes, Joseph Harris as per do, James Devin as per do, Robert Shelton as per do, Clk of Pittsylvania Court as per Ticketts
To my services &c
Jno Hampton, Junr
To John Hampton Exor DR
To 1 Negro boy 1800 & raising the same 9 years
Thomas Hampton To Jno Hampton, Exor. DR
To 1 Negro Boy born 1801 & raising same 9 years

1803 Augt 18 To my attending Pittsl Court in a law suit and Expenses until Oct. 1811 Inclusive amounting to δ18.13.7 1/2
To be paid in equal proportion by the above John Hampton jun & Thomas Hampton
James Hampton proportion of Sail of Stock amounting to δ18.14.0
Preston Hamptons proportion of Do
James Colquitt Do of Do
George Young Do of Do
John Hampton do of do
Pittsylvania County to wit

We do hereby Certify that we have agreeable an order of Court to us directed, Settled and adjusted the acct Current of John Hampton, Exor. Of Thomas Hampton, Dec'd and do find the same as above stated. Given under our hands this 16th Nov. 1811
Ro. Harrison, Joseph Morton, Thos Marshall, Mathus Cabiness
Recorded: November 18, 1811

**A/C Book 4, Page 408                    Thos. Pistole's list of Sales**

A list of the Sales of the property of Thomas Pistole Sen Deceased made by Henry E. Wilkinson & Thomas Pistole, Executors viz:

1811
March 21  20 Gallons brandy Sold John Pistole
15 gallons do  do  to Ditto
1 young hepher sold to Do
1 small yearling sold Chs. Pistole
1 Sow and pigs sold James Crenshaw
4 sheap sold to John Newbell
60 gallons Cyder sold to S. Walker
 60 gallons do sold John Eudaley

Sept 27
1 Steer Sold to William Townes, Senr
1 hepher sold to William Harris
1 Cow Sold to Ben Morris
Total: 24.13.2
Sold by us Henry E. Wilkinson, Thos. Pistole, Exors.
Recorded: December 16, 1811

**A/C Book 4, Page 409          Brown's Inventory**

An Inventory & appraisment of Henry Brown, Dec'd

33 ½ Barrels Corn, 1 Stack top fodder & Shucks, 1 Stack Blades, 1 ditto ditto, 3 sows & Pigs, 1 Cow bell & Calf, 1 loom, 1 Grind Stone, 1 Sythe & Cradle, 3 pole axes, 2 hilling hoes & 1 grubing hoe, 1 Frow, 2 plow hoes (old), 1 Foot addz., Drawing knife, 2 augers & hand Saw, 1 half Bushel measure, 2 raw hides, 1 Small pot and hooks, 1 oven & lid, 1 Colter & Haymes, 2 old barrels, 1 old Saddle & bridle, 1 pewter bason, 1 pewter Dish, 4 plates & 2 knives & forks, 1 pewter Dish, 1bed Stead, 1 700 Slay, 1 350, 1 gum & feathers, 1 piggin, 1 old pine chest
Total: £22.17.9
Pittsylvania County
In Conformity to an Order of Pittsylvania County Court bearing date October Court 1811 we have appraised the Estate of Henry Brown, deceased, as shown us agreeable to the above list which amounts to twenty two pounds, 17/9 exclusive of the corn at nine Shellings per barrel the quanitity of which is not ascertained at this time and we do report accordingly. Given under our hands this 11th day of November 1811.
Will. Smith, Robert Waller, Stephen Clement
Recorded: December 16, 1811

**A/C Book 4, Page 410                    Tanner's account of Sales**

A list of the sales of the estate of Mathew Tanner, Dec'd began the 27th day of February 1810 By Creed Tanner the Executor of the Same

Creed Tanner-To 1 pair money Scales & horse, 1 pair sheep shears, 1 Piece of Steele, 1 pair of Stilllyards,

1 flax hatchett, 1 lot of tools, 3 reap hooks, 1 raw hide, 1 bottle Crocas, 1 pair horse phlegms, 1 lot tin ware, 1 lot of books, 13 oz spun tow, Basket, 1 pair of Scales & 2 baskets, 1 old hogshead

Joseph Flippin 1 piece of Steele

Daniel Mottley , Jun 1 lamb

Benjamin Burgess Dr piece of Iron

Garret Ford 1 well Chain

Lucy Tanner DR Shovel & R. hooks, 1 oven, 1 ox Cart , 10 barrels of Corn, 10 barrels of ditto, 3 chairs, 2 Ditto, 1 Sugar box, 2 Slays, 2 Jugs, 1 earthen dish, 2 butter pots, 1 lot of pewter, 1 Soop spoon, tallow & wax, 1 lot wood ware, Candle Stick, 1 chest & 2 vials, 1 flax wheel, 1 pair of Cotton Cards, 1ditto, ditto wool, 2 pair of harnesses, 1 bag of cotton, 1 basket of Cotton, 1 lot of baskets, 1 bag of cotton, 2 tubs, flower tub & 1/2 bushel, parcel of tow?., 2 tubs & wheat, Tops & Shucks of 1000 lb of fodder, 10 lb bacon, small barrel & bags, 4 shoats, 2 barrels, 2 tins, bridle

Sylvany Gardner DR 1 parcel of Coopers Tools, plough, 2 hoes, 1 Coulter & Stock, 1 piece of leather, 1 pair fire dogs

Moses Grigsby 1 pair of hames & traces, 1 pair of Cards, 1 Cotton wheel

Willliam Stimpson 1 lot of tools

Anderson Rowel 1 skillet, 1 bed & furniture, 1 Candle Stick

Francis Duly 1 pot & ladle, 1 stack of oats, 1 stack do, 3 chairs, 1 bay filly, 1 Cutting knife

Nathan Cunningham 1 Oven, old irons, 4 earthen plates, 1 Side of leather

Daniel Bryant 1 Sithe blade

Tunis Coles Sen 1 plough hoe

Joesph Mottley Sen 1 Cask, 1 hiefer, 5 bee gums, 1 Cask, 1 well bucket

Will. Dobtson 4 sheep, 4 sheep do, 1 table

Stokely Turner DR 1 bull, 1 heifer, 1 Ditto, 1 ditto ditto, 1 bull & heifer, 2 heifers

Thos Tanner DR 1 brass morter, 1 grid iron, 2 piggins, 1 sorrel mare, 3 barrels corn, 1 Negro girl

Barton Terry Jr 1 Cow

Abner Lynch 1 Steer, fodder

John Hendrick 1 Sow

Stephen Hardy 5 hogs

The Rev'd Geo Dodson 2 raw hides

Josiah Shelton 5 barrels corr

Nehemiah Kello 1 bed & furniture, 1 case & bottles, 1 Cupboard, teapot & mug, 1 Jug & pitcher

John Waller 1 Shot gun, 1 lot of pewter

William Burgess 1 pitcher

Elisha Bryant 1 brass cock, 1 bason, 1 bason & tin, 1 do do, 1 chest, looking glass, leather, 1 pair cotton Cards, 1 band box, 3 chairs, 1 side of leather

Asa Tanner 1 Cow, 1 lot of hogs

Spencer Adams 1 pair of shoe brushes

John Ford DR fodder

John Patterson DR 1 filly

Heath Gardner 4 barrels of Corn

Also Sales made the 3rd day of April 1810

Allen Caldwell DR 1 dram glass & Caster

Nathan Cunningham 1 lot of Crockery ware, 1 chamber pot, 1 decanter, 1 skillet

Creed Tanner DR 1 lot of crockery ware, 3 barrels & 3 pr harnesses, 1 lot of Iron, Jointer Iron, lot of glasses, 1 X cut saw

Thomas Tanner, Jr 1 lot of crockeryware, 1 bottle & 1 table, 1 basket & barrels, 1 cupboard, 7 beds & furniture, 1 Sad iron, 1 Case knives & forks, 1 tray & **griller**, 1 real, 4 sheep & 2 labs, 1 pot rack, 1 Cow & Yearling, 1 table cloth & towel, 1 do do, 1 basket &c

John Duly DR Churn & lard

Asa Tanner DR 1 lot of lumber

Robt White 1 bead stead & furniture, 2 hogs, 1 sow & pigs

Frances Duley 1 lot of tinware, 1 funnel & coffee mill

John Hendrick 1 Churn

John Patterson 1 butter pot

Geo Shelton 1 Barrel, 1 wheat

Mrs Bryant DR 1 Skillet

Abner Lynch DR 2 barrels of corn

Vincent Hardy DR 1 pot & hooks

Floyd Tanner 1 barrel

A list of Sales made the 21st December 1810

Creed Tanner DR 1 lot of old tools, 1 do do, 1 Cow & yearling, 1 Oven, 1 rawhide, Tubs, 1 lot of tools, 1 Sithe

Absolam Hendrick 1 lot of tools

John H Hendrick 1 grind Stone

Nathan Cunningham 2 hogs

William Oliver 1 yoke of Oxen

Thomas Tanner Jur 1 Sorrel mare

Thomas Cooper DR 1 flax wheel

Creed Tanner
Recorded January 20, 1812

**A/C Book 4, Page 412        Report of Geo Sutherland's Est**
In obedience to the annexed Order of Pittsylvania County Court, we have examined the account Current of John Sutherlin & Geo Sutherlin, former administrators of Geo Sutherlin, dec'd, and find a balance of $9 37 Cents to be due to the said administrators. That the sum of $376 "5.2 which appears to be due to the decedant's Estate from the said administrators was accounted for with the executors of the said Geo Sutherland, deceased, in a credit of the amount of Sales of said Estate with the Executors of the said Geo Sutherland Deceased, in a credit of the amount of Sale of said Estate with the Executor of the said Geo Sutherland, deceased, which will appear in the settlement of their acco. Current. Given under our hands and Seals this 14$^{th}$ day of Nov 1811
Will. Yancey, Daniel Sullivan, Hez. Puryear
Recorded: January 20, 1812

**A/C Book 4, Page 413        Waller's acct. Curt.**

The Estate of John Waller, Senr., Dec'd, DR In account with Samuel Walker, Exor. CR

1809-To Expenses of five Hhds. Tobacco, Carriage and expenses of too ditto, Cash paid Jesse Atkinson for coffin, paid Joel Mann per acct, Henry Pell Ditto, paid William Stamps Ditto, David Fields ditto, paid J. Stimpson ditto, the Surveyor ditto, Sheriff Pittsy. For tax 1809, Joseph Flippin per acct., Wm Slayden ditto, John Stamps do, Jos Slayden Do, Joseph Flippin Do, Robert Waller Do, Noel & A Waddill Do, John Walters do, Thomas Ruffin Do, William Shelton the amt of a Judgment.

1810- March 3  Paid John Waller Jun, Will. Stamps, Gur. of Pleasant Waller, Ep. White, Gur of Liddy White's children, Pheby Boulton, Creed Tanner agent for R. Waller, Wm Walker for Carriage, 3 Hhds Tobacco to Richmond, Charles Colley, A Waddill for carriage 1 Hhd. Tobo. To Richmond, Rebecca Waller, James Walker for carriage one Hhd. Tobo. To Richmond, Thos. Clark attorney, Funeral charges, Clerk of Pittsy. for fees, Creed Tanner per acct., Paid Stokely Turner, Thomas Shelton, James Colquhoun, Harris & Brown, Major Price his Legacy, Clerk Pitts., Pheby Boulton amt of Judgmt., The amt of Samuel Walkers acct for Smith's Work
Paid William Beavers, T Shelton for Jos Slaydon's bond, Robert Walters per acct. , W B Banks atto., Doctor Rawley White, Wm Walker, Clerk Rockingham N C, Clerk Pitts., Charles Pistole, John Waller Jun per acct rendered from Jas Colquhoun & Co, John Waller, Jun

Contra

1809

By Jas Colquhoun bond, 6131 lbs refused Tobacco sold, 1350 ditto, 982 for, Joseph Slaydens bond & Int, Cash received of Sollomon Stimpson, Cash of Asa Thomas by Rebecca Waller's Bond, Samuel Walker's acct. due the estate, Cash found in the house of the Dec'd , Cash paid Jas Colquhoun by Jno Waller Sen for Samuel Waller, Eppa White, John Walter's bond for Rawley White's acct, One loan office ceretificate sold for , The Court allows the Executor for his services
Total: δ30.18.7
Pittsylvania County
In obedience to an order of the worshipful Court of said County, we have proceeded to examine the Vouchers of Samuel Walker, Executor of John Waller, Dec'd, and find the sum of thirty pounds eighteen Shillings and seven pence due the said estate from Said Executor agreeable to this Vouchers &c Rendered us. Given under our hands
J M Williams, Rich'd Jones, Joseph Flippin
Recorded: February 17, 1812

### A/C Book 4, Page 415                              McLaughland's Inventory

An Inventory of the Estate of Charles McLaughland , Dec'd, Taken 12$^{th}$ Day of Nov 1811

1 fat hog, 2 ditto, 4 shoats, 3 do, 6 pigs, 1 old horse, 1 heiffer, 1 Cow, 1 Yearling, a parcel of flax, a parcel of Corn, Hay say 18 barrels, a parcel of nubbins say 2 ½ barrels, 2 stacks of blades say 800 lb, a parcel of Tobo. say 675 lb., 1 Top fodder stack, Shucks, a parcel of Sheave oats Say 350 lbs, 3 sheep, 2 Do, 1 Do, 1 Loom, 6 bushels wheat, 1 old barrel, 2 old bags, 1 Do, 1Do, Coopers tools, old flax wheel,1 old Saddle, 1 Do, 1 half bushel 25 lbs., 2 washing tubs, 2 pails & 2 piggins, 1 Riddle & sive, old Sifter, 2 pewter basons, 1 Do, 5 pewter plates, 1 pewter dish, 1 Do, 9 Spoons, knives & forks, pott & hooks, 1 Dutch oven, 1 Saddle, 1 Trowel, 1 foot adds. draw knife, 2 iron wedges, 1 broad ax, frow, hand saw, hammer &c, 3 augers, 1 chizle and gouge, 1 pole ax, 2 old grubbing hoes, 1 old hilling hoe, 1 Do, Double Swingletree, 2 old plow hoes and Swingletrees, 1 Colter & Stock, 3 bells, 5 chairs, 1 gum & Lott, 1 Cask, 1 Hhs, 1 bagg, 1 table, 1 Cubbard, 1 sugar box, 3 bowls, 1 bottle, 1 mug, 1 Do, Teapot, mustard pot, 1 Cannister, 4 plates, 1 Pitcher, butter pot, Jugg, a parcel of old books, 2 flat irons, 1 Shot gun, Case of Razors, 1 bed and furniture and Stead, Do, furniture & Cord, 1 pr Stillard, 6 geese, 1 flask, Cash $2.42, pr geer, warping bars & Spooling frame
Total: δ209.2.9 1/2
This is to certify that the foregoing is a true inventory of the estate of Charles McLaughton, Dec'd as taken agreeable to an order of the Court of Pittsylvania to us as directed. Given under our hands this 12$^{th}$ Day of November 1811
Robert Clopton, Bartin Terry, David Terry
Recorded: February 17, 1812

### A/C Book 4, Page 416                              Farmer's Inventory

An Inventory and appraisment of the personal estate of Thomas Farmer, Deceased taken the 6$^{th}$ of Dec 1811. Viz:

6 old hoes, 2 old plow hoes & 1 Coller, Sundrie carpenter & Coopers tools, 1 spade, 2 clevices &one pin, 1 old bell, 5 axes, 2 malaxes & 1 iron wedge, 1 old wagon & gear, 4 Cows & 3 Calves, 3 young Cattle, 18 head of hogs, 9 sheep , 1 bay mare, 1 Sorrel horse, 1 Small bay mare, 1 negro man Charles, woman Sylva, 1 negro woman, 1 ditto do Chaney, 1 Ditto girl Sarah, 1 blue Sow, 6 hogs, 1 pig, 1 grind Stone, 1 large pot, 1 Ditto, 1 oven & hooks, 1 Small skillet, iron pot, 1 oven & lid, 3 pails,1 chirn & 1 barrel, 2 Sifters , 2 powdering tubs, Sundrie tubs, 1 Cutting knife & box, 1 Sithe & Cradle, 1 X Cut Saw, 2 old barrels, 1 loom, 1 Small wheal, 1 old barrel & old wheal, 1 bed bedstead,, 2 Juggs, 1 flax wheal, 2 old pine Chests, Square table, 1 Cotton wheal, 1 Side Saddle, Cubard & Contents, 1 bed bedstead & furniture, Coffee mill, 1 pr. Stillards, 1 pr fire tongues, 3 basons, 3 dishes & ½ doz. Plates, 1 old Chest, 1 earthren mug,, 1 bowl, 1 butter pot, 1 Sugar box,  2 earthen dishes, 1/2 doz. Plates, 1 mug, 6 spoons, 5 knives & 6 forks, 1 Holy Bible, 1 hymn book, razer hone,  1 looking glass, 1 pine table, 1 pr spoon molds, 6 old Chairs, 1 bead furniture & 2 beadsteads, 1 pr old saddle bags, 1 old razor & Case

In obedience to an order of the worshipful Court of Pittsylvania to us directed we have appraised the personal estate of Thomas Farmer, Deceased to us shown as above First being duly qualified.
Ralph Smith, Chs Clement, John L Adams, Charles Callaway, Sr

1 small Sow & 6 pigs, 1 pr fat (sic) irons, 1 Candle mold, 1 old bryer sithe, 1 small tin water, 2 old slays
Total: δ565.1.0
Recorded: February 17, 1812

**A/C Book 4 Page 417         Inventory of David Patrick's Estate**

The estate of David Patrick In account With Sam'l Pannill

1810
Septem. 19 - 16 lbs Sugar, 1 Knife, 1 doz. needles, 1 lb Coffee, 2 Butter potts
Value paid Miss Salley Patrick (in Goods)

October 13 - 15 lb Iron, pd Enock Organ
October 31 Cash paid John Turner Exor. of Benjamin Lankford for 20 Barrels Corn per Rect, Amt paid ditto for 6 Barrels ditto Sold on a credit per Rect.

Nov 3 - 2 Chest Locks, 2 Thimbles, 2 pare Locks, 1 piece ck Cotton 20 yards, 1 ditto ditto 20 yards, 5 yards ditto, 100 10 dy Cut nails, 4 lb cheese, 1 doz. Needles, 1/2 Bushel Salt
Cash paid Cornelious McHaney for 8 Barrels corn per Rect.

Nov 12 - 1 Side upper Leather, 12 ½ lb Sole Leather

Nov 14 Nathan Betterton for 15 ½ lb Butter
Nov 21 1 Sack Salt, 41 Bushel Bran
Nov 22 1 Butter pott, 18 ½ lb Sugar, 10 lb Coffee, ¼ lb Allum, 40 Bushels Bran
Nov 27 Cash paid Wm Clark for 1 Cow
Nov 29 1 lb copper rap, ¼ lb Pepper, 1 pr Steilyards, 1 pair Cards
Nov 30 Thomas Fox for Turning per Bill & Rect., ½ lb allspice, 32 Bushels Bran

December 4 - William Worsham for his Nett, part of Tobacco made in 1809 per Rect.
Dec 6 - 27 Bushels Bran
Dec 11 - 400 8 dy wood nails
Dec 29 4 ½ lb Crawley Helle/Stolle, 1 paine windsor Glass, Cash paid John Hunt for Schooling Fanney Patrick per Rect

1811
Jany 1 - amount your Smith's acct for 1810
Jany 2 - Samuel Nowlin for his acct per acct & rect.
Jany 8 - James Pemberton for Tax per Rect
Jany 23 - 45 ½ Bushels Bran

Februa 4 - 32 lb Iron, 55 Bushels Bran, 1 almanack, Tickler, 1 Bunch Bees, 1 Curry comb, 100 8 dy cent nails
Feby 15 - 23 lb Cotton
Mar 11 - 2 Tumblers, 1 lb pins
Mar 23 - 1 paper ink powder, 65 Bushell Bran
Mar 25 - 1 Bushel Flax Seed
April 3 - Joseph Uhane for making Tobo. Hhds per Rect.
Apr 11 - 2 Gallons molasses, 18 ¾ lb Cotton, 100 8 dy nails
Apr 16 - Cash paid Clerk of Pittsylva per Tickets, Ditto paid ditto per ditto

Apr 24 John Turner for Haling corn from Lankfords per Rect.

May 4 - 1 ½ yards Cambrick, 1 quire paper
May 8 - Cash paid Sam'l Noulin for Carriage & Ferriage of 1 Hhd Tobo to Lynchburg per Rect
May 15 - Cash paid John Organ for Surveying whepring Land per Rect
May 16 - Cash paid Sam'l Noulin for 31 feet top Fodder per Rect
May 17 - 20 lb Sugar, 2 Gallons Molasses, 42 Bushels Bran
May 20 - George Dejarnatt for Plank & Leantting per Rect

June 3 - 1 Sack Salt, 22 ½ lb Iron
June 12 - 6 yards calico, 1 Jug, 1 hand saw, 2 1/2 yards divity, 1 Knife 1 doz. maskes
June 18 - Cash paid Turning up 5 Hhds Tobo
June 27 - 1 yard Callico

July 10 - 1 Barrel Herrings
July 15 - Cash paid Wm Whitlow for 1 Cotton wheel per Rect
July 27 - Edward Douglass for Halling 4 Hhds Tobo to Lynchburg per Rect, Cash , 1 oz. Arontea?

August 12 - 3 lb Bees Wax, Balance for 5 ½ yards Substring, 1 Vial Jacop, 1 mug, 1 oz nuns thread, 100 4 dy nails cut
August 13 - 4 ¾ lb Loaf Sugar, 1 frying pan
August 22 - Cash paid Wm Clark Sheriff of Pittsylva. Tax & per Rect.
August 23 - 50 lb Sugar, 1 yd indio cotton
August 27 - Cash pd. Wm Clark Sheriff of Pittsylv.your tax for 1811 per Rect.

Sept 12 - Sam'l Pannill & Co for Season 1 mare to Boxer due 25$^{th}$ Dec 1810, 100 8dy cut nails, 2 chamber pots, the 6$^{th}$ Instant per man George, 9 ¼ Harness leather, 9$^{th}$ Instant, 5 per Cent Commission allowed for Trouble, Expense for collecting £136.15.2 since Settlement 4$^{th}$ Septer 1810
Balance due the Estate of D L Patrick Enclusive of 5016 lb Tobacco unsold

1810 Sept 4 - By Balance due per acct Settled by the Commissioners to be returned to Pittsylvania Court
Sep 23 - 6 ¾ Gallons Brandy Rec'd of Wm Raine on act rent 1809

Nov 22 - 137 ½ Gallon Brandy

1811
Jany 29 - Cash rec'd of George Pannill, Exor of Wm Pannill, per Jenmial Pannill
June 13 - 5016 lb tobo. your part of 5 Hhds inclusive of overseers part made in 1810 to be accounted for agreeable to Sales when Sold
Enoch Organ for 1/6 part of carriage and turning up 6 Hhds.
July 6 119 38/60 Bushels of Wheat abt. to Stand as credit the 6$^{th}$ Dec 1810 the time the last of the crop was delivered.
Moses Craddock for so much rec'd 17$^{th}$ January 1810 on acct rect fir 1809

Sept 11 Cash rec'd of Wm Clark for Tobo. put in his Hd.
Sept 19 By Int on 432 12 1 ½ from 4$^{th}$ Sept 1810 till this day.
1811
Apr 19 By Balance & debit exclusive of 5016 lb Tobo unsold as stated above.
Total: £421.12.4 ½
Pittsylvani County
In obedience to an Order of Pittsylvania County Court dated August Court 1811, We have Settled the account Current of Sam'l Pannill Exor. of David F Patrick deceased agreeable to the written Statement & have compared the Same with the Vouchers and report a Balance due the Estate of D F Pataraick of four hundred and twenty one pounds 12/4 ½ exclusive of five Thousand & 16 pounds of Tobacco which is listed as a credit in the Within account & yet remains unsold.

Given under our hands this 19th Day of September 1811
Wm Smith, Joshua Stone, Philip L Grasty
Recorded: March 16, 1812

**A/C Book 4, Page 421**                                                                 **Pannil's acct Currt**

The Estate of David Pannill In account with Sam'l Pannill

1810
Novem 9th To amt paid John Shelton for a trip to the Western County collecting runaway Debts per Rect.
Decm 18 Cash paid P R Gilmer per Rect

1811
February 13 Cash paid John Dabney atto. fee &c vs Sinns admr. per Rect
March 8 Cash paid James Graham for advertising the lands of Henry Brown & Joseph Leak per Rect
April 13 Cash paid Clerk of Patrick per Ticketts
April 16 Cash paid Clerk of Pittsa. Per Ticket, Ditto paid ditto per Ditto
May 15 Cash paid Sam'l Irvine bals. of Cost of said per Rect, Cash paid for 2 Clerks tickets, Campbell
June 26 Cash paid Sheriff of Henry per Ticket, Ditto paid Jailor of ditto per ditto
August 22 Cash paid William Clark Sheriff of Pittsylva. per tickets
Septem 19 - 5 per cent allowed for trouble and Exps. on Collecting £323.17.7 ¾
Paid Bethenia Pannill widow of the deceased per rect
Heirs of David Pannill for this sum transferred to their acct with their Guardian

1810
Sept 8 By Cash rec'd of John Bruce for John Dabney
Oct 24 Cash rec'd of Gabriel Penn per Peachy R Gilmer atto, Ditto Rec'd of Abraham McMillon per Ditto, Deduct Lawyers Commission
Oct 25 Stephen Lankford for amt his Debt
Novm 9 Amt rec'd of Wm Jones (uncle &c) in horse flesh in Kentucky, Ditto rec'd of Ditto in ditto, Ditto rec'd of Ambrose Jones in Ditto, Cash Rec'd of Mary Todd, Cash rec'd of Thomas Todd for bala. Of Cash sent to pay Tax of Land D. P. Sold to S. Calland
Dec 5 Cash rec'd of William Henderson
Dec 14 John Turner for so much assumed in part Samuel Irby's Debt per Rect.
Dec 18 Cash rec'd of Gabriel Penn for P R Gilmer

1811
March 20 Cash rec'd of Grasty and Pannills, Cash rec'd of Chloe Shelton, John Lewis & Abraham Shelton for their note dated 18th Instant and due 1 March 1812 with Interest from the date in full for Chloe Shelton's Debt
June 18 Cash rec'd of Lewis Jones per acct. , Cash rec'd of James Linn per William Wimbish admr. on part Execution per rect.
July 6 Cash rec'd of Sam'l Irby per John Turner Jr
Augt 21 Cash rec'd of James Linn per Wm Wimbish admr. per rect
Augt 22 Cash rec'd of Geo McNealey
Sept 19 Cash rec'd of Gaines & Beggarly per Wm Clark Shff.
Pittsylvania County
In obedience to an Order of the County Court of Pittsylvania bearing date August Court 1811, We William Smith, Joshua Stone, Senr & Philip L Grasty named in the said Order have Settled the account Current of Samuel Pannill, Exor of D. Pannill, Dec'd, with the Vouchers as exhibited in the said account as herewith Stated and find the same to be balanced on this day. Given under our hands this 19th day of September 1811
Wm Smith, Joshua Stone, Philip L Grasty
Recorded: March 16, 1812

A/C Book 4, Page 423                                    Sam'l Pannill's Gdn Acct

DR The heirs of David Pannill, Dec'd, In a/c with Sam'l Pannill, Guardian

1810
Sept 4th 1 Thimble for Eliza L Pannill
Nov 13 Francis Chumbly, Const. for attaching Fredk Shelton's property for rent in 1808 per rect.
Dec 25 1 new Ogno. shirt for Negro Dick, 1 pr yarn Stockings for ditto
Dec 28 1 qt brandy, 1 oz alloes, medicine for Negro Sally , 1 hat furnished Negro Jack
Dec 29 Sam'l Pannill & Co for 2 blankets for Negro Patt & children

1811
Jany 14 1 quart port Wine for Negro Letty
Feby 13 Cash paid Cost of Suit Crump vs S Pannill, Guardian per rect. from John Dabney
March 2  1 oz. alloes, 1 qt. Whiskey for Negro Letty
April 16 Cash paid Clerk of Pittsylvania per Ticketts, Bethemia Pannill for expenses from 1st Jany. 1810 per Rect.
May 15 Cash paid Doctor G Cabbell for medicine for Negro Letty per rect.
July 6 - 1 V. E Vitrol, 1 lb Sugar, Ginger for Negro Letty
Aug 22 Cash paid William Clark Shiff Pittsylva per ticket, Ditto paid " " Tax per his acct.
Aug 27 Ditto paid Tax for 1811 per Rect.
Sept 12   Samuel Pannill & Co for Cash paid Rich'd Jones for E S Pannill per Rect, ditto   ditto for 1 blanket furnished Negro Peter 1st Jany. 1810.
Sept 13 Cash paid Layton Yancey, Sheriff Tax per rect
Sept 19 5 per cent Comms. allowed for Trouble & Expenses on Collecting £493.4.1 ¾ rec'd since Settlement 4th Sept 1810
Balance due the Orphans

1811
Sept 12 By Amount bought from Contra
Samuel Pannill & Co for Cash they rec'd of John Lewis on acct. Rent for 1810
Sept 19 Interest on δ40.0.0 which was received & omitted in Settlement in September 1810.
Interest on £2111.2.4 1/2 from 4th September 1810 till this day
Estate of David Pannill for this sum transferred from that account.
Sept 19 By bal. due as above

CR

1810
Sept 4 By balance due per acct. settled by the Commissioners and returned to Pittsylvania Court. Hire of Negroes Jack & Dick for 1809, Ditto ditto for 1810 due at the end of the year
Sept 10 Cash rec'd of Rich'd Goggins in full for his Note and Int.
Oct 24 Cash rec'd of Thomas Stone in part of hire for Peter
Dec 15 Benjamin Jones Sen for hire of Negro Richardson for 1807 per Note rendered.
Ditto ditto for hire of said Negro for 1808 & Interest on Note rendered
Ditto ditto for hire of said Negro for 1809 and Interest on note rendered
Ditto ditto for hire of said Negro for 1810 due 25th December 1810 per Note rendered
Dec 29 Samuel Pannill & Co for balance of Thomas Stone's note & Interest for hire of Negro Peter

1811
Jany 26 Cash rec'd of Charles Lewis per Jno East & Drury Casey in part for rent of Hollow Plantation for 1810
By Isaac Tines for his note & Interest for hire of Negro Letty for 1810 rendered
Apr 16 Samuel Pannill & Co for 1 month hire of Negro Betty
May 3rd Cash received of Issac Coles for his note & Interest for hire of Negro Peter for 1810

Sept 12 Samuel Pannill & Co for Cash the received of Wm Dave Sen. the 21st of Dec last
Ditto ditto for ditto they received of ditto the 12th of June last
Ditto ditto for ditto they received in full for note & Interest rendered him 30th Aug last
Pitttsylvania County
In conformity to an order of the Worshipful Court of Pittsylvania to us directed bearing date August Court 1811, We have Stated and Settled the Guardian account of Samuel Pannill, Guardian of the Orphans of David Pannill, dec'd, and compared the same with the Vouchers and report a balance due from the Guardian to the Orphans of Twenty five hundred and thirty pounds, Eight Shillings & 11 ¾ agreeable to this within Statement. Given under our hand this 19th day of September 1811
William Smith, Joshua Stone, Philip L Grasty
Recorded: March 16, 1812

**A/C Book 4, Page 425                                        H Barksdale's Inventory &c**

22nd February 1812
In obedience to an order to us directed from the Court of Pittsylvania, have met and being first Sworn, proceeded to appraise the personal Estate of Henry H Barksdale, Dec'd, as follows. To wit:

Two feather beds & one Counterpin, One chaney press, two tables, Five Setting chairs, A parcel of old books, Two trunks, Pots & a pair of Pot Hooks, One spinning wheel, three hogsheads, Four lite Casks, Eight old hoes, Three grubbing do, One coalter, One Cutting Knife, one draw &c and one steel for cuttings, One pair of Hames, two plows & one Swingletree, A parcel of old Iron, One ax, One Loom, One Cow

We the appraisers agreeable to an order of the Court of Pittsylvania hath this day proceeded to appraise the above property being all that is delivered to us by Mrs Molley Barksdale, and stated by her the above contains a/cthe estate of the above deceased and being called on by the Sheriff for all the estate that was in the possession of Henry H Barksdale at his death which she acknowledges to be eleven Negroes, one yoak of oxen, and two beds and two head of cattle which said property she claims as her own & childrens and refuses to deliver to us to be appraised.
Thos. Anderson, Step. Coleman, Willis Glass
Recorded March 16, 1812

**A/C Book 4, Page 427                                        Rich'd Bennetts Inventory**
Pittsylvania County. We the appraisers of Richard Bennet, Dec'd, properly has made & proceeded as the law directs agreeable to list that the Executors has shown us

3 dutch ovens, 3 pots & hooks, one pair of fire dogs, 1 skillet & frin pan , 3 pot racks and fourteen pewter plates, 4 dishes, 6 basons & 3 spoons, one Shoner and Earthen Dish, 2 earthen pitchers, 1 loom and Sundry Wooden Vessels, one Negro woman Sarry & two children, 1 fellow George, Lucy and two Children, Nancy a girl, 2 axes, 1 waggon and gears, 4 head of horses, two Cows and 1 Calf, 8 head of hogs
half Dozen Chears, one desk, one book, one coffee mill & candle stick, one pine chest, one warnot chest, Sugar box & bottel, one bed and furniture and Waggon Cloth, one Side saddle, three beds &c, one bottle and Small Skillet, ½ dozen knives & eight forks and Candle box, one lantern & Earthen tea pot, Sundry Earthen Ware and Glasses, Two spinning wheals, One looking glass & Candle moles, One pair of fire tongs & Shovel, One pair of fire dogs, Sundry Iron tools, Three plows and Coalter & ten hoes, 5 geese &one bottle, pare of Saddle Bags, one pair of Stillards, one Gun and one Saddle, three thousand weight of Tobacco & decanter, one Grid Iron, 2 beds and furniture & barrel, table
Daniel C Edward, David Vance, John Witcher
Recorded March 16, 1812

**A/C Book 4, Page 428                    Keziah Sparks acct Curt**
The Estate of Keziah Sparks, Dec'd, In acct with Adam Sutherlin, Committe thereof DR
1811 Cash paid William Tunstall, Esq.

1810 July  1/2 barrel corn delivered the decadant.

1812 Jany 18 Paid William Dunkin & Thomas Sparks per acct. & Rect

1811 March Support of 1cow and yearling 28 days, 2 days work of my ox Cart and driver, Paid William Tunstall for the Copy of the Inventory

Jany 18 1812 My Trouble of feeding Stock hogs 28 days

In obedience to the annexed Order of Pittsylvania County Court we have examined, Stated and Settled the account Current of Adam Sutherlin, Committee of the Estate of Keziah Sparks, Dec'd, and find the said Estate indebted to him the above sum of $12.41 cents, we find also that he has accounted with Larkin Ford, administrator of the Estate of the said Keziah Sparks, dec'd per his rect for all the Estate belonging to the said Deceased except the Sundry articles mentioned in the list herewith returned which we deem a Sufficient acco. for the balance. Given under our hands this day and date above written.
Wm Yancey, Carter Mickelburrough, Redmond Fallon

A List of Sundry articles belonging to the Estate of Keziah Sparkes dec'd which is comprised in this inventory thereof which was sold by Larkin Ford, administrator of said Estate and not Complied in his receipt for the balance of the said Estate and used for the Support of the decedant's Children and Support of stock &c viz:

3 Barrels Corn used by the family & support of Stock
2 Fattend hoggs used by the family
1 Ditto Claimed by M. Brooks Sparks & used by him
3 Turkeys used by the family, 4 1/2 gallons Brandy used by ditto
1 pair pot hooks belonging to one of the legatees and given up
1 piggin claimed by Edmund Sparks & delivered him
1 pewter plait melted & not sold in the day sale
1 Jug, drawing knife, wedge, and 1 pr traces which was in the possession of Mat. B Sparks, one of the Legatees who has never delivered them & refuses to do so
1 hand saw of no account & an old with other old lumber
2 Frigen Irons and one open ring sold by the administrator
1 pole ax Sold by ditto
1 1/2 Gallons brandy used the day of Sale
March 1, 1811 – Then received of A Sutherlin, Committee of Keziah's Sparks, dec'd property:

3 barrels of corn, 1 top stack and shucks, 1 blade stack, 4106 lbs blade fodder, 1 cow, 5 hogs and 10 pigs, the pork of 2 hogs - 145 lbs , 6 geese, 7 moby Stands, 2 Cyder Casks, 15 gallons brandy, 1 cask, 2 feather beds, 2 bead quilts,2 Counterpins, 1 pine Cupboard, 1 Walnut table, 2 bead steads, 2 coten wheals, 1 flax wheel, 1 iron pott, 1 dutch oven, lead and hooks, 1 loom, one chearn, 1 skillet, 2 old flat irons, 1 piggin, one looking glass, 1 six hundred slay, 2 pewter dishes, 2 old basons, 7 old pewter plates, 6 old spoons, 1 sugar box, 2 candle sticks, 4 chairs, 2 teapots, 1 jugg, 2 gees, 1 bottle, 1 Cullender, 1 Womans Saddle, old books &c, 1 plow hoe, 1 ax, 1 weding hoe, 2 hand saws, 1 tomhock, 1 Iron Spice Mortor, 1 hackle, 3 ducks, 1 bread tray, pair of shears, 2 small augers, 3 small barels, 1 old sythe blade, 1 pare of old cards, 1 bell, 12 lbs of cotton, 2 fish gigs, the Sole of 1soope spoone, old Scraps of Iron &c,
I say rec'd by me blade Stack
Enterlined                              Larkin Ford, Admrs.
Recorded: March 16, 1812

**A/C Book 4, Page 430**                              **Woody of Blades Gdn Acct**
In obedience to an order of the Court of Pittsylvania County to us directed, we have examined and Settled the Guardian account of James Woody to the orphans of Joseph Blades, Dec'd. To wit:

Joseph and John Blades – And find that the said Woody has received the Sum of eighteen pounds, sixteen Shillings and ten pence from the Sale of a Negro in the County of New Kent sold by the Sheriff of that county for sundry purposes. We also have viewed an acct of James Woody for sundries furnished the orphans to the amount of Four pounds after deducting the four pounds we are of opinion that the balance of

the δ 18.16.10 should go to the said Woody, Guardian for the trouble and expenses in prosecuting a Suit to recover the said £18.16.10
Given under our hands this 13th day of February 1812.
Rich'd Jones, John Walters, Sto. Turner
Recorded: March 16, 1812

**A/C Book 4, Page 430                                                                 Dupuy's Gdn Acct.**
DR   Polley Dupuy orphan of John Dupuy Dec'd In acct current with Robert Dupuy, her Guardian.
1810
July 10 To cash paid Sheriff of Pittsa.
Sept 28 - Expenses incur'd at the Division of the estate of John Dupuy, Dec'd
Cash paid James M Williams, Commissioner of the Revenue for transfer of land
Dec 27 - Paid for Expenses of hiring Negroes, Cash paid for Clerks Ticket in the year 1810

1812
March 21- Cash paid Thomas H Clark
April 18 - cash paid J Lansdown, Commission at 5 per cent, To Balance per contra

Contra

1811 Dec 25 - By Basler Irby for the hire of a Negro named Chloe, Layton Wood for hire of Negro Delpha

1812
Mar  Cash rec'd of Jno Keesee, Jun
April 18 Bal due the Guardian
Pursuant to an order of the Worshipful Court of Pittsylvania County bearing date March Court 1812 directing us to examnine, date, settle, & adjust the account of Robert Dupuy, Guardian of Polly Dupuy orphan of John Dupuy, Dec'd, with the said Orphan and after examing the account and exhibits produced to us, we found a balance of one pound, one Shilling and five pence as stated within due Robert Dupuy, Guardian of Said Orphan. Given under our hands this 18th of April 1812.
J. Lansdown, Joel Willis, Champness Terry
Recorded April 20, 1812

**A/C Book 4, page 431                                    Robert Wynne's acct. curt**
DR  The Estate of Robert Wynne, deceased, With Thomas Worsham, admr of said Estate CR

To cash paid William Yancy as per acct, to ditto ditto Nathaniel Wilson, to ditto ditto Isaac Hill ditto, to ditto ditto John Barnett  ditto, Samuel Stone per account, ditto ditto Thompson Robertson per ditto, Joseph Cowen, John Noble, Thomas Barnett, William Beavers, Harris & Brown, Gregory & Fravell, Robert Harrison, William Johns, Peter Irby, Jesse Munday, Thomas Worsham, William Tunstall, Thomas Harris on an Execution Book, John Smith on ditto ditto, James Colquhoun as per acct, Ditto William Yancey, William Tunstall Tickets, to ditto for Thomas Worsham Expenses going & returning from the County of Brunswick, to Commission allowed the admr. for transacting the business of the Estate of one half per cent on δ 266.1.5, To Cash paid William Tunstall, to ditto ditto Phil P Adams, to entering on record 10/6, By cash of William Yancey,  John Worsham, Isaac Hill, Alexander Brown, Robert Ferguson, William Linn, Eppa Stone,  Thomas Worsham, William Stanfield, Daniel Brice, William Walker, Thomas Stewart, Stockley Turner, Richard Gowen, Thomas Worsham, James D Patton, Hickman Spiller, Thomas B Fontain, John Farguson, Lewis Gatewood, Joel Man & Sam'l & Scott, John Barnett from Robert Edwill.

In obedience to an order of the County Court of Pittsylvania made at the August term A.D. 1810, we have Stated and Settled the account Current of the Estate of Robert Wynne, Dec'd with Thomas Worsham, his Administrator, as will appear above and find there is a balance of fifteen Shillings & eight pence half penny remaining in the hands of the said Admr. Given under our hands this 5th of March A D 1812
Francis Dabney, John Noble, Nath. Wilson
Recorded March 16, 1812

**A/C Book 4, Page 433**             **Thos Watson's Inventory**

An Inventory of the Estate of Thomas Watson, Dec'd:

! Negro Woman, Gin, and her child Henry, 1 ditto named Betty and her child, Joe, 1 Negro woman Judy, 1 Boy Simon, 1 negro girl Sary, 1 Boy named Sampson, Lucy nothing, one Red Steer, one one horned Cow, 1 milk and cider Cow & Calf, 1 bell, Cow & Calf, 1 Red Hefer, 1 Black do white face, 8 sheep, 1 ox Cart, 1 bay mare, 1 Sorrel mare, 1 Still, 1 bed &c, parcel of pewter, 1 poplar table, 1 chest, 1 flax wheel, old chest, 4 chairs, Grind Stone, frow, wedge & old Saw, 1 cotton wheel, 1 pot, 1 Dutch oven, 1 skillet, 2 water vessels

Total: $ 515.0.0

Persuant to an order of the worshipful Court of Pittsylvania, We the Subscribers have appraised the Estate of Thomas Watson, dec'd, as appears from the foregoing statements. Given under our hands the 16$^{th}$ day of March 1812.

Samuel M Lovell, Wm Rawlins, Daniel Dunbar

This day Samuel M Lovell, Wm Rawlins & Daniel Dunbar made oath before me.

Thomas H Wooding, a Justice of the Peace for said County to the foregoing appraisement to the best of their Judgment

16$^{th}$ of March 1812

Tho. H Wooding

Recorded March 17, 1812

**A/C Book 4, Page 435**             **C Shelton's acct Current**

DR the Estate of Crispin Shelton, deceased, in acco with Susan Shelton, Exec, Charles J & Abra. C Shelton, Executors

1807

January 2- Pd Sam'l Pannill & Company in full Bond and Acct per State.

Feby 7- Wm Barnes in full of Bond

Feby 17- Exrs of Daniel Pannill, deceased, bala. Exor. & Bond per Stat.

May 18- James Whitehead in full a/c, Expense of Sale, John Lewis in full per a/c

1808 May 16 John Dabney fee per a/c, do do per rect am'd May 18.1807

1807 May 19 Amt taxes per a/c

June 15 – Sheriff's ticket, Richard Johnson full amt Judg. vs us as Security for William Shelton

Sept 15 Henry Ward per bond, Doctr Madison per acct and rect.

Sept 21 – Samuel Yates do do

Oct 23 Thompson Robertson do do

Nov 14 Avory Mustaine per bond, Rich'd Johnson per bond

Dec 21 David Hunt per bond

1808

Feby 21 Francis Dabney per rect. For fee

March 21 Robertson Shelton, Executor of Chloe Shelton, deceased, per bond, Wm Yancey Shff Commission on debt from Tavanor Shelton which has since been rec'd and credited in this accout, Wm Tunstall fee bill

May 16 Wm Wimbish admr of James Linn, deceased per State.

June 11 To Pd John Smith per a/c and rect., Sheriff's ticket per do

Dec 19 Wm Yancey fee bill

1809

Jany 31 – Joseph Motley, Exor, in full Judgment

May 15 Wm Leigh prect expenses going to Georgia to Collect debt due from Lumkin, Doctor Fitzgerald per a/c and acct, William Ward per acct.

1810
March 17 – Benjamin Gosney per bond State &c
July 27 – William Tunstall fee bill
Nov 23 - John Dabney per rect., Wm Leigh per do
Nov 27 – Leroy Shelton per a/c and Rect., John Shelton for 10 barrels Corn amt March 14, 1807

1811
Aug 1 - For inserting 1 notice in the Star, do do do in the Prep.
Aug 19 – Cash deposited to pay cost of Suit Johnson vs Saml & others, in full my proportionable part a debt recovered vs me as Exor as joint Secy. for Ro. Shelton, to David Pannill Exors

1812
Feby 29 - Samuel Pannill per rect, Avery Mustaine amt May 15, 1807 per a/c and rect.
April 16 – to Balance due as per Contra

1807
Jany 2 – 209 ½ pounds machine Cotton Sold S. Pannill & Co,
Feby 7 –Cash rec'd for 1 Hhd Tobo. note 1373 lbs
April 29 – do do do 1426 lbs, deduct John Shelton's part as overseer, Deduct carriage ferriage and Expenses
May 19 - Cash received for Militia Claims, Mary Martin per Claim
June 13 – Cash rec'd of Zacheriah Irby in full his a/c
Aug 18 - Rec'd of Vincent Shelton Bala. his a/c per State., Amount Sales made 14th of May last
Oct 19 – Rec'd of James F Johnson in Full his a/c per State., By cash received of Samuel Irby in full

1808
Dec 19 – Do Stokeley Turner in full his debt per Shffs State.

1809
Jany 20 " of ditto for Tickets paid for him By cash rec'd of Shff. Infull of Exor vs William Shelton for money paid, Rich'd Johnson as Secy. for which a Suit is now pendending Jas F Johnson Ptiff.
Sept 29 – Cash rec'd of the Exor. of Crispin Shelton, Sen, deceased, in full of Legacy

1810
Nov 23 - Cash rec'd of E Jones in full a Judgment vs Tavernor Shelton & said Jones

1811
July 15 – Cash rec'd in closed from Tho. W Cobb (Georgia, payment in full of a Debt vs Joseph Lumpkin, admr. per State. Deducting postage

1812
April 16 – By balance due the Estate
Pittsylvania County
In obedience to an order of the County Court of Pittsylvania bearing date March Court 1812, we have Stated and Settled the account Current of the Estate of Crispin Shelton, Dec'd with Susanna Shelton, Extrix, & Charles J Shelton and Abra. C Shelton, Exors per account within Stated and have Examined the Exhibits accompanying the Same and find no receipt for a part of the Debt of £ 117.6.5 paid Jas Motley, Exor say to the amount of £ 19.4.4.. but such papers as will authorize us to insert the amount as paid and do report a balance of nine pounds, ten Shillings and 9/3 due the said Estate the Exors., Extrix prefering any Compensation that may be allowed them for trouble and Expenses to be laid over till a future time of Settlement. Given under our hands the 16th day of April 1812.
Wm Smith, Philip L Grasty, Samuel Stone
Recorded: April 20, 1812

A/C Book Page 438                                              Jas Henderson 's Inventory

Inventory of the Estate of James Henderson, Dec'd, the 31 January 1811 by Wm Smith, Exor

1 Negro Man Peter, one Negro man Laud, one Negro woman Dinah and child Sally, one Black mare, 1 bay mare and filly, 1 Bay mare, 1 Red Cow and Calf, 1 Red Cow broken horn, 1 red Cow & pide Calf, 1 Brindle Cow & Calf, 1 Brindle Cow & Yearling, 1 Red Cow, 1 Black Cow, 1 pided Cow, 4 Yearlings, 4 Sheep and 1 bell,1 black sow, 3 barrows and 1 sow, 1 Shoat, 5 pole axes, 10 old weeding and hilling hoes, 3 mattox and 1 grubbing hoe, 2 old hatchets, 2 Coulters, 2 old plow hoes, 1 pair Iron Wedges, 3 Clevis & pins and 2 swingletrees, 2 pair traces and haymes, 3 pair iron traces, part of 1 log Chain, 1 hand saw and 1 pair do , 1 X cut saw, 1 froe, 1 foot adze, 1 auger and drawing knife.

1 lot old irons, 1 old Straw knife, 2 Curl boxes & hackles, 3 Bells old and 1 Collar, 1 old sieve, 1 pair old Cart wheels & Irons, 1 Bed and furniture, 1 do do, 1 Still and Worm, 1 flax wheel, 1 do do, 1 Chest, 6 reap hooks, 1 mans saddle, 6 pewter basons, gallon, 7 ditto ditto 2 qt, 2 ditto ditto and 1 porringer, 3 large pewter Dishes, 3 smaller pewter dishes, 16 pewter plates, 1 Ladle and soup spoon, 13 pewter spoons, 2 pewter measures & 1 Candle mold, 1 Safe Eur. & glassware, 5 knives & 6 forks, 1 pr steelyards, 1 pr spoon moulds, 1 Iron trivet, 1 Book Shelf & tins, 2 Iron Candle Sticks, 1 Sad Iron, 1 Family Bible & 4 other books, 1 pewter bason 3 qt, 1 Walnut cupboard and contents, 1 shot gun, 1 pine chest, 1 do do, 1 small walnut table, 1 pine table, 1 do do, 1 walnut chest, 1 small trunk, 1 looking glass, 5 Jugs, 3 butter potts, 11 Chairs, 1 case & 5 bottles, 1 pair Sheep Shears, 1 tin trumpet, 1 pine cupboard, 1 pr fire dogs, 1 large pot and hooks, 1 small pot, 2 pots and hooks, 2 ovens & hooks, 1 do, 1 Skillet & lid, 1 Skillet, 1 mortor & pestle, 1 frying pan, 1 Gridle, 2 Skimmers & 1 fork, 1 Brass kettle, 1 iron pot rack, 1 old pot, 1 grind Stone, 2 Casks, 8 old tubs, 1 Cotton wheel, 1 do do, 3 old Slays, 2 Shovels, 1 tub, 4 piggins
Total: £ 383.4.6
Persuant to a Commission from the County Court of Pittsylvania bearing date January Court 1811, we Joshua Stone Sen, Philip L Grasty and Wyatt Haley, being first Sworn have appraised the Estate of James Henderson, Dec'd, agreeable to the foregoing list. Given under our hands, this 31$^{st}$ day of January 1811.
Joshua Stone, Sen, Phillip L Grasty, Wyatt Haley

A parcel of the corn, a parcel of Tobacco not prized
One Hhd Tobo. prized & on the plantation, Stocks, blade, fodder, Top fodder wheat & oats
Will. Smith, Exor. Of Jas Henderson, Dec'd

1811 January 31 Received of Wm Smith, Exor. Of James Henderson, Dec'd, the property agreeable to the above list, also one bed & furniture which was given to me by James & Wm Henderson which was not appraised.
Mary (X) Hnderson
Test   John Buckley
Recorded: June 16, 1812

**A/C Book 4, Page 441**              **James Henderson's acct of Sales**
Account of Sales of Sundry Property the Estate of James Henderson, dec'd, sold the 17$^{th}$ of December 1811
Wm Smith, Exor.

William Henderson – 1 Froe, drawing knife & old augers, 1 Mattox, pr log Chains, 3 pair traces, 2 pr Haymes, swingletrees, 1 grubbing hoe & Mattox, 2 pr axes, 2 Ditto, 3 Iron wedges, 1 X Cut saw, 3 pewter basons, 5 p. plates, 4 basons, 1 of 1 bason Dish & 1 plate, 1 bason & dish, 1 pewter measure, Candle mold, 1 black mare, 1 pr moulds, 1 Copper still, cap & worm, 1 hackle, 1 addze, 3 Slays, 1 belt & Collar, 1 Skimmer & Saddle, 1 Laddle & fork, 1 Coffee pot, 1 gun, 1 bed & furniture, 1 ditto ditto, 1 blanket, 1 Copper tea kettle, 4 old books

John Buckley – 4 hoes, 1 plow hoe & 3 Clevices, 1 pr hand saws, 1 oven & lid, frying pan & skillet, 1 lot old Irons & 2 cart boxes, 1 Cotton wheel, 1 straw knife & box, 1 pr old Cart wheels & irons, 8 Ea. Plates

James Henderson – 3 hoes, 2 Coulters, 2 plow hoes, 3 basons, 5 tablespoons & 15 spoons, 3 basons & 1 ladle, 2 large p. basons, 1 Griddle & grid Iron, 1 oven & lid, 1 brass kettle, 1 Grind Stone, 1 Sorrel filly, 5 barrels Corn, 1 red Cow & Calf, 1 Walnut Chest, 1 pr Steelyards, 6 reap hoops, 1 mortor & pistole, 2 pair sheep Shears, 1 tin measure, 1 pitcher, 1 butter pott, Walnut table, 4 Chairs, 1 bed Coverlet, 1 Counterpin, 1 Set Cup & Saucers, 1 mug & Saucers, 1 Cow sold at private sale, 274 lbs beef

Catherine Shackleford – 2 bells, 1 Jug & butter pot, 1 Safe, 2 Shoats

Bartlett Greenwood - 1 Man's Saddle

Nelson Tucker – 1 Sad Iron

Samuel Nowlin - 7 pewter plates, 1 red Cow, 1 White back heifer, 1 Steer yearling, 1 heifer yearling

Daniel Fisher – 1 pot & Hooks, 1 pine Chest, 2 Casks

William Whitlock - 2 Iron pots racks & Shovel

Francis Irby - 1 Pot & hooks, 1 oven & lid, 1 large pot & hooks, 4 old tubs

John Dews – 1 Bay mare

John Douglass – 5 barrels Corn, 5 barrels ditto, 1 tub & 2 piggins

Mary Morgan – 5 barrels Corn

Andrew McHaney – 1 Red Cow broken horn

Stephen Dove – 1 white faced Heifer

Charles L Adams – 4 sheep & bell

Mary Henderson - 1 pine Chest, 1 pine Cup'd., 1 lot tins, 1 looking glass, 1 pine table, 1 ditto ditto, 2 tubs, 2 Ear. pitchers

William Smith - 2 Iron Candle Sticks, 4 shoats

John Faris - 1 tin bucket & Skimmer, 1 Lanthorn, 1 Cullender, tin pan & Candle moulds, 1 Sugar box, 1 flax wheel, 1 Jug & Butter Pot, 1 Case &c, 5 bottles, 1 half bushel, 1 Hhd & Barrel, 1 pipe & barrel, 4 Chairs, 1 blanket, 1 lot Ear. Ware, 6 plates, 2 mugs, 1 tea pot, tumble, decanter & Cri. Pot, 1 rawhide, 2 ditto

George Boyd - 4 tin Cups, 1 pine Hhd

Stephen C McDaniel – 1 Black sow & 6 pigs

Jesse Buckley - Parcel of Tobacco out of whch John Compton is entitled to 1/7 part as overseer when collected.

Philip L Grasty – 1 heiffer sold you
Recorded: June 16, 1812

**A/C Book 4, Page 444**                          **Eliza Adams' Inventory**

An Inventory of the Estate of Eliza Adams, Deceased
1 loom, 1 cotton wheel, 1 pot & hooks, 1 Skillet, 1 Dutch oven, 1 pail, too piggins, 1 bole & 1 tray, 4 Chairs, 1 bead & furniture, second bead & furniture, 1 flax wheel, 1set nives & forks, 1 Cannister, too tins,

pepper box, mug & bucket & looking glass, Too butter pots, 1 lot of earthen ware, 1 pewter dish, half dozen doz. Plates & too spoons, 3 puter baisons, 1 pair of Cotton Cards, 1 chest, 1 grey mare, 1 saddle cloth, 1 table & nife box, 1 cubbard, 1 meal tub & churn, too bead sleds, 1 sow & her pigs, 1 red pied cow.
Appraised by us, being first sworn
Henry Glass, Thos. Chattin, Thomas Davis
William Vaden, admr.
Recorded: June 15, 1812

**A/C Book 4, Page 445                                            Jno Shelton's acct Cur.**
The estate of John Shelton, Dec'd, In acct Current with Joel & Abraham Shelton, Exors.

May 12, 1814 - To Cash paid Daniel Shelton Sen, Young Shelton per acct., Clerk Pittsylvania per Ticket, Young Shelton per Rect.

Nov 1 Ditto West D Hurt for Crying at Sale per account
Nov. 10 Ditto Claybourn Shelton per Rect.

1805
Aug 3 – ditto Jacob Saunders Smith's acct., Ditto John Lewis for Spirits
Dec 31 Paid Abraham G. S acct

1806
Feby 17 – Cash paid Pannill's, Exors. for Adam Pace?

July 24 Paid Sto. Turner & Co.

July 26 ditto ditto ditto, ditto Wm Lewis per Will, ditto Tunstall Shelton Do, Ditto Joel Shelton for Services, Ditto William Tunstall per Ticket

1807
Sept 11 Cash paid Sheriff paid for Abraham Shelton by Robertson

1809
July 15 Cash paid Sheriff of Pittsylvania, Cash paid Sheriff of Pittsyvania 12$^{th}$ May 1804,

Nov 1804 by William Lewis for amt. bal at Sale, Isaac Coles for Do, Beverley Shelton Do, Daniel Shelton Jr Do, Abraham Shelton Sen to John Do, Young Shelton Do, Henry Sanders Do, Vincent Shelton Do, Edward Douglass Do, Henry R Shelton Do, Clayborn Shelton Do, Robertson Shelton Do, Griffith Dickenson Do, West D Hurt Do, Wyatt Shelton Do, Absolum E Hurt Do, Armistead Shelton Do, Joel Adams Do, George Butcher Do, William Coe amt. bot at sale, Joseph Mayes Do, Capt. William Shelton Do, John Greggory Jun, Stephen Harris, Henry Keatts, William Haymes, Fannie Shelton, Samuel Irby, Willis Shelton, Tunstall Shelton, Claybourn Shelton, Lettice Shelton, Transper Tobacco, Amt of Debt Brot forward

In obedience to an order of the worshipful Court of Pittsylvania County to us directed we have examined the account of Joel Shelton & Abraham Shelton, Exors. of John Shelton, Dec'd, with the Estate of the said Decedant together with the Vouchers agreeable to the within Stated account and do find that a balance of Sixty four pounds, five Shillings, and five pence half penny is due the said Estate.
Isaac Coles, Vincent Shelton, Samuel Stone
Recorded: July 20, 1812

**A/C Book 4, Page 446                        Nathan Curry's Inv**
November 12, 1807
We the subscribers being sworn according to law do return the following as a true Inventory of the estate of Nathan Curry, deceased

8 heads of cattle, 1 yoke of Steers & Cart, a parcel of potware, a parcel of pewter, 1 tea kettle, knive box, knives & forks, a parcel of Water vessels & churn, 1 Cask, 2 Butter pots, 1 grind stone, 1 pasil of geese, 1 pare of Haymes & hanes, 1 bee hive, a parcel of iron working tools, a parcel of old tubs, 1 plow & some other tools, a parcel of hoggs, 2 Colts, 2 Saddles, 1 bed &furniture, 1 bed & furniture, 1 bed & furniture, 14 lbs of feathers & 2 jugs, 1 old trunk & table, 1 cupboard & furniture, 1 pare of Stillard, 1 chest, 1 stat & 3 Chairs, 1 little Truck, a set of Smith tools, 1 set of rods & vice, 1 pound of good Smith's tools, One Sorrel mare, Bonds & A/C rendered, 2 head of sheep

Total:  £137.13.5

Isaiah Morton, John Payne, Gelbert Burnett

Recorded:  February 10, 1808

# GLOSSARY

**Accompt** – Archaic form of account.

**Adz** – Cutting tool with thin arching blade used to trim off surface of wood.

**Alfin** – Old speeling for orphan; from original account. May also be spelled "alpin."

**And Iron (andiron)** – Used as support for wood in a fireplace.

**Assumset (assumsit)** – An oral or written promise or contract.

**Auger** – Carpenters tool for boring holes longer than those made by a gumblett.

**Axeltree** – Rounded bar used to support wheels of a carriage.

**Bareshare Plow – (bar share plow)** – Plow that cuts furrow slice at bottom and side.

**Barrow** – Male hog castrated before it reaches sexual maturity.

**Battle Door (battledore)** – Long handled paddle for placing bread in, or taking it out of, an oven.

**Beek/Beck (beak) Iron** – Pike or taper end of blacksmith's anvil.

**Bread Hoe** – a griddle, usually iron, that batter is spread on for baking.

**Britch/Breach (breech) Bands** – Part of back of harness.

**Broad Ax** – Used to split or hew logs. Had wide blade tapering to narrow where it joined the handle.

**Cadder/Cader** - Can be grain or child's cradle.

**Calliminco Shoes (calamanco)** – Shoes made of a European woolen fabric of satin weave in plain or striped design.

**Carboy** – Large glass bottle enclosed in box or wicker work.

**Cleveses** – "U" shaped piece of metal with ends perforated for pin and used on end of plow.

**Clock Reel** – A rotary type of yarn winder.

**Contra** – Against; contrary or opposite.

**Cooper** – Maker of barrels or casks.

**Crows** – Bar or iron with one end slightly bent and sharpened to a beak; used as lever to pry.

**Curb Bridle** – Chain or strap passing under lower jaw of a horse and fastened to upper ends of the branches of the bit. Used primarily for controlling an unruly horse.

**Cuttoe/Coutear** – Large knife worn as weapon.

**Denny John (demijohn)** – Large bottle with bulging body and narrow neck that holds from three to ten gallons. It is usually encased in wicker or rush that has one or two handles made of the same material. Used for convenience in transporting.

**Diaper Table Cloth** – A linen type of fabric with small and simple pattern formed by different directions of the thread to make varied reflections of light from surface.

**Dowlas** – Coarse linen cloth now nearly replaced by calico.

**Drawing Knife (drawknife)** – Tool having blade with handle at each end used to shave off surfaces – can be for shaving off wood or the hoof of a horse.

**Drum** – Sieve or cylindrical box or receptacle.

**Durants** – Woolen material sometimes called "everlasting"; or fabric composed entirely of wool.

**Dutch Oven** – Cooking vessel about nine or ten inches in diameter, made of cast iron with bail handle, three short legs and flanged lid. The flanged lid made it possible to heap hot coals on top for even baking. Reflecting ovens (open on one side to face heat) were often called Dutch ovens.

**Ells** – Measure of length, as in cloth. English Ells is equal to 45 inches.

**Fair Calf Skin/Fair Leather** – Leather that is free from blemishes and often used for gloves. The fairest skins were taken from calves or kids and often used as parchment.

**Fellow (A Wheel)** – To make a wagon wheel fit together – where exterior rim of wheel is supported by spokes and curved pieces of wood are joined together to form circular rim of wheel. There were times when the entire wheel had to be soaked in a creek to make it pliable.

**Ferkin** – Small wooden vessel or cask usually for butter or lard.

**Fire Dog** – Same as And Iron.

**Fleams** – A surgical type of instrument that may be used for bleeding a horse or lance the gums.

**Frizens** – Used in making leather soft.

**Frow (froe)** – Cleaving tool with handle at right angle for splitting cask staves and shingles.

**Fulled Cloth** – Cleansed cloth. Cloth was washed in hot water and soap to remove dirt and some grease; was then beaten with fuller's earth (an absorbent clay). The cloth then had to be washed again and stretched and hung over rods. The surface was then curried to raise the nap, with the dried pod of the teasel plant often used to get the desired effect.

**Fustain** – Formerly cotton and linen cloth – now a kind of coarse twilled cotton.

**Gimp** – Narrow ornamental fabric of silk, wool or cotton, often with a metallic wire or sometimes coarse cord running through it. Used in lace as a heavier thread to outline the finer threads of the lace. Used in trimming for dresses, furniture, etc.

**Girth** – Band or strap which encircles body of horse or other animal to fasten a saddle.

**Glover** – Person who made gloves.

**Gound** – Early spelling of gown.

**Gumblett (gimlet)** – Small tool with screw point to bore holes.

**Hackle** – Comb for dressing flax, hemp, raw silk, etc.

**Hair Trunk** – Trunk covered with fur on the outside, with smooth side of hide/leather to inside of trunk.

**Hames** – Curved piece of wood or metal to which Traces are fastened.

**Hessians** – Kind of high boots with top extending to just below the knee; may be ornamental and have tassel.

**Hogshead** – Large cask or barrel, with shaft through center, that permitted tobacco to be rolled to market. Could also be made to hold liquids.

**Holland Cloth** – Linen fabric originally called from province of Holland – unbleached fabric called "brown Holland".

**Hone** – Stone used for sharpening a cutting edge such as a razor.

**Howell** – Cooper's tool used especially for smoothing wood to make casks or barrels.

**Keeler** – Very broad shallow tub especially one for holding milk or for washing dishes.

**Jacklin (jackline)** – King of rope on a line.

**Lancett (lancet)** – Surgical instrument usually with two edges and point like a lance – could be used for opening an abscess or bleeding.

**Martin Gale (martingale)** – Strap fastened to horse's girth.

**Mill** – 1/10 of U. S. cent or .0010.

**Moby Stand** – "Mobby" is a spirituous liquor distilled from sweet potatoes or fruit juice used for distilling brandy. A Moby Stand held beverages.

**Muslinnet (muslinet/muslinette)** – Sort of thick muslin or light cotton cloth.

**Nankeen** – Cloth of firm texture and durability; yellowish-brown in color.

**Noggin** – Small drinking vessel – mug or cup.

**Ochre** – A native earth with mix of hydrated oxide iron with properties of clay. Extensively used as a pigment; usually red or yellow, can be used in making a paint.

**Oznabrig (osnabrig)** – A type of coarse linen, originally made in Osnaburg, Germany; now a stout coarse cotton fabric used for overalls, sackings, etc. Often shortened to "osna."

**Pea** – Sliding weight used on a steelyard.

**Pheaton (phaeton)** – Light four-wheeled carriage with or without a top.

**Pied** – Two or more colors in blotches on an animal – could be just black and white.

**Piggin** – Small wooden pail or tub with an upright stave as a handle.

**Plunder** – Personal property or household goods.

**Poringer (porringer)** – Dish for porridge or similar food; especially a bowl or cup that might hold soup from which children were fed.

**Portmanteau** – Case or bag for carrying clothing or other necessaries when traveling. Originally of a form suitable for carrying on horseback.

**Pottle** – Bottle used to hold liquids and equal to two quarts.

**Quire of Paper** – Loose sheets of paper packed together, formerly four sheets folded together into eight leaves, fitting one within another as the sheets of a book.

**Replevy (replevin) Bond** – A writ by which goods wrongfully taken are ordered to be returned.

**Riddle** – Sieve with coarse meshes, as one for separating grain from chaff.

**Rood** – Square measure equal to ¼ acre or 40 square rods.

**Runlet/Runlett/Rundlett (rundlet)** – Old liquid measure or small barrel equal to about 18 gallons.

**Sad Iron** – Flat or smoothing iron heated on top of stove to press clothes.

**Salamander** – Various articles used in connection with the fire such as a flat round iron, with handle, to be heated and set over pie, or other food to brown the top; or large poker or iron used red hot for igniting certain substances.

**Scantling** – Small piece of lumber (can be used as stud or house framing).

**Scythe** – Long curved blade with sharp edge, on long bent handle, used for mowing grass, grains, etc.

**Shalloon** – Woolen fabric of twill weave, used chiefly for linings.

**Shoat** – A young hog.

**Snaffle** – Bridle bit with mouthpiece of one or more links; used for horse bridle.

**Spancil** – A rope hobble for horse or cow.

**Steelyards** – Form of balance, with arm that is notched, indicating weight.

**Sugar Box** – Wooden box or chest that stood on legs, with sloping lid on top, that held sugar.

**Swift** – Turning reel for winding yarn, thread, etc.

**Swingletree (singletree)** – Pivoted or swinging bar to which traces of harnessed horse are fixed.

**Tare** – To weigh as in wool.

**Tennon (tenon) Saw** – A fine-toothed saw for cutting tenon joint in wood. The tenon is the projecting piece of wood left by cutting away the wood around it. This piece of wood is inserted in the mortise (hole) for joining two, or more, pieces of wood.

**Tickler** – Small pocket flask for "just a dram" of whiskey, or small weapon such as a knife or pistol.

**Toe (tow)** – Coarse & broken part of flax, hemp or jute separated and ready for spinning.

**Traces** – Strips, chain or rope of harness extending from collar to swingletree attached to cart or carriage that is to be drawn by horses.

**Truckle Wheels** – Small wheel, as a pulley wheel.

**Trumpery Iron** – Iron used for decorative work.

**Ullage** – To fill a wine or whiskey cask properly; to fill up to the bunghole.

**Weathers (wether)** – A ram, usually castrated before maturity, or even when only a few weeks old.

## INDEX

AARN
- George 145
- Adam 57

ADAMS
- Charles L. 5, 168
- Eliza 168
- Geo. 25, 107, 108, 139, 140, 141
- George 50, 95, 138, 139
- Joeb L. 151
- Joeb T. 151
- Joel 169
- John 24, 96, 152
- John, Jr. 103
- John L. 158
- N. 7, 8
- Nancy 63, 64, 65
- Nathan 7, 8, 51, 52
- Phil P. 164
- Robert 94
- Spencer 155
- Tim 111
- William 69
- Wm. 16

ADKINSON
- Thomas 147

ADKISON
- Will 104

AKIN
- John 113, 115
- Joseph 124
- Taply 104

ALEXANDER
- Ro. 57
- Robert 12, 54, 57, 63, 91, 128

ALLEN
- Hartwell 40
- L. B. 121
- Lewis B. 121, 133
- Richard 133
- W. A. 59, 61

ALLSUP 78

ANDERSON
- Jacob 100
- Richard 124
- Thomas 6, 67, 102, 124, 134
- Thos. 81, 117, 162
- William 118, 121

ANGLIN
- Caleb 48, 147
- Susannah 48

ANTHONY
- Mark 151

ARMISTEAD
- Samuel 94

ARNERTT
- Jo. 110

ARNOLD
- Henry 38
- James 63
- James, Sr. 91
- Jas. Jr. 54

ARTHUR
- James 34
- Jesse 104

ASHLOCK
- Mrs. 63
- R. 64

AST
- Mr. 110

ASTIN
- James 139
- William 25

ATKINSON 133
- Henry 46, 86, 87
- Jesse 156
- Reg. 111
- William 89

AUSTIN
- Joseph 144

BABER
- Joshua 22

BAGGERLEY
- David 15

BAILEY
- Charles 16, 83
- Cris, 16
- Tho. 55
- Thomas 56

BALL 13, 15, 38, 69

BALLINGER
- Benjamin 3

BANKS
- Henry 13
- W. B. 156
- William B. 92
- Wm., B. 15, 38, 137

BANNISTER
- Edward 4

BARBER
- Shadrack 128

BARGER
- Jacob 70
- Jacob, Sr. 16

BARKER
- Anderson 99
- Ste. 46

BARKSDALE
- B. 46
- Beverly 36
- Henry 115
- Henry H. 162
- Molley 162

BARNES
- James 14
- Wm. 165

BARNETT 137
- Curri 109
- Currie 120
- John 164
- Joseph 118
- Tho. 112
- Thomas 87, 164

BARON
- Josiah 133

BATES 102
- James 23
- L. H. 102
- Lucy, H. 23.103
- Mathew 103
- Matthew 23, 24
- Mr. 24
- Nancy, D. 24

BATTERTON
- Nathan 22

BAXTER
- James 109
- John 119
- Thomas 118, 119
- Thos. 111

BAYNE
- Richard 115, 116

BEAGERLY
- David 104

BEAL
- Shadrack 101, 134

BEAVERS
- Capt. 28
- Jos. 16
- W. 1, 78, 123, 147
- William 27, 28, 133, 156, 164
- Wm. 109, 122

BECKE
- Wm. 50

BECK
- Saml. 94
- W. 70
- William 14, 94
- Wm. 16

BEGGARLY 160

BEIRNS
    Churchill 50
BENAUGH
    George 21
BENNETT
    Bartlet 116
    Hezekiah 96
    James 116
    John 9, 152
    Richard 151, 162
    Richd. 136
    Thomas, F. 116
    Thos. 152
BENSON
    Selby 88, 109
BETSEY 124
BETTERSON
    Nathan 158
    William 76
BINGHAM
    Edmd. 31
    Edmund 23
BLACK
    Abraham 23
    Jim 109
    John 55, 56
    Peter 121
    Thomas 101, 134
    William 57
BLADES
    John 163
    Joseph 163
BLAKE 134
    William 101
BLAKELEY 78
BLAKELY
    J. 7
    James 8, 112, 113, 144
BLANKS
    Joseph 93
BLEAKLEY
    James 112
BOATMAN
    Eliza 14
BOAZ
    Shadrack 20, 148
BOHANNON
    Henry 102
BOLING
    John 95
BOLLING
    William 39
BOOTHE
    Eppy 27
BORDEN
    James 68

BOULDIN
    Thomas 42, 43, 114
    Thos. 44, 113, 114
BOULTER
    Mrs. 85
BOULTON
    Pheby 156
BOWLING
    John 96
BOYD
    David 125
    Georg 84
    George 168
BRADFORD
    David 113, 114
BRANCH (water feature)
    Lick 6, 47
    Lick 6
    PoleCat 47
    Spring 71
BRICE
    Daniel 164
BRIM
    Churchel 107
    Churchill 108
BRISON
    Jno. 15
BROOKS
    John 12
BROWN 87, 111, 124, 133, 137,
        156, 164
    Alex 28, 87, 123
    Alexander 133, 164
    Harris 36
    Hart 124
    Henry 153, 160
    John 124, 146
    Tho. 137
    Thomas 46, 146
    William 125
    Wm. 33
BRUCE 115
    Betsy 26
    Elizabeth 27
    James 5, 13, 115, 124
    John 38, 70, 82, 92, 160
    Lucy 26, 27
    R. 27
    Robert 25, 26, 27
    Thomas 26
    Thos. 27
    Ward 13, 15, 17, 25, 26
BRYANT
    Daniel 154
    Elisha 155
    Mrs. 155

BUCKLEY
    Jesse 76, 168
    Jno. 124, 125
    John 124, 167
BUCY
    Edward 88
    William 87
BULLINGTON
    Robert 104
BUMPAS
    Robert 15, 21, 22
BURCH
    Dandrige 133
    Elish 101, 134
BURGESS
    Benjamin 154
    William 147, 155
BURNETT
    Benjamin 94
    Dodson 8
    Gelbert 170
    Geo. 1523
    Godfree 92
    John 110
    Richard 32
    Thomas 147
    Thomas, J. 34
    Wm. 34
BURNS
    William 41
BURSEY
    Edward 112
BURTON 112
    Elisha 19
    James 120
    Jas. 110, 112, 121
    William 95
    Wm., B. 87
BURT
    Wm. 112
BURWELL
    Henry 20
BUSEY
    Edw. 120
    Edward 118, 119
    Severn 112
BUTCHER
    George 169
BUTLER
    P. 63
CABBELL
    Doctor G. 161
    George 56
CABBLER
    Wm. 139

CABINESS
  Mathus 153
CABLER
  Wm. 138
CALDWELL
  Nathan 155
  Wm. 110
CALL 124
  William 124
CALLAHAN
  Bowker 79
  Jas. 79
  R, /S. 79
CALLAND
  Anna 77
  Booker 76, 77, 78
  Elizabeth 76, 77
  James 76, 77, 78
  Mrs. 78, 79
  Ralph 76, 77, 78
  S. 160
  Saml. 79
  Samuel 39, 74, 76, 77, 78
CALLAWAY
  Anna 76, 77
  Charles 82
  Charles, Sr. 158
  Doct. 75
  Elizabeth 76, 77
  Henry G. 76, 77, 78, 89
  H. G. 79
  James, Sr. 92
  Will. 79
  William 76, 77, 78
CALLUND
  Saml. 113
CAMPBELL
  A. 4
  Abraham 5, 7, 52, 53
  E. 7, 8, 52
  R. 7, 8
  Richd. 52
CAMRON
  Daniel 23
CARTE
  John 115
CARTER
  Jo. 81
  John 113
  Joseph 125
  Juduthun 138
  Lawson H. 43, 44
  Lawson L. 44
  Linen 102
  Pressley 118
  Saml. 35

CASEY
  Drury 161
  Thomas, Jr. 106, 139, 140
Caswell (NC) 109, 110
CHALK LEVEL 13, 91, 130
CHAMBERS
  Tho. 7
CHANDLER
  Daniel 118
CHANEY
  Abraham 7
  T. 35
  Thomas 2, 35
CHAPMAN
  Rebeckah 79
  William 88
CHARLES 118
CHATTIN
  Thos. 169
CHEATHAN
  Abia. 44
CHELTON
  Abel 50
CHICK
  Anderson 6, 129
  Harden 33
CHILTON
  Abel 79
  Wm. 111
CHIRNHALL
  Reubin 91
CHRISTINA 50
CHUMBLEY
  F. 134, 148
  T. 134
CHUMBLY
  Francis 14, 161
CHUMLEY 124
CHUMNEY
  Francis 27
CLABORN
  Mr. 144
CLABOURN
  Nathaniel H. 133
CLAIBORN 27
CLAIBORNE
  Nathl. H. 115
CLARK
  C. 125
  Christopher 124
  Peter H. 31
  Thomas H. 164
  W. 29
  William 21, 109, 125, 148, 160, 161

CLARK (contd.)
  Wm. 109, 125, 129, 130, 158, 159
CLARKE
  Wm.
CLEMENT
  Daniel 101, 134
  Hugh 10
  Isaac 81
  Stephen 10, 45, 153
  Vachel 60
CLEMENTS
  Vachel 82
CLERK
  Wm. 137
CLOPTON
  Jno. 19
  Robert 71, 96, 141, 157
  Robert, Jr. 98, 99
COBB
  Tho. W. 166
COBBS
  Robert 54
  William 56
  William W. 57
COBLER
  William 50
  Wm. 49
COBS
  Wm. W. 57
COE
  Francis P. 16
  William 169
COLBERT
  Lemuel 14
COLEMAN
  Betsy 150
  Chloe 149, 150, 151
  D. 19, 78
  D. B. 115
  Daniel 116
  Danl. 111, 115
  Joel 150, 151
  Johnson 150
  Lucy 150, 151
  Permelia 150
  Polley 151
  Polly 150
  Polly W. 149
  Salley 151
  Sally 150
  Spilsby 150, 151
  Step. 48, 146, 162
  Stephen 23, 145, 150
  William 149, 150, 151

COLES 6
    Isaac 6, 24, 30, 38, 80, 96, 125, 149, 161, 169
    Isaac, Jr. 15
    Tunis Sr. 154
COLLEY
    Charles 141, 156
COLLINS
    John 82
    John Sr. 128
    Thomas 15, 21, 23, 55, 56
    Thos. 57
    William 22, 55, 56, 90
COLQUHAUN 16, 63, 110, 112
    James 27, 79, 87, 133, 137, 156, 164
    Jas. 122, 157
    Ro. 15
    Thomas 64
    Waller 40
    Walter 15
COLQUIT
    James 152
COLQUOHOUN
    James 73
COMPTON
    Caleb 15
    Joshua 92
    Wm. 14
CONNER 107
    John 108, 140
CONSTABLES
    Sam 46
CONWELL
    Mrs. 137
    Samuel 137
COOK 85
    Geo. 137
    George 20, 104
    Harmon 4, 126
COOKE
    Thomas 57
COOPER
    Thomas 156
CORNWELL 85
    Francis 20, 49, 133
COTTRILL
    Andrew 27, 28
    Ann 27
COUNTIES
    Campbell 15, 39, 41, 56, 57, 69, 70, 127, 130, 160
    Franklin 38, 130
    Guilford (NC) 61
    Halifax 13, 37, 40, 42, 47, 68, 69, 70, 115, 129, 130

COUNTIES (contd.)
    Henrico 15
    Henry 13, 69, 124, 130, 131, 160
    New Kent 163
    Patrick 12, 13, 41, 42, 129, 130
    Rockingham (NC) 156
COWAN
    Jo. 109
    Joseph 164
COX
    Charles 152
    George 13, 16, 70
    Jno. 124
    John 124
    Lewis 111, 120
    Philip 120, 121
    Philip Jr. 111
    Philip Sr. 109, 147
    William 11
CRADDOCK
    Ann 22
    Anne 56
    Elebeth 23
    Jno. 3
    John 21, 82
    Moses 159
    Nathaniel 69
    Richard 82
    William 22, 23, 82
CRAINE
    James 40
CREEKS (watercourses)
    Lick 47
    Little Sandy 47
    Pudding 95
    White Horne 6
    White Thorn 42
CREEL
    Elijah 35
CRENSHAW
    James 153
    Nathl. 125
CREWS
    James 84
CROFF
    Henry 40
CROSS
    Henry 14
CROWDER
    Wilmouth 42
CUNDIFF
    Elijah 31
CUNNINGHAM
    Nathan 154, 155, 156

CURRY
    Nathan 169
CURTIS
    Reubin 139, 140, 142
DABNEY
    Doctor 111
    Francis 164, 165
    Geo. 147
    Jno. 91, 124, 134
    John 39, 56, 69, 80, 90, 107, 110, 115, 124, 132, 160, 161, 165, 166
    Samuel 147
DABNY
    John 57
DALEY
    Francis 35
DALTON
    Jas. 120
    John F. 34
    Thomas 13
DAMSON
    Go. 111
    Go. B. 112
DAN'L. 110
DANDRIDGE
    West 91
DANIEL
    Martin 17
    Mathew 139, 141
DANVILLE 36
DARNING
    William 10
DAVENPORT
    Thomas 65
DAVE
    Wm., Sr. 162
DAVID
    John 84
    Thomas 169
DAVIS
    Frankey 85
    George 10, 11, 67, 92
    H. 33
    John 85, 104
    Thomas 123
    William P. 10
    Wm. P. 16
DAWSON
    Geo. B. 112, 119
    Go. B. 112
    Jo. B. 23
    Jon. B. 76, 125
    Jona. 125
DECKENSON
    G. 64

DEER
  Gilbert 137
DEJARNATE
  Geo. 13
  George 21, 22, 23, 143, 146, 159
  James 125
DEJURNETE
  George 117
DEURMAN
  John 23
DEVENPORT
  Thomas 125
DEVIN
  James 152
  Robert 112
  Robt. 4
  William 125
DEWS
  John 168
  Reuben 13
  William 123
D. F. P. 54
DICKENSON
  Griffith 142, 169
DICKERSON
  Griffith 81, 82
DICKINSON
  G. 66
  Griffith 30
DILLARD 124, 125
DILLEY
  Francis 141
DISMUKES
  E. 63
DIX 110
  James 37, 147
  John 121
  John, Sr. 119
  Larkin 111
  Mrs. 112
DIXON
  Hall 112
  Henry 118
  Thomas, Jr. 111
  Wm. 111
DOBTSON
  Will. 154
DODSON
  Calab 114, 115
  Elisha 73
  Geo. 19, 141, 148, 154
  Geo., Sr. 98, 142
  George 105
  Mr. 110, 112
  Mrs. 112

DODSON (contd.)
  Presley 73
  Rawley 105
  William 87, 88, 121, 122
  Wm. 141
DOSS
  Ambrose 82
  H. 111
  James 101, 134
  John 124
  Patsey 70
  William 124
DOUGLAS 63, 64
  Edward 21
  John 21, 22, 83
DOUGLASS
  Edward 128, 159, 169
  Edward L. 101
  John 101, 168
DOVE
  Leonard 31, 40
  Robert 130
  Stephen 22, 168
  William 25, 26, 92
  Wm. 27, 129
DOWNS
  Leven 87
DOWRIS ?
  Levin 118
DRY FORK 66
DUDLEY
  Armstd. 14
DUES
  William 123
DULEY
  Frances 155
DULY
  Francis 35, 154
  John 155
DUNBAR
  Daniel 165
DUNKIN
  William 163
DUNNING
  William 82
DUNN
  James 94
  Thomas 94
DUPUY
  Jessee 124
  John 17, 19, 47, 147, 164
  Polley 14, 18, 48, 147, 164
  Robert 164
  Sally W. 18
  Susanna 18

DURRARN
  Grigory 19
DUVALL
  Lewis 57
DYER 136
  Hanson 49
  Joel 104
  Wm. 49
EADS
  John 5, 10
  Wm. 57
EASLY
  Robert 100
EAST
  Jno. 161
  Joseph 33
  Obedience 44
ECHOLS
  Abe 18
  William 97
EDDINGS
  William 42, 113, 114
EDDS
  John 13
EDENFIELD
  W. 57
EDWARD
  Daniel C. 162
  Daniel 53
EDWARDS
  Daniel C. 53, 86, 87
  James 144
EDWILL
  Robert 164
ELLIOTT
  Jas. 51
  Jno. 7, 8
  Peter 51
  Saml. 51
  Simon 51
  Thomas 51
  Thos. 117
  William 51
ELLIS
  Wiatt 70
EMMERSON
  James 94
  John 125
EPPERSON
  Francis 37
  John 42, 44, 113, 114, 115
  Jon 43
  Littleberry 63
EUDALEY
  John 153

FALLON
    Redmond 163
FAMBORUGH
    James 31
FARGUSON
    Covington 119
    Jacob 105
    Jo. 119, 121
    John 164
    Robert 118
FARIS
    Cloe 124
    John 168
    Nathaniel 40
FARLEY
    Daniel S. 119, 121
FARMER
    Hubbard 19, 136
    James 18, 93
    Martin 24
    Thomas 13, 157, 158
    Thos. 5
FARRIS
    Amos 38
    Caleb 10
    Mrs. 124
    Nathaniel 10
    Nathl. 148
FARTHING
    Dudley 23
FAULKS
    John H. 130
FEARN
    Mary 118, 120, 121, 122
    Polly 110
    T. 87
    Thomas 109, 112, 122
    Thos. 117
FEARNE 110
FEARS
    Pleasant 21
FENDLY
    Abraham 94
FERGUSON
    Js. 109, 110
    Milllicent 49
    Robert 49, 164
FIELD 124
FIELDS
    David 156
FIGG 132
    John 68
FINDLEY
    Abraham 140
    Robert 50

FISHER
    Daniel 92, 130, 168
    Thomas 36
FISHNICK
    James 44
    Jonas 43
FITZGERALD
    Doctor 165
    Edm. 152
    Edmd. 59, 61
    Edmond 18, 103
    Jno. 47
    John 49
FLIPPIN 47, 85
    Jo. 137
    Joseph 20, 72, 73, 86, 136,
        137, 154, 156, 157
FOUNTAIN
    Thomas B. 164
FOUNTAINE
    Martha 13
FORD
    E. 35
    Elisha 35, 36
    Garret 154
    Henry 30, 35, 36
    Jarrald 35
    John 35, 142, 155
    Larkin 147, 163
FOX
    Thomas 158
FRANKLIN
    Joseph 23
FRAVELL 164
FREEMAN
    John 36, 43, 44
FRISSEL
    Nathan 130.131
FRIZZLE 70
    N. 14
FULTON
    James 20, 87, 142, 148
FUQUA
    Saml. 12, 13, 14, 15
FUQUAY
    Moses 125
FURGUSON
    Jo. 120
GAINES 160
GALLION
    Mitchell M. 33, 63
GALLIONS
    Mitchill M. 91
GARDNER
    Heath 7, 155
    Silvany 154

GARDNER (contd.)
    Silveing 109
    William 20
GARDNOR
    Silvany 97
GARNER
    W. 20
GARRETT
    John 145
    Thomas 137, 148
GATEWOOD 63
    Dudley 111
    Dudly 118
    James 79, 119
    Jas. 121
    Lewis 164
    Tho. 113
    Thomas 87, 114, 147
GEO. 110
GEORGE
    Jno. 125
    Jonadab 54
    Jorden 14
GEORGIA (state) 165, 166
GILBERT
    George 62
    John 6.33, 62
    Preston 5, 33
GILLISPEE
    Ann 114
    Anne 113
GILLMORE
    P. R. 70
GILMER
    P. R. 160
    Peachy R. 160
GILMORE
    Mr. 145
    P. R. 131
    Peaches 131
GILPIN
    Rodham 105
GITTON
    Jas. 111
GIVIN
    James 29
GIVIMS
    James 27
GLASCOCK
    George 97
    Ro. 118
    William 97
GLASS
    Daniel 22
    Eillis 93
    Henry 23, 169

GLASS (contd.)
    Willis 136, 162
GLENN
    Mrs. 65
    Nathan 31, 34, 39, 81, 82, 83, 142
GOGGINGS
    Robt. 82
GOGGINS
    Richd. 161
    Robt. 83
GOIN
    Richard 110, 118
    Sherward 112, 118, 121
GOOLSBY
    A. 142
GORDON 78, 124
    J. M. 33
GOSNEY
    Benjamin 166
    Henry 26, 108
GOSSAGE
    Daniel 111
    Wm. 111
GOSSNEY
    Benjamin 10
GOWEN
    Richard 164
GRAHAM
    James 160
GRANSTY
    Thomas 25
GRASTY 11, 40, 41, 70, 71, 92, 131
    P. L. 55, 134
    Phil L. 125
    Philip L. 12, 17, 41, 42, 45, 55, 56, 65, 67, 68, 71, 91, 92, 93, 101, 134, 135, 149, 160, 162, 166, 167, 168
    Phil. S. 125
    Thos. 27
GRAVES
    Peyton 32, 131, 132
GRAVLEY
    William 145
GRAY
    Adin 95
    Samuel 105
GREEN
    Berriman 130
    James 104
    Jos. F. 94
GREENWOOD
    Bartlett 168

GREGGORY
    Jno., Jr. 16, 169
    Jno., Sr. 16
GREGORY 164
    John 38
    Mrs. 110
GRESHAM 138
    Laben 138
GRIGGORY
    Josiah 124
GRIGORY
    John 82
    William 82
GRIGSBY
    Moses 154
GUNN 112
HADEN
    Anthony D. 110
HAGOOD
    John 115
HAIL
    Sibert 139
HAILEY
    Joseph E. 124
HALE
    Benj. 124
    William 104
HALEY
    Ambross 35
    Ann 102, 134
    Jos E. 117, 134
    Joseph E. 6, 101
    Lovelace 105
    Sarah 102
    Theo. 101
    Theophilus 100, 133, 134
    Wyatt 101, 134, 167
HALL
    Harry 140
    Henry 138, 139, 140
    Sebert 140
    William 18
    Wm. 105
HAM
    David 89
    Obediah 125, 136
HAMES
    Joseph 53
HAMICK
    David 6
HAMMON 110
HAMPTON
    James 152
    John 152, 153
    John, Jr. 152
    Preston 152

HAMPTON (contd.)
    Thomas 152, 153
HAMRICK
    Benjamin 124
HAMS 137
HANDERSON
    Mary 168
HARDWICK
    Pleasant 132, 133
HARDY
    Benjamin 96
    George 98, 99
    Jesse 96
    John 96
    Joshua 40, 70
    L. 8
    Lewis 96
    Nancy 96
    Polly 95
    Preston 96
    Reubin 96
    Rodah 99
    Rosanna 98
    Sarah 96
    Soloman 96
    Stephen 7, 96, 154
    Vincent 96, 155
    William 95
HARNESS
    Tho. 7, 8
HARPER
    Jesse 114, 115
HARRIS 87, 133, 156, 164
    Benjamin 1
    James 136
    John 14, 39, 40, 71
    Joseph 152
    May Lin 152
    Nancy 148
    Nathaniel 68
    Peter 104
    Peter H. 104
    Peter M. 104
    Robert 138
    Samuel 147, 148, 169
    Thomas 103, 164
    William 153
HARRISON
    Andre 111
    Andu. 118
    Answorth 97, 116, 145, 146
    Ro. 139, 141, 153
    Robert 140, 164
    Saml. 57
    T. 52
    Thomas 109, 118

HARRISON (contd.)
  Thos. 111
  William 139, 141
  William K. 36
  Wm. 57
  Wm, Jr. 140
HARRISTON
  George 70
HARSTON
  Geo. 125
HART
  James 19, 96
  Jas. 49, 113
HATCHETT
  Jasper 144
  Joseph 53
HATTON
  Jesse 136
HAYMES
  William 35, 143, 169
HAYNS
  Joseph 90
HAYS
  George 38
HENDERSON
  James 124, 167
  Mary 167
  William 160, 167
HENDRICK
  Absolam 156
  John 154, 155
  John H. 35, 156
HENRY
  Francis 135, 146
  John 105
  Mary 146
  P. 79
  Patrick 33
HERNDON
  George 13, 31, 32
  Heston 111
  Silas 72
HIGGENBOTHUM
  Reves 105
HIGGINBOTHAM 24
HIGH
  Freeman 99
HILL
  Isaac 46, 111, 120, 132, 133, 164
HILLYER
  James 37
  Jas. 133
HINTON
  Richd. 46

HISTEN
  Silas 109
HODGES
  Chas. 33
  Jesse 96
HODGSON 13
HODNETT 102
  Ayres 100, 103
  Elizabeth 99
  James 99
  John 58, 71, 99
  Lucy 58, 71, 99, 100
  Nancy K. 103
  Wilson 99
HOGDON
  John 70
HOLDEN
  Delaney 23
HOLLAND
  John 114, 115, 147
HOLLOWAY
  Anthony 20
HOLT 141
  Thos. B. 98
HOPKIN
  James 89
HOPKINS
  J. 80
  Jas. 33, 76, 78, 146
HORNBRICK
  David 90
HORSES
  Boxer 62
  Quick Silver 62
  Whip 62
HOSKINS
  John 41
  Thomas 125
  Wm. 14
HUBBARD
  Clark 55
  John 113, 114
  Reubin 84
  Robert 23
  Ruben 21
HUDSON
  Jerry 111
  John 118
  William 113, 114
HULE
  William 104
HUMFREYS
  Benj. 119
HUMPHRIES
  Benj. 121

HUNDLEY
  Caleb 33, 89
  John 14
HUNT
  D. 125
  David 12, 17, 70, 92, 124, 125, 165
  G. 125
  Gilbert 81
  James 38
  John 10, 45, 84, 158
  Nathl. 125
  Samuel 82
  West D. 169
  Wm. 124
HURT
  Absolum E. 169
  Jas. 127
  John 16
  Moses 125
  West, D. 13, 14, 16169
HUSER
  Christon 73
HUTCHERSON
  Walter 15, 16
HUTCHINGS
  Christopher 51
  M. 51, 53
  Moses 51
IRAINER 14
IRBY
  Abraham 81
  Basler 164
  Charles 23
  Chas. 61
  David 14, 82, 83
  F., Sr. 81
  Francis 81, 83, 101, 168
  John, Jr. 23
  Peter 83, 101, 134, 164
  Rebecak 82
  Saml. 16
  Samuel 9, 82, 83, 160, 166, 169
  William 18, 24, 82
  Wm. R. 83
  Zacha. 16, 82, 92
  Zacheriah 166
IRVIN 38
  Sam 24
IRVINE 69, 130
  Saml. 160
ISRAIL 13
JAMES
  Thomas B. 91

JEFFERS
  Joshua 112
JEFFERSON 78
JEFFRYS 37
JENKINS
  Daniel 82
  John 16, 40, 55, 70, 81, 82
  Mrs. 124
JENNINGS
  Saml., H. 124
  Saml. K. 124, 134
JIM 118
JINKINS
  John 70, 97
JOHN
  Robert 56
JOHNS
  Abraham 4
  Doctor A. 90
  Elizabeth 4
  Isaac 4
  Jacob 4, 144
  Jos. 4
  Judith 4, 145
  Polly 4
  Ro. 14
  Robert 15, 83, 142, 143
  Tho. 4
  Thomas 145
  William 164
JOHNSON 166
  Chas. 69
  F. 81
  James 58
  James F. 124, 166
  James T. 124
  Josiah 94
  Oba. 64
  Obadiah 63
  Philip 38
  Richard 165
  Richd. 165, 166
  William 141
  Woodson 128
JOHNSTON
  Richard 36
JONES
  Ambrose 160
  Benjamin, Sr. 161
  E. 24, 166
  Emanuel 23
  Jacob 55
  Nathaniel 39
  Rich. 29
  Richard 105, 119, 121, 147
  Richd. 152, 157, 161, 164

JONES (contd.)
  Rowland 70
  Tho. B. 23
  Thomas 24
  Thos. 24
  Thos. B. 24, 96
  Wm. 124, 125, 160
JORDAN
  L. 111
  Samuel 120
JORDEN
  Saml. 111
  Samuel 87
KAY
  Henry 32, 122
KEATTS
  Charles 11, 12, 40
  Chas. 16
  Curtis 9, 11, 12
  Henry 9, 169
  James 9
  James G. 11, 108
  John 9, 148
  Parkskell 45
  Pascal 45
  Richard 10, 11, 108
  Thomas 9, 11, 12
KEESEE
  Jesse 84
  Jno., Jr. 164
  John 131, 132
  Jeremiah 4
KELLO
  Nehemiah 155
KENN
  M. 13
KENT
  John 63
  Luke 125
KENTUCKEY 76
KENTUCKY 14, 160
KERBY
  Moses 46, 76
KESEE
  Jesse 31
KING
  Peyton 30, 133
  Royal 30
KIRBEY 146
KIRBY
  B. 52
  Moses 53, 104
  Nathaniel 135
  Nathl. 104, 146
LACKEY
  Geo. 14, 70

LAMB
  Walter 49, 124
LAMPKIN
  Geo. 87
LANDON
  N. 124
LANDSDOWN
  J. 164
  Johnson 35
LANIER 70
LANKFORD
  Ben. 14
  Benja. 149
  Benjamin 131, 158
  Stephen 160
LANSDOUN
  Johnson 133
LAWLESS
  John 133
LAWSON
  Smith 18
LEABRYSON ?
  Go. 111
LEAK
  Jos. 16
  Joseph 92, 160
LEE
  Alex. 112
LEFTWICH
  Jesse 92, 136, 138, 140
  Jessee 133
LEGRAND 83
  Agness 2
  John 2
LEIGH
  B. W. 130
  William 111
  Wm. 165, 166
LEPARD 146
LESTER
  F. 124
  John 23, 38
  Joshua 14
  T. 124
  William 82
  Wm. 124
LEVERSTON 127
LEVESTON
  Sarrah 56
LEVIN
  Wm. 125
LEWIS
  Charles 27, 92, 124, 129,
    131, 145, 161
  Charles, Jr. 39, 42
  Chas. 125

LEWIS (contd.)
- Chas, Jr. 12
- Chs, . 15
- Edward 112, 124
- George 103
- James 14, 38, 82
- John 16, 23, 37, 38, 39, 42, 69, 122, 129, 141, 160, 165, 169
- Levi 7
- Sarah 96
- William 13, 27, 98, 169
- William, Jr. 25
- Z. 45
- Zachareas 83
- Zacharias 142
- Zachs. 27, 34

LEXINGTON (VA) 109

LIKEN
- William 119

LINN
- James 14, 18, 18, 38, 39, 40, 60, 61, 62, 63, 65, 71, 130, 160, 165
- Jas. 16, 59, 60, 67
- Nancy 65
- Samuel 70
- Will. 133
- William 49, 108, 119, 121, 164
- Wm. 112, 133

LINTECOMB
- Thos. 24

LINZY
- William 24

LOGAN
- D. 115
- David 115
- James 14

LONG ISLAND 33

LONG
- Jesse 8
- John 5
- L. 8

LORTON
- Robert 120, 121, 122

LOVE
- James 16, 31, 84
- Ro. 16, 40, 91
- Robert 15, 16, 38, 39, 70, 83, 92, 130, 131, 136

LOVELACE
- Nathaniel 123
- Thomas 123

LOVELL
- John 15

LOVELL (contd.)
- Saml. 69, 70
- Samuel M. 165

LOVETT
- John 70

LUCK
- John 33, 62
- Richd. H 33
- Sarah 63

LUMKIN 165

LUMPKIN
- George 132
- Joseph 166
- Sharp 66

LUMPKINS
- George 111
- John 112
- Thomas 122
- Thos. 121

LYLE 144, 145

LYNCH
- Abner 133, 154, 155
- John 54

LYNCHBURG 13, 24, 54, 56, 57, 91, 122, 128, 159

LYNN 136, 140
- Wm. 139

LYON 13

MACAN
- John 152

MADDING
- John 137, 142
- Thomas 141
- Thos. 98

MADDIN
- Jno. 8

MADISON
- Doctr. 165

MAHAN
- Alexander 19, 89, 127

MAHON
- Henry 114

MAN
- Joel 164

MANN
- Joel 156
- Robert 125

MANNING 125

MARKHAM
- John 6
- ary 6, 117

MARKS
- Joseph 1

MARSHALL
- Daniel 90, 127
- John 90

MARSHALL (contd.)
- S. 14, 15
- Saml. 13
- Thos. 153
- Wllis D. 80

MART
- Joseph 19

MARTAINE
- William 92

MARTIN
- Abraham 50
- Abram 93
- Agness 94
- George, Sr. 130
- John 93
- Livicey 31
- Mary 166
- Milly 31
- Patsey 93
- Thomas 31
- William 83, 93

MATHERLEY
- Israel 133

MATHEWS
- Luke 94

MATTHEWS
- Luke 16, 70
- Thomas 94

MATTOCK
- John D. 132

MAY
- Wm. 3

MAYES 85
- Champness 27
- David 48
- Fleming 148
- Flemming 149
- J. 149
- Jos. 149
- Joseph 148, 169
- L. 149

MAYS 85
- Armisted. 47
- Champion 26
- David 47
- Eliza. 26
- Elizabeth 27, 130
- Fanny 47
- Flemming 108
- Garder 47
- Gardner 47
- Gardner, Sr. 47
- Jos. 134
- Jos., Jr. 26
- Joseph 11, 23, 101
- Joseph, Jr. 27

MAYS (contd.)
   Patsey 47
   Polly 47
   Rhubin 47
   Sally 47
   Smith 47
   Wm. 2
MAYSE 152
McALLESTER
   William 62
McCADIN
   John 147
McCAIN
   Jas. 65
McCALLESTERR
   William 91
McCATLESTER
   Wm. 57
McCLANAHAN
   Frs. 15
McCLELAN 13
McCLELAND
   Thomas 89
McCRAW
   A. 125
   Wm. 115, 152
McCRITCHARD
   Jno. 16
   John 15, 40
McCULLOCK 13
   Jeremiah 11, 45, 83
McDANIEL
   Absalam 28, 29
   Clemt. 19
   D. 42, 43, 44
   Drury 43
   Mrs. 124
   Stephen C. 168
McDANIELS 13
McDANNALD
   Joel 119
McDONALD
   Joel 111, 112, 117, 118
McGRAW
   Wm. 124
McGREGGER
   Daniel 38
McGRUDER 78
McHANEY 125
   Andrew 21, 22, 23, 90, 91, 143, 168
   Andrew, Sr. 21
   Cornelious 55, 158
   Terry 82
McLAUGHLAND
   Charles 157

McLAUGHTON
   Charles 157
McMILLON 131
   Abraham 160
McNEALEY
   Geo. 160
McNELEY
   Geo. 16
   George 39, 41, 71, 130
   William 38
   Wm. 14, 15
McNELY 91
   Geo. 92
McNICHOLES
   Donald 82
McROBERTS
   Tho. B. 124
   Thos. B. 66
MEAD 38, 138
   Wm, J. 140
MEADOR
   James 17
MEASE
   Philip 86
MEDCALF
   Spencer 14, 38
MEEKES 48
MICHELBOROUGH
   Henry 71
MICHELL
   David 119
MICKELBURROUGH
   Carter 163
MICKLEBERRY
   Carter 28
MICKLEBOROUGH 132
MICKLEBURROUGH
   Carter 137
   Rob. 29
   Robt. 28
MIHELLOS
   John 24
MILLER 13
   Ro. 81
MILLS (place)
   Lynch's
MITCHEL 109
MITCHELL
   Gidean 132
   Gidion 79
   Henry 13
   James 82
   Jane 92
   Letty 13
   M. 70
   Michael 38

MITCHELL (contd.)
   Michail 39
   Reubin 70
   Robert 14, 92
   Rubin 41
   W. C. 123
   William 20, 31
   William M. 123
   Wm. 13
MITCHILL
   James 129
MOERMAN
   William 57
MOODY
   Blanks 125
MOORE
   James 14, 15, 16, 23
   Rev. 133
   Thomas 35, 144
MORGAN
   Hanes 145
   Haynes 123, 125
   M., Mrs. 134
   Mary 123, 168
MORRIS
   Ben 153
   William, Sr. 94
MORTON 70, 78
   Isaiah 170
   Isiah 104
   Joseph 68, 153
   Josiah 68, 69, 103
   Lucy 113
MOTLEY
   Daniel 59, 105, 154
   Jas. 166
   John 18, 63, 105
   Joseph 165
   Saml. 59
MOTTLEY
   David 99
   John 151
   Joseph 99
   Joseph, Sr. 154
MUNDAY
   Jesse 164
MUNFORD
   Wm. 124
MURDOCK
   James 80, 122
MURPHEY
   William 95
MURPHY
   James 35
   John 130
   William 108

MUSE
   Caty 87
   Joel 104
   John 135
   John, Sr. 104
   Samuel A. 104
   Thos. 127

MUSTAIN
   Avery 34, 84
   John 102, 134
   Polley 27
   Thomas 83

MUSTAINE
   Avery 166
   Avory 165
   Drury 148
   Polly
   Thomas 69

NANCE
   James 139, 140

NAPIER
   Champion 142

NASH
   John 105

NEAL
   Abra. 61, 64
   David 48, 59, 60, 61
   Joel 15
   Mrs. 59, 61
   Ste. 59, 60
   Stephen 60, 61, 62, 145
   Thomas 60, 61, 62

NEGRO – A
   Aamey 43
   Aba 75
   Abbey 77
   Abraham 44, 51, 77, 114, 123, 151
   Abram 53, 72, 73, 75, 88, 104, 108, 113, 115
   Abrams 43
   Adam 73, 151
   Agg 148
   Aggey 5, 75
   Aggy 33, 47, 48, 77
   Agness 75
   Agy 46
   Ailey 72
   Ailsey 151
   Alfred 73
   Allen 30, 47, 48
   Alley 131, 149
   Amanda 33
   Ame 75
   Amey 42
   Amy 46, 108, 114, 115

NEGRO – A (contd.)
   Anaby 151
   Anderson 53, 93
   Ann 48
   Anna 53, 132
   Anny 77
   Anthony 141
   Asa 132

NEGRO – B
   Baccus 62, 127
   Barnett 59, 93
   Bathsheba 53
   Beasau 143
   Beck 151
   Bedford 101, 134
   Belly 75
   Ben 6, 51, 73, 108.132
   Benjamin 75, 77, 96
   Bett 51
   Bette 62
   Betty 30, 53, 64, 65, 75, 77, 126, 138, 139, 152, 161, 165
   Bill 137
   Billey 6, 17
   Billy 33, 77
   Bird 47
   Bob 6, 50, 53, 75, 77, 147
   Bobb 137
   Braneer 132
   Byrd 49

NEGRO – C
   Cabel 33
   Caesar 6
   Candice 132
   Cango 144
   Carter 35, 84, 132
   Castelleo 33
   Catey 126
   Cato 51
   Cealy 46
   Cely 53
   Cesar 47, 48
   Chaney 33
   Charistian 77
   Charity 47, 48
   Charles 30, 33, 123
   Chloe 75, 77, 116, 164
   Christian 76, 89
   Christiana 139
   Cindy 75
   Clary 71, 75, 77
   Cloe 135
   Coleman 131, 149
   Condy 53
   Cotter 21

NEGRO – C (contd.)
   Creasey 76
   Creasy 77, 89
   Cretia 72, 88
   Cupet 85
   Cupid 73, 123
   Cyller 48

NEGRO – D
   Dafney 59
   Daniel 59, 71, 73, 75, 77, 89
   Darby 62
   Darker 1
   Darkie 75
   David 30, 75, 77
   Davy 131
   Dean 30
   Delpha 164
   Delsey 75
   Denes 93
   Dice 69, 61
   Dicey 5, 24
   Dick 25, 50, 75, 77, 88, 92, 103, 108, 129, 161
   Dilee Rucker 62
   Dinah 75, 167
   Doll 35
   Dolly 75, 77
   Dols 116
   Dorcas 33, 89
   Drewry 41

NEGRO – E
   Eady 149
   Easter 46, 64, 65, 66, 67, 71, 88.93, 96, 132
   Eda 49
   Eddy 139, 140, 141
   Ede 50
   Edith 93, 144
   Edmond 48
   Edmund 53, 131, 149
   Edy 30, 75, 77, 131
   Emanuel 46
   Esther 50
   Euclid 64, 65, 66, 67

NEGRO – F
   Fanny 76, 77
   Federick 123
   Fillis 132
   Frances 131
   Francis 149
   Frank 19, 75, 77
   Frederick 30

NEGRO – G
   Gabriel 25, 75, 77
   Garland 143

NEGRO – G (contd.)
    George 25, 53, 58, 62, 64, 65, 66, 67, 76, 77, 89, 144, 159, 162
    Gill 123
    Gin 165
    Grace 143
    Grey 6
    Gruff 33

NEGRO – H
    Hallaway 33
    Hanah 97
    Hanar 46
    Hannah 53, 62, 71, 73, 75, 77, 85, 89, 143
    Harry 33, 34, 49, 51, 73, 75, 77, 84, 89, 104, 116, 126, 139, 140, 141, 148
    Henry 25, 143, 165
    Hester 144
    Humfrey 131
    Humphey 149
    Humphrey 149
    Hurt 72, 88

NEGRO – I
    Isaac 50, 96, 132, 138, 139, 148
    Isbel 62, 73, 77
    Isbell 71, 76
    Isham 123

NEGRO – J
    Jack 5, 6, 33, 46, 51, 64, 65, 67, 75, 76, 77, 92, 104, 129, 131, 144, 149, 161
    Jacob 25, 53, 64, 65, 66, 67, 150
    James 47, 48, 71, 75, 77, 116, 143
    Jancy 108
    Jeanil 123
    Jenn 62
    Jenney 33
    Jerden 104
    Jere 47, 59
    Jere George 62
    Jeremiah 76, 77
    Jerry 73, 143
    Jesse 47, 48, 93, 116, 150
    Jessy 48
    Jim 62, 65, 66
    Jim Thornton 64, 65, 66
    Jincey 59
    Jinney 71, 77, 151
    Jinsey 75
    Joe 150, 165
    Joel 143

NEGRO – J (contd.)
    John 47, 48, 64, 65, 66, 72, 88, 141, 143
    Jonathan 62
    Joseph 71, 96, 123
    Joshua 21
    Juda 19
    Judah 75
    Jude 50, 88
    Jude Viry 108
    Judith 93
    Judy 25, 69, 77, 165
    Juno 51, 132

NEGRO – K
    Kajah 6
    Kiah 30

NEGRO – L
    Laney 108
    Laud 167
    Lawson 141
    Leah 148
    Leonard 75, 77
    Lett 64, 65
    Lette, 62
    Letty 47, 48, 66, 141, 161
    Levina 132
    Lewis 6, 24, 51, 71, 75, 77, 116, 126, 142, 144
    Libby 75, 77
    Lily 104
    Lina 132
    Lindey 75, 77
    Lindley 97
    Lindy 77
    Little Humfrey 131
    Little Peter 35
    Little Sary 25
    Liza 148
    Long Jim 64, 66
    Lorenzo 75, 77
    Luce 33
    Lucey 33
    Lucretia 132
    Lucy 30, 35, 46, 47, 48, 50, 62, 75, 76, 77, 89, 97, 107, 108, 132, 141, 148, 150, 162, 165
    Lydia 33, 76, 77
    Lymus 88

NEGRO – M
    Major 33
    Manuel 35
    Mary 33, 35, 46, 53, 73, 75, 77, 85, 116, 132, 145
    Matt 89
    Mike 75, 77

NEGRO – M (contd.)
    Milley 25, 33, 75, 117
    Milly 30, 77, 123
    Mingo 108
    Miriah 35
    Molley 76
    Molly 77
    Moses 19, 47, 48, 59, 71, 76, 77

NEGRO – N
    Nan 5, 62
    Nancy 71, 88, 97, 137, 162
    Nat 65, 75, 77
    Ned 33, 76, 77
    Nell 48
    Nelley 47
    Nimrod 77

NEGRO – O
    Obediah 77
    Old June 132
    Osborne 49
    Osburn 140, 141
    Ozburn 139

NEGRO – P
    Pat 132
    Patience 43, 44, 114, 115
    Patrick 33, 76, 77, 89
    Patsey 53
    Patt 161
    Pattey 5
    Patty 73
    Pegg 144
    Peter 25, 35, 73, 75, 77, 85, 104, 108, 123, 150, 161, 167
    Peyton 53
    Phebe 53
    Phibby, 25
    Phil 132
    Philip 75
    Philis 73
    Phill 69
    Phillip 77
    Phillis 17, 33, 53, 59
    Phoebe 123
    Pigg 25
    Polley 17, 75
    Polly 77
    Prew 30
    Primus 5, 103
    Printer 77
    Prirrter 75

NEGRO – R
    Rachel 35, 47, 48, 75, 77, 89, 93, 131, 144, 149
    Randolp 75

NEGRO – R (contd.)
   Randolph 76, 77, 89
   Ratley 71
   Reah 73
   Reas 85
   Reubin 62
   Rewbin 88
   Rhoda 96
   Richardson 161
   Rilah 75
   Ritah 77
   Ritter 101, 134
   Rob 50, 108
   Robert 47, 48, 142
   Robin 108
   Rose 53, 76, 77
   Rutha 137
NEGRO – S
   Sal 137
   Salley 116
   Sally 30, 75, 77, 161, 167
   Sam 53, 59, 89, 135, 144, 151
   Sampson 165
   Samuel 19, 25
   Sarah 53, 62, 75, 77, 89, 141, 143
   Sarry 162
   Sary 25, 165
   Shato 148
   Sias 77
   Sillar 17, 47
   Silva 73
   Silvey 85, 103, 116
   Silvy 137, 152
   Simmons 131, 149
   Simon 57, 58, 62, 165
   Solomon 1
   Sophia 53
   Sopia 46
   Squire 46, 75, 77
   Stefiny 103
   Stella 33
   Stephen 53, 71, 75, 77, 88, 92, 123
   Stuart 33
   Sucky 129
   Sukey 75, 77
   Susan 75, 89
   Sy 73
   Sye 85
   Syller 53
   Sylva 46, 143
NEGRO – T
   Tabby 143
   Tamer 53

NEGRO – T (contd.)
   Tarmar 104
   Ted 150
   Thornton, Jim 66
   Tiller 33
   Toby 66, 67, 123
   Tom 6, 35, 46, 84, 108, 144, 148, 150
   Turner 5
NEGRO – V
   Vanny 129
   Vilett 116
   Viney 144
   Voilette 88
NEGRO – W
   West 33
   Wheler 131
   Wiley 71
   Will 30, 53, 58, 123
   William 75, 77
   Wining 143
   Winney 48, 65
   Winny 47, 104
   Wright 123
   York 35
   Zoe 108
NELSON 137
   James 44, 46, 113, 137
   Jas. 46, 114
   Mrs. 137
   Nathl. 95
NESON
   James 49
NEWBELL
   John 153
NOBLE
   Jno. 109
   John 164
NORMAN 140
   Ro. 49
   Robert 139
NOULIN
   Saml. 159
   Briant W. 40
   Bryan W. 131, 132
NOWLIN
   David 24, 103
   Mary B. 24
   Mrs. 24
   Saml. 127, 143
   Samuel 129, 158, 168
   W. 16
NUNILEE 145
NUNNELEE
   Edward 40

NUNNILEE
   Edward 125, 144, 145
   John Edward 145
O'KILBY
   Mr. 110
OAKS
   Robert 23
OLD BUCK 118
OLDAM
   John 152
OLIVER 40
   Ben 38
   James 15
   William 156
ORGAN
   Enoch 22
   Enock 158
   John 159
ORKES
   Robert 70
OVERBY
   James 67
OWEN
   Drury 14, 40
   John 136
   Obadiah 2
   Obediah 107, 108
PACE
   Adam 169
   Spencer 14, 130
PALMER
   L. 111
   S. 111
PAMPY 119
PANILL
   David 24
PANNELL 11
PANNILL 40, 70, 71, 92, 136, 169
   A. J. 63
   Bathena 129
   Bethemea 91
   Bethenia 30, 41, 68, 70, 92, 130, 160, 161
   D. 42, 64, 65, 66, 70, 81, 124, 129
   Daniel 165
   David 12, 13, 17, 26, 27, 30, 38, 41, , 64, 66, 67, 68, 69, 70, 71, 91, 92, 93, 115, 124, 129, 130, 131, 160, 161, 162, 166
   E. S. 161
   Elizabeth L. 129
   Elizabeth S. 129

PANNILL (contd.)
   Eliza L. 161
   George 128, 159
   Jenmial 159
   Jere. 128
   Jermiah 54
   John 63, 65, 66, 67, 124
   Mrs. 30
   Nancy 63, 66, 67, 82
   P. S. 91
   S. 70, 124, 133
   Sal. 54
   Sam. 62
   Saml. 12, 55, 58, 63, 67, 70, 71, 81, 124, 127, 128, 129, 158, 159, 160, 161, 165
   Samuel 12, 13, 17, 21, 22, 26, 27, 41, 42, 56, 57, 66, 68, 69, 89, 91, 92, 93, 115, 122, 130, 148, 162, 166
   Samuel C. 38
   T. 66
   William 40
   Wm. 128, 159
   Wm., Jr. 15
PARHAM
   William G. 38
PARKER
   William 39
PARKS
   Joseph 152
PARNILL1 41
PARRISH
   Abraham 137
   Jno. 4, 144
   Nich. 33
   Nichs. 4
   Richard 94
   W. 144
PARSON
   John 136
PARSONS
   Saml. 14, 16
   Saml., Sr. 16, 40
   Samuel 39
   Thomas 23
   William 70, 136
PATRICK
   Behathaland F. 57
   D. F. 56
   D. L. 159
   David 158
   David F. 6, 54, 55, 57, 58, 62, 63, 89, 91, 127, 128, 159
   Fanney 158

PATRICK (contd.)
   Jno. F. 125
   Mrs. 56
   Salley 158
   Thos. F. 124
PATTERSON
   Jno,. 7
   John 40, 82, 155
   William 11, 142
PATTON
   James 139
   James D. 29, 37, 49, 94, 95, 107, 110, 120, 122, 133, 147, 164
   James L. 111
   Jas. D. 72, 87, 112, 121
   Js. D. 109
PAUL
   Mrs. 110
PAYNE
   Catherine 122
   Charles 72, 87, 88, 118, 119, 120
   Chas. 51
   Giles 122
   Jo. 110
   John 112, 170
   Leana L/S. 87
   Leanna L. 121
   Leannah L. 88
   Leop'd. Mo. 110
   Mrs. 110, 133
   Philimon 133
   Philip 33
   Philt. 133
   Ro. 37, 79, 94, 110, 140
   Rob. 46
   Robert 95, 106, 139
   Thos. 32, 38
   William 46, 80, 144
   Wm. C. 110
PEAY 78
PELL
   Henry 137, 156
PEMBERTON
   James 55, 56, 128, 130, 158
   Jas. 56
PENN
   Gabriel 131, 160
PERKINS 13
   Abraham 139
   Henry 50, 108
   Nicholas 107, 124
   P. 124
   Peter 14, 15, 16, 38, 70
PETERSBURG 2

PETTY
   Davis 137
PHARES
   Pleasant 31
PHILIPS
   Thompson 102
PHILLIPS
   Thompson 100
PIGG
   John 94
PISTOLE
   Abraham 133
   Chs. 153
   James 118
   Jno. 118
   John 153
   Thomas 146, 147
   Thomas, Jr. 146
   Thomas, Sr. 153
PITTS
   Riche 90
   Richie 116, 117, 146
PLEASANTS 13
POLLEY
   Joseph 39, 83
POLLY
   Miss 109
POOR
   Abra. 15
POORE 13
   Adam 14
POSEY
   Robert 23
PRATTIN 137
PREWIT
   Byrd 125
PRICE
   Daniel 79, 87, 111, 121
   Danl. 51
   Fountain 94
   Maj. 112
   Major 118, 120, 156
   Meredith 119, 121
PRINGLE
   William 39
PROCTOR
   Richd. 51
PULLIAM
   Drury 148
PULLIN
   Thomas 151
PURYEAR
   Hez. 122, 151, 156
   Hezekiah 1
   Hezh. 112, 133
   Hezk. 72

QUIN
    John 94
QUINN
    Zero 118
RAGLAND
    William 30, 36, 142
    Wm. 35
RAGSDALE
    Thomas 108, 140
    Thos. 5, 138
RAINE
    Wm. 128, 159
RATCLIFF
    Benjamin 149
RATLIFF
    , Benj. 110, 119
RAWLINS 64
    Thos. 140
    Wm. 136, 140, 165
RAY
    Francis 119
READ
    Jean 36
    Thos. 36
REID
    Reid 78
REINE
    William 57
REYNOLDS
    Joseph 89
    Nancy 8
    Richard 8, 147
RICE
    David 68, 95, 107, 139, 141
    Josiah 23, 102, 134
    Wm. 134
RICHARD 147
RICHARDS 37
    D. 37
    Durrett 36, 37
    H. 125
    J. 8, 52
    Jesse 7, 8, 52
    Jos. 7
    Joseph 21, 51
RICHARDSON
    James 88
    Jas. 122
    Rubin 40
    Thomas 148
    William 118
    Wm. 112
RICHMOND 38, 130, 156
RICKETTS
    Wm. 7
RIDGEWAY
    James 125
RIEVES
    Peter 9
RIPLEY
    Heza. 16
    Hezk. 14
RIVER (watercourse)
    Banister 48
    Bannister 6
    Dan 76, 78
    Pigg 146
    Sandy 14, 39, 70, 76, 78
    Stinken 66
RO. 110
ROACH
    Burdet 31
ROBERTSON
    Christopher 1, 3, 137
    Christopher, Jr. 3
    E. 8, 52
    Edward 21
    Edwd., Jr. 134
    Geo. 3, 16, 138
    George 23, 28
    J. 13
    James 119
    Jos. 15
    Joseph 13, 16, 39
    Mary Amy 21
    Thompson 23, 122, 136, 164, 165
    William 70, 95
ROGERS
    John 36
    Joseph 2
    William 93
ROLANDS 64
RONALD
    Andrew 80
ROPER
    William 82, 83
RORER
    Abraham 131, 132
ROSS 63, 64
ROWEL
    Anderson 154
ROWLAND
    Ferd. 112
    Henry 65
    J. 134
    Jesse 91
    Jesse, Sr. 14, 41
    John 15, 16
    John, Sr. 41, 101
    Mrs. 65
ROWLIN
    John 82
ROYAL
    Jno. 125
RUFFIN
    Thomas 156
RYBURN 39
SALLY
    Jno. 13
    John 14, 15
SAML. 164
SAMUEL 147
SANDER
    Jesse 82
SANDERS
    Henry 169
    Jacob 24
    Jeremiah 82
    Wm. 16
SAUNDERS
    George 11
    Jacob 122, 136, 169
    John 16, 40
    Mrs. 65
    Richard 118
    Wm. 14, 15
SAWYERS
    James 18, 138, 139, 140
    Maj. 133
    Wm. 8, 140
SCOTT 164
    John B. 125
    Samuel M. 92
SCRUGGS
    Drury 21, 22, 44, 83
    Drury Sr. 9
    Grose 21
    John 139, 140
    Langhorn 9, 21, 22, 23, 134
    S. W. 134
    Thomas 22
    Warfield 101
SCURLOCK
    Mr. 63
SELF
    Thomas 39, 40
SHACKLEFORD
    Catherine 168
    Morice 147
    Thos. 76
SHAW
    Alexander 105
    Charles 137
    Evans 137
    John 100
    Nathaniel 105

SHAW (contd.)
  Pat 105
  Robert 105
  Thomas 105
SHEALDS
  Wm. 15
SHEETS 19
SHELTON 136
  Abra. 15, 38
  Abra. C. 165, 166
  Abraham 40, 68, 160, 169
  Abraham, Sr. 169
  Arm. 80
  Armistead 12, 122, 169
  Armsd. 125
  Armstad 24
  Bev. 14, 15, 16
  Beverley 32, 79, 80, 169
  Beverly 40, 122, 125
  Beverly G. 24
  Beverly, Jr. 122
  Charles 2
  Charles J. 165, 166
  Chloe 38, 39, 41, 160, 165
  Chris. 34
  Chs, I. 34
  Clayborn 169
  Caybourn 169
  Coleman 16
  Cris. 16
  Crispin 16, 33, 39, 40, 79, 80,
    122, 124, 165
  Crispin, Sr. 166
  Daniel 70, 95, 96
  Daniel, Jr. 169
  Daniel, Sr. 169
  Danl. 125
  Fannie 169
  Frederick 42, 129
  Fredk. 161
  Gabl. 14, 15, 16
  Gabriel 40, 68, 122
  Gabriel, Jr. 40
  Gabrl. 32
  Geo. 155
  George 7, 27, 28, 96
  Henry R. 134, 169
  James 141
  James, Sr. 142
  Joel 15, 169
  John 7, 15, 47, 68, 98, 142,
    160, 166, 169
  John, Sr. 49
  Josiah 35, 154
  Lemuel 16
  Leroy 14, 39, 82, 140, 166

SHELTON (contd.)
  Lettice 169
  Randolph 95
  Richard 16
  Richd. 15
  Ro. 166
  Robert 152
  Robertson 16, 165, 169
  Roy 95
  Ste. 16
  Susan 165
  Susanna 34, 166
  T. 156
  Tavanor 165
  Tavernor 166
  Thomas 35, 47, 97, 141, 156
  Thomas, Jr. 49, 141, 142
  Tunstall 95, 96, 169
  V. 125
  Vincent 12, 13, 30, 79, 80,
    81, 83, 122, 166, 169
  Wiatt 122
  William 156, 165, 166, 169
  Willis 96, 169
  Wm. 8, 36, 142
  Wm., Capt. 16
  Wyatt 82, 169
  Young 95, 96, 169
SHIPPARD
  Benjamin 133
SIMPSON
  J. 156
  John 15, 31
  Thomas 84, 148
  Thomas, Jr. 31
  Thomas, Sr. 31
  William 31, 136
SIMS
  Elijah 112
SINNS
  160
SLATE
  Mary 105
  Saml. 6
  Samuel 7
SLAUGHTER
  Doctor T. 127
SLAYDEN
  Daniel 17, 35
  Jos. 156
  Joseph 73, 157
  Wm. 156
SLAYDON 85
SLAYTON
  Lucy 142

SMITH 64
  B. 45
  Bartlet 15
  Booker 46
  David. 36
  Edward 87
  George 88, 89
  Hezekiah 87
  Jno. 46
  John 13, 164, 165
  Joseph 40
  Mrs. 127
  Orlando 37
  Peter 118, 119
  Ralph 158
  Saml. 46
  W. 27, 63
  Will. 153
  William 12, 14, 17, 25, 29,
    38, 39, 65, 67, 81, 91, 92,
    93, 101, 128, 130, 131,
    134, 149, 162, 168
  Wm. 13, 16, 27, 31, 41, 42,
    55, 62, 68, 69, 71, 80, 125,
    129, 135, 160, 166, 167
SNEED
  Wm. 152
SNODDY
  John 135
SONTE 39
SOYARS
  James 21, 28, 51, 151
SOYERS
  James 147
  Tat., Majr 87
SPARKS
  Edmund 163
  Keziah 135, 147, 148, 162,
    163
  M. Brooks 163
  Mat. B. 163
  Thomas 163
SPEARS 80
SPENCER
  David 55
SPILLER
  Hickman 132, 164
  William 132
SPILTER
  H. 110
SPRAGGINS 78
SPRATTEN
  George 147
SPURLINE
  Henson 16

SPURLING
   Henson 15
STAMP 85
STAMPS
   John 24, 105, 147, 156
   Timothy 102
   Will.156
   William 156
   Wm. 114, 115
STANFIELD
   William 164
STEEL
   John 6\
STEELE
   John 16
STEPHEN 57
STEWART 19
   James 70, 124
   Jas. 113, 114
   Nevin 15
   Thomas 72, 87, 111, 164
   Thos. 87
STILL
   John 87
STIMPSON
   Sollomon 157
   William 154
STOCKTON
   John 32
STOEKAS
   Allen 53
STOGDON 69
STOKES
   Silvanus 17, 19, 118
STONE
   Benja. 131
   Clack 63, 91, 128
   Epp. 118, 119, 121
   Eppa 164
   G. 133
   Isaac 50
   J. 124
   Jno. 61
   Jno., Jr. 83
   John 15
   John, Jr. 12, 15, 16
   Jon. 59
   Joshua 6, 65, 71, 80, 91, 92, 93, 115, 116, 123, 125, 149, 160, 162
   Joshua, Jr. 135
   Joshua, Sr. 12, 14, 15, 17, 67, 128, 129, 130, 131, 134, 160, 167
   Saml. 55, 63, 68, 71, 129

STONE (contd.)
   Samuel 27, 128, 130, 131, 149, 164, 166, 169
   Thomas 161
   Thomas C. 70
   William H 31
STORES (building)
   Stinkin River 61
   Thos. Bouldin 43, 44
STOUT
   Bailey 89
STRANGE
   Francis T. 104
   James 103, 104
   Smith 104
   Susanna 104
   Susannah 103
STREET
   Bailey 67, 129
   Paul 129
SULLIVAN
   Daniel 72, 87, 156
SUMMERHAY
   Robert W. 149
SUTHERLAND
   A. 7
SUTHERLIN
   A. 8, 163
   Adam 162, 163
   Adams 28, 29
   Geo. 156
   George 3, 28, 29
   James 28, 29
   John 3, 28, 29, 156
   Thomas 3, 28, 29, 118, 119
   Thos. 110
   Willaim 29, 132, 133
SUTTERLIN
   Adams 135
SWANN
   Thos. 111
SWAN
   Thomas 139, 140
SWEPSTONE
   John 13
SYDNER
   E. 122
SYDNOR
   E. 80
SYM
   Patrick 136
TALBOT
   David G. 56
TANER
   Lucy 154

TANNER
   Asa 155
   Creed 17, 30, 49, 72, 73, 86, 97, 108, 136, 137, 153, 155, 156
   Floyd 155
   Lucy 97
   Mathew 97, 108, 153
   Thomas 97, 109, 155, 156
   Thos. 133, 154
TATE
   Betsy 105
   Caleb 15
   Nathan 19
TAYLOR
   Creed 111
   James 122, 136
   Jane 122
   Oba. 14
   Obediah 136
TEMPLE
   William 16
TENNISON
   Ignatious 110, 118
TERRY
   Bartin 157
   Barton, Jr. 154
   Benj. 59
   Benj., Jr. 59
   Benjamin, Sr. 35
   Champ. 105
   Champness 18, 48, 59, 60, 61, 62, 71, 152, 164
   David 99, 157
   Elizabeth 105
   J. 18, 105
   Jere. 43, 99
   Jeremiah 71
   Jerre. 105
   Jerry 44
   John 105
   Joseph 105, 115
   Mathew 119, 121
   Matt. 37
   Nat. 70
   Nathaniel 100
   Wm. 105, 125
THACKER
   Jos 14, 15, 16
   Joseph 40
   Nathaniel 19
THOMAS 109, 120
   Philip 93
   Asa 36, 37, 42, 43, 44, 73, 113, 114, 115, 147, 157

THOMAS (contd.)
   Charles 147
   Chas. 36
   E. 64
   Jacob 37
   John 36, 37
   John, Sr. 94
   Joice 36
   Nathanael P. 42
   Nathl. 36, 37
   Nathl. P. 114
   William 37, 43, 52, 114, 115
   Wm. 8
THOMPSON 13, 107
   Ann 112
   Jennings 5, 21
   Saml. 3
   Samuel 138, 139, 140
   Washington 2, 96, 147
   William 35, 36, 146
   Wm. 125
THOMSON
   William 135
THORNBURY 13
THOMAS 109
THRUSHER
   John 31
THURMAN
   Allen 33
   Richard 13
THURMAND
   Allen 14
THURMOND
   Nathan 16, 40
   Nathan, Sr. 39
TIFFIN
   Thomas 106, 140, 141
   Thos. 138, 139
TIFFON
   Thomas 105
TINES
   Isaac 69, 161
TODD
   Mary 160
   Thomas 160
   William 66, 81
TOLAR
   Joseph 32
TOMPKINS
   Edm. 95
TOWNES
   William, Sr. 153
TOWNS
   Halcott 94
   Holcott 95
   William 120, 121

TRAVIS
   Jno. 111
   Wm. 111
TUCK
   Mr. 64
TUCKER
   Anderson 50, 108
   Martha 11
   N. 117, 122, 134, 143, 146
   Nelson 9, 45, 83, 168
   Pleasant 110
   Robert 9, 11
   William 9, 70
   Wm. 11
TUNSTALL 64, 65, 66
   Edm. 134
   Edmd. 101
   Edmund 17, 38, 39, 81, 82, 83.134
   John 82
   Will 76, 122, 133
   William 15, 31, 162, 163, 164, 166
   Wm. 80, 138, 140
TURLY
   Thomas 136
TURNER 141
   George 3
   John 10, 22, 23, 56, 90, 158, 159
   John, Jr. 160
   S. 116
   Ste. 115
   Sto. 12, 13, 14, 36, 61, 80, 81, 86, 115, 142, 147, 164, 169
   Stockley 18, 164
   Stokeley 166
   Stokely 116, 154, 156
   Stokley 38, 48
   Stookley 124, 125
   Wm. L. 68
TWEDEL
   Abigail 46
TWEDELL
   Benj. 46
   Mrs. 46
TWEDEL
   William 46
TWEDWELL
   William 44
TWIDLE
   Abigail 137
TYNES
   Isaac 40

TYRE
   Josiah 99
UHANE
   Joseph 158
VADEN
   Sil. 35
   William 169
VANCE
   David 32, 162
VAUGHAN
   James L/S. 93
   Mr. 56
   Wm. 81
VENABLE
   Richd. N. 37
VOSS
   Greenberry 118
WADDILL
   A. 156
   John 152
   Noel 72, 73, 102, 156
WADE
   Henry 101, 134
   Henry, Sr. 54
WALKER 78
   Doctor 124
   James 35, 156
   Jeremiah 104
   Robert 148
   S. 153
   Samuel 17, 30, 46, 49, 73, 97, 109, 133, 137, 147, 156, 157
   V. 65
   Vincent 10, 45, 148
   Vinct. 14
   William 76, 89, 164
   Wm. 156
WALLER 47
   Benj. 63
   Benjamin 22, 56, 57, 58
   Hamton 136
   J. 8
   Jane 136
   Joel 85
   John 72, 73, 85, 86, 155, 157
   John, Jr. 156
   John, Sr. 156, 157
   Jonas 7
   Pleasant 86, 156
   R. 156
   Rebecca 156, 157
   Rebeckah 85
   Robert 101, 134, 153, 156
   Samuel 157
   Willaim 35, 70, 136

WALLER (contd.)
   Wm. 34
WALLINGTON 125
WAL
   Richard 41
WALL
   Johnson 36
WALROND
   Reubin 105
WALTEN
   Benjamin 10
WALTER
   Ro. 137
WALTERS
   , Archibald 141
   Jackson 30, 136
   Jno. 37
   John 42, 43, 156, 157, 164
   Rob. 47
   Robert 72, 73, 86, 156
   Robt. 19
WALTON
   Anne 139
   Wm. 51
WARD
   George 113
   Henry 165
   John 21, 22, 34, 82
   John, Jr. 44, 84
   William 165
   Wm. 124
WARE 107
   Bezaleel 133
   William 50, 108, 117, 119, 140
   Wm. 107, 112, 138, 140, 148
WARF
   Roger 113, 114
WATKINS
   Bej. 19
   Ben 137
   Benj. 47, 141
   Benjamin 35
   Jno. 139
   John 141
   Saml. 4
   Wm. M. 115
WATSON
   James 147
   John 2, 40
   Richd. 140
   Tho. 7, 8
   Thomas 52, 165
   Wm, Jr. 16
WAYNE
   A. 33

WEAR
   William 118
   Wm. 112
WEAVERS 13
WEBSTER 13
WELLS
   Mathew 145
   Thomas 39
WEST
   George 3, 44, 117, 146
   John 130, 131
   Joseph 40
   Owen 3
   Robert 119
WHIT
   William 112
WHITE
   Doctor 124, 125
   Ep. 156
   Eppa 157
   John 12, 110, 125, 147, 156
   Liddy 156
   Lydea 85
   Lydia 86
   Oliver 33
   Rawley 141, 156, 157
   Robert 133
   Robert F. 99
   Robt. 155
   William 11
   Wm. 45, 133
WHITEHEAD 11
   Cary 83
   James 165
WHITLOCK
   Achiles 36
   Achilles 114
   William 136, 168
WHITLOW
   William 90
   Wm. 159
WIATT
   Thos. 57
WICKHAM
   John 38
WIER
   Bazabil, Sr. 146
   Bazaleel 114
   Bazalul 115
   John 44
WILKERSON
   W. 44
   Wm. 73
WILKINS
   Rob. 36

WILKINSON
   Henry E. 146, 153
   Tho. 44
   Thomas 137
   Thomas, Sr. 133
   Thos. 27, 46, 114, 115, 146
   William 119, 120, 123
   Wm. 27, 46
WILLIAMS 78, 107
   Charles 25, 117
   Elisha 94
   J. 69
   J. M. 19, 60, 62, 96, 157
   J. W. 99, 103
   James M. 18, 47, 85, 105, 116, 164
   Jno. 15, 16
   John 125
   Joseph 125
   N. C. 100
   Permecious 95
   Perminias 107
   Perminius 108
   William 19, 20, 40, 41, 70, 91, 125
   Wm. 14, 15, 16, 130
WILLIAMSON
   Elisha 31
   John 95
   Polly 95
WILLIS
   Joel 164
   Ster. 70
   Sterline 69
   Stew. 13
   Thomas 14
   Thos. 16
   Wm. 14
WILLS
   Mathew 144
WILSON
   Colo. 152
   Ellis 138, 139
   Henry 29, 45, 123, 133
   James 29, 45, 133
   Jesse 2
   Jno. 3, 25, 105, 147
   Jno. Pat. 110
   John 28, 29, 45, 46, 50, 87, 107, 108, 125, 133, 137, 138, 139, 140, 141
   Martin 133
   Mead 50, 139
   Meade 138
   Nat. 109, 147
   Nath. 133, 164

WILSON (contd.)
   Nathaniel 109, 133, 164
   Nathl. 29, 87, 137, 139, 140, 141
   P. 25, 49, 105, 106, 138, 139, 140
   Peter 49, 50, 105, 106, 107, 108, 138, 139, 140, 141
   Thomas 133
   William 49, 133, 139, 141

WIMBISH
   H. 70
   John 64
   John, Jr. 64
   Mary 105
   William 100, 130, 160
   Wm. 16, 38, 41, 42, 165

WIMBUSH
   Jno. 65
   Jno., Jr. 65
   John 24, 59, 61, 63, 66
   W. 66
   William 24, 59, 60, 61, 62, 63, 65, 67

WINTERS
   John 111
   John, Jr. 8

WITCHER
   Jno., Jr. 86
   John 21, 31, 53, 87, 162
   Will 87, 104
   William 53, 86
   William, Jr. 46
   Wm. 32

WOMACH
   Allen 103

WOMACK
   Allen 24, 96, 117

WOOD
   Layton 164

WOODEN
   James 125

WOODING
   T. H. 125
   Tho., H. 136
   Thomas H. 165
   Thos. H. 13, 53

WOODSON 110
   Allen 23, 82
   Jesse 64
   Jos. 63
   Wm. 24

WOODY 164
   James 163

WOOSLEY
   Saml. 71
   Samuel 70

WORSHAM
   Berry 79
   Daniel 119
   F. 8, 52
   Francis 7, 8, 53
   Henry 38, 82
   John 79, 107, 111, 121
   Lucy 52
   Ludwell 120
   P. 7, 8, 52
   Thomas 72, 79, 146, 164
   William 22, 23, 56, 158
   Wm. 90, 127
   Thomas 107

WRIGHT
   James S. 147
   W. 46
   Wm. 27

WYNN
   Mrs. 112

WYNNE
   Robert 87, 164
   Robt. 28, 147
   Stith 51

YANCEY
   Layton 161
   Will. 133
   William 132, 144
   Wm. 87, 107, 122, 163, 165

YANCY
   James 116
   Shf. 137
   W. 80
   Will. 156
   William 39, 56, 164
   Wm. 55, 109, 112

YANSEE
   Wm. 145

YATES
   Elijah 117
   George 117
   Samuel 27, 165
   Stephen 35

YEAMAN
   John 20

YEAMANS 78

YEATTS
   Joseph 14
   Saml. 14, 25
   Samuel 31
   Ste. 15
   Stephen 14

YOUNG
   George 152
   Wm. 151

Gayle Beverley Austin

Gayle was born and grew up in Pittsylvania County, Virginia. After graduating from Chatham High School, she attended The College of William and Mary receiving a degree in history and government. Now retired and living in the suburbs of Orlando, Florida, Gayle finally has time to pursue her love of history. She is the web master for the Pittsylvania County Gen Web project and is presently working on the Land Taxes of Pittsylvania County from 1788-1801, Court Order Book I and several Deed books of the county.

www.ingramcontent.com/pod-product-compliance
Lightning Source LLC
Chambersburg PA
CBHW080432230426
43662CB00015B/2256